ANOTHER FEG

Jim Green MBA

DEDICATION

This book is dedicated to my family, especially my wife Elaine and my children and their children and their wider families who continually love and support me. Also, the people of Ferguslie and Paisley who inspired me to write. I would also like to dedicate this book to the University of Glasgow, my academic Alma Mater.

There is no doubt that the people I met during my life enriched it and were fundamental in my long-term survival and success. Most of those times were a matter of being in the right place at the right time which enables me to use a new word for those "sliding door moments"

Superordinancy

A derivative of its cousin
Supercalifragilisticexpialidocious. ☺

ACKNOWLEDGEMENT

To my family and friends who provided emotional support, encouragement, and understanding throughout the writing process.

Individual mentors and teachers who have influenced my writings and provided guidance whether formally through education or informally through feedback and encouragement.

The various editors including my daughter Emma who helped me improve the content, and the Amazon publishing team.

Fiona Parrot my Creative Writing tutor at the University of Glasgow who introduced me to the most awesome and inspirational books in literary history.

Feggie Memories on Facebook which continually reminds me of the energy and affection that exists between the new and older generations.

All readers of this book and any feedback will be noted and appreciated.

The people of Ferguslie and more generally the People of Paisley who have quite rightly earned the name "buddies" my buddies.

To the late John Byrne who's art and creative energy was fired up by his life and times living in Ferguslie, probably the most awesome "Feg" to emerge from its streets.

To Camillia Riva from the Fine Art Society Edinburgh who gave permission to use the John Byrne painting (Stranger in Paradise) on the front cover.

To Isaac and Paul at Kindle Books Publishing team at Basecamp 3

Table of Contents

INTRODUCTION

This book attempts to record my life and my family since 1950. It describes the impact of being born and brought up in Ferguslie Park, Paisley. I began authoring the book in 2004, during my fifties, while attending a creative writing course at the University of Glasgow under the tutelage of Fiona Parrot.

I chose to write in the first person rather than the third, hoping it would better serve the narrative. Being a "Feg" seemed to offer few advantages, as there remains a social stigma associated with being from or living in Ferguslie. However, this book provides an account of my life in Ferguslie from 1950 to 1971. I have also accepted the "Americanization" of word spelling despite my Scottish appreciation of the English language.

I also change individual and organization names in order to protect the innocent and guilty. (*You know who you are!*)

Having researched and learned so much about my family history I became aware of how much is lost to the past because most ordinary people do not tell their story. I wanted to tell my story as raw, exciting, and sometimes boring before some AI app. did it for me.

The artwork on the front cover was created by John Byrne, commissioned by me to depict Ferguslie Park. Like me, John is also a "Feg." he called the picture "A stranger in Paradise" which shows how he really felt about his life as a young art student living in Logan Drive (Ferguslie) and was inspired as I was by life as a "Feg." I dedicated this artwork to my late father whose name was painted by John Byrne on the frame of the canvas he is holding in the picture.

People of my generation who lived in Ferguslie and the surrounding area were demonized and discriminated against during their lives where it was routine to be excluded from jobs or subject to careless whispers as a social underclass. Part of the Council Scheme called Graigmuir Rd was called the "Undesirables" to the shame of the Local Council. I have used the local vernacular language for effect.

Another Feg

I apologize in advance for any profanity used for literary effect. I also apologize for any part of this story that might upset the reader or cause offence. It will be for others so disposed to write their version of life as a "Feg."

Despite my Ferguslie background, I have been fortunate to achieve a good life and consider myself as blessed. I attended university, became a lecturer, and even found myself at No. 10 Downing Street and the Queen's Garden Parties. I travelled extensively, developed a successful business, lost it, and eventually got declared bankrupt.

I married Elaine, the love of my life and my compass. Together, we have three wonderful children and ten awesome grandchildren. I am privileged to now live in a lovely country house n o t t o o f a r from Ferguslie.

Jim and Elaine his wife of 53 years(2025)

After my bankruptcy, I faced a long and arduous climb out of financial and personal difficulties. This part of my journey led me to leave Scotland and move to a farm in Denmark to try and rebuild my life.

My new life involved working offshore in some of the harshest environments of the North and Irish Seas, where I sought to save

2

lives during real emergencies. I later returned to the UK, living and working in the Lake District, London, and eventually Aberdeen, where I became involved in security matters both onshore and offshore. This work brought me into contact with covert organizations and organized crime—not for the first time in my life.

I have faced significant danger over the years, including being attacked twice by gangs and shot at on two occasions. I have come close to death at least twice. I have also been politically active, serving as a candidate for the Scottish Parliament and as an election agent and coordinator for Ken MacIntosh, the Scottish Parliament's Presiding Officer (Now Retired) and Rt Hon Jim Murphy, the former Secretary of State for Scotland and a cabinet member under Prime ministers Tony Blair and Gordon Brown.

With the Rt Hon Jim MP at the Houses of Parliament London

Nevertheless, the true success of my life lies in my family. We live in and love the countryside, only a few miles from my true alma mater, Ferguslie.

Part Two of this book, Fishing for Spanners, takes the reader on a journey of survival after near-death experiences to a better life. It explores themes of family, business, optimism, and the founding of the *Purple Sox Club.

Jim Green the Author

CHAPTER 1:
THE NE'ER-DO-WELLS

1950

January–February:

Mum and Dad begin courting, but finding places to go is difficult; they mostly spend time in parks or at the cinema.

March:

Mum becomes pregnant with me.

April–May:

They break the news to their parents. Dad secures a job at the Linwood Paper Mill, and their wedding banns are posted at the Paisley Registry Office.

July:

Mum and Dad marry at Ferguslie Manse on McKenzie Street, Paisley, next to the old Ferguslie School and opposite the Catholic School huts. They initially move in with both sets of parents but soon begin searching for a place of their own. Eventually, they rent a kitchen in Dad's Aunt Maggie's house on Brown Street, Paisley, for 5 shillings a week, plus a contribution for electricity and gas. The flat is on the top floor of a four-storey tenement. Mum, now heavily pregnant, has to stop working at McCallum's Dye Works on Abercorn Street.

August–December:

Mum struggles with the stairs in Brown Street, and both parents try to stay warm in the damp room and kitchen. On 20th December, Mum's waters break, and Dad calls a taxi to take her to Barshaw Maternity Hospital on the outskirts of Paisley, near the county border with Glasgow. At 9:15 pm, I am born, weighing 7 lbs. The attending midwife is Nurse Van der Bomm.

Mum and Dad name me James, after Dad and his father. Mum is an attractive blonde, and Dad is a handsome ex-soldier, de-mobbed in 1947. They make a striking couple and are deeply in love.

The Day the Author Was Born.

Jimmy (Dad) was about to put the last batch of mortar mix for the day into the large diesel-driven mixer when Martin, the site foreman, shouted him over to the site bothy (Office).

Martin was a big, strong man with a black moustache. He wore an old, greasy skipped bonnet to cover his balding head. He was the old-fashioned type of ganger who'd punch you out if you stepped out of line. However, one man he wouldn't tackle was Jimmy, given his reputation as an Army boxing champion. "Yer wife's been taken intae hospital! The wean's on its way, so ye better get yersel up there pronto—and make sure yer back onsite the morra!"

"Right-o, Martin, I'll be here the morra—nae problem."

It was late December 1950, and a bitter cold wind blew through Jimmy's de-mob greatcoat. The toes of his wellington boots were frozen, the cut-up rags he used instead of socks soaked in the day's sweat. He knew he'd be just as quick walking to the hospital on the outskirts of town as waiting for a bus. His walk was punctuated with short bursts of running, pulling his brown ex-army beret tightly over his full head of black curly hair. As he approached the hospital grounds, his eyes locked on the ward lights, hoping Ellen was okay and the wean was a healthy one.

Barshaw was an old mansion house converted into a maternity hospital.

Jimmy ran up the solid stone steps, worn down in the middle from years of use, and headed straight to reception. "Ma name's Green! Is ma wife awright? Has the wean been born? Is it okay?"

"Calm down, Mr. Green. I'll get the ward sister to speak to you."

Jimmy paced anxiously at the entrance to the ward, wincing as he heard the screams of women in labour.

Sister Mackenzie, crisp in her uniform, complete with cap and watch pinned to her tunic, approached him.

"Mr. Green," she said, extending her hand, "congratulations! You have a lovely wee boy, and your wife is fine."

Jimmy, accustomed to bad news, was skeptical. "Fine? I've heard that word before. Are ye sure she's no lying in there bleedin' tae death or somethin'?"

"Would you like to see them?" "Aye, I wid."

"Follow me to Ward Five."

As Jimmy entered the hospital proper, his senses were overwhelmed by the smell of carbolic, the cries of newborns, and the sight of women in pink hospital gowns. It was a long way from the building site he knew so well. He wished for a moment for the diesel fumes and the clatter of the mixer. Ellen was propped up on three pillows stamped with the Barshaw Hospital insignia.

Jimmy grabbed her face with his cement-stained hands and kissed her hard and long.

"James! For the love of God, I've jist had a wean!" she winced, clearly in discomfort.

Jimmy loved Ellen more than anything. While some men welcomed separation, Jimmy missed her as though she were a vital organ. "Is that him there?"

"Aye, it is, and he's jist been fed, so dinnae disturb him." "Do not disturb him? Ye must be joking'!"

Jimmy approached the baby cot and carefully lifted the little bundle, wrapped in a white knitted shawl. He marveled at the tiny fingers peeking from the swaddle.

"Jesus Christ, Ellen, wid ye look at that wee finger—and that wee nail!"

"Aye, he's beautiful, if I say so masel. The ither women hiv been droolin' ower him. He's a wee blondie." Jimmy carried the baby to the bay window, lifting him towards the indigo night sky.

"Look, God, this is ma wean. Look after him aw his life fur me. Thanks, God, and al no let ye doon either."

He kissed his son's forehead, cradled him close, then gently placed him back in the cot.

Ellen propped herself up. "Whit are we gonnae gie him fur a name, James?"

"Oh, that's easy, hen. He'll be named efter ma faither—anither James for the clan."

"Ah hiv tae confess, I've been callin' him wee Jamie since he wis born. I'm glad we agree." As they spoke, Sister McKenzie entered and announced the ward was closing so mothers could rest.

Jimmy hugged Ellen tightly. "I'll be back the morra night, hen."
"Don't be coming in here wi' drink in ye."

"Wid I dae that noo?"

"Aye, ye wid." Jimmy stepped into the frosty night air, gazing up at the stars, bright like diamonds in the clear sky. He couldn't stop smiling, doing a little dance unseen by the town's good people.

"Fuckin' yes! Yes! Yes! Fuckin' yes! A wee boy—me, a faither! Ya beauty!" He jumped on a tram as it gained speed.

"C'mon, you, get oan or get aff!" the conductress barked.

Jimmy laughed. "Am only half oan this bus—can I get half fare?"

She smirked. "Right, you, c'mon, sit doon!"

As he settled in, Jimmy shouted to the top deck, "I've jist become a faither!"

A middle-aged man offered congratulations and a Capstan cigarette. Jimmy lit it, savoring every puff, still grinning ear to ear.

Later, he burst through his mother's door. "Maw, yer a granny!" Isa Green hugged him tightly, her excitement mirrored by the rest of the family. Beer was fetched, sherry poured, and toasts raised to wee Jamie.

By Christmas, Jimmy's son was safely ensconced in his granny's home, doted on by all. Isa, having lost two sons in her life, was utterly in love with this little boy.

1951

January–March:

Mum struggles to pull her pram up the four flights of stairs every time she goes out. She takes me out of the pram and places me in the cot, hoping Dad will bring it up before it gets stolen. The pram is a brand-new Silver Cross, bought by Grannie Green (Isa).

Grannie Green (Granny Isa)

April:

Dad leaves his job at the paper mill as the night shifts leave Mum feeling very isolated. He takes up a laborer's job on post-war housing construction schemes around Paisley and Glasgow.

May–December:

Mum and Dad continue searching for better housing. When the severe winter shuts down building works, Dad is laid off. They are forced to move to a model lodging house on Abercorn Street, next to the rat-infested River Cart. This place is notorious as a slum for "ne'er-do-wells" (poor people without means).

The Ne'er-do-wells location Abercorn St Paisley

In 2023, I revisited the site on my brother Charlie's 70th birthday. Shockingly, there were still rats running around the bins of the nearby nursery

My brother Charlie

1951

January:

I am breastfed by Mum, and despite several chest infections, I thrive under the love and care of wonderful parents.

Mum visits her mother's house on New Sneddon Street daily, just a five-minute walk from their attic room on Abercorn Street. These visits are a relief for her. On weekends, Mum and Dad make the longer trek to 101 Ferguslie Park Avenue to visit Grannie Green.

March–December:

As the weather improves, I thrive further. Mum scrubs the room and kitchen daily, though they have little furniture. Mum's green and cream houndstooth wool coat and Dad's suit often make trips to the pawnshop on New Sneddon Street.

During this time, Dad strikes up a friendship with Walter Gibson, the caretaker at the lodging house. Walter becomes quite famous as the author of two books: "Heiland Laddie" and "The Boat." The first recounts his life as a young soldier in the Argyll and Sutherland Highlanders, rising to Sergeant Major. The second describes his survival when his troop carrier was torpedoed by the Japanese, leaving only four survivors after days adrift at sea.

As Dad was also an ex-Argyll, they bonded. Walter was always polite to Mum, who was only 22 years old, and often helped her carry the pram up to the attic flat.

1953

January–June:

Dad resumes work on the building sites. Mum becomes noticeably larger in October as she falls pregnant again. Walter Gibson lobbies Renfrewshire County Council to get the family a house in Ferguslie.

July–November:

I become aware of my new brother, Charlie, born on 6th June at Barshaw Maternity Hospital. A membrane covered his eyes at birth, which the midwife kept as a lucky charm, believing it would protect a sailor from drowning.

Adjusting to having a sibling, I miss Mum's undivided attention. On one occasion, I hit Charlie over the head with his feeding bottle, and when Mum questioned the source of his crying, I innocently declared, "Me no did it, Mammy."

December:

I experience my first memory of Christmas, receiving green and red pirate boots with an integrated toy knife and a small plastic horse that walks down an incline on its own. Mum becomes pregnant once more.

1954

January–April:

Life continues in the model lodging house until Walter Gibson persuades the council to allocate a home for the growing family. In April, we move to 2 Killoch Avenue in the infamous Ferguslie housing scheme in Paisley. Uncle Robert helps transport our meagre possessions on the back of his British Rail Scammel wagon.

May–August:

Our new home, a ground-floor flat, has one bedroom, a living room, kitchen, and bathroom. It is filled with light, a stark contrast to the dim attic bedsit on Abercorn Street.

Outside, there is a well-maintained garden with flowerbeds and a nearby play park on Candren Road, equipped with swings, monkey bars, and a chute. Opposite the park, new houses are being built. I play with the clay from the excavations and sometimes with Mum's cousin's boy, James Noble.

The local area includes Blackston Road, leading to Menzies Post Office and licensed grocers. However, the infamous Graigmuir Road nearby is home to poverty, alcoholism, and chaotic lifestyles—a Council made ghetto. In the fifties Graigmuir Road was known as the "Undesirables"

During the summer, the funfair (Cardona's Shows) arrives at St James's Park, previously a racecourse. The magical experience of lights, music, candy floss, and rides like the waltzers and ghost train stays with me. Dad takes me to see the circus, complete with elephants, tigers, and Coco the clown. After the show, Dad carries me home on his shoulders—known as a "collie-backie"—a memory I still cherish. I can still remember the scent from his hair.

23rd August:

My sister, Ellen Rosina Armstrong Green, is born at home. The birth is difficult, with the cord wrapped around her neck three times. She is born blue and immediately transferred to Killearn Sick Children's Hospital near Loch Lomond.

It is impossible for anyone to visit her, so Dad telephones daily for updates. Mum is frantic and terribly upset.

Eventually, we got this little pink bundle back from Killearn, and the whole family doted on her. Charlie and I were allowed to help with bathing and changing her. It was then I noticed that the baby was different—she was deformed and didn't have a "willie," or as my mum called it, a "doodle."

September–December:

Family life resumed with all five of us. Dad was laid off again from building work and became a bookie's runner during the winter to pay the rent on the house.

That Christmas, we had a real tree, which we got from Robertson's fish shop in Falcon Crescent, about a five-minute walk from Killoch Avenue. The tree was decorated with coloured lights, glass baubles, and a silver-and-pink pinnacle. Mum placed it in an old soup pot, weighted it down with half-bricks from the nearby housing scheme, and wrapped the pot in red crepe paper. She also hung decorations from the ceiling and walls.

This was a magical time for Charlie and me. I don't remember the presents, but I do recall getting a bag of gold foil-wrapped chocolate coins and a tangerine.

1955

January–February:

That winter was bitterly cold. We had a coal fire, which felt magical, warm, and comforting. I often visited Grannie Isa, who lived just 400 yards away at 114 Ferguslie Park Avenue.

March:

My father's comrade from the Argylls, Willie, and his wife, Belle, moved into the opposite ground floor flat next door. Mum and Belle seemed to get on at first, but tensions soon began to rise over minor disputes about the washing line and cleaning the close. Meanwhile, Mum became pregnant again.

April:

As the house only had one bedroom, Charlie and I slept on a bed settee in the living room, while Ellen slept in a cot in Mum and Dad's room.

One night, Charlie and I were jumping up and down on the bed settee. I brought my foot down on a glass tumbler hidden among the bedclothes. I don't remember feeling any pain, but I had effectively severed my little toe, which was hanging by a sliver of flesh, and there was a lot of blood.

Dad wrapped my foot in a towel and took me by bus to the Royal Alexandra Infirmary on Crow Road, Paisley, where they stitched my toe back on.

May–June:

Charlie and I spent most of our time playing together. We often went for walks to Kyle's Farm or caught sticklebacks and tadpoles in the Candren Burn, keeping them in a jam jar.

Sometimes, I played on the construction site of the new housing scheme off Blackstone Road, behind the church halls. One day, I fell and gashed my leg badly on a piece of metal, leaving a large hole. Mum, worried about taking me back to the hospital so soon after the toe incident, bound the wound herself. Remarkably, it healed on its own without stitches.

Another Feg

Mum also relied on me to run errands to the local shops. On one occasion, someone on roller skates collided with me, nearly breaking my nose. I still remember the salty taste of my own blood.

CHAPTER 2:
DARK CLOUDS BURST

July–August:

Relationships between the Greens and the neighbors continued to deteriorate. On one occasion, Mum saw Belle our next-door neighbour telling her son William to hit me with a stick.

This led to an intense argument between Mum and Belle. By the time Dad got home from work, Mum was furious and unburdened herself to him. My Dad had only one way of dealing with problems: his fists. When Willie returned home from work, Dad confronted him, telling him to control his wife. An argument broke out, and Willie ended up on the receiving end of Dad's fists. Belle, who tried to intervene, was shoved onto her backside during the scuffle.

Reprisals didn't take long. That Friday night, Mum and Dad went to the cinema in Paisley town centre, leaving Gran Green to baby-sit us. Willie the neighbor was from a large Irish family, had his father and two brothers waiting for Dad when he returned home. As they approached, Dad asked them to let Mum past so she could get into the house.

What followed was a fight heavily weighed against Dad. Dad, a former regimental boxing champion for the Argylls, held his own, but four big Irishmen were too much, even for him. Eventually, they knocked him unconscious and dragged him into Willie's house, out of sight.

Inside, Mum was screaming while Gran Green urged me to climb out of the ground-floor window and run to fetch my uncle Sammy, Dad's younger brother. I ran as fast as I could while Mum and Gran Green banged on the neighbour's door, demanding to see Dad.

It didn't take me long to reach Sammy, who now lived with Grannie Isa at 114 Ferguslie Park Avenue, just opposite 101, where they had recently moved.

Sammy Green was one of the most feared men in Paisley, built like an ox and known for his strength and willingness to use violence. As it turned out, the bookie's runner job was a two-man debt-collecting team—Dad and Sammy.

Sammy grabbed a wooden fencepost from a garden during the short run back to Killoch Avenue. I tried to keep up, but Sammy was unstoppable. When he reached Wullie's house, he didn't bother with the door. Instead, he picked up a galvanized bin and threw it through the window, shattering the frame and glass. Using the 4x4 fence post, he cleared the rest of the broken glass, climbed onto the coal bunker beneath the window, and disappeared inside.

I covered my ears with the yelling, screaming, and the sounds of thuds and crashes. Gran Green took me inside, away from the noise.

Sammy knocked out Willie's father and one of his sons before rescuing Dad. The other two were left in pools of blood. The common close and both houses were splattered with it. By the time the police arrived, Dad was conscious again, hanging over the kitchen sink with a very sore face while Sammy washed his own blooded knuckles under the same tap.

The police sergeant assessed the situation quickly, called an ambulance for two of Sammy's victims, and issued everyone a caution. No charges were filed; in Ferguslie, reporting every fracas would have overwhelmed the police cells and the courts.

After that, relations between the families at 2 Killoch Avenue became icy. Mum and Dad began searching for a larger house for us to move to.

September–December:

Life carried on without further incidents. Christmas came and went peacefully. Dad continued supplementing his income by doing debt collection for the local bookies who were running an illegal operation.

1956
January–April:

I was eventually separated from my dear mother and brother when I was enrolled at Graigielea Primary School. The school was about a half of a mile away, further up Blackston Road, next to the manse where Mum and Dad had been married.

The school smelled strongly of carbolic soap. I remember the warm glow I felt after drinking the free school milk; sometimes, I managed to get a second bottle if there were any spares. I particularly loved the creamy top of the milk—after all, as they say, as it resonated with me "the cream always rises to the top"

Meanwhile, Dad found work in construction with James Y Keanie and Sons Ltd as a builder's labourer. It was backbreaking work, carrying a hods with up to 22 standard bricks, often climbing timber ladders to deliver them to scaffolding. By the time he got home, he was too tired to play with his growing family or chase debts for the bookies.

When he wasn't working, Dad would spend his weekends at the football, cheering for Paisley's St Mirren FC at Love Street before heading out to collect debts.

CHAPTER 3:
ON THE MOVE

Mum and Dad arranged a house exchange with a family at No. 94 Ferguslie Park Avenue, moving to a three-bedroom upper villa apartment. The previous occupants had been an elderly couple and their daughter. Tragically, the old man who lived there had fallen down the stairs and died. Thankfully, no one mentioned this at the time, as it might have made navigating the stairs more unnerving.

The young Green children at 94 Ferguslie Park Ave 1950

I transferred to Ferguslie Primary School, just around the corner from Graigielea School, and directly opposite the Catholic school huts. My teacher seated me next to a girl named Margaret Robertson in the Primary Two class, housed in the "wee school"— an annex building between Graigielea and the larger Ferguslie Primary School, which had a bell tower that rang out to signal the start of the day. The headmaster, Mr. Wilson, wore a black academic cloak and commanded profound respect. His presence in the classroom was both awe-inspiring and intimidating.

Ferguslie Primary School Paisley

We had new neighbours. Below us lived the Slavin family, who had four sons and were also of Irish descent. Opposite, on the lower floor, was Mrs. McCracken and her daughter, while opposite on the upper floor was Mr. and Mrs. Bowes, their daughter, and their son-in-law, Richard Hutton. Through the party wall lived Mrs. Simpson and her two daughters, and below her was the elderly Mrs. McFarlane and her son, John. These families were mostly refugees from the Clydebank Blitz during the Second World War.

The view from our front window included a row of houses and bus stops on either side. To the left was a large triangular garden, well maintained with neatly trimmed grass and vibrant flowerbeds. At the back, we had a shared grass green for drying clothes, though our front garden section was little more than compacted dirt and broken bricks. The Slavin's had a small patch of grass and half a hedge.

Our first winter at 94 FPA

October to November:

As autumn set in, Mum's pregnancy became more noticeable, and we gradually settled into our new home, which desperately needed redecorating. The wallpaper was grimy, and the kitchen walls were painted a dull bottle green.

The kitchen itself was basic, with a coal bunker, a meat press (Cold Cupboard), a gas boiler, two sinks, an old cooker, and some painted shelves—one of which held the gas meter above the cooker.

With winter approaching, Mum would buy a few bags of coal from Canavan the coal merchant. I vividly recall the red-faced man in his work clothes and studded leather back cover, laboriously hauling a hundredweight of second- class coal up the stairs. He'd dump the coal into the bunker with a loud thud, leaving a cloud of coal dust in his wake. Mum refused to buy the more expensive steaming coal briquettes he carried on his big red flatbed wagon.

December 1955:

Mum's tiredness meant we had to help with Christmas preparations. By tradition, we put up decorations on her birthday, the 13th of December. This year, however, Dad, Charlie, and I took on most of the work. On the 21st, my little brother, Samuel Stewart Green, was born at Barshaw Hospital in Paisley.

Naming our new sibling sparked debates among Mum, Dad, and Grannie Isa. The family rule was that Dad named the boys, and Mum named the girls. True to form, Dad named him Samuel after our uncle and Grannie Isa's Stewart family. Later, Mum subtly influenced his destiny by ensuring everyone called him "Stewart." However, in the fullness of time our Stewart preferred to be called Sam.

Christmas and New Year were magical times. Our home would be beautifully decorated, and extra food filled the cupboards. On Christmas morning, presents were laid out on separate chairs in the living room. My younger siblings were too little to fully grasp the excitement, but as the years passed, Christmas became a much-anticipated event in our household.

1957

January:

Winter was harsh, and coal supplies were limited. To conserve fuel in the evenings Dad would transfer the remaining burning coals from the living room fire onto the fire in their bedroom, filling the house with acrid coal smoke.

Charlie and I shared a double bed in the "wee back bedroom," while Ellen had her own room, and Stewart, for his first six months, slept in a cot in Mum and Dad's bedroom.

When the coal ran out, Dad resorted to burning old shoes and coal dross mixed with water to "back up the fire." This kept us supplied with hot water for our weekly Sunday baths. Outside, the smog was so dense that Mum wrapped scarves around our faces to filter the air. By the time I reached school, my scarf would be stained black with soot where my mouth was.

February:

Mum announced she was expecting another baby. In my innocence, I protested, saying we already had enough babies.

March to April:

Both Charlie and I developed bronchitis. My condition worsened to the point where I had to stay with Grannie Isa, who had already experienced the heartbreak of losing two sons and was determined to nurse me back to health. She made me a bed next to the fire in her living room, rubbed my chest and back with camphor oil, and fed me hearty Scotch broth. Within two days, I began to recover.

On the first day Grannie Green crafted a makeshift vest for me out of a freshly skinned pigskin she bought from the local butcher, stitching it together with twine to keep me warm and protected. By the end of April, my chest was clear, and I returned home.

On 15th April, Caroline Isabella Stewart Green was born in Mum and Dad's bedroom. Ellen was thrilled to finally have a little sister. Mum breastfed all her children but had to stop after six months, as the pain became unbearable. She was given tablets by the doctor to dry up her milk.

Grannie Isa became even more involved with our family, and Charlie and I spent much of our free time at her house, enjoying her nourishing soups and unconditional love.

June-December:

Life became much harder for Mum and Dad financially, and Dad started working more hours for various building companies. On weekends and evenings, he and Sammy continued with the debt collecting work. Charlie and I spent a lot of time with Uncle Sammy, who helped us with spelling and learning. This was done with small cards which were inserted into the lining of packets of Brook Bond tea, where you could also collect savings stamps and stick them onto a collection card by licking and sticking them. Chewing gum cards also served as our encyclopedia. I became more aware of my family after Christmas in 1957.

I have three brothers and two sisters, a Mum and Dad, a Grannie Isa (Grannie Green), Grandpa Green, Grannie Nellie Armstrong, and Grandpa Joe Armstrong. I also have Uncle Sammy, who is not married and lives with Grannie and Grandpa Green. Mum tells me she has two sisters: Auntie Margaret, who is married to Uncle Tommy Allan, and they have two sons, my cousins Jim and Thomas Junior, who live in Scott Avenue, Johnstone; and Auntie Alice, who is married to Uncle Gordon Minkley, and they have two children, my cousins James and Michelle, who live in Crich, near Matlock, in England. I also have Uncle Joe Armstrong, who is married to Jean, and they have two sons, my cousins David and Craig, who live in Linwood. I have Uncle Robert, who is married to Auntie May, and they have a large family of cousins: Robert, Joseph, Anne, Gordon, Caroline, Fiona, and Lizzie, who live in Glenburn, Paisley. I also found out I have Auntie Jennie, who is married to Uncle Matt, and they have two cousins, Oliver, and Isobel (the Tannahill's). Auntie Esther (Dad's younger sister) is married to Uncle Jimmy, and I have three cousins—John, Jim, and Scott (the Burns). Jennie and Esther also live in Abercorn Street, Paisley. I also have and auntie Jessie who is married to a man called Andy Carr. Auntie Jessie is probably on the spectrum with learning difficulties, and I can only remember her telling me that I was a "cheeky we bugger." My great-grandfather Charles Green is also still alive and lives in Glenburn with my Dad's aunt Nessie and Great uncle Jock McKenzie.

By 1957, I had over 40 living family members.

Charlie was affectionately known as "peas and barley" by Sammy. After a couple of years of Sammy's educational programme with the cards, Charlie and I could tell you about every country in the world, their capitals, currency, crops, exports, etc., just by looking at the flag. Our young brains soaked it all up. When Charlie was in his final class at primary school, he won first prize and was the school Dux (top student). I didn't do as well but received third prize: a French dictionary and a book for special subjects, Swiss Family Robinson by Daniel Defoe.

1958

As I look back, there was so much happening. I became more aware of my position as the oldest son, which was important, as Mum, especially, would rely on me to help with housework and running errands (fetching groceries). So, Charlie and I would help by grating carrots and turnips into big pots of soup, putting coal on the fire, and especially going to fetch the "messages." (groceries). This was a complex task depending on what was needed. Mostly it meant going to Galbraith's store in Falcon Crescent, and a typical list would be:

Galbraith's:

A plain loaf.

Half a pound of Stork or Echo margarine, 2 tins of Granny's tomato soup.

A packet of Brook Bond tea (green pack with stamp), 2 x 3lb bags of potatoes.

1 packet of "indigestive biscuits" (as I miscalled them), 6 oz of chopped pork.

6 oz of corned beef,   Half a pound of cheese.

A packet of Daz or OMO washing powder (whichever had a free plastic flower, usually a tulip or daffodil).

A cake of Sunlight soap; A packet of OXO cubes and a big onion

A packet of Dairylea cheese in a round box.

Galbraith's Butchers:

Half a pound of round sliced sausages, and pound of mince.

Half a pound of beef or pork links and a pound of lard (beef fat).

Robertson's Fish Shop:

4 slices of white fillet and a packet of fish dressing.

McMenemy's General Store:

I handed over a note to George, the owner, and he gave me a brown parcel. It took me years to find out that it was a packet of large Dr White sanitary towels. When I got older and became embarrassed, it became Charlie's job with the note.

On Friday Nights:

Mum would send me to get fish and chips from Broon's fish and chip shop, which was also in Falcon Crescent. Although Dad usually got paid on a Thursday night, it was Friday night before we celebrated the incoming wage.

3 fish suppers

2/6d worth of chips (Two Shillings and sixpence).

4 fritters (Potato slices in fried batter).

A jar of Silverskin pickled onions and a bottle of brown sauce.

A bar of Caramac white chocolate.

A bottle of Barr's Iron Brew or Vimto juice.

On Saturday Mornings:

If Dad had worked more overtime or we had more income, the treats continued, and I was sent to McLeod's Dairy, also in Falcon Crescent, to get:

A dozen rolls and a half a pound of chopped pork.

A print of fresh butter (half of a pound) and 6 cream puffs pastry.

2 pints of milk (normally we got our milk delivered, but we always needed more at weekends).

Sometimes I was sent to the Paisley Cooperative Manufacturing Society (PCMS) shop for basic food and butter biscuits. I would have to give a note to the assistant on my Mum's share book number, which was 32987.

If I was getting groceries for Grannie Isa, then her number was 23437. I have trouble now remembering pin numbers, but these numbers are an indelible imprint on my memory.

Falcon Crescent was a hub of activity, with people of all ages throughout the day. There was also a draper's shop, and later, Robertson's fish shop became a betting shop.

When Money Ran Out

Mum always did her best, but sometimes we simply ran out of food, so I was dispatched to Grannie Armstrong's in Abercorn Street, where she would give me a note for Field's Store in Old Sneddon Street. I suppose Mum would pay her back from her family allowance, which she collected from Menzies Post Office on Blackston Road every Tuesday. She had a book full of vouchers that were date-stamped and handed over for cash. This was known as family allowance.

I know Mum loved to visit Grannie Maw's, but usually, only when Grandpa Joe was at work. On occasion, however, he was on the night shift, and we had to be incredibly quiet. On one occasion, he got up wearing his nightshirt, displaying his pale but strong ex-footballer's legs, and closed the door to the old scullery. He emerged minutes later and went straight back to bed. It's only now that I realise he was having a pee in the sink.

Walking to Grannie Armstrong's

The walk from our house in Ferguslie Park was quite long. We would walk half a mile along the scheme, past Nellie Gray's shop (Nellie's), which was open all hours – well, from 07:00 to 21:00. Nellie's head was always shaking, and it took me years to realise she probably had Parkinson's disease, or some other ailment. Nellie allowed 'tick' (credit) to some of the poor souls living in the scheme.

We then turned at St James's Station, right into Greenhill Road for 100 yards, then left into Clark Street, passing the big Greenhill Hotel on the corner, followed by Stirrat's Dairy. A few yards more, and we passed Mrs. Ferguson's house, our headmistress at Ferguslie School, which had a large monkey tree in the garden. Moving up Clark Street, after the bridge, it became heavily industrial. A&F Craig's engineering works was where welding flashes could be seen from the street, and the clanging of air caulking guns could be heard as they dressed the welds on the metalwork. Onward, past Haldane's Chemical Works and the timber yard, where Charlie and I would always try to find a good stick for making swords.

At the end of Clark Street, the continuation was Albion Street, which ran parallel to Love Street Football Ground. We walked to the end, turned into Love Street, and continued for about 50 yards until we turned right into Wallace Street, passing the intersection with Old Sneddon Street, and down towards New Sneddon Street. Here, we came to an old, disused playground next to the old St James School. This school and playground with a Maypole were where my mum had grown up as a little girl, near Carlyle Quay on the banks of the River Cart.

This location held historical significance, as it was the first place in Britain where American troops disembarked during the First World War.

Passing Carlyle Quay on the left, we took a narrow pathway next to the old school, where we could peer through the broken windows into the old chapel on the ground floor. Then, we approached the old iron-riveted cantilevered frame bridge. It was painted grey and had two tracks with metal block teeth that engaged the curved part of the frame on the school side. Charlie and I would call these block teeth "Mars bars."

The River Cart was rat-infested, and you could see the rats swimming by, their movements leaving a V-shaped wake in the water.

One day, as we crossed the bridge, Mum said, "Hurry up, or the monster will get you." Charlie and I were petrified. "What monster, Mammy?" she told us that beneath the bridge sat a horrible monster with one red eye and one green, dragging chains that it used to capture children who played on the bridge. I was much older before I stopped taking the long route into town to avoid the bridge, and even then, I didn't waste any time. Mum was worried that we might fall off the bridge into the River Cart, as many children had in the past.

After crossing the bridge, we turned left into Abercorn Street and made our way past the farm, where hens roamed freely into the street. On the opposite side of the road to number 77 was where Grannie Maw Armstrong lived. Auntie Jennie and Uncle Matt Tannahill, along with my cousins Isobel and Oliver, lived at number 98, while Auntie Esther and Uncle Jimmy Burns lived at number 96. Abercorn Street was an industrial area, with two rows of old grey sandstone tenement properties. One shop, owned by the Fields family, was just one door up from number 77. Grannie Armstrong lived one floor up in a room and kitchen.

Also in the street was McCullum's Dye Works and White's Engineering Works, where machine tools for global export were made. This is where my grandfather, Joe Armstrong, worked as a radial arm driller.

Inside My Grandparents' Room and Kitchen

The room had a bed recess, and the scullery had a Belfast sink with a gas geyser water boiler and a gas cooker. Apart from that, there was a tallboy cupboard and two chairs. On the cupboard was a miniature barrel in wood and brass, which I think was a biscuit barrel. On the old, tiled fireplace, there were two seashells, about the size of a boy's fist, which, when placed against your ear, Grannie said, you could hear the sea. I was always amazed by this, as it was true. In the corner, behind the door, was an upright piano.

The door into the flat was a heavy panel door, and inside, on a hook, was a large, heavy black metal key for the outside toilet, which was located on the landing, half a flight of stairs down.

Going to the Toilet

Going to that toilet was not a pleasant experience for several reasons. It was usually cold and smelly, and we had to use newspaper or, if we were lucky, Izal paper, which was extremely hard. There was a large hole in the door, so the last thing you wanted to see was someone's eye. Often, the seat was wet, so we would put down the newspaper, which would leave an ink print on your rear end. Finally, there was the chain and handle, which was so old and dirty, I'm sure it harbored all sorts of germs.

The room and kitchen were so small that Charlie and I would often be sent outside to play, usually in the back court, which had open middens – large, oblong, galvanized containers with two handles for the binmen to empty into the rubbish carts. (This provided plenty of food for rats.)

Cartvale Lane and the Docks

Sometimes, Charlie and I would venture into Cartvale Lane, which was a fork in the road just up from the old swing bridge. The first building was the head office of McCullum's Dye Factory, and further down the road was the dockside, where timber from all over the world was unloaded.

After a cup of tea, Mum would start the long trek back home, with Charlie and me out in front, and Ellen and Stewart hanging onto the pram, which had Caroline safely inside, away from the barking dogs and drunks who loitered around the Fountain Gardens in Love Street, as we made our way home.

CHAPTER 4:
THE STORIES WE WERE TOLD

The Stories We Were Told:

From as far back as I can remember, Mum told us stories. They began to be remembered in 1959 and developed over the next few years. Here are the ones I can recall.

Grandpa Joe, Footballer:

This is a true story. I know that Grandpa Armstrong served in the HLI during the First World War. As a young man, he worked as a riveter in the shipyards in Govan, where he met Grannie Maw (Helen Lowe). After the war, he started playing professional football, and played for various teams, such as Stenhousemuir, Royal Albert, Saltcoats Victoria, and eventually St Mirren at Love St. According to the stories, he was a good defender and occasionally played the man rather than the ball. Opposition crowds regularly booed him when he did this, to which his response was always the "V" sign. He played for St Mirren in the late 1920s.

It is more than likely that Grandpa Joe was affected by his experiences in the war, as I know he drank heavily. Although he always had a job, after his death, papers were found showing that he was paying back loans to a money collector in Well St Paisley. This may be an unfair reflection on him, as we know Mum received help from them with food bills. I do know, however, that when I was about 10 and visiting Grannie Armstrong, I was misbehaving with my cousins, Robert, and Joseph, while eating a bowl of soup served by Grannie Maw. Grandpa Joe skelped me on the ear for "sluchttering" in my soup. I left quickly and never went back to 77 Abercorn St while he was alive.

When he was drunk, he was very unpredictable. He would burst into Al Jolson songs, using a frying pan as a banjo prop. If my aunt and uncles weren't paying attention, he would bang them on the head with the frying pan. Another story was that when the family were having a sit-down meal at the table, Auntie Mag asked for more butter. He dug out a large slice of butter from its dish and decorated Auntie Mag's mouth with it. On another occasion, my Dad had the habit of visiting 77 Abercorn St on New Year's Day with a drink for Joe. On this occasion, he was a day late, and Joe jumped on his back. "Where the fuck have you been?" he shouted, slapping Dad on the back of his neck and bursting a boil that Dad was growing, sending pus all over the place.

I know this paints a bleak picture, but he had been raised by my Great Grandparents, Robert Armstrong, a soldier (Colors Sergeant) from Ayrshire, and Alice Roche, a middle-class piano teacher from Dublin. They were both devout Catholics, well-dressed, and lived in McKerrel St in Paisley, next to the old Grammar School. Joe could play the piano and was certainly a character, but I do think his war experiences left a lasting mark on him. I know for sure that Mum was afraid of him, and my cousin Robert Armstrong told me that Grannie Maw once had a big bruise on her chest where Joe had poked her during an argument. So, Joe was a complex character, sometimes brutal but probably damaged by the horror of the trenches.

Grannie Maw, Artist's Model:

This story may not be true, but apparently, when Grannie Maw was a young woman from Govan, she had long, lustrous red hair, on which she could sit. She was also in service in a big house in Govan, where the owner was an artist who painted her portrait. The portrait was apparently displayed for some time in the Kelvin Art Galleries in Glasgow. One thing I do know is that my two daughters inherited that long red hair.

The Cement Mixer:

Mum told this story in such a graphic way that I believe it to be true. During the Second World War, my Auntie Mag had been assigned to work at Babcock & Wilcox Engineering Works in Renfrew. On Fridays, she would get paid, and Mum had been sent to French St in Renfrew, near the main offices, to collect her wages.

As Mum stood waiting, a construction lorry carrying equipment and men on the back of it turned to go up a lane off French St, which had an entranceway with an overhead beam. A large cement mixer struck the beam and was dragged off the lorry with one of the men, falling on top of him and crushing his chest. Mum witnessed this man's last breath, a very graphic death scene, which marked her for life. She was only 13 years old at the time.

The Bull:

This is another story I believe to be true . During the early part of the 20th century, cattle were driven from Gilmour St Station in Paisley town centre along Love St to the slaughterhouse in Mossvale, which was at the back of Love St football ground. On one occasion, a bull bolted away from the herd and found its way into New Sneddon St, with an angry farmer in hot pursuit. Eventually, the bull was cornered by the farmer with a big stick at Carlyle Quay, in front of Mum's house. To escape the beating, the bull charged into the common close just as Mum was coming down the stairs. She was petrified at the sight of this huge, sweating, snorting bull being beaten by the farmer. An elderly lady in the house below rescued her by pulling her inside and closing the door. Mum would have been about 10 years old when this happened.

The Monk Ghost:

Mum would tell us a story about how she was coming down the stairs at her house in Carlyle Quay when she saw an apparition — a monk holding a prayer book. She was startled and gasped. The monk disappeared, leaving behind spiraling puffs of smoke. This is an interesting ghost story, as the building was constructed on the site of an old monastery affiliated with Paisley Abbey. It could have been the active imagination of a young girl — who knows? But the story certainly spooked us kids.

Shrapnel:

This story from 6th May 1941 is true. In our Ferguslie kitchen, on a shelf, there was a jar filled with various bits and pieces, including a large splinter of metal about 3 inches long and 1 inch wide with rough edges. Mum told us that during the German bombing of

Clydebank, she was running to the air raid shelter with the siren blasting in her ears to the Fountain Gardens local park with her mother and father. This piece of shrapnel ripped through her coat and began to smolder. Grandpa Joe attended it by removing the coat as they ran. The shard remained in our family for many years before it disappeared. The fact is, though, that the shrapnel didn't come from Clydebank, but rather from a bomb that fell just a few hundred yards away in Mossvale Paisley, where it had taken out two houses. Joe didn't want his little girl to know that the bomb had been so close to their house. The Germans were targeting the Paisley gas tank. One of the bombs missed the gas tank and hit a nearby first aid post and killed all the doctors and nurses and others a total of 92 people.

Paisley Gas tank, target for the German bombers WW2

Little Nell:

Mum would tell us the story of the little match girl who sold matches on the cold streets of London during winter to earn money for food for her sick little brother. She tried unsuccessfully to sell her matches in the bitter cold of Christmas Day, lighting them to warm her hands. As she wandered through the streets where grand mansions stood, she could see wealthy families inside, feasting on tasty food and wine, sitting in front of roaring fires. The next day, the dust cart man found a bundle in the gutter, frozen stiff. No more matches from the little match girl. We were all reduced to tears, especially Ellen, our sister, who had an incredibly soft heart.

Uncle Joe:

Uncle Joe Armstrong was Mum's oldest brother. He was a soldier and very fit; according to Mum, he could walk down all the stairs in their house on his hands. The story goes that while he was fighting in Italy during the war, he and two other soldiers captured an entire mountain full of Italian soldiers, about 1,000 of them. This may have happened, as many Italians surrendered to the Allies as soon as they saw Mussolini hanging upside down with his girlfriend on the banks of Lake Como. It was also reported that while a comrade was cleaning his gun, a shot was fired, and it entered Joe's cheek and exited his neck without damaging any arteries or his spine. He did have a scar on his cheek, but I'm not sure if this part of the story is true.

Auntie Alice:

Auntie Alice was Mum's older sister, but younger than Auntie Mag. Mum didn't have much to say about Alice, other than the fact that she loved her more than Mag, and that she had a gentle nature. Auntie Alice met Uncle Gordon Minkley during the war and moved away to England, where she had two children, Jim and Michelle.

School Prizes and Certificates:

Mum had an old worn brown leather handbag, a little larger than a normal one, about the size of a small briefcase. Inside this bag were several certificates Mum had received when she was at school. Every now and then, she would take them out and show us these beautifully embossed certificates for English, Arithmetic, and so on. She would also tell the story of when a large, fancy-dressed doll was given to someone in her class at school. I don't think she received the doll, because all her life, Mum loved to cut out and dress up paper dolls.

Heavy Horses and Fights at the North Pole:

Next door to Mum's house at Carlyle Quay was a stable yard, or carter's place, with several horses and carts. Heavy horses were the main means of transport in the twenties and thirties. Mum would tell us about the horses sweating and twitching, leaving piles of dung in the streets. One story she told was about when she was a little girl, and she saw a carter whipping his horse to pull a heavy load up St Mirren Brae in the centre of Paisley. She said that no matter how hard the carter used his whip, the horse just sat down and refused to get up. This story left an impression on me about hard taskmasters and work.

Working in McCullum's:

Mum had only a few jobs after leaving school, one of which was working in a sweet shop in Paisley High St, near the YMCA building. During the war, she worked in the laundry on Seedhill Rd and giggled with the other girls when they found pictures of naked ladies in the POW laundry basket. After the war, she got a full-time job at McCallum's Dye Works as a machinist. She met my Aunty May there, and that's how May met her husband, Uncle Robert, Mum's brother. Mum didn't talk much about this job, but I think my grandfather's cousin, Charlie Donovan, who was a foreman colorist at McCallum's, may have helped Mum get her first job. The Donovan's and the Armstrongs have a long, good history together.

The Armstrongs (Mums family) late 1940s

Mum behind Grannie Armstrong

Uncles Joe and Robert missing

as they were serving during the war

Robert Armstrong, my great-great-grandfather (GGG), was in the army in Ireland during the Easter Rising (1916) troubles and was based at Blackrock Barracks south of Dublin. His comrade was Charlie Donovan's father. They met up with Alice and her sister Emily for dates, and eventually, after the troubles, they all returned to Scotland, where they married and settled down. Donovan and his new wife, Emily, moved to Clydebank, and Robert and Alice settled in Paisley. GGG Armstrong got a manager's job at the Cartvale Chemical factory, while Donovan became an insurance salesman. Sadly, he only lived for a few years, dying of tuberculosis, leaving behind a wife and three children. It was Robert Armstrong who helped this family survive. So, old Charlie Donovan was merely repaying a favour by helping Mum get her job.

During the war, Charlie Donovan's son, Charles Jr, joined the RAF, and in his pocket, he kept a picture of his young blonde cousin, Ellen, in his tunic. I like this idea, as I met Charles Jr in the nineties, and he was a great man, then a retired director of British Gas.

Monkeys and Men Fighting:

At one time, Carlyle Quay was a busy little harbour, and many of the men returning from seafaring had exotic tastes and hard drinking habits. Mum would talk about local people having pet monkeys and other exotic animals brought home. On the corner of most streets in that area there were many pubs, one of which was called the North Pole. Mum said that when this pub was busy, fights would often break out, and the men would spill out into the street. She could hear the noise of headbutting and fistfights before the Black Maria police van arrived, and the men were duly truncheoned to the ground and carted off to Paisley Gaol (jail).

Carlyle Quay with the house where mum was born on the left

CHAPTER 5:
MY FATHERS TEARS

1959

January - February

It was another bleak winter, with freezing smog and deep snow. I can vividly remember scraping the ice from the inside of my bedroom window, where beautiful fern-like patterns had formed from the damp air in the room, a result of our breath and lack of ventilation. In early February, I visited Grannie Green and noticed that Grandpa Green was unwell. He had been wounded during the First World War when mustard gas damaged his lungs and eyes during the battle for Passchendaele in Belgium.

He was only able to breathe with about a third of his lungs. Every night, he would cough up dreadful green lumps of catarrh and often struggle to catch his breath. His skin had an almost blue tinge as he fought to breathe, a battle that had plagued him since 1918 when he was exposed to mustard gassed.

I can still picture his notched bayonet, tucked away in a drawer in Gran's bedroom.

On the 1st of February, I visited Grannie Isa and Grandpa Green with my Dad, who was obviously concerned. The smog was so thick I could hardly see ahead of me, so I clung tightly to my Dad's hand. When we arrived, Grandpa Green looked very unwell. Grampa, Dad, and Sammy were discussing horse racing bets, and Dad wrote out a bookie's line for Grandpa Green, signing it with his nom de plume "Punty." Whenever you wrote out a line for the bookie, you had to include your nom de plume. Dads was "Bunty."

Grandpa Green passed away that night from chronic emphysema and heart failure. He was only 59. I never saw my Dad cry, but I know he did, and I could sense it affected him deeply. There was a large family gathering at Grannie Isa's house, 114 Ferguslie Park Ave, and I was there. My Dad took me into the bedroom where my grandfather lay. A plastic device was holding his chin up, and his skin had taken on a bluish pallor. No one said he was just sleeping— "He's deed, son." A few days later, the smog lifted, and we could finally see Grandpa's coffin as it was taken towards Hawkhead Cemetery in Paisley. At the purvey, everyone was kind to me, and I remember receiving lots of pocket money.

Grandad Green 1958

Grannie Isa was completely grief-stricken, but she soldiered on. Mum and Dad let me stay with her frequently for the next few years, until I reached puberty. Mum had gained so much weight that it was hard to tell whether she was pregnant again, but she was, at least five months along, though she didn't talk about it.

March - June

I was always aware that it was 1959 because our teacher, Mrs. Cowan, required us to write the date in the margin of our books every day. When I started school in Primary One, I was given a small slate tablet with a wooden frame and a French chalk stick to write with. By 1959, we had moved on to pencils, and later, at the big school, we had pens, ink, and blotters. My writing was a mess, the nibs digging into the paper. Dad would tell me to write by going up light and down heavy, confusing me by saying that's how his late brother had done it, and that he won prizes for his writing.

So, the story goes that my Dad's older brother, Charles, was exceptionally bright and was set to be promoted to Camphill Senior Secondary. However, he contracted appendicitis, which turned into peritonitis. It then burst, and he died.

The most significant event of the year, however, came on the 15th of June when my sister, Anne Denise, was born at 94 Ferguslie Park Ave. I now had three sisters. Dad may have had a French girlfriend named Denise when he was stationed in the south of France, waiting to be transferred to Palestine. He was very insistent on this name for his daughter.

Dad and Denise *Theory* June (1946)

It took a few days for the mood to lift in the Regiment. However, as they moved towards the Middle East and the weather warmed, the young Argylls began to think more seriously about combat.

"Whit's it like tae kill a man, Sarge?"

Jimmy genuinely wanted to know. He'd fist-fought in the streets of his hometown, Paisley, but when a man had had enough, that was it – you let him go. He'd seen other men go berserk during a fight, with bystanders having to pull them off their victims to stop them committing murder.

Sergeant Aitcheson had seen his fair share of combat, having fought the Germans, and he'd killed plenty of men.

"Killing is different each time, never the same twice. If you drop a man at, say, fifty yards, he might only be wounded. In fact, most shots don't usually kill outright. If you're lucky and hit him in the head or face, there's usually a big pink blood burst, and sometimes you can see the brains flying through the air. If ye have to finish him off, then the bayonet is best—straight through the heart. If you're low on ammo, you'll need the bayonet a lot. It's awful messy, and most men die slow. I've seen me hitting them over the head with big rocks or the rifle butt. It makes a crunchy noise, and they squeal like hell. The fact is, lads, some of you will be good at it, some of you will like doing it, and some of you will be vomiting all over the place. But remember this: it's you or him. It's better to be a bad bastard than a dead one."

"Aye, Sarge, I've heard that somewhere before! "The troop ship tied up at the naval base at Toulon on the south coast of France. The men were given 12 hours of short ship leave. A 10-tonner and a troop carrier were to travel east to Hyères along the Boulevard de Strasbourg to collect some supplies for the final leg of the journey to Palestine.

Jimmy found himself among ten of his company, on his way to help gather supplies from an agreed pick-up point in the market area of Hyères. It was warm, and the sea view was spectacular. The Argylls were dressed in short-sleeve order, with khaki shorts and heavy webbing belts.

When they reached the market depot, the troops jumped from the back of the covered truck.

Since leaving Perth in Scotland, Corporal Ronnie Syme, now sporting two full stripes, had been put in charge of the mission to pick up stores.

"Right, men, fall in and follow me," he ordered, leading the two columns of men towards the main market office. The area was packed with army vehicles loading up. Syme stood the men at ease outside the office door. With a clipboard in hand and all the necessary paperwork, he entered and approached the desk.

"I'm looking for Denis Martinez," he announced.(Thinking it was a man)

A tall, sallow Frenchman took the papers and spoke in French to his colleague, a shorter, sallow Frenchman.

"You must come with me, Sir," the taller one said in good English.

"Are you Denis?"

"Ah non, Sir." His English slipping, he pointed to a striking woman, Denise Martinez, who was overseeing another loading operation across the yard.

"Well, fuck me, is that no a sight for sair eyes?"

Denise Martinez had been commissioned by the British Navy Overseas Procurement Office and was based locally on the Giens Peninsula in the South of France. Before her commission, she had spent the entire war fighting with the French Underground. She was not only formidable but also exceptionally attractive.

The men outside had already spotted her, giving the compulsory wolf whistles, unaware that she was the Commanding Officer of the Depot.

Jimmy, paired up with Wully Connell at the front of the two columns,

couldn't help but stare.

"Jesus Christ, have you ever seen a better-looking woman than that?"

"Very nice." Jimmy understated his reaction. As he watched Denise, he felt something new wash over him. It could have been that she was the first truly feminine woman he had seen since basic training—or maybe something else. The result was that he was temporarily mesmerized.

"Squad, at the double, over here to the big white building!"

Denise checked Corporal Syme's paperwork, ignoring his feeble attempts at small talk. She then organised her warehouse staff and the Argylls to start loading the 10-ton truck. She stood back in a shaded area of the warehouse, watching the young soldiers. Jimmy soon became the focus of this experienced French woman's attention. She watched his muscular arms and powerful physique as he loaded the truck. Every chance Jimmy got; he smiled back at her. She observed the whole operation until it was complete.

As the truck began to pull out of the yard, Jimmy etched her image into his memory. She was tall, about 5ft 9 inches, just slightly shorter than him. She had deep brown hair and blue eyes, a classic hourglass figure, and wore navy shoes that matched her pencil skirt. Her open-necked blouse was pale blue, like the Mediterranean sky.

But it was that sexy smile that captivated Jimmy. From the back of the truck, he waved to her. She waved back and blew him a kiss.

Jimmy had to be restrained from jumping out of the truck.

"Did ye see that? She blew me a kiss! If it's the last thing I do, I'm coming back here to get her."

When they returned to the ship and offloaded the supplies, the men were called to order at the quayside.

The Commanding Officer, Colin Mitchell ("Mad Mitch of Aden"), addressed the Regiment from a small portable rostrum.

"Attention, men!" There was a thud of boots on the ground.

"Alright, at ease, men." (Another thud of boots.)

"As you know, we were scheduled to embark tomorrow morning for our destination. H.Q. has advised us to wait for strategic supplies being shipped overland, and they'll be here on Sunday. This means you'll all be given a mixture of light duties and extra shore leave." A huge roar of approval went up.

"Any breach of discipline will be severely dealt with. I'll leave your NCOs to brief you on what is required." He dismounted the rostrum and disappeared back onto the ship.

Jimmy was burning to get back to Hyères and see if he could get close to Denise.

"C'mon, Sarge, let me go on the supply run or maybe get some leave," Jimmy tried to be persuasive.

"Private Green, don't even try to beg me, it doesn't suit you." "Anyway, you're on a special mission, so forget about Denise." The rest of "C" company erupted into laughter, bellowing D-E-N-I-S-E, Sergeant!"

Jimmy shot a quizzical look at his Sergeant. "Special mission, Sergeant?" "Aye, the Colonel's asked me to provide four soldiers for onshore escort duties."

"Escort duties, Sarge?"

"Get yourselves cleaned up and changed, ready for official escort duty at 18:00 hrs. tonight."

Tam Aitcheson had chosen his four best soldiers for the job: Private Jimmy Green, marksman and regimental boxer; Private Jimmy Stevenson, radio operator; Corporal Ronnie Syme, his right-hand man with combat experience; and Private Alan Walls, driver.

After a short briefing, they prepared for the mission. At 18:00, they were in a small convoy of two army cars, heading east.

The colonel sat in the rear car with the Regimental Interpreter and two officers from the ship: the Captain and the First Officer.

"This is all very mysterious, Sarge?"

"Naw, it's no. The officers are meeting at a small hotel on the Giens Peninsula for some military business and dinner. All we have to do is make sure there are no fuckups. Now shut the fuck up."

The men were dressed smartly in lightweight uniforms, with their Glengarry bonnets cocked at an angle, nearly ready to fall off their heads. They wore white webbing belts, kilts with the "swinging six sporrans," red and white- diced army socks, and boots polished to a mirror shine.

They breathed in the salty Mediterranean air, thickened by the salt fields of the peninsula, as the convoy drove down towards the town of Giens. The cars pulled uphill, revealing a stunning panorama of the Mediterranean as they neared the town and entered Avenue des Stemes. The two cars stopped outside the Hotel Lune de Neil.

The guard escort jumped out quickly, took up their positions, and the officers passed between them, entering the hotel.

Jimmy tried to keep his gaze forward, but his eyes kept drifting to the activities inside. The officers were shaking hands with others and being guided into the bowels of the building, where a large official dinner table awaited, with panoramic views of the Mediterranean.

Jimmy's heart skipped a beat as his eyes focused on the divine figure approaching the entrance.

"Denise," he gasped.

She was with another woman, dressed in chic evening wear: pale blue, a gold clutch handbag, and white high heels. Her belt was tight and matched the bag.

As she entered the hotel, they gave a smart salute, and she smiled sweetly at him, brushing past him as she did.

Jimmy nearly fainted. His eyes followed her into the hotel until she disappeared. He inhaled the air, as if drawing in her scent like the last drag of a cigarette.

"Fuck me, that was her. That was Denise."

"Calm down, Jimmy. She's well out of your league, pal. A woman like that only has eyes for the brass."

Tam Aitcheson called them to "At ease." The men relaxed and held their rifles at a side angle.

"You two relax and have a fag. I'll be back in fifteen minutes."

Jimmy and Ronnie Syme stepped to the side of the hotel, where they could lean over the wall, gazing out at the azure, blue sea as they lit up. From there, they had a clear view of the official dinner table laid out on the patio, again with the Mediterranean in the background. Denise was sitting opposite Colonel Mitchell, clearly enjoying herself. Jimmy wished he could be down there, but he knew it would never happen.

He tried to make small talk with Ronnie.

"Aye, I haven't got a clue how to use cutlery. Ma maw always just gave us a spoon."

"How the fuck can you eat steak with a spoon, man?" "I don't know, I've never had a steak in ma life."

"C'mon, Jimmy, don't take the piss. You must've tasted a steak, pal!"

"Naw, a lot o' mince, but never a steak."

"When we get out of the army, I'm treating you to a steak. My Uncle Andy's a butcher."

They finished their cigarettes and returned to relieve their comrades.

At the official dinner table, there were about ten male officers, two female officers, and four other female escorts. All of the men were in uniform, while the women wore elegant evening dresses suitable for a summer evening. The meeting's purpose was to discuss the ongoing relationship with Navy supplies and the logistics in place and concern over spies. After the business was concluded, the group sat down to dinner. Denise was seated opposite Colonel Mitchell. In a charming mood, she spared him the trouble of using his schoolboy French by speaking perfect English in a middle-class accent.

"Can you talk, Colonel, about your duties in the Middle East?"

"Sorry, Mademoiselle, but I'm afraid that's classified." He had already noticed that she wasn't wearing a wedding ring.

"So, what can we talk about?" she pressed. "I would like to propose a toast first." Everyone raised their glasses.

"To the *entente cordiale*," the group said in unison.

"Could I add, Colonel? Thank you for liberating my country."

"May I also suggest that you call me Denise?" she added with a smile.

"We can indeed, Denise and your beautiful companion?" "This is Mademoiselle Abarrane Teluskin."

Colonel Mitchell gave a mental check without showing it, then politely extended his hand across the table to shake Abarrane's. He smiled.

"Enchanted, my dear."

He had studied the Middle East situation for four years and knew immediately that "Teluskin" was a Jewish surname. He grew wary, knowing both Jews and Arabs were hostile to the British Army in Palestine.

Denise had already made up her mind about Colonel Mitchell within the first five minutes. She didn't like him. His piggy looks and short stature were physically so different from the young Argyll she had been fantasizing about.

My father James Green 1ˢᵗ Battalion the Argyll and Sutherland Highlanders

The rest of the evening passed with polite, superficial conversation. As the evening wound down, Denise placed her hand on the Colonel's cuff.

"I wonder, Colonel, do you have soldiers who can dance the Highland sword dance?"

"Yes, we do," he answered, his curiosity piqued.

"I was wondering, since your ship does not leave until Monday, if you would like to come to a small private garden party at my house in La Tour Fondue, only a few kilometers from here?"

"We would be delighted, Mademoiselle." The Colonel made a note of the arrangements, and he and his officers followed Denise out toward the entrance, where their guard detail was waiting. Denise stayed close behind, inspecting the men.

She stopped in front of Jimmy. "What is your name, soldier?"

Jimmy glanced at the Colonel for permission to answer. The Colonel nodded.

"Private Green, Ma'am." "Your first name, please?" "Jimmy, Ma'am."

"I think the translation would be Jacques Vert! Or Vert Jacques," she smiled.

"Can you do the Sword Dance, Jimmy?" "Yes, Ma'am."

"Good. Then maybe I'll see you tomorrow."

The next day, Sergeant Aitcheson organized a dance rehearsal on the quayside. It was a warm, beautiful day, and the mood among the men was upbeat.

The men selected for the garden party included the regimental band and six of the best dancers, including Jimmy. The same officers attended, minus the ship's officers who had to prepare the vessel. Now, this was strictly Argyll business.

As the small convoy veered left before the town of Giens, the men caught sight of the turquoise-blue sea of the Azure Coast. The truck's flaps were rolled up, allowing the warm air to flow through, and members of the band loosened their collars. They proceeded down a dirt track road toward a large country house just off the beach, surrounded by Mediterranean flowers.

The house was built from local stone with a terracotta Roman tile roof and encircled by fully grown dragon trees. The front garden was awash with blooming blue dawn trumpet flowers that surrounded the windows and doorway.

The garden walls were lined with large clumps of yellow senna flowers and red China roses. Someone clearly loved this place.

Denise ran out from the side of the house to greet her guests. There wasn't a single man who didn't have a smile on his face. They were a long way from a dreary wet grey day in Glasgow.

This time, Colonel Mitchell received a r e s e r v e d kiss on both cheeks.

Denise was in high spirits, bubbly and clearly looking forward to the party.

The Argylls were directed to a large garden at the side of the house, which overlooked the sea. A designated area had been set aside for the display, with a row of tables laden with food and wine, courtesy of the store's facility in Hyeres. Around fifty people were there—family, friends, and some French Navy officers.

Colonel Mitchell had tried to gather some intelligence on Abarrane Teluskin, but none was forthcoming.

Denise opened the party by thanking everyone for coming, with a special thanks to the Regiment and Colonel Mitchell. She then outlined the plan for the day and the entertainment, which would feature the dancers and the pipe band.

The event began with Pipe Major Sean McGinn calling the band to attention, followed by tuning up. The band then played several Scottish airs, their haunting melodies creating a striking atmosphere in the Mediterranean setting. There were solo piping and drum displays, followed by a break for refreshments. Most of the young soldiers had never seen such an abundance of food, having been raised on war rations. Sergeant Aitcheson kept a watchful eye on the men, reminding them of the importance of discretion and the potential dangers of careless talk. They had all been briefed beforehand on the proper conduct.

Denise, typically cool and composed, was unusually excited to mingle with the young Argyll soldiers. She found herself drawn to Jimmy in particular.

"What dance are you going to perform for me, Jimmy?" she asked. "Just a selection of Strathspeys and Reels, Ma'am," Jimmy replied. "Would you show me how to do that?"

"It would be a pleasure, Ma'am," Jimmy smiled, as did the rest of the men.

As Denise moved on to speak with others, the soldiers muttered amongst themselves, sharing thoughts they knew better than to voice too loudly.

"That lady is pure class, boys."

"Dream on boys!" Ronnie Syme, standing nearby, made sure the men kept their thoughts to themselves.

The dancers took their positions as the pipers began the introduction. The young soldiers looked resplendent in short-sleeve order, Black Watch kilts with belts, highland hose stockings, and black lace-up dancing pumps. They raised their arms in the classic Highland dance position, their hands held above their heads to resemble the antlers of the great stag. Denise was mesmerized, charmed by every movement. She watched, captivated by the muscles in their legs, the sheen of sweat on their faces, and her imagination running wild with thoughts of what lay beneath their kilts. The sight of men in kilts had always stirred something in her.

After the display, Denise approached the Colonel.

"Colonel, my dear Sir, may I borrow one of your men for a moment? I'd like to discuss the dancing," she said with a playful smile. "Of course, Mademoiselle, c'est la vie."

"C'est la vie, merci son kilt," Denise replied, then turned to Jimmy.

She pulled him from the crowd and led him upstairs into her boudoir. The moment they entered, it was clear what was about to happen. Before he knew it, Jimmy was on the bed, his kilt pushed up around his chin. Denise, filled with overwhelming excitement, was beyond control. It was a frenzied, passionate encounter—one that would leave a lasting memory for Jimmy, especially every time he looked at his Glengarry. For the rest of his life Jimmy was never far from his Glengarry.

(End of Theory)

In April 1959, something else remarkable happened: St Mirren, the football team that the entire family supported, won the Scottish Cup at Hampden Park. It had only been a few months since Granddad Green had passed, and the victory became a symbol of joy for the family. They celebrated with dancing and drinking, and for the first time, Jimmy saw the adults in his family so happy. The victory was even recorded in the newspapers:

25/04/1959

Final   Hampden Park Attendance : 108,591

St. Mirren 3 Aberdeen 1

Team: - Dave Trotter, Davie Lapsley, John Wilson, Jackie Neilson, Jack McGugan, Tommy Leishman, Jim Rodger, Tommy Bryceland, Gerry Baker, Tommy Gemmell, Alistair Miller

This is the last crowd over 100,000 for a match not including one of the Old Firm (Rangers and Celtic).

The game and the players were discussed endlessly afterward, and they became local heroes.

Another hero of that time was John "Cowboy" McCormack. Known as "Cowboy," McCormack started boxing in 1950 at the age of fifteen. By 1956, he held the Scottish and A.B.A. Light Middleweight titles as an amateur and earned the bronze medal in the light middleweight division at the 1956 Summer Olympics in Melbourne, Australia.

He compiled an impressive amateur record of 103-6, with 51 knockouts. McCormack (also another Feg) lived at the top of the Ferguslie scheme and was a regular on the bus to town. Jimmy vividly remembered sitting opposite him on the bus, recognizing him by his brown leather kit case.

July-August

It was a sizzling summer, and we got seven weeks off school, so we played football non-stop in the cow park at the back of the rows of council houses. Sometimes in the evenings, groups of men would gather to play cards or pitch and toss for money. When the police van appeared on the old dirt track near the railway, they would scatter quickly, looking for the lookout to give him a good kicking.

All the kids knew each other, and we'd often head to the "Cowboy Valley," a stretch of waste ground with small hills and trees next to Clark Hunter's Cooperage, which smelled fantastic. Sometimes Charlie and I would embark on adventures up to the Glennifer Braes or out to the "Black Hill's" near Inkerman or the Moss to collect tadpoles. Once, we ran away for a day, and when we returned, we got a real roasting. Apparently, two boys had been killed when a wall collapsed at the back of those tenements on Brown Street. Someone had put our names in the frame, and journalists were waiting at the door when we got home safely.

We also played on the bing , which was the local rubbish dump near Abbotsinch Aerodrome (now Glasgow Airport). We found all sorts of things, including hypodermic syringes, which we filled with water from puddles and used as water guns during water fights. We were early "dump kids," I guess. On one of these trips, Charlie lost his shoe in deep mud while we scrambled across the main train line to avoid a train on the way to Greenock. He was limping on the hard ground and stones, so he climbed onto my back all the way home. I always smile when I hear the old Searchers song, "He Ain't Heavy, He's My Brother."

Our summer days were never without incident. Usually, Charlie would slice his leg, or we would cut ourselves, or some of the other kids would break bones. As the oldest, I'd have to take them to the Royal Alexandra Infirmary (RAI) for stiches or plaster casts. After a few years, all the nurses knew me by my first name.

The truth was that Mum and Dad were flat out just trying to survive, so we were well-loved but totally feral.

September - December

Back to school, and the process of handing down clothes from the older kids to the younger ones began. Mum would buy me clothes that were at least one size too big, and anything I had—especially my school uniform—would be passed down to Charlie. Ellen was lucky as the only girl at school; her clothes were new, and Mum would always tie a ribbon in her hair. At Christmas, Dad would take me up to the Barras in Glasgow's east end on Christmas Eve to get toys for all the kids. This meant walking about a mile to the top of Ferguslie Park Avenue, passing under the arched railway bridge, and then a short walk to the main bus route into Paisley, which led us through to Glasgow.

Dad had a good pace.

We'd get on the tram opposite Brown's Brickwork Factory, which rattled and buzzed its way through Paisley town centre and along Paisley Road West into Glasgow. Eventually, we'd reach Clyde Street. Dad would point out the Carrick tea clipper, then a club for ex-naval officers, and the large cranes, which he called "Derricks."

We'd proceed toward the Barras via the Salt Market and arrive at the pitching stalls where the Barrow Boys shouted to sell their wares. I found it all exciting, and by the time we were done, we had presents for everyone, including me. I wasn't so sure about Santa anymore, though, wondering if he'd bring me anything because I knew from last year that he left presents at Gran Green's.

Dad asked me to wait at the bus stop for a minute while he popped into a pub on Clyde Street. He told me not to let anyone steal the presents I was carrying. Standing outside, I could smell the beer, smoke, and listened to a pleasing, manly buzz coming from inside.

On the tram ride back home, Dad explained that as I was a big boy now, I should know there was no real Santa. He asked me to sneak the presents into the house and hide them in the wardrobe in his room, so the others wouldn't figure out what was going on.

As we travelled back, the tram windows became steamed up. The diffused light outside looked like something out of a Monet painting. I wiped it away with my hand and noticed the nicotine-tinged droplets run down the walls.

When we got home, I hid the presents in the wardrobe. Mum made me a cup of sweet milky tea and a piece of toast with melted margarine.

On Christmas morning, the living room was transformed. There were bundles of presents on every chair and couch. We were all so excited, and Santa had forgot to bring me my present: a Lone Star silver Buntline Special gun, complete with a spinning barrel and six bullets that fired caps. I did eventually get this from my son Jamie for my 60th birthday present who remembered my story (thanks Jamie).

Dad smiled and said, "Maybe there really is a Santa, son."

CHAPTER 6:
THE BEST GRANNIE IN THE WORLD

1960

We now had a boys' room and a girls' room. In the boys' room, Charlie, Stewart, and I all slept in the one big double bed. In the girls' room, Ellen and Caroline slept in a double bed, and Anne slept in a cot.

In the boys' room, we had a chest of drawers and a gas fire, which had little cones that glowed when the gas was burning. However, no matter how cold it was, this fire produced very unpleasant fumes, and I think both Mum and Dad knew it was a real health risk. So, we never complained about the cold, and sometimes we got hot water bottles for our feet, which were lemonade bottles filled with hot water from the kettle wrapped up in an old towel. Grannie Green owned one of those earthenware bottles, which she used all the time because she would get night cramps. Sometimes when I stayed with her, I got to sleep in her bed, and she would wake me up so I could rub her cramped leg for her. This only happened occasionally, and most of the time when it was cold, she would wrap my feet up in her long nighty, and I would fall blissfully asleep in her warmth and love.

Before coming to bed, she would go into the cupboard in the front bedroom and take out an old school picture. She'd hold it in her hands for a few minutes before putting it back. It was a photo of her son Charles, who had died when he was only 10 years old of peritonitis. I inherited this picture years later, and you can clearly see her finger marks where she held it over the years, the only image she had of him.

Something magical happened this year. It had been a year since Grandpa Green had died, and Grannie Isa had reached the age of sixty. She was now a pensioner from the Paisley thread mills, which was owned by the Coats & Clark family in Paisley. This brought in extra money with her widower's war pension and her old-age pension, so she bought a TV.

It was an Echo model with a solid walnut cabinet, fancy knobs, and dials. I remember sitting and watching the black and white images mesmerized by the flickering pictures in her front room. People came from everywhere to see it, some of whom had got dressed up as if it were a special occasion, which, on reflection, it was.

Over the next few years, Charlie and I enjoyed programmes such as the Watch with Mother series, Rag Tag and Bobtail, The Wooden Tops, Andy Pandy, and Bill and Ben the Flower Pot Men. Later, we watched Emergency Ward 10, Wagon Train, Bonanza, and Z Cars.

Back at home, we nagged Mum and Dad to get a telly, but it was just too expensive. So, we huddled round the old crystal-set radio and listened to Radio Luxembourg.

Caroline was now getting bigger and showing off a beautiful head of exceptionally light brown curls. Grannie Green was very fond of Caroline and commented on her beautiful locks within earshot of Ellen. So, later that day, Ellen decided to give Caroline a haircut, much to Mum's horror, as Ellen had managed to remove all the curls and hide them behind the cooker in the kitchen. Another case of "Me no did it, Mammy."

A few weeks later, Ellen was standing near the kitchen cupboard that we called "the meat press," and Dad was trying to retrieve something from the top shelf when a heavy metal cobblers last for shoe repairs fell off the shelf. It just missed Ellen's head and embedded and gouged out the concrete floor.

During the winter months, another problem kept happening. Every now and again, the lights would go out or the gas would get cut off. This was because we had both utilities on pay as you go meters. Mum would normally feed them with a shilling for the electricity or a "wooden thrupenny bit" for the gas. Sometimes, she wouldn't have a shilling in her purse, and neither would Dad, so I was sent out to Grannie Green's to borrow one or go round the neighbours with change to get one. Usually, this would mean Mrs. Hamilton or Mrs. Simpson next door. I would knock on their heavy door with the knocker and ask, "Please can I have a single shilling for my mammy?" Sometimes, I would get not only a shilling but a piece of fruit or a biscuit as well.

On Tuesdays and Thursdays, the mobile grocer's van would park outside our house. Davy Douglas was one of the first men to have a mobile shop in addition to his main shop in Hunterhill on the other side of Paisley. His green van was always welcome, as he would allow Mum to get "tick," which she would pay back on Friday from Dad's wages when he was working. Usually, he would come at lunchtime when I was home from school. The list of groceries was usually the same: two tins of Grannie's tomato soup, Dairylea cheese, a loaf, and a block of Stork or Echo margarine. This was for the children's lunch. During the summer holidays, I would sometimes get to travel in the van to the top of the scheme to help deliver orders to the elderly or young mothers who couldn't get out of the house. On the way back, Davy would go into his bag and give me a florin (2 shillings)(10p in 2025) and a Cadbury chocolate bar.

At school, I was progressing well and had joined the football team and the chess club. The football team played in a maroon V-neck strip, white shorts, and maroon woolen socks. We would meet every Friday after school in Mr. Bowie's classroom for a briefing. He would tell us who we were playing and the venue, appoint a captain, and hand out the strips. The captain usually got the "cudger," which was the leather and bladder ball, to take home and get it "dubbened" for the game. Dubbin was a natural wax for waterproofing the ball.

My problem was that I didn't have any boots, and any chance of getting a pair was zero. I usually nagged Mum. Dad chipped in, saying, "You've got boots." He went into the girls' room and opened the shoe press (cupboard) and produced an incredibly old, worn pair of brown leather boots, which didn't have studs but bars on the soles. These boots had been given to us by Mrs. Ferguson, the primary school headmistress, along with a batch of clothes, including wine-coloured blazers from her two sons, who went to the John Neilston School in Paisley Oakshaw St.

The game was scheduled for 10:00 on Saturday morning at St James's Park playing fields, commonly known as the "Racecourse." It was freezing cold when we arrived, and the pitch was very muddy, especially in the goal areas where I would spend a lot of time in the left-back position. As the game progressed, the "cudger" got heavier as the dubbin layer wore off from thousands of schoolboy kicks.

I spent a lot of the time during the game lying on the ground after sliding in the mud or getting knocked down by some of the bigger boys, now blessed with an increased level of testosterone.

Eventually, there was a free kick on our goal line, and we formed the wall. The other team's captain, who was a powerful player, hit the ball as hard as he could, and it struck me full on the face, which I had turned to one side. It knocked me clean out, and I even saw stars. Lying on my back, Mr. Bowie shoved smelling salts under my nose, and I was immediately awake but groggy. It was then he noticed my boots. Mr. Bowie, a polite gentleman who also ran the chess club, commented, "We'll have to do something about those boots, James."

At the end of the year, we had a gymnastics display, which was hilarious, as the boys had these baggy white shorts and vests in fifty shades of grey (behave!!!), and the girls had to run about with their blouses tucked into their fleecy navy-blue knickers. On this night, the mums and Dads had been invited, and Mum was there. One of the agility exercises was to walk along a narrow beam, pass a beanbag underneath after every step, and then stand up and repeat until you had walked the full length of the plank. Every boy fell off, and I was last to go. When I cleared the whole beam, all these folks applauded and cheered me, and it made my mum immensely proud, as she professed on the way home. "I knew MAJIM would do it." I thought for years that my name was Majim because Mum always referred to me as Majim, meaning my Jim.

When you have no money, you must barter, and to my shame, I usually bartered Charlie's toys or cards. So, the next time I played, I had a pair of second-hand boots with studs, and Charlie had fewer toys and cards.

The boy who lived next door was called Richard Hutton. He lived with his mum and Dad in his gran's house, Mrs. Bowes. Now, Ferguslie was a very tough and rough place, so this middle-class family was out of place at No.

98. I can remember Mr. Hutton playing his piano in the back bedroom. Richard would always help us make up our football teams, and sometimes I think local folk would try and steal the coal from Hutton's bunker. Other than that, this family had some relatives who would sometimes visit, and they were always an attractive bunch. The Hutton's only lived there for a couple of years, and then the house was occupied by the Cree family.

Our neighborhood was also very vibrant. There were things happening every day, especially in the summer when cows from the cow park decided to pay us a visit, as there was little or no fence around the cow park. We tried to milk them, but eventually the farmer would appear, and the cows would be herded back to the grassland.

The cow park was our playground, bounded to the south by the housing scheme of Ferguslie. To the west was the Candren burn, too deep to cross but not too deep to play in if you had wellies. To the north was the supply railway track for the Linwood car factory, where thousands of Hillman Imp cars were exported south. I would stand and be amazed as all these futuristic cars, in many colours, rattled past on their journey. To the east were the prefab houses—hundreds of temporary post-war accommodations for the homeless.

One summer, Charlie and I found a little kitten that had badly infected eyes. We took it into the house to show Mum. When she saw it, she exclaimed, "Poor wee thing, it would be better deed," and told us to take it out of the house, wander it, and come back to wash our hands.

About that time, there was a local man with a couple of boxer dogs who, on reflection, was training them as fighting dogs. I had heard these awful animal screams one morning as they ripped a cat to pieces in the cow park. So, this little cat was not going to suffer the same fate. Charlie and I took the cat over to the burn and threw it in, hitting it with half bricks until it was dead.

When we got back and told Mum, she was horrified, but we had taken her at her word, and the cat was better off now that it was dead.

On Saturday mornings, Charlie and I would take lemonade bottles back to the shops and collect the deposit. Usually, this was enough money to go to the Paisley baths for a swim. It cost a penny halfpenny to get the bus from Ferguslie to Paisley Library, then quickly down Storie Street.

When you paid for your ticket, you had to decide whether you wanted the small pool or the big pool. The small pool, which only cost 4 pence, was my favourite, as it wasn't as deep and had a lot of light. If it was busy, you didn't get a cubicle and had to undress and leave your clothes on a bench at the side of the pool. The water was always warm, and I could swim forever there with Charlie. The pool attendant would usually chase you out after an hour, and so, with very wrinkled fingers, we would get dressed, roll up our trunks in our wet towel, and climb back up Storie Street hill to the fish and chip shop, where we got two bags of chips and a pickled onion.

We would then proceed into the High Street, and walk past the library and museum, the Regal Cinema, and into Wellmeadow Street. Turning the corner into Walker Street, we would reach the "Yankee Mags" shop. The smell of new comics was so nice, and we could take our pick of any of the Marvel heroes, usually Batman or Superman.

We would spend every penny and walk all the way home with no money for the bus. When we got home, we were given big bowls of soup and bread, then it was out to play until 9:00 pm, back in for a big cup of sweet tea and toast, then bed. I can't remember ever not being able to get to sleep.

As I got older, I became more aware of the people who lived around me in our street. Most of the families were big families, with five to seven children. In our immediate vicinity, there were the Slavin family, who lived downstairs with seven children. Mrs. McCracken had moved away, and the Donald family moved in next door. Upstairs from them were the Cree family. A total of 24 kids, all next door to each other.

This meant that disease spread amazingly fast throughout families, especially when most of the kids were feral and played on the dumps. The main hazards were polio and, later, the Thalidomide scare. But it was a matter of routine for us to get measles, mumps, scarlet fever, scabies, influenza, flea bites, eye infections, cuts, and broken bones.

I got tested for various diseases and was already immune. Mum was very against us getting any injections or medication, so most illnesses were allowed to run their course, or a Granny cure would be used, such as a sugar soap and bread poultice to draw the pus out of boils.

Jimmy Strong, who lived four doors away, had contracted polio. He was on two calipers, so we just played him in goals, where he was hard to beat with his sticks. His sister, Linda, would organize concerts in the back garden, where the local kids would dance or sing songs, and the shy ones would recite poetry or tell jokes to bring in the crowd.

There were other visitors in the street, and when they appeared, it would stop Mum in her tracks. The first was the Brown Lady (the colour of her uniform), a community health nurse who came to see the family in general, especially Mum and the kids. In fairness to Mum, we never went to bed dirty or without clean clothes, and the housework was easier as we didn't have a carpet and had little furniture. What we did have was clean and tidy, but it was always stressful for Mum because, in those days, children could be taken away from their parents for minor reasons.

The other visitor was the Grey Lady, or sanitary woman, who had the job of inspecting your house and garden. If they weren't kept properly, you could be rehoused to Graigmuir Road, where the "undesirables" were sent to Scotland's worst ghetto.

I guess we must have been all right because we were never rehoused, but if we had been, we would only have been moving around the corner, as Graigmuir Road was just a stone's throw away.

Granny Green and Mum warned me not to go into Graigmuir Road ever, but the first chance I got, I went for a look. The street was about a quarter of a mile long, with houses and tenements, and ran parallel to Ferguslie Park Avenue. At one end, there was an oval with tenements that were four stories high. This was the main part of the ghetto, and the streets were covered in broken and crushed glass. No garden was kept, and many windows didn't have curtains. Some were broken and boarded up. Children were everywhere, in very ragged clothes, and some were covered in sores that had been daubed with iodine, leaving a brown or purple stain on their shaved heads. Some little kids were running around with just vests on, with no nappies. The place was full of dogs barking, and I could hear loud music and people shouting. There were no cars. The garden fences were mostly torn down, and the split-pole fencing was being used for firewood or as weapons. Sometimes, the kids would have a tin can hammered flat on one end to make a tomahawk.

It seemed like a million miles away in my mind, but in fact, my Gran's house, 114 Ferguslie Park Avenue, was on the corner with Graigmuir Road, and next door was the close at No. 2 Graigmuir Road. She once took me to visit her friend, called "Nellie," who was incredibly fat and had legs as thick as an elephants, where her shoe strap bit heavily into her swollen, fluid-filled foot.

The local council came up with a great idea to remove the stigma surrounding the people of Graigmuir Road, who struggled to get jobs or credit. They renamed the street, which became Holborn Avenue, and the oval became Ardmore Oval. They couldn't have gotten things more wrong, and it took years to learn the lesson. These people were desperate, so they stole and committed crimes and if that wasn't successful, they got drunk on cheap wine from Menzies Licensed Grocer shop in Blackston Road.

House by house, the chaotic infection spread until they had to demolish the whole street. But by then, it was too late; it had already spread to the main scheme, and before long, the whole place had to be rebuilt. But it took a few years.

There were some welcome visitors in the street from time to time. Charlie, the ragman, with his battered bugle, who gave us balloons for old rags. The Whelk man, who gave you a little bundle of cooked whelks in a newspaper cup and a small pin to winkle them out, allowing you to taste the salty morsels and spit out the little hard cover from the whelk shell, all for a penny.

But best of all was Mr. Whippy, the ice cream man. When Mum had the money, she would let us get a cone, and she would have a shell or double nugget, which she would squeeze and lick and share with us. When the Jaconelli ice cream van came, Mum would get a double nougat and a few cones, or sometimes a shell, which she shared with us.

Paisley had a large Italian population, including the following families: Conti (of Tom and Nina Conti fame)

Pieraccini

Cardosi

Lazarini

Nutini (of Paolo Nutini)

Corri

Pirelli

Jaconelli

Coia

CHAPTER 7:
FISTS AND FIRE

1961

January-September

There were plenty of people willing to help with our large family. My Grannie Green, who had taken a second job after retiring, worked in Ross's Canteen which was attached to the Anchor Thread Mills. Every day after her shift, she would get off the bus, cross the road to our house, and bring bags filled with leftovers from the canteen. So, while we weren't spoiled with luxuries, we were clean and probably reasonably well-fed. There were no regular sweets, but at school, we got free milk. Most of the time, we walked or ran everywhere, so we were incredibly fit kids.

Mum and Dad had more money now, which we assumed was thanks to the generous family allowance, now covering six children.

At the weekends, Dad and Sammy would dress in their finest— extremely expensive suits—and disappear for two days. Charlie and I were always happy to polish their shoes for a half crown, which was about 12.5 pence in today's money (2025).

What we didn't realise at the time was that Dad and Sammy were serious debt collectors for all the Paisley bookies. Both ex-army, they were skilled with their fists and had a reputation that matched. They worked on a price list detailing the escalating costs of recovering debts. It started with a visit and became progressively more violent, depending on the size of the debt and how long it had been outstanding. Plenty of people in Paisley feared these brothers. However, we remained blissfully unaware—until one night when Dad came home, his shirt spattered with blood. I never knew if Mum understood the full extent of what he was doing, but the extra money was certainly a relief to her.

I idolized Dad. He was handsome, with his outdoor tan and immaculate weekend dress. He was also tough—an enigma, never offering much advice or explanation.

Yet, he had a playful side. I remember jumping on his back and wrestling with him on the floor. At night, we were washed in the deep sink in the kitchen. I would sit there, playing with a plastic cup and the soapy bubbles, lost in a soft, foamy dream. One evening, something in the corner of my eye jolted me back to reality. Dad had silently crept up on me, wearing an old black Rexene school helmet. He just stood there, smiling. I nearly jumped out of my skin.

We also had an ongoing battle with mice. Dad would sit for hours in the kitchen, perched on a small white chair in the dark, armed with a water gun filled with bleach and a bit of cheese as bait. He'd wait patiently before springing into action—blinding the mouse before finishing it under his foot.

Around this time, Dad was working on another construction site and had a habit of wrapping his feet in strips of cotton cloth from old ripped-up sheets instead of wearing socks. After work, he'd come home, pull off his boots or wellies, and unwrap his feet. I would usually drop the cloth strips into the sink to be washed before they were hung over a string stretched across the living room fireplace to dry overnight.

One weekend, I had gone into town and, like most boys, bought myself a penknife. It had an emerald-green pearlite handle, and I was quite pleased with it—until Mum saw it.

"Let me see that," she said, eyeing it suspiciously. "It's green."
"Aye, Mammy," I replied.

"That's a very unlucky colour. Get rid of it."

Mum wasn't usually so superstitious, which unsettled me. I set the knife on the mantelpiece above the fire in the living room, hoping she'd forget about it.

That Sunday, Dad was at work. When he returned, he went through his usual routine—unwrapping his feet and hanging the cloth strips out to dry over the fire.

A few weeks earlier, we had bought a television on pay-up terms. It must have cost a lot because, that night, I woke to a commotion outside my bedroom. Dad was trying to wake Mum while simultaneously running out of the house with the TV.

Mum got up, and we had to get all the children outside. The main living room was on fire. The cloth strips had caught alight, setting the wooden mantel ablaze. It was a miracle that Dad smelled the smoke in time. We all got out safely, as did the television.

I remember the fire brigade arriving, putting out the flames, and then staying overnight at Granny Isa's. The next morning, the newspapers were at our door, and the firemen were still there, ensuring the fire was fully extinguished. They had pulled out the charred wooden fireplace and left it against the back wall of the outside stairs. As I peered over the stairs at the charred wreckage, I spotted something embedded in the burnt mantelpiece—my melted new penknife.

"I told you that was an unlucky colour," Mum said.

Looking back, I had to agree. Perhaps I should have renamed myself 'Gleen.'

Now, we faced another problem. Most of our clothes had either been burned or ruined by smoke damage. With no other options, we went to school in whatever we had left. By the end of the day, our kind teachers had sent home large bags of second-hand clothes for us.

As a young, newly post-pubescent boy, I wasn't particularly thrilled when Mrs. Ferguson, the headmistress, handed me a pair of maroon school shorts. Her sons attended the fee-paying John Neilson school, which had a maroon uniform, and I was now expected to wear their cast-offs. Still, it was a generous act, and we had nothing else, so I wore them.

In April, I was lucky enough to be gifted a racing bike from my Auntie Jenny—without any conditions that I had to return to the Salvation Army. I would set off on grand adventures, cycling to places as far as Langbank and Greenock, wearing my maroon shorts and my green Cub Scout hat.

One day, I got caught in torrential rain. By the time I made it home, the dye from both my hat and shorts had run. The next morning at school, my teacher asked why my hair was green and my legs were pink. I told the story, and the entire class—teacher included—

laughed their heads off. However, I got a gold star for being self-effacing and honest and funny.

October

October brought the excitement of Halloween. In the baker's shops, Halloween cakes lined the shelves—sponge cakes covered in brightly coloured icing, each topped with a cheerful face. Two mounds of cream formed the cheeks, hidden beneath another layer of icing. I longed to bite into one, to taste the sweetness and let the cream melt in my mouth.

At school, we made Halloween drawings—witches sketched onto black paper with coloured sticky shapes to bring them to life. After school, we dressed up, usually as pirates or wise men from the nativity, making do with whatever we could find—a tea towel for a headscarf, pieces of rope for a belt, and a smear of soot from the fireplace for effect. If we could get hold of an old turnip, we'd carve it out, light a candle inside, and carry it around on a string attached to a stick.

Charlie and I would go door to door, singing our Halloween song: *"Can you wash a sailor's shirt?*

Can you wash it clean?

Can you wash a sailor's shirt?

Please, for my Halloween."

Sometimes we were invited inside, but more often, we stood at the doorstep. I can't recall ever being turned away, and we usually came away with an apple, an orange, or a handful of monkey nuts (unshelled peanuts).

One year, as we made our way home, a group of older boys ambushed us and stole all our treats.

November

November meant bonfires and Guy Fawkes Night. For weeks leading up to the fifth, we gathered anything that would burn—old furniture, fallen branches, broken wooden fences, even discarded hut panels. Rival neighborhoods often stole from each other's piles, and more than once, we'd come home from school to find our bonfire ransacked. Anything that could be repurposed was taken, though I don't recall if we ever placed a "guy" on top. We just wanted a fire.

We always hoped for dry weather so we could light it. When we did, the flames roared so fiercely that we could feel the heat through the windows of our house. One year, it cracked the glass on nearby houses, and after that, we had to move the bonfire further away.

Fireworks were rare—an occasional rocket or zigzag if we were lucky. Most of our entertainment came from "squibs," small penny bangers. With no adults around to supervise, accidents were inevitable, and at least one child would end up with burns.

We stayed up late, watching the fire until it smoldered down to glowing embers. Before bed, we had to take a bath to wash off the soot smell of smoke.

The next morning, we'd poke at the ashes with sticks, searching for charred remnants of metal buried in the remains.

December

The winter of 1961 brought heavy rain. Ferguslie, being low-lying, flooded overnight. By morning, the water had crept up to the first step of our house. Outside, the street was like a lake. As children, we wanted to wade through it, but we were warned about raw sewage. Instead, we stayed indoors, watching as the flood slowly receded, leaving a scum line on the lower walls of every building.

Then came the snow. One afternoon, it fell heavily, blanketing the world in white. By evening, it was eight inches deep. Stepping outside, I noticed the eerie silence—until I moved. Each step created a crisp, squeaky crunch beneath my feet.

The landscape had transformed. Above me, an inky blue sky stretched endlessly, not a cloud in sight. The full moon cast a glow so bright that it felt like daylight. Unable to resist, I ran to the cow park where we played football. Falling backwards into the deep snow, I made my first snow angel.

The next morning, the schoolyard was a battlefield of snowball fights. The slush didn't deter us, though some unlucky kids ended up with icy missiles to the face or snow shoved down the back of their necks.

It was around this time that I sat the "qually"—the eleven-plus exam that determined whether I'd go to senior or junior secondary school. I remember feeling nervous, and an odd rash appeared on my arms and legs—small, red, circular marks. My mother took one look and announced it might be ringworm. I was sent straight to a skin specialist at the Western Infirmary in Glasgow, where I was prescribed a cream.

After the exam, the rash vanished.

Two days later, the snow had turned to hard ice. We made slides everywhere—on pavements, in schoolyards, even on the way home. Not a single sledge in sight, just the sheer thrill of gliding across the frozen ground.

CHAPTER 8:
THE QUALLY

1962

In January, I received a letter from my teacher, Miss King, to give to my parents. It had to be signed and returned. I was used to getting the big brown envelope each year— the dreaded school report— with its Unsatisfactory/Good/Very Good/Excellent marking system and little ribbons of paper containing notes on my performance.

I remember my mum and Dad telling me that I had passed the "qually," but the problem was that this meant I would be going to Camphill Senior Secondary. That required an entirely new uniform—something my parents simply couldn't afford. It was history repeating itself; the same thing had happened to my Dad when he was twelve.

Thankfully, Granny Isa came to the rescue. She bought me everything I needed from Stirling and Stevens department store in Paisley, which allowed families to pay back the cost in weekly instalments.

The paper was signed, and my future changed. I did get a good education. When I returned the letter to school, a few days later Miss King announced the pupils who had passed the 11+ and would be going to Camphill. The rest would receive a junior secondary education.

Camphill Senior Secondary School Paisley 2C boys

I'm the only boy without a tie

We were also told who the prize winners were and, most importantly, who had won the school Dux, the top mark in the school. Nessie Kennedy won the first prize every year, and all through primary school, I had never won anything, unlike Charlie, who racked up prizes annually and eventually won the Dux prize in his time.

Nessie was the top girl and won the Dux prize. Margaret Easton took second place, and then, to my utter disbelief, my name was called out. James Green—top boy, third prize. That moment was life changing. I had never thought of myself as a prize winner.

Looking back now, I realise I was a little bit in love with Miss King. Just before the Christmas break, I had spent my pocket money on a cheap little bracelet for her as a present. Maybe, just maybe, that had worked in my favour. I base this suspicion on the fact that once I moved up to senior school, I never won another prize.

Miss King then announced a special award for General Subjects— and, once again, it was for James Green. Me. I couldn't wait to run home and tell my mother. For years, I had lived in Charlie's academic shadow, but now I was a winner. Mum came to the prize-giving, beaming with pride as I collected my awards. The First Boy prize was a Collins French Dictionary, and the General Proficiency prize was Daniel Defoe's Swiss Family Robinson.

I remember Mum saying how clever Charlie was, winning prizes every year, but now her Jim—her Majim—was clever too.

When Miss King read out the names of those heading to Camphill, I felt a surge of pride:

Nessie Kennedy, Margaret Easton, Helen Digney, James Green,

Howard Chapman, Kenneth Gibb, George McKenna, and Wilma Carson.

We were pleased with ourselves—until we saw the reaction from those who hadn't passed. It wasn't the kids who took it the hardest, but some of the parents.

Our next-door neighbours, the Slavins, were particularly displeased. Their son Johnny, who had been in my class, didn't pass, and this created a major rift between our families. The older Slavin boys, Frankie, and Tommy, started bullying me and Charlie.

"You think you're better than us," they sneered.

Charlie suffered the worst of it, often getting his arm twisted by one of the older brothers. One day, Mum said to me, "You're the eldest. You need to protect your brother and sisters."

"But they're all bigger than me," I protested.

Mum glanced at the wooden pole next to the coal bunker. "Don't be afraid to use a stick."

That was all the permission I needed. They say the firstborn male child is the alpha with survival instincts. I don't know about that, but I had no problem creeping up behind Johnny and giving him a whack with the stick—a heavy thing, more like a baseball bat. It nearly took his ear off.

So began a tit-for-tat battle over the next few days. Eventually, one of the older Slavin brothers twisted my arm up my back so hard that it nearly broke.

Mum waited until Dad got home and unburdened the day's troubles. That night, Dad got up from his chair, walked straight out, and started banging on the Slavins' door. I followed, but he pointed at me to stay on our stairs.

One of the younger boys answered.

"Is your faither in?" Dad asked.

"Daddy, Mr. Gleen is at the door!" The younger Slavins had trouble pronouncing our surname, so they called us the Gleens.

Big Tam Slavin eventually appeared. "Whit is it, Jimmy?"

Dad took one step inside and, with a single punch, sent Big Tam flying up his own hallway.

"Sort your wife and family out," Dad said, holding up his fist. "If they hit any of oor kids again, you'll get mair o' this." Showing his clenched fist.

That settled it. No more dirty tricks. Peace reigned. Well, almost. There were still fights. But I had vengeance in my heart for the arm-twisting Tommy.

My chance came while helping our new neighbour, Noel Donald, build a fence in his back garden. My job was to hold the post while Tommy used a ten-pound hammer to drive it into the ground.

When we reached the final post, I asked, "Can I have a shot with the hammer?"

Tommy held the post.

I brought the hammer down—right onto Tommy's hand. I have never, in my life, heard anyone scream like that.

From then on, Tommy kept a respectful distance, claiming I was crazy and should be locked up. We never had any more trouble with the Slavins.

Seeing my Dad in action, and then dealing with the Slavins myself, I was always ready for a fight. I was never frightened I got a buzz from it.

One sunny day, we were playing football when Ian McConnachie roughed up Charlie. I pounced like an animal, pounding his face until I was dragged off. Billy Carson, also guilty of the crime, got the same treatment.

Later, Ian's mother came to our house, complaining about the state of his face.

Mum simply said, "That's what he gets for being a bully."

From that day on, Ian kept to the other side of the road when I was around, and bullying became less of a problem.

Then, in February, just as I was about to start at Camphill, we got word that the school was too full. We'd have to spend five months at a prep school first.

The prep school was none other than Mossvale Junior Secondary—better known as the "Mosey."

The "Mosey" was the most feared and hated school in Paisley at that time and the only uniform I had was my pristine Camphill one—the very thing they despised.

The Slavins were laughing now. This time, it was me who wasn't.

With great trepidation, I put on my uniform and made my way to secondary school for the first time. The jeers started before I even got inside, and Camphill boys were being plucked from the crowd and dragged to the toilets for a good dunking in the manky (disgusting) toilet bowls. Just as I was about to become a victim, Howard Chapman appeared—soaked in smelly toilet water, with a seriously busted-up mouth and teeth. Turns out they had smashed his face onto the rim when he resisted. That put an end to the ceremony. For the next four months, Howard was in the dental hospital, and when he finally returned, his smile looked more like crazy paving than teeth.

As the weeks passed, nobody so much as said "boo" to me. I thought my reputation had preceded me, but it turns out my mum had spoken to Mrs. McCrone, whose son was the feared Gerry McCrone—the same lad who had helped redesign Howard's smile. Unbeknownst to me, Gerry was my bodyguard, keeping trouble at bay from the shadows.

We settled into our lessons—Latin, Greek, French, Math's, English, History, Geography, Art, Technical Drawing, Physics, Chemistry, and Woodwork. Miss Kunzel would drone on, reciting amo, amas, amat, while we mischievously called back amamus, amatis, amant. She also taught French and Greek, and, with her all-black matron's gown and gangly frame, she looked like Popeye's girlfriend Olive Oil. I spent most of her lessons gazing out the window and dreaming.

We weren't the only ones in Prep School; there were others from West School, but we made up a well-behaved class, kept in line by the dreaded Lochgelly tawse—a 10mm-thick heavy chrome leather belt used to strap kids' hands. It hurt like hell (more on that later). My time at Mossvale wasn't too bad. I managed to get through Prep in Greek and Latin before eventually dropping them, and we even had a field trip to Renfrew Airport. There, I saw a

French twin-engine Caravelle, which I later built as an Airfix model— without sniffing the glue. (How did kids figure out you could do that?)

By April, I had joined the Cub Scouts at Anchor Mills in Paisley. Every Thursday evening, I'd take the bus—three pennies (thrupence) from outside our house in Ferguslie. I'd get off at Paisley Cross, follow the river Cart pathway to Cotton Street, then cross the old bridge in front of Paisley Abbey and walk down the other side of the Cart to the old Anchor Mill gatehouse. The gatekeeper always let me through as soon as he saw my green cub uniform, McKenzie tartan neckerchief, and wolf cub woggle.

Inside, the cubs were lined up in Sixes—I was in the Tawny Six. The supervisors took their names from Rudyard Kipling's Jungle Book: our leader was Akela, and we had Kaa the snake, Baloo the bear, and Rikki- Tikki-Tavi. We would take our oath to the Queen, unfurl the Union Flag, and dedicate ourselves to the wolf cub pack. Akela would call out:

"Dib-dib-dib!"   And we'd respond:

"Dob-dob-dob!"

Then it was time for games—British Bulldog, treasure hunts around the mill grounds (where we could hear the Anchor Mill Pipe Band practicing), or badge-making sessions. I worked on badges like Signalers, First Aider, and Knot-Tying, but the one I remember best was the less macho "Household" badge—boiling an egg, peeling a potato, polishing a brass candlestick.

After a year, I earned my first star on my cub cap, symbolizing one eye open. Two years in, I had both eyes open—meaning I was ready to become a Scout. I was promoted to Seconder (with one yellow stripe on my arm), then Sixer (with two stripes), overseeing six other boys.

The cubs were brilliant. We saved money through the Cubs' bank and funds, went on sausage hikes, and paraded with the veterans and Boys' Brigade on Remembrance Day. Years later, Akela (Jim Davey) and Kaa (Irene) got married and moved to Canada, where they did magnificent work for the Inuit people. By pure chance, I met Irene again in 2005—she was living as a guest with my mother's cousin in Pinner, Charlie Donovan. (But that's a story for another time.)

Somewhere in the middle of my cub years, my brother Charlie joined. Having him there every Thursday night was brilliant. We did everything together trekking up the Gleniffer Braes, playing in Cowboy Valley, exploring the local Black hills or the racecourse at St James's Park. We covered every point on the compass around Paisley.

But our time in the Cubs ended abruptly after a fight with the Pierochinni brothers—the sons of the local chip shop owners, where Charlie and I always stopped for chips and pickled onions on the way home.

Sundays meant Sunday School, but ours was a bit different—it was run by the Salvation Army. Every Sunday, a big green double-decker bus rolled into our estate, picking up about seventy kids and taking us to the Salvation Army Hall in Paisley's west end. We sang songs on the way, streamers hanging from the windows, then sat through happy Christian songs and Bible lessons.

After a few weeks, Charlie, Ellen, and I gave our hearts to Jesus. This presented a bit of a problem for me—I had just hit puberty, and the real attraction was the young, pretty Salvation Army officer in uniform. She wore black nylons and suspenders. (How did I know? I'd developed a habit of "accidentally" dropping my pencil on the floor.)

After a few weeks of this, guilt set in. I asked my mum if I could stop going— I wanted to play football with the lads on Sundays instead. The whole thing had been Auntie Jenny's idea, terrified that the devil would catch our souls. Mum just said, "Alright then," and when Jenny protested, she stonewalled her. Soon, none of us were going. I had been measured up for the "Blood and Fire" uniform, but someone else would have to wear it.

In September, I finally got to Camphill—the school everyone called "The Prison" because it looked exactly like one. Inside wasn't much better. The school motto was "Onwards and Upwards"—which, given the steep climb to the top of Camphill (built on an old Roman hill fort), felt very literal.

On our first day, we were assembled in the boys' shed (girls were now segregated) and placed into classes based on ability. The clever ones—how did they know? —were put in 1A. Then came 1B, 1C, 1D, and finally my class, 1E. I had been top boy at my last school, yet somehow, I found myself in the bottom class with all the other Ferguslie lads.

Camphill was a good school, but discipline was strict. I was strapped regularly, forced to write out hundreds of lines, and subjected to the taunts of Andy Hammond, our English teacher.

"Green, you are a slubberdegullion!" he'd bark.

I didn't dare ask what it meant at the time. Later, I discovered it had three definitions:

A filthy, slobbering person; a sloven; a louse. A worthless person.

A drunk or alcoholic.

Lucky for me, I assumed he was just showing off his vocabulary rather than calling me all three at once.

At Camphill, nobody was called by their first name. I was simply "Green." Unlucky for some.

I scraped by, doing the bare minimum of homework, and spent my weekends on my bike.

Then, in Christmas 1962, my Dad bumped into his old army comrade, Jimmy Stevenson, from their time in Palestine with the Argylls. Jimmy was now manager of Hay & Co, a grocery shop in Paisley, and he needed a part-time boy. The shop was only a ten-minute walk from Camphill, so at twelve years old, I had a part-time job. Jimmy was great, and he paid me £2 and 10 shillings for 4 days through the week and Saturday all day. I gave all this money to my mother. Jimmy taught me the grocery trade, how to bone hams and string wrap them for slicing, how to peel the wax cloth off cheeses and cut with a cheese wire, how to cut and print butter with butter pats, how to grind coffee and serve other delicacies like desiccated coconut, glace cherries, and stem ginger.

I loved working on a Saturday all day as I was now a grown-up, and I learned to be confident with work and dealing with people. There was no political correctness, "what can I do for you today, dear?"

"Oh! you're such a handsome boy. Can I have half a pound of butter, please?" "Would you like Danish salted fresh butter or perhaps some New Zealand?"

"Make that Danish salted, please." When these butter lumps ran out, I had to get another one onto the counter. The kegs came with proper staves and cane hoops and weighed 112Lbs, which is a hundred weight. I do not know how I did it as I was only 7stones, but as a young boy, I could lift that awkward keg from the shop floor to the counter in one lift. I then used a meat cleaver to cut the cane hoops, and the wooden staves just collapsed. I then had to lift the butter on its timber base from the counter to the butter shelf by hugging it and walking with it to the shelf.

Jimmy was particularly good to me and trusted me. I remember I found a five-pound note on the floor one day, and I took it to Jimmy immediately. He gave me a hug and said good boy and said, "Come and see this." The front and back shops were separated by a partition, which had shelves on the shop side with packets of Brooke Bond and Poona Kandie or Darjeeling tea.

On the back side, there were big packs of Westburn Sugar. Jimmy moved one of the packs to one side to reveal a hole in the partition, which overlooked the till and front shop. The reason that Jimmy was so delighted was he had to trust his staff, and I know he did not want to have to tell my Dad that I was light-fingered. On one occasion he caught a female assistant loading her sister up with groceries and undercharging. I had to tally up the groceries in the bag as Jimmy checked the till money. The assistant was instantly sacked, and incredibly she was lucky Jimmy did not get the Police, but a valuable lesson to me about other people and the wee hole in the wall.

Every Saturday night, when I finished my shift, Jimmy would give me something to take home to the family. Sometimes, it was cooked meat cuttings or broken biscuits, but Mum was always delighted with six kids to feed.

Another Feg

During the school holidays, I got to work full time and got paid £5 for the whole week and £7 10 shillings if I worked on stocktaking on a Sunday. Mum was always delighted with the extra money, and I got to keep 5 shillings as pocket money.

At Christmas time, Jimmy would make up a hamper for the family with a large tin of cooked ham in jelly which was a favourite for us as it did our Christmas Dinner.

CHAPTER 9:
BOOKS AND MORE BABIES

1963

Mum was looking heavier again—she had put on weight, but it wasn't long before she told us she was expecting another baby. I could see she was struggling. Dad had been laid off from his job on the building sites due to one of the worst winters on record, and his only source of income was debt collecting. Charlie and I did all we could to help—fetching messages (groceries), starting and maintaining the coal fire, making beds, preparing food, and helping with the washing.

It will be another year before we got our first Rolls Rand washing machine. Until then, dirty clothes were boiled in a gas-heated boiler, which invariably singed off my eyebrows when it ignited. We used a boiler pole (the same one Johnny Slavin got clubbed with) to lift the scalding clothes into the deep sink next to the boiler. After rinsing them, we fed one end of each garment through the rollers of an Acme wringer, which was clamped onto two blocks that separated the deep sink from the shallow sink. Both sinks, made of white glazed earthenware by Shanks of Barrhead, had seen better days their edges were chipped and broken.

That winter was particularly harsh. With Dad not working, Mum kept us warm in bed by piling old coats on top of the blankets. It was so cold inside that when we breathed out, we pretended we were smoking. At school, we looked forward to our bottles of milk—they gave us a comforting glow on a freezing day.

Using the Acme wringer took skill. The trick was to turn the handle exactly right to squeeze out water without popping off the buttons. I usually managed, but Charlie was less careful, which meant Mum had plenty of sewing to do when the clothes dried. We had a jar full of mismatched buttons as a result. Once the clothes were wrung out, we carried them in a big plastic basket to the back green, where four clothes poles and some rope stood ready. Mum always did the hanging herself, but if it started raining, all hell broke loose as Charlie, and I scrambled to bring the washing in. It was understandable— each of us only had one change of clothes. To her credit, Mum kept both us and the house exceptionally clean.

Despite her efforts, big families in housing schemes were prone to all sorts of illnesses and afflictions. Kids pass infections and viruses easily. Head lice were a constant problem. If one of us got them, two things happened: first, Mum doused our heads with a bottle of Suleo head lice lotion and left it for an hour. Then came the dreaded metal Derbac comb. The lotion stung the nose, but the stainless-steel comb was agony on the scalp. Mum sat by the fire, combing through our hair, scraping our scalps until it hurt. Each time she pulled out dead nits and lice, she wiped them onto newspaper, then tossed it into the fire, where the lice crackled and popped as they burned.

When my sisters got scabies, the health visitor arranged for the entire family to be painted in treatment, and all our clothes and bedding had to be fumigated. I ran away and stayed with Granny Isa. We caught colds and flu every winter, so there was always a big brown bottle of camphor oil on the shelf, next to an equally big bottle of calamine lotion. Occasionally, we'd get big, red, lumpy spots on our bodies. Mum called them heat spots, but years later, I realized they were flea or mosquito bites. Living in a council housing scheme next to fields meant we had mice, which required a cat—and where there was a cat, there were fleas.

On 11th April, Mum went into labour. After a long, difficult delivery, she gave birth to my brother, Steven, weighing an astonishing 12.5 lbs. I remember seeing him in his pram in Mum's bedroom—this golden-haired baby, already looking three months old. Mum tried to feed him herself, but within days, he needed Ostermilk 3, the formula for babies three months and older.

Within days, Mum was back on her feet, running the family. Life became busier than ever. The girls loved pushing Steven's pram and helping with his baths, fascinated by his umbilical cord as it blackened and fell off. Charlie and I had the less glamorous job of pre-washing nappies stained with luminescent yellow poo, steeping them in Napisan. Disposable nappies didn't exist. Sometimes, when rinsing them in the toilet bowl, one would slip from our grasp and vanish down the pan. Mum would count the nappies and sigh, "I'm sure I had a dozen, and now there are only nine."

Feeding bottles were sterilized in Milton bleach solution. One of my jobs was to heat a needle and widen the hole in the dummy teat to accommodate Steven's appetite.

We had a special white chair for baby baths—an old kitchen chair with the legs sawn off so Mum could sit comfortably while bathing the baby by the fire. If Dad wasn't using it to stalk mice, it was also used to wash the younger kids in a plastic basin.

By then, I was working after school, on Saturdays, and during the holidays. My chores fell to Charlie, who, like me, just got on with things without complaining. But sometimes, it was too much. I remember one occasion when he just left. It was pouring rain, and he sat in the back field on a big rock, wearing a red cowboy hat, getting soaked to the skin. Mum asked if I knew where he was. When I looked out the window, I saw him sitting there, unmoving. Charlie was highly intelligent, with a deep perception of what was happening in our lives. He devoured information, collecting cards and toy soldiers, which he played with for hours.

To my great shame, the deal I made with Richard Hutton, our next-door neighbour, to trade Charlie's cards and soldiers for a bike was unfair. Charlie reluctantly agreed. We both learned to ride it, but it was a terrible trade for him—I'd take off on the bike and leave him behind. Incidents like this made Charlie tough, and he got his revenge later.

One task I continued was exchanging Uncle Sammy's library books every Tuesday evening, as the shops in Paisley closed early, but the library stayed open. Sammy was generous with pocket money—me and Charlie could usually expect a florin or a silver half-crown—but we had to earn it, either by running errands or polishing his shoes.

Paisley Library was a haven for me. I loved the atmosphere, the scent of books, and the studious expressions of people in the reference section. Sammy only wanted Westerns, but after swapping his books, I started borrowing for myself. That's when my thirst for learning began. Today, I can read up to three books at a time and find the internet almost magical, but back then, knowledge only came in hard copy.

One of the first books I ever read was Isaac Asimov's I, Robot. Written in 1950—the year I was born—it sparked in me a love for technology, development, and progressive thinking. Asimov was a visionary. I admired his clear, unambiguous writing. From there, I moved on to design, psychology, and art books. I enjoyed a good novel, but my real focus was knowledge. Somewhere in the back of my mind, I'd heard the phrase "Knowledge is Power"—and when you're the eldest of seven children, living in one of the most deprived and chaotic housing schemes in the UK, you start looking for a way out.

You start looking for a way to change things for the better. The sheer workload for Mum was never-ending, and she began to fall ill. She had six children to care for, and we had no modern conveniences—a washing machine, no hoover, not even an electric iron. Ours was an old cast-iron type that had to be heated on the gas ring in the kitchen.

In June 1963, Mum was admitted to the Cottage Hospital in Johnstone for a much-needed rest. With Dad still working, we were all sent to stay with relatives. Charlie and I went to live with Aunty Mag, Uncle Tommy, and our two cousins, Jim and Robert, in Scott Avenue, Johnstone. Ellen was sent to Aunty Esther and Uncle Jimmy Burns, along with our cousin John. Meanwhile, Granny Isa took in the rest—Caroline, Stewart, Anne, and Steven.

While staying in Scott Avenue, Charlie, my cousins, and I spent a lot of time playing in the local park, which had a pond. One day, I stood on a broken bottle and suffered a deep cut to my foot. Luckily, Aunty Mag was a nurse and expertly patched me up.

When Mum came out of hospital, she looked noticeably better, and some changes were made at home to help her. Dad bought her a washing machine, a hoover, and a new iron. We also replaced our old, mismatched chairs and couch with a modern three-piece suite. Neighbours like Mrs. Strong and Isa Donald started taking more of an interest in our family, and my aunties— Mag, Esther, and May—visited more often. But no one was as reliable as

Granny Isa, who continued to help out with housework and ensure we had enough food.

By September, life had more or less returned to normal. That's when Granny Isa decided to visit her cousins in America—Sam Stewart and his wife, Peggy. Off she went, and I was lost without her. She gave me something special: unconditional love. I knew Mum and Dad loved all of us, but Granny Isa had lost two of her own children, Billy and Charlie, and I felt she poured that unused love into us, especially me. When she wasn't around, I felt her absence keenly.

Granny Isa in America with Sam Stewart

When she returned, she brought back loads of presents. I still remember the pure cotton shirts and crazy ties. She also brought back triangular pennants from America with names like Minnesota, Buffalo, Ohio, and Chicago, which I proudly tacked up above my bed. Most memorably, she gifted me a chemistry set (I still have the metal box to this day) and a Kodak Brownie 127 box camera. The first picture I ever took was of Granny Isa, proudly posing in her American outfit.

While Granny Isa was away, Mum agreed to make Uncle Sammy his tea. A few days in, Sammy asked if he could have a bath. Mum told me to run it for him and lay out a clean towel. Sammy was enjoying his soak when he reached for the cake of Lux toilet soap resting on the rim of the bath. The next moment, he let out a scream in agony, an open safety pin had been embedded in the soap, and he had ripped his arm and shoulder on it.

He leapt out of the bath, dripping with blood, soap, and water, hastily got dressed, and stormed out of the house, convinced someone had deliberately put the pin there. It took weeks before he calmed down enough for us to visit him again and resume our shoe-shining duties for pocket money. When he told my Dad what had happened, Dad simply remarked, "Just as well he decided to wash his shoulder first rather than his testicles"—though he used a much cruder word for that part of anatomy.

Uncle Sammy was a remarkable character, likely somewhere on the autistic spectrum. He was tough, highly intelligent, and wickedly funny. He never married—having been jilted, he never took another chance on love. Instead, he devoted himself to me and Charlie, treating us almost like his own sons. He taught us skills, showed us how to do things properly, and spent time with us. If he was in a bad mood or had been drinking, we knew better than to go near him.

One of the things I remember most was Sammy teaching us how to polish shoes Army-style. He had a full kit—three different brushes, three cloths, a box of matches, and a tin of black Cherry Blossom shoe polish. He used a stiff brush to remove the dirt, a medium-soft brush to apply the polish, and a soft brush to work it into the leather. Then came the burnishing process: a yellow duster, followed by corduroy cloth, and finally another duster for the finishing touch. The last step involved melting a fine layer of polish on the toe cap with a match, then burnishing it repeatedly until the shoes gleamed like patent leather.

Sammy had been called up for military service and ended up in the less glamorous NAFFI Corps. Nevertheless, he was a fine physical specimen and, like my Dad, an Army regimental boxer. After leaving the service, he became a slater and plasterer for Hugh Allan & Son. One day, he fell through a roof and instinctively grabbed a live electric cable to break his fall. If he hadn't been so fit, he would have died that day. But he survived—and went on to care for Granny Isa for the rest of her life.

Sammy also had a different kind of influence on me those library books. He was one of the few men I knew who read books. He had a passion for those cowboy novels and never once complained about my selections. He also read quickly, so I had to go every week. But he made it worth my while, giving me extra pocket money.

It was during these visits that I continued browsing books for myself. I eventually joined the library and received my own little membership card and blue carrier slip. These library books were infinitely more engaging than The Poets' Quair or the dull school history books that felt completely irrelevant to my life. School should have been opening doors for me, not closing them.

Charlie, too, had a door opened for him—by one of our teachers, Dr James McCullum, who taught religious studies. He recommended a book called The Cross and the Switchblade. It would become truly relevant to Charlie later in life, inspiring him so much that he became one of the few pupils to score 100% on a Religious Studies exam.

The Cross and the Switchblade was written in 1962 by Pastor David Wilkerson with John and Elizabeth Sherrill. It recounted Wilkerson's first five years in New York City, where he ministered to disillusioned youth caught up in drugs and gang violence. The book became a bestseller, with over sixteen million copies distributed in more than thirty languages and was eventually made into a film. Charlie now has his own church in Edinburgh where he is Pastor for the local community and supports local homeless people.

Another Feg

In late September, on a particularly sunny Sunday evening, I noticed something happening outside. Looking out the window, I saw a commotion about 200 yards from our house—something involving a caravan and a trailer. A crowd was gathering.

Mum told me to go see what was happening. As I left the house, an ambulance arrived, and men were shouting for people to stand back. I soon learned that one of the Doyle family boys, Graham, who had a mental disability, had been caught in the gap between the car and the trailer. His clothes had snagged, and he had been dragged along the road before the driver finally stopped. He wasn't dead, but he was severely injured. Even from a distance, I could see blood and shredded skin on the road like potato peelings.

After the ambulance left, one of the men from the prefabs brought out a bucket of water and washed away the blood and torn flesh. It was weeks before Graham got out of hospital, his body and face covered in substantial skin grafts.

In October, I received a truly special gift from my cousin Oliver Tannahill— a racing bike in pristine condition. It had Sturmey Archer gears, a hub dynamo, a pump, and a stunning satanized cherry metallic finish. To this day, I have no idea why Oliver gave it to me. If I had been him, they'd have had to pry it from my cold, dead hands in Charlton Heston style.

CHAPTER 10:
BAD BOSSES AND BARE-
KNUCKLE FIGHTS

1964

Early in 1964, Jimmy Stevenson was transferred from Hay & Co Ltd (Grocers) to another branch in Glasgow. He lived in Govan, and I remember him visiting my Dad in Ferguslie. They went out for a drink, but that only happened once or twice. I never saw Jimmy again until I was 40, when I ran into him outside the Linthouse Housing Association in Govan. He was clearly unwell and asked me to tell Dad he was asking for him. He died very shortly after that.

The impact of Jimmy leaving was immediate—all the little treats stopped. I also got a new boss: Glasgow hard man Jim Butterworth. He was rough with me. On one occasion, he pressed an extremely hot knife against my bare arm. My reaction was instant, as always, and he was lucky the knife didn't end up in his neck. He must have thought better of it in the following days, because he gave me some of his old trendy bum-freezer jackets—but I never wore them.

He also brought in some new weekend staff, including a biker named Andy (Drew), who was totally wicked. One day, while we were in the front shop, he asked, "Are you hungry?"

"Always," I replied.

He nodded toward the slicing machine. "Want some of this roast pork?" I said yes and started to shove a huge thick slice into my mouth. Then he shouted, "Mr. Butterworth! Jim is stealing meat off the machine!"

Bastard. He needed that job and clearly thought his chances would be better with me out of the way. But karma played its part—one day he was there, and the next weekend he was gone killed on his motor bike.

It's always a fact that bigger boys bully younger ones, and this happened to me many times. I always recall a quote from the TV series Daniel Pike, played by Scottish actor Roddy McDowall. In one scene, he's accused of being a mean bastard, and he retorts, "Aye, I am—and it was people like you who made me mean."

That summer, Jim Butterworth got the sack, and we got a temporary manager, Rose Feghan. She hired another boy from my school, David Taylor. It was good to have company, and David was a decent worker— when he wasn't nicking chocolate finger biscuits.

Rose, however, was clearly an alcoholic. She would leave at lunchtime to prop up the bar at the George, a pub across the road on Causeyside Street. This wasn't just a drink—she would get wrecked. She'd come back barely standing, and on one occasion, she even fell into the bins. Agnes, the full- time shop girl, was seriously concerned, while Dave and I just laughed— until the day Rose, in her alcohol state of delirium accused us of plotting to kill her.

By then, customers were starting to notice. Her husband came to collect her every day after closing. She also relied on me to do the books, the banking, and the weekly reconciliation form that had to be sent to Hay & Co's head office.

One day, the regional manager visited. When he saw the state Rose was in, he sent her home. She never came back.

My next boss was Hugh Harvey, who was like Jimmy Stevenson but very middle class with a lot of charm, especially for the Ladies he was ex-RAF.(Brylcreem Boy) He was particularly good to me and continued my education not so much on the grocery side but on business, people, and life. If he ran out of stock on a particular product, he would send me around all the other grocery shops to get a price and see what the sale items were. He called them lost leaders. It was a bit of local market analysis, but he would get me to buy up stock and bring it back to the shop, where he put the price back up and, I am sure, deprived the competition of further sales.

On Sundays, Mum would wash my white nylon grocer's coat, and I would take off on my bike. I remember being away all day and getting a very deep tan on my legs. I had my little puncture repair kit and often would take the wheel off and do my own repairs using the rubber patches and glue, then finishing off with a dusting off the repair with French chalk before carefully levering the tube and tyre back onto the rim without pinching the inner tube. I would then pump it up, and away I would go, happy to be on my own and free from any people or stress.

In the evenings I could hear the trains travelling to and from Linwood with the Hillman Imps and occasional big, muffled explosions and light flashes which came from the Royal Ordinance factory at Bishopton 3 miles direct north of our house. My Granny Isa and Grandfather worked there during the 2nd World War and sometimes we could smell the burnt cordite.

Over the years we became familiar with the industrial smells around us. If the wind were blowing from the west, we got the smell of Forrester's Knackers yard, where animal bones were processed it smelt foul, and we would pray for a change in the wind. If the wind blew from the north, we got the farm smells, steam train smells and cordite. If it was from the east, we got whisky barrels or paint smells from Clark and Hunters Cooperage. If the wind blew from the south, we got the gas works or, on occasions the Robertson's jam factory smells of marmalade and strawberry jam.

Dad had got a job building the new extension to the new Linwood car factory extension to cope with the Hillman Imp production. On Thursday nights, if he was working late, mum usually needed his wages to buy food, so either me or Charlie would go to meet him and get some money to take home. Mum would sometimes ask us to get balls of wool to make clothes as the pickup point was near Galls, the wool store in Causeyside St. On this occasion, the pickup point was going to be at the back of the factory in Linwood and as I set off this time on my own, an excessively big thunderstorm came over with heavy rain and black skies. I was soaked instantly. The location was about three miles away, involving going under the Train line for the cars and negotiating several farm tracts and rough marshland to get to the back of the site. The thunder was overhead, and I could almost feel the lightning as it sizzled onto the rail tracks and other farm buildings and pylons.

Another Feg

I was halfway when I heard my mother shouting my name. She thought the better of it and decided it was too dangerous and decided that if I were going to get hit by the lightning and get killed, then she would get killed with me. That is what motherhood is really all about (I am sure every mother would agree). It is worth noting something about this area of Paisley as it was the area where the book (From Scenes Like These was written by Gordon Williams.)

When I was not working in the shop, I had a second job with a local man called George McIndoe, who had a makeshift mobile shop that sold groceries in the newly built Linwood, which was a domicile town for the workers of the car factory. He would drive into the scheme, which was still being built, park up the van and let Johnny Slavin do all the running up and down the maisonette flats and houses to supply groceries to the good folks inside. Sometimes, they gave us a tip, but mostly not. At the end of our shift, George would take us back home and give us 5 shillings and a Mars bar. We would usually get picked up after school and had no dinner, and we would be burning a lot of calories we did not have, so we asked George if we could have the Mars bar at the beginning of the shift and he said no. This caused a substantial change in our modus operandi. First, we would steal a Mars bar and eat it when we were out of sight. Then we started taking cigarettes, only one packet each, and when I got home, I hid them under my mattress, not knowing what to do with them. I came home one night to find Mum with a very not-pleased look as she had found the fags. Then the dreaded words "wait till your Faither gets hame."

I felt very sheepish and did not like the idea of being a thief, so I sat on the living room couch until Dad got in. He had a conversation with Mum and said right, you show me the fags. I went into the bedroom and lifted the mattress, and there he saw an Aladdin's treasure of about a hundred packets of cigarettes all makes, Players, Capstan, Woodbine, Embassy all tipped and untipped. He instantly clenched his teeth, and I prepared for a thick ear but no such action, the clenched teeth were to hold back a smile at his luck of having his own in-house Tobacconist shop. He said not do that again and replaced the mattress down, he also actually clapped my head and said, "Wis, he not paying you enough"? To which I replied, "Naw, Dad."

Working in the construction industry was a dangerous game as this was before the Health and Safety at Work Act, and Dad got a few injuries for which he had industrial claims, one of which presented him with compensation for a twisted ankle. It was not a lot of money, but enough to pay for a holiday for us all to go to a holiday home in Port Seaton on the east Coast of Scotland near Portobello. He contracted George McIndoe to drive us all in his minibus to the holiday campsite. When we got there, it was a little grey hut with a pitched roof and three bedrooms. There was no toilet and no running water, and the cooker needed a gas cylinder. Charlie and I fetched the water in big plastic containers and took the younger children back and forward to the toilet block. One other luxury we had was a small Baby Bambi transistor radio, and I can remember Mum and Dad leaving me to watch the kids while they went to a local lounge for a drink. I was trying to tune into Radio Luxemburg or the pirate station Radio Caroline to see if I could hear Beatles music as they were fast becoming a phenomenon. The only songs I can remember were the Beach Boys and a group called the Applejacks (Have I the Right to Hold You).

Charlie and I would head off to wherever adventure was, and that was at the harbour at Port Seaton, where we would use a fishing rod we found to catch little sprats. One day, we decided to go to Edinburgh Zoo, which we did by bus and without incident. Mum and Dad did not fret if we disappeared off on our adventures.

When we got home, a new problem was brewing as Johnny Slavin had been apprehended by the police for allegedly stealing from George McIndoe. I didn't know if Johnny had put my name in the frame or if Dad had spoken to George, but nothing more was heard of it (thanks Johnny). That was enough for me to decide that stealing was an unbelievably bad idea.

By September, I was working in the shop on Saturdays, and by the time I got on the bus home in the evening I was always relieved to rest my feet. As the Western SMT bus turned the last corner into Ferguslie Park Avenue, I saw a big crowd gathered around our house. Earlier that year, the Hutton family had moved away to

Clydebank, and the Cree family had moved in. Roy and his wife had five kids, and as usual, these often-caused fights with the parents. That Saturday, Anne Cree had called my sister Ellen "a wee hoor," which sparked a rammy (fight) between my mum and Mrs. Cree.

It didn't take long for me to find out that my Dad and Roy Cree were having a bare-knuckle fight in the back garden to settle things. The washing area had been roped off between the four clothes poles like a makeshift boxing ring, and the two men were squaring up. This was just how some people in the scheme resolved issues. Roy was a known criminal with serious Barlinnie prison time under his belt for violence against women. Dad, on the other hand, was an ex-army boxing champion who spent his weekends using rough stuff to collect gambling debts for the local bookie syndicates.

Roy never stood a chance. I don't think he even landed a punch before Dad thumped him several times, sending him crashing to the ground. His face just exploded—burst lips, a broken nose, and cuts around his eyes. Dad's hands were covered in blood, despite wrapping them in handkerchiefs. Women were hanging out of their windows, screaming. Dad stood over Roy and asked if he'd had enough. Roy just raised his hand in defeat.

Breaking through the crowd, Dad got patted on the back by onlookers before heading inside. He washed his hands at the sink, then sat down to a dinner of beef ham, mashed potatoes, and beans, all washed down with a glass of milk. Afterward, he quietly rolled up a very thin cigarette using Rizla papers and Golden Virginia shag tobacco. I asked him what it was all about.

"Ask your mum," he said, then added, "Shut the door." Which I did—from the outside.

That night, Roy responded by locking his wife out. Through the early hours of the morning, she called out, "Roy, let me in! Please let me in!" But he left her to sleep on the doorstep in the cold until daylight.

Winter was setting in again, and we took in extra coal. Some of the lumps were too big for Mum, Charlie, or me to lift, so we had to break them up with a hammer (actually it was an old axe which we called a hatchet) that was always kept by the coal bunker. One day, Stewart was watching me smash up the coal, keeping the bunker lid partially down to stop the dust from covering the kitchen.

Mum told me to give Stewart a shot, so I passed him the heavy hatchet. He whacked away at the coal for ages while Mum and I let him get on with it. Eventually, he came into the living room looking more like a chimney sweep. We ran to the kitchen—coal dust and shards of coal covered everything. Some pieces were even sticking out of the margarine tub like porcupine quills. It was a long time before Stewart was trusted to break coal again.

Being the older brother gave me a certain status—generally, the younger kids did as they were told. I also got to stay up later and was considered a "licensed" adult. One night, after all the other kids had gone to bed, I was sitting with Mum and Dad when Stewart wandered into the room, sleepwalking. He went to the corner and started peeing up the wall.

Mum just gently led him back to bed without a word. I was left to clean up the mess, which wasn't too bad since we had no carpets, just a square of wax cloth in the middle and black-painted borders on the floorboards.

Dad had started decorating the kitchen, laying red-and-white twelve-inch floor tiles in a chessboard pattern. We also got a red Formica table and chairs. It was a significant improvement, and Mum encouraged him to do more in other rooms.

Back then, wallpaper had to be hand-trimmed because of the border on both sides of the pattern. That job fell to Mum, Charlie, and me. Each roll was about 50 feet long, and we had seven rolls for our main room—so that was 700 feet of trimming. Armed with scissors, we got to work. Mum was the quickest, but we all ended up with blisters.

You can imagine our disappointment when we woke up to find Dad had hung the wallpaper upside down.

It was not the first time either. Once, he decorated the bathroom with seagull- themed wallpaper, but the seagulls were all flying upside down. When I pointed it out, he was not pleased, and it stayed that way for a long time— until some adults noticed, and Mum finally convinced him to change it. She picked up new wallpaper with a fish theme.

We were all nervous to check. Sure enough, the fish were upside down, too.

When I told Dad, he marched me into the bathroom. "Why are they upside down?" he demanded.

"Because the bubbles from their mouths are going the wrong way down," I said.

Dad squinted at the paper. "That's not bubbles," he grumbled. "Oh? What is it then?"

"They're being sick," he muttered.

Dad was never going to be a painter and decorator. Neither was Uncle Sammy.

One time, he was wallpapering Granny Isa's bedroom while I helped with the pasting. I handed him a roll while he stood on a short step ladder. The paper started creasing, and no matter how much he tried to straighten it, it wouldn't lie flat. Suddenly, it tore.

That was the last straw. Sammy's famous temper flared, and he ripped the entire roll straight off the wall in a fit of rage. I made myself scarce after that.

The family was becoming less of a distraction for me as I was working and beginning to enjoy music especially the Beatles and fashion. At lunchtime at school, a small crowd of us would make our way into Paisley town centre center and have lunch in the Deep-Sea fish and chip shop or Cardosi's café where we could listen to the top music charts and drink Coca-Cola. Sometimes we would go to Cuthbertson's music centre or Boots store to hear the new releases in the sound booths. As a working boy with money, I could afford fashionable clothes, and it was the sixties, and girls were remarkably interesting especially when the miniskirt appeared.

CHAPTER 11:
FIRST LOVE AND MORE FIRES

1965

At school, the Camphill pupils held parties, and I was always invited, having a wonderful time. But I began to notice a stark difference in the material wealth of their homes compared to mine.

We had some decorations and a few modern conveniences, but we had no car no phone, and Dad didn't drive. Some of their houses had pianos, fridges, and carpets. So, when I finally asked Lizzie Brown out on a date, I was so embarrassed about our house that I got my Granny Isa to host tea for her, giving me time to improve the décor at home. I never mentioned this to Mum or Dad—I just started buying pictures from sales and cleaning and tidying the house.

Eventually, I introduced Lizzie to my family. My sisters just stared, Mum tried to make polite conversation, and Lizzie and I spent the whole hour blushing.

Lizzie and I dated for about a year. I gave her a gold friendship ring, which I suspect was actually a wedding ring, and we spent that year snogging our way through. I vividly remember one occasion when I decided to walk all the way from Ferguslie to Foxbar to visit Lizzie, who lived there so we could go for a walk. I wanted to look my best for her—I was very fashion-conscious, wearing grey hipsters with a white belt, a tab shirt with a gold collar clip, and London toe shoes. All I needed was for Mum to finish the Arran knit jumper she had been working on for two years, using 00-size knitting needles.

She stayed up all night on Saturday to finish it. When I put it on, it was fantastic—big and chunky, with a traditional Arran pattern in pure white wool. It was a perfect fit as I set off on my long trek to Foxbar.

By the time I reached the Red Road at the top of Ferguslie, the jumper had begun to stretch, now hanging halfway down my legs.

By the time I arrived at Lizzie's house, it had reached my knees, and the sleeves were a good 30% longer. When Lizzie opened the door, I immediately took the jumper off—it was fast turning back into a sheep.

I was invited to her house in Ivanhoe Road, in the Foxbar housing scheme, where I met her mum, Dad, and siblings. They were a nice family, and, of course, they had a piano. Lizzie's Dad was a tall man who asked careful questions—exactly what I'd do if my own daughters brought home a boyfriend. I don't know if my answers were the right ones, but all I know is that Lizzie and I saw less of each other after that. After the school holidays, she had a new boyfriend from Kilmarnock, and her old boyfriend, Alan Stirling, was still hovering around.

I got all my 45s records back which I had lent to Lizzie and asked for my ring, which I promptly threw away. I've always had a thing for jewellry—even now, I still buy it for my wife and kids. It's in my DNA, but that's another story. I did go back days later and actually found that ring in a garden.

In April, I came home from work on a Saturday night to find my family in a state of absolute joy. Mum was ecstatic, and the kids were practically wetting themselves. It turned out Dad had scored 23 points on the Littlewoods football pools—the maximum points possible that weekend. He had gone to the Pools shop in George Street to lodge a phone claim.

Mum was already dreaming aloud—at last, we could buy a house out of Ferguslie, a little bungalow on Glasgow Road. We could go on holiday to America, wear great clothes, and Dad could buy his dream car.

When Dad got home, he had clearly had a drink and was in high spirits.

"So, how much have we won?"

"We'll find out on Wednesday night when the dividends are published in the back of the Evening Times newspaper" he said.

The days dragged by, and in our minds, we'd spent that money a thousand times over.

Finally, on Wednesday, Dad came in with the paper and slumped into his chair, his face heavy with disappointment.

"How much did we win?" I asked.

He held up the newspaper, and I read: £28 and 10 shillings. Underneath, it said: Rule 23 applies—whatever that meant.

It turned out that so many people had won that the dividend was dismally low. Our dreams evaporated. The next day, Mum had dark circles under her eyes—not because Dad had hit her (that never happened), but because disappointment is a major stress factor. And there would be plenty more of that in the years ahead.

Back at the shop, Mr. Harvey had a few special customers for reasons unknown to me. One of them was Mrs Mack, whom he obviously liked. Every Thursday, I had to deliver her grocery order to her home in Foxbar. This meant carrying a heavy egg carton box—about three feet long, eighteen inches wide, and eighteen inches high—filled with all sorts of food and provisions.

I'd catch the bus near the shop, placing the carton under the stairs for the ride. At the stop near her house, I'd haul it out and lug it uphill for 200 yards, then up to the top landing of a four-storey tenement. Every week, I dropped it off, and never once was I offered a glass of water or a tip.

The prefabs were only a few hundred yards from our house at No. 94. I should mention the type of people who lived there and in our general neighborhood were all good folks and generally took diligent care of the property and gardens unlike the folks in Graigmuir Rd.

During the Second World War, Clydebank was blitzed by German bombers. Many were killed, and even more, lost their homes—mainly sandstone tenements. These people became, in effect, war refugees, and they were given priority for the newly built houses in Ferguslie. Our next-door neighbours were all from Clydebank.

Housing demand was so high that prefabricated houses had to be built, not just in Ferguslie but also in Hunterhill and Gallowhill. The prefabs were single storey but surprisingly comfortable, equipped with fridges, gas, and electricity. They were timber structures with corrugated asbestos roofing.

Another Feg

I recall two occasions when these little houses caught fire. The first was when the Stafford family's prefab, about 300 yards from ours, went up in flames.

It was around 8:00 p.m., and most families—including us, were watching television. We did have a TV by then. Suddenly, our picture started flickering and crackling, so, as usual, Dad asked me to adjust the long white aerial. As I approached the TV, which was near the window, I noticed flames shooting through the roof of the Stafford prefab.

Dad and I ran out towards the fire. The police and fire brigade had miraculously arrived—despite the fact that hardly anyone had a phone. The fire was raging, with glass breaking and little explosions popping inside. Then came a massive explosion, sending flames fifty feet into the air—it must have been the gas main rupturing.

The police held us back, but we saw George Stafford, blackened and cut from jumping through the front window to rescue his wife and two kids. The next day, I saw him walking past our house. Normally, he walked straight-backed, but on that day, his chest was pushed out with pride—and rightfully so. He had no house, but his family was alive.

Ferguslie had its fair share of stray dogs. Licenses weren't needed, and vet insurance wasn't a thing, so packs of dogs roamed the streets, raiding bins. When a bitch was in heat, it wasn't a pleasant sight—sometimes dozens of dogs would catch the scent.

One summer, a pack of about twenty dogs was chasing a single bitch when a fast-moving lorry ploughed into them. Some were killed instantly, but around seven lay writhing on the ground, their intestines and bones exposed.

Jimmy McCurdy arrived with a hammer. Without hesitation, he moved from dog to dog, smashing their skulls to put them out of their misery. When he finished, he dragged the carcasses to the nearest gutter. Then he sat down on the pavement, covering his blood-splattered face with his hands and cried.

One of our new neighbours was Nick Donnachie and his family—his wife, Irene, and their children: Jane, Billy, Tony, and Kim.

They lived in the downstairs house across our pathway. Nick was an Irish Catholic from Bundoran, County Donegal, Éire (the Free State). A young father, he was fit and good-looking, with a muscular physique and thick black hair. He was hardworking and tough as nails. I liked the Donalds, especially Irish Nick.

DNA discovery I am Ancient Irish on BBC program Scotland's DNA

I was always happy to help him in the evenings when he was flush paneling the old doors in his house. My job was to hammer in the small panel pins while the glue was setting. He also had a tape recorder, and sometimes he'd invite half a dozen of the local lads over to listen to music and record songs. The first time I heard my own voice on tape, I was completely unimpressed. I used to recite lines from the Katie OXO cube adverts, but I didn't sound the way I imagined.

Nick was full of life—sometimes too full of it. He was the type to wreck his motorbike on country roads and end up in a hedgerow or, when my Dad got him demolition work, to sit on the very beam he was cutting and fall straight through the roof. His body and face were covered in scars. One Friday night, there was a commotion outside when Nick and Tam Slavin decided to race up and down the street—completely nude. They were both full of wine, and it was the best entertainment ever.

One evening, Irene was working the twilight shift and was counting on Nick to be home in time to watch the kids. But he was late and had left the fire on in the house. Irene asked Mum if she could keep an eye on the children until he got back, and Mum, in turn, asked me to do it. I was sitting on Nicks's couch in the living room when burning soot started falling down the chimney. I quickly got the kids out and sent them upstairs to our house.

A heavy black plume of smoke and a fireball erupted from Noel's chimney. My Dad rushed in and tried to smother the flames with an old carpet rug. The room was filled with smoke, and we both started coughing and spluttering. We opened the windows and doors to let air in. Then came the unmistakable sound of the police.

"Mr. Donald?" the officer enquired. My Dad answered, "Aye."

(in an Irish accent)

"I've radioed for the fire brigade. They should be here any minute."

And sure enough, I could hear the bells outside in the street. The firefighters arrived, went up in the turntable ladder, and sprayed down the chimney until water splashed into the fire grate below. The thick black smoke turned to white steam, and the fire was extinguished.

The whole street had turned out—nosey neighbours and curious kids everywhere. The police officer turned to my Dad.

"You know you can get fined for this, Mr. Donnachie?" Dad just shook his head.

As the police and fire engine pulled away, I started cleaning up the room. Then Nick appeared, breathless.

"Christ, Jimmy, I'm sorry I was late." My Dad just looked at him.

I smirked and said, "It's Mr. Donnachie to you."

We all burst out laughing.

A few months later, Nick asked me for a favour. He handed me a small triangular parcel wrapped in cloth and brown paper and told me to hide it somewhere safe—where no one would find it. He made me promise not to tell anyone about it. I thought the whole thing was thrilling, so I took the heavy parcel and hid it under the floorboards in my room.

It took me a few days to work up the courage to peek inside. When I finally unwrapped the brown paper and the oily rag, there it was—a Browning 9mm handgun made in Belgium. No bullets. I quickly wrapped it back up and shoved it under the floor again.

We all knew Nick was Irish, but he never spoke about home. We knew he had a brother who was a doctor, but he didn't like to talk about his past. So, we assumed he was an IRA runaway. I handed the parcel back days later and Nick gestured to keep my mouth shut.

Around this time, Charlie had decided to call off my debt for selling all his toys and cards, so I'd given him my beloved bicycle. He'd had it for a few weeks when, one day, he rode it to Hunterhill, where Auntie Jennie lived. On the way back, speeding down the road, he hit a kerb stone and went flying. He was pretty badly grazed and bruised, and the bike was wrecked. It took me weeks to get it back and then repair it. But by the time it was ready, Dad needed it for work. Just like that, my bike became the new family transport.

We had a normal Christmas in 1966. Then, Mum announced she was having another baby. I was embarrassed to tell my friends at school, but the people in the shop thought it was lovely news.

Just before New Year, Mum had a dream that really unsettled her. In the dream she saw her mother, but she had a bad limp, her nose was falling off her face, and she was floating over a wall. Mum was always having dreams and was deeply superstitious. If a dog howled in the night, she'd say someone was going to die. If she dreamed of fire, she'd say bad news was coming quickly.

Dad had dreams too—nightmares. As an old soldier, he had seen things he wished he hadn't. He once told me about a soldier he trained with at Stirling Castle when he was with the Argylls. The poor lad had been on guard duty at night and on the firing range during the day. He'd pocketed a bullet and later used it to blow his brains out in the regimental toilets. My Dad said his brains were stuck to the ceiling.

New Year and Hogmanay (New Years Eve) came and went without incident. Well, except that I got a belt on the ear for calling it a "sweetie Christmas"—and rightly so. My mum and Dad were doing everything they could just to keep us afloat, and there I was, stuck in my own teenage bubble.

CHAPTER 12:
CAR CRASH AND ANGELA GOES TO HEAVEN.

1966

It was January 3rd, a few days after Mum's dream, when we got the news that Granniemaw, my two cousins, Robert and Joseph Armstrong, and Uncle Joe Armstrong had been in a bad crash on Beith Road. They had all been hospitalized. Joe got off with just a bad gash to his leg, but Granniemaw was severely injured—her leg was broken, and she had serious head injuries, including lacerations to her head and nose. Uncle Joe suffered fractured hip and chest injuries, but it was Cousin Robert who fared the worst, with a bad concussion and severe facial injuries that required 100 stitches.

It was New Year, and he had been visiting Auntie Mag and Uncle Tommy in Scott Avenue, Johnstone. On the drive home, in icy conditions, he lost control and crashed into a wall at high speed.

They were all in hospital for weeks, but Granniemaw was the first to be discharged. She came home badly limping, leaning on a stick, with scars that formed a large horseshoe shape on her forehead and lacerations on her nose where it had been partially detached.

I visited Robert a few weeks later once he regained consciousness. The original stitching had been done with catgut, and it was so bad that a plastic surgeon had to remove the stitches and redo his entire face with fine stitching. I don't think Robert ever fully recovered from the trauma of that accident, though he went on to marry and have a family.

At the start of the year, we got a new boss in the shop. Mr. Harvey had left, and May Keenan took over. She was sharp, well-dressed, and always had her hair done—she stood out from other women. I was very fond of May, and she was particularly good to me. The new staff she introduced made the biggest impression on me. She brought in May McGuinness, Billy Jones, her sister Betty, and, on Saturdays, a boy named John Reid.

John, who came from Gallowhill, was fascinating—He had strong opinions about music and culture and a clear idea of what he wanted from life. A few years later, he would go on to become Elton John's manager.

Billy Jones was a lot of fun—slightly effeminate, but he always brought great energy to the shop, making it a lively place for both staff and customers. May also brought my brother Charlie in to help, but the most significant change came when she introduced her daughter, Elaine, into my life.

For the first few months, up until April, Elaine and I just flirted, and I was so happy. But then I got brought back down to earth with a hard bang.

I often worried about Mum, having all these babies and managing so much work, so one day, I had a conversation with her. I suggested she consider not having any more children. When you're fifteen, you know nothing about the world, and I regret ever saying it—it upset her deeply. If I'd said anything to Dad, he'd have probably given me a thick ear.

It was mid-April, a Sunday, when Mum went into labour. She had been having contractions for some time, and the doctor wanted her to go to hospital—she was in her mid-forties and suffering from high levels of fluid retention. I was sent out to call an ambulance.

I ran to Falcon Crescent, about 400 yards away, where there was a telephone box with a payphone. These phones were complicated compared to today's ones—you had to press Button A, insert money, then press Button B. But in an emergency, you just dialed 999.

The phone booth had been vandalized. I tried to get through, but I wasn't sure if I had succeeded, so I ran nearly a mile to the other end of the Ferguslie housing scheme to try again. That phone was vandalized too. In desperation, I ran to the west end of Paisley, another two miles away, and finally managed to get through.

By the time I got home, two ambulances had arrived. Doctor Pat McCusker was there. When I stepped inside, my Granny Isa was in the house, the doctor was with my mum, and Dad was sitting in the living room, rolling a cigarette.

It was late evening, and the doctor decided not to move Mum but to let the midwife stay with her. She was still having contractions when all the kids, including me, went to bed.

I could hear Mum's discomfort and moans as I lay in bed. Eventually, I fell asleep.

At around 5:00 am, I woke with the feeling that something was wrong. I got up to go to the toilet, but when I entered the bathroom, I froze. The bath was filled with blood-stained sheets and afterbirth. Granny Isa wasn't quick enough to stop me from seeing it. She pulled me out of the bathroom and hugged me.

Dad was sitting in the kitchen, crying. That's when I found out— the baby had been stillborn.

Mum had been sedated, and the night doctor had arrived earlier to assist with the birth.

At around 8:00 am, Dad broke the news to Mum. Even now, writing this, it still upsets me.

Mum and Dad had seven children, all fit and healthy. This baby should have come into a big, happy family. Dad had even bought a brand-new coach-built Silver Cross pram. There was a lovely new cot, stacks of fluffy nappies, Zac cream for its bottom, Johnson's baby powder that smelled wonderful, and fancy pram sheets and covers with silk fringes.

Granny Isa got us all up, washed, dressed, and made breakfast.

Then Dad called all us children together. He told us the baby was a little girl—Angela— and that she had gone straight to heaven. He led us to the bedroom where the new pram was. We gathered around as he lifted the pram cover.

"She's perfect," he said softly. "Not deformed. So, if anyone asks, you tell them she was perfect."

Angela lay there, still, and peaceful, her tiny lips-tinged lilac.

Later that day, a black van arrived. A man in a black coat went into the back bedroom and left carrying a black hold all.

I went to Mum's room, where she lay in bed, staring out of the window. I watched as the man put the bag into the van and drove off slowly.

Mum turned to me. "Where's my wee Angela?" she asked.

"Heaven," I whispered.

She turned away and sobbed h a r d into her pillow.

Mum never truly got over it. In the immediate aftermath, she sank into a deep depression, sitting at the window for hours, staring out. Visitors came and went, but she was inconsolable.

I asked Dad where the man had taken the baby.

He said, "She's with Granddad Green in heaven," he said.

That event affected us all, though we didn't realise it fully at the time. It left an unspoken weight on us, a subconscious awareness that life and death shared the same bed.

Eventually, we stopped talking about it, and so did our friends and neighbours.

The rest of that year drifted by. The kids grew, and Charlie excelled at school—he was now at Camphill with me. But Angela's death had left something in me, something I didn't understand yet.

Back at school, I decided the sixpence every pupil had to pay when a window got broken was unfair. I had never broken a window, yet I had been paying sixpences since 1963. So, one day, I wrapped my school scarf around my fist and smashed five or six windows.

One of the younger boys identified me.

I was given six of the best—the Lochgelly leather strap, swung with full force.

Three lashes from the Rector. Three more from his Deputy.

Each strike drew great pain and the last one blood. My hands swelled, and welts climbed up my wrists. The pain was searing, but in my mind the injustice of it was worse.

I cursed them under my breath.

They could only give six lashes in one go, so I was told to return the next morning for another six.

I was also warned I might be expelled and also my parents were going to be called.

What really scared me was the thought of having to tell Dad what I had done. I knew I had let them—and myself—down and only added to their troubles. I walked home slowly and went straight to bed, in the same room where Angela's body had lain in state just two weeks earlier. I've always believed that when kids act like that, something deeper is disturbing them.

I fell asleep quickly, only to be shaken awake by Dad. He asked what was wrong, and I told him. He looked at my wrist, then left the room without a word.

The Rector, and his Deputy got the fright of their lives when Dad took time off work to confront them about the state of my wrists. I wasn't privy to any of the whole conversation, but within hours, I was assured there would be no further punishment and no possibility of being expelled. In fact, I would be given extra support to help me through my exams. God bless you, Dad.

For me, there was a welcome distraction in Elaine, the boss's daughter. I asked her out in late April, and our first date was at the Regal Cinema in Paisley, where we watched My Fair Lady with Rex Harrison and Audrey Hepburn. Love blossomed, and we became inseparable—I simply couldn't bear to be apart from her.

At the same time, we were becoming increasingly aware that we might be leaving school the following year, so getting a job and planning for the future were becoming important. Though we were always welcome at home, Elaine and I loved spending time alone, just kissing and chatting. When it was cold, we would visit her aunties and uncles, and sometimes, we'd babysit her young cousins—the Taylors or the McMillans. On summer days and evenings, we would walk everywhere together, heading into Paisley town centre or wandering through the better housing areas, fantasizing about one day living in Thornley Park or Potterhill.

I was also getting to know Elaine's wider family, including her Dad, James, and her brothers, John and James.

John was a cooper, and he was dating Elaine's friend Cath Gordon. He had a real spark to his personality—a drummer in a band called The Talismen, he would sometimes set up his drums in the back garden, playing alongside other musicians like my cousin, Robert Armstrong, who was on guitar. John also had a Lambretta scooter, and we got on great.

The thing I noticed most about him was his hands. They were covered in the hardest, dirtiest callouses I had ever seen. Coopers did hard work making barrels, and because they were often on piecework rates, making money meant working fast—which meant callouses. But the upside was that most of the Paisley coopers were always well-dressed and had money in their pockets.

We made a great foursome. When the girls went off to Weston-super-Mare for a girls-only holiday, John and I stuck together for the duration. We got to know each other better, and we even swapped clothes.

Elaine's mum and Dad were in Blackpool for the week, so John and I had the house to ourselves. We loved music, and John would set up his Paiste Classic red mother-of-pearl drum kit, letting me practice alongside him. Sadly, I haven't a musical bone in my body, but it was brilliant just listening to him play. It was even better when the girls came back, and we returned to our usual dating routine.

Sometimes, we'd visit the Taylor family in Gordon Street. Davy Taylor was a big character—a motor mechanic with countless hobbies, including photography, electronics, and gardening. I was always trying to get hold of electronic parts for his projects. He was great company, always full of stories, and the first man I ever had genuinely interesting conversations with about life.

He had even converted his van into a camper van, taking his young family off to the Highlands whenever he could. Isobel, his wife, was an absolute delight. She would make us huge toast-and-cheese sandwiches with sweet tea while she and Elaine got down to some serious chatting. Meanwhile, Davy and I would try to solve the world's problems. Their kids David Junior, Yvonne and Linda were also brilliant—full of character.

At New Year, we made the rounds visiting family. I had already been to Elaine's Aunt Betty's, spending time with her husband, Tommy, and their kids—Tommy Junior, Eleanor, and Peter, who had Down's syndrome. They were such a loving family.

On New Year Eve 1966, we all went to Elaine's Uncle Charlie's house on Tennent Road, Paisley, for a party. They asked me to sing a song, and—somewhat to my own surprise—I gave Nobody's Child a go. They loved it, which was unexpected, given that I had never sung in my life before.

We had far too much to drink, and as John, Elaine, Cath, and I made our slow journey back to Glenburn on foot, we reached the top of King Street—a steep hill climb. At that point, John, and I both desperately needed to pee, so we let the girls walk ahead. That's when we spotted an old lorry tyre.

Drunk as we were, it seemed like a brilliant idea to roll the tyre up the street. However, we quickly lost control of it, and it started racing downhill towards Clavering Street—a steep slope leading down to Well Street. We tried to catch it, but I fell flat on my backside. Meanwhile, John looked on in horror as it bounced off cars, walls, and fences.

Just as I got up, I walked straight into the silver buttons of a giant of a police sergeant. I was nicked.

John luckily escaped and vanished into the night, and I was unceremoniously dragged off down the hill to inspect the damage, praying I hadn't killed anyone. The tyre had travelled miles by the time we found it. I was knackered but sobering up remarkably fast.

The sergeant made me roll the tyre all the way back up the hill to where we had found it. Then, he marched me into the mini police station at the top of King Street.

"What's your name?" "What's your address?" "What school do you go to?" "What's your pal's name?"

Most of the answers were easy, though I refused to snitch on John. But when I mentioned Camphill School, that caught his attention.

He told me he had been educated at Camphill, too, and asked if I understood the momentum of a rotating body on an inclined plane. Something about the force of gravity, acceleration, and weight rendering the moving object high- impact, with potentially devastating effects.

I just shook my head.

I won't repeat what he said next, but I've never been in trouble with the police since.

He wrapped up his lecture by asking my name again.

"I know your Dad. I should have a chat with him."

I froze. I honestly thought I was about to get a baton over my head. Instead, he just opened the door and told me to beat it.

Not a great start to 1967.

CHAPTER 13:
LEAVING HOME

1967

Elaine and I were growing closer, and I loved spending time with her family—especially her grandfather, John. A First World War veteran, he had lost a leg in battle, but he remained a true gentleman, always cheerful. He lived with Elaine's family at No. 84 Glenburn Road, in the small front bedroom, which always smelled of tobacco and bay rum.

On Sunday mornings, May would make a huge Scottish breakfast, and afterward, we would try to coax her Papa into telling us stories about the war. He had a set of German razors, each engraved with a different day of the week, he claimed that he had been offered them from a soldier whose life he had spared. Like my father, John had been an old Argyll. He lost his leg during the Salonika campaign in the Dardanelles. The wound became infected, and after multiple operations to remove the gangrene, they had to amputate above the knee.

Following his recovery, he spent time on the Isle of Skye and then at Erskine Military Hospital before resuming his trade as a saw doctor and eventually an inspector at Babcock and Wilcox. I loved sitting with this kind old gentleman and listening to his stories. My own grandfather, James Green (Bunty) , had passed away, and I hadn't seen my Grandfather Joe since the day he belted me on the ear.

It was exam time at Camphill, and since Elaine and I were the same age, she was also sitting her O-levels exams at St Margaret's Convent School on Renfrew Road in Paisley. I took seven subjects, Elaine six, but the truth was, we were more consumed with each other than with our studies. In the end, I think we both managed five or six passes.

I had already made up my mind to leave school, despite my French teacher's pleas to continue and sit my Higher Certificates.

Elaine's teachers encouraged her to stay on as well, but we both decided to leave.

Leaving school was simple. On the last day, I walked out through a side door I had never noticed before. It led past an old graveyard and church, the same one where Ronald Reagan's ancestors had once worshipped and buried. I never looked back.

Around this time, Elaine's mum came to my door in Ferguslie, distressed. Her father, Charlie McMillan, had passed away, and she asked if I could open the shop for her. I left immediately for Causeyside Street. It was a sad time— Charlie wasn't that old, and he was well loved. I did my best to comfort Elaine, but that kind of pain lingers.

Elaine decided to go to college to study secretarial courses, while I began attending interviews for apprenticeships. Mum always said, "An engineer's sweat is worth a guinea a drop," so when I was offered an engineering apprenticeship at Babcock and Wilcox Ltd in Renfrew, I took it. The only catch was that it was with their Construction Division, meaning my training would take place in Tipton, in the Black Country near Birmingham in England.

I was due to start in August, and when I got the job offer in July, we put it out of our minds—until the day arrived. The shop folks bought me a lovely lamb's wool jumper as a farewell gift, and at home, I knew Mum wasn't happy about me leaving, but Dad was pleased. An apprenticeship was a good opportunity, even if it took me away from home.

I was set to leave on Sunday from Glasgow Central to Birmingham New Street, where the other Scottish apprentices would gather. On Saturday night, I spent my last hours with Elaine. When the time came, I promised to write every day and reminded her that it wouldn't be long before I'd be home on leave. I dragged myself away, walking just a few hundred yards to the bus shelter. As I stood there waiting, Elaine suddenly came running down the hill, tears streaming down her face. Big, fat mascara-soaked drops fell onto my new jumper, and it was gut-wrenching. They say parting is such sweet sorrow, but really, it's just raw emotion—for young lovers, for all lovers, for anyone who truly cares.

Saying goodbye at home was just as hard. My little sisters grilled me: Why are you leaving us? Charlie, meanwhile, stayed quiet, I think probably pleased that he would now get my bed and wardrobe.

The next morning, Dad agreed to take me to Central Station. I hugged Mum, and she had a little cry as I left Ferguslie behind. The train ride from Gilmour Street in Paisley to Central was mostly silent. Dad was a tough man, but I knew he must have been wondering what would happen next to his firstborn son.

We arrived early, so Dad and I took a walk around the block, passing under the Heilandman's Umbrella—the railway bridge over Argyle Street. There, we met Frank Call, one of the construction administrators, who would be travelling with us.

Eventually, the moment came. I said my goodbyes to Dad and boarded the train, finding a window seat with some of the other apprentices. Dad didn't walk away immediately. Instead, as the train pulled out of the station, he started walking alongside it, waving. I watched him, and at that moment, I realised—he had been here before, when he left home to join the Army in 1941.

God bless him.

I was on my way. The train rattled through Carlisle, Preston, and Wolverhampton. Along the journey, I made friends with Joe McCrystal, John McNee, Jim Picken, Willie Sullivan, Willie Gallagher, Willie Bell, and Angus McLeod.

When we arrived, a bus picked us up and took us to 13 Pritchatt's Road, Edgbaston, on the outskirts of Birmingham. The house was an old Tudor- style rectory, with a warden called Mr. Gush who lived there with his wife and daughter.

Two instructors from Babcock and Wilcox, Tom Smith and Jim Raeside, met us. They explained where we'd be sleeping—in the dormitory upstairs— outlined our expected behaviour, mealtimes, and informed us that a bus would pick us up in the morning at 06:30.

After they left, I took my kit upstairs and chose the top bunk near the window, which overlooked the ornamental gardens below Pritchatt's Road was next to Birmingham University and Queen

Margaret's Hospital, about half a mile from the famous Edgbaston cricket ground. PJ Smith took the bunk below mine.

Once I'd settled in, I left the house to find a phone box so I could call Elaine. It never occurred to me to contact Mum and Dad—besides, they didn't have a phone anyway.

I dialed 0141 884 4318, feeding a fortune in coins into the greedy machine. When my cash ran out, I had just enough time for a quick goodbye and an "I love you" before the line went dead.

Back at the house, Mr. Gush was already struggling to get this lively bunch of lads ready for dinner. The place had a grand, old-world feel, with plenty of oak paneling. But the real surprise was the food—absolutely fabulous. Most of us came from council estates and had never seen such a feast: steaks, roast potatoes, vegetables—like Christmas dinner every with the full English breakfasts w h i c h kept me going all day.

The first morning, I was up early showered, dressed, and downstairs for breakfast. Then, a bell signaled that the bus had arrived. It left promptly at 07:15. It was an old single-decker coach, the kind of holiday bus you'd take to Blackpool. Most of the lads dozed off for the hour-long journey through heavy traffic towards Tipton.

Babcock and Wilcox in Tipton was a transport depot with a welding school attached. At the back of the site, a brand-new training school had been built. Once inside, Tom Smith got us kitted out in blue boiler suits, safety boots, gloves, and hats. We were given toolboxes with some basic tools: a Rabone Chesterman 12-inch rule, a ball-peen hammer, a bastard file, and a smooth file.

"All your other tools, you'll have to make," Tom told us.

Upstairs, our newly painted lecture room had a view of the industrial Albion Works, railway lines, and heaps of scrap metal. We were given an overview of what lay ahead, including one day a week at Dudley Technical College to study engineering.

One of our first tasks was to handle a small piece of freshly polished mild steel, then return it to an envelope and sign our names on it. This test determined if we had "rusty fingers"—some people, due to high acid sweat, left fingerprint-shaped rust marks on steel. If that happened, you'd never become a an engineering fitter, as high-value tools like slip gauges—precision instruments worth a small fortune—couldn't be risked in your hands. Those with rusty fingers were destined for welding or plating. Luckily for me, I became a fitter.

Next door, the welding school flashed and sparked all day. Hundreds of unemployed men had been encouraged to train in gas and electric welding for the power station construction projects across the UK. They looked like gladiators in their gauntlets, leather shoulder protectors, and visors. I often wondered how many later suffered from welder's lung or arc eye before these conditions were accurately diagnosed.

After my first week, I sat in the lecture room thinking, what on earth have I done?

The instructors decided I should take Math's and Higher English at Dudley Tech, as the general craft course wouldn't challenge me enough.

Each evening, when we got off the bus, we'd race to the post box to check for letters from home. I always got one from Elaine, and I'd dash to my bunk, savoring every word. After dinner I retreated to the study where I would pen my love letters to Elaine. For the lads who received little or no post, moods would sink. It created tension—sometimes even fights. Big Angus once launched a chair at me, just for amusement.

On our first Saturday off, a group of us—me, Joe McCrystal, and PJ—took the bus into the center of Birmingham. We visited the Bullring shopping centre, snapped a few photos, and explored Brum and the Spaghetti Junction. On the way back, we got off at The Green Man pub in Harborne and chanced our arm at ordering pints of lager and lime.

It felt great—free, earning money, and living in the adult world. Our wages? £4 seven shillings and sixpence, plus a 25-shilling away-from-home allowance.

In the evenings, after lights- out, we'd try to scare each other with ghost stories.

Without proper supervision, some of the lads took things too far. One Saturday night, they smashed a shop window in Harborne. That brought the police to Mr. Gush's door, triggering an investigation. Some of the worst troublemakers were sent home for good. Babcock and Wilcox picked up the bill for the window repair.

The following Saturday, I treated myself to a trendy gold and green full- length kaftan. It was the hippy sixties, after all—we all wanted to wear cowbells, put flowers in our hair, and go to San Francisco. Unfortunately, the lecturers at Dudley Tech didn't share my enthusiasm. They ripped the piss out of me in every class.

The music of the time was incredible. Tony Blackburn's Top Twenty on the new Radio One set the tone for our days. A Hole in My Shoe by Traffic played in my head for weeks.

Me and PJ were the only guys who weren't on cannabis or LSD. I completely missed out on the sex, drugs, and rock 'n' roll. Honest.

By the end of the first month, the boys had split into two groups— one looking for trouble, the other (my lot) trying to avoid it.

By the time I boarded the train to Glasgow, I'd already made up my mind— I was going to find another job.

When I arrived home, Elaine was waiting for me at the station, wrapped up in a yellow fur-lined hooded parka. I stepped off the train in pale blue jeans and a lime green jumper.

We walked all the way from Gilmour Street Station to Ferguslie, where you'd have thought I was Elvis with the way the kids and Mum fussed over me. Ellen reminded me that Charlie was the new 'wee Daddy.'

Mum handed me a couple of letters that had arrived, and when I opened them, one was from Kilpatrick's Electrical Group, offering me a job as an electrician. That was it—my problems were solved. I had a job to go to, and Elaine and I could live happily ever after.

We had a long weekend where I stayed at Elaine's house in Glenburn, and on Monday, I travelled back to Birmingham. The next day, I handed in my notice. Some of the boys were genuinely upset, and PJ and Joe tried extremely hard to change my mind.

I worked for one more week, and before I left, I was given a message to contact Alec Scott, the B&W Construction Division Personnel Manager who had hired me a few weeks ago. I had already agreed on a start date with Kilpatrick's, so in the week in between, I went to see Alec Scott. He was a nice man and told me he was sorry to see me go to another company, asking if I'd reconsider. I think he didn't want the other boys to 'get infected' by what he called the 'homesick virus.' I admitted that, yes, I was a little homesick and missed my girlfriend, but I had another job offer.

He told me I had scored the highest marks amongst the intake of boys and that B&W needed apprentices like me. He suggested I speak to the Renfrew site's Training Manager, John Higgins, while I was on-site. So, I walked over to the training school, and after a short chat, John Higgins offered me an apprenticeship on the spot.

A week later, I joined B&W and signed the big employee register kept in the Plant Offices at the top of Porterfield Road. Every B&W employee for 100 years had signed that book.

At home, the arguments started over whether I should get my bed and wardrobe back. My siblings were no longer babies and had become very feisty. I decided I should stay at Elaine's at the weekends. Mum was overjoyed to have me back, but Dad thought I might have wasted an opportunity.

The Renfrew training school ran on almost British Navy rules, with strict punctuality. We all wore blue overalls, made our own tools and toolboxes, and had to paint them battleship grey with a brass nameplate. It was expected that once we had completed our time, we would go to sea as junior engineers, obtain our steam and diesel tickets, then progress from fourth engineer to chief engineer. After a few years, we'd return to Babcock's as supervisors or managers.

Jimmy Connell, the training administrator, produced this huge set of indentures—about the size of a tabloid newspaper and made of parchment. He explained that these had to be signed by my parents and a witness, as I was being formally bound as an apprentice by Babcock's and had to follow their rules and regulations. I took the papers home; Dad signed them, and Uncle Sammy was my witness. It all felt very official. I returned the indenture to Mr. Jimmy Connell.

The boys had already been preselected for their trades, and I was allowed to continue as a fitter. I was enrolled at Reid Kerr College for Math's and Physics and sent once a week to Carbrook Street Annex in Paisley's west end.

I also got my old job back at the shop and, apart from spending most of my time with Elaine, my greatest delight was running home from college on Tuesday nights to watch Star Trek.

My daily routine during the working week was to get up early so I could catch the Babcock bus, which left every morning at 07:15 from the roundabout near 148 Ferguslie Park Avenue. Dad would make me breakfast—hard toast soaked in Stork or Echo margarine and a cup of sweet tea. Thanks, Dad.

One morning, Dad invited me to look in the sink. A mouse had fallen in and was running around frantically, unable to escape.

Dad said, "Your maw won't want to find that, so you need to kill it." "Naw, you kill it."

"Don't be daft. Just do it."

Eventually, after pushing the words of Robert Burns out of my head—Wee sleekit, cowrin, timorous beastie, O what a panic's in thy breastie—I drowned the mouse after several attempts.

Mice were a constant problem in our house, and our cat wasn't nearly as diligent as it should have been. One night, while we were watching TV and Elaine was visiting, a mouse started climbing up an old mesh fireguard. I took off my shoe and dispatched it, which sent Elaine into a total panic—she leapt onto the couch in horror.

Cats came and went in rapid succession since they were mostly feral. When my Grandad Green was alive, he'd deal with a new litter of kittens by putting them in a bag made from an old sheet, adding a stone, and taking them to the River Cart. In those pre-Whiskas days, people simply couldn't afford to keep cats or get them dressed to stop kittens being born.

Now that I had re-established myself at Babcock's Renfrew, I set about making new friends and exploring Babcock's world. The training school was well established, and all the boys (there were no girls) had to clock in every morning at 08:00 sharp. If you were even a minute late, you'd be 'quartered,' meaning you lost 15 minutes' pay. Employees were only allowed to be quartered twice in any month and if so you would be issued a warning letter and if you got two warning letters in any year you got a final warning letter, and any further lateness would mean you would be fired.

The training school was divided into sections:

Machine Shop The Plating Shop The Welding School Electrical Section The Fitting School.

There was also a separate office facility with a lecture room upstairs. Most of the boys arrived in the morning already wearing their navy boiler suits, keen to look like working men and show that they had a job.

Each section had its own instructors, and the training school had a Chief Instructor, George Feely. A new welding school was under construction next to the existing building, as demand for welders had increased due to North Sea oil work. The plan was to rotate the boys over a year so they could learn all the trades before moving into the main factory shops. I was extremely impressed with the setup, but my heart sank when we were told that all the fitters would be housed in '222 Store'—an incredibly old, dilapidated building next to the bridge in the centre of the factory grounds—until the new welding school was complete.

Our instructor, Louis Arcari, was a short, no-nonsense older man—half Scottish, half Italian. He led us into this Dickensian-looking building and warned us to stay in the middle passageway. The reason? On either side, spot welders worked furiously, sparks flying as they welded thousands of studs onto power station pipes. They were on piecework, meaning no time was lost as they carried out their repetitive, industrial 'spark dance.'

We pressed on to the end of the building, where a work area had been laid out with metal benches fitted with vices, along with some wooden benches. The weather had turned cold, but overhead steam radiators clanked and banged with the pressure and steam hammer in the pipes, at least providing some warmth.

Louis set us on our first exercise: take a piece of black bar steel, cut it square, file and polish all sides, then stamp our names onto it using metal punches. Once completed, we had to present it for marking.

Most fitters know that there are several types of files, and one of the roughest is called a 'bastard file.' We quickly learned why—filing was a bastard. But it was what we did, constantly.

We made every tool we needed: hacksaws, try-squares, punches, footprints, spanners, surface gauges, centre finders, and depth gauges. When we weren't making tools, we were on test pieces. After cutting and polishing the first piece of metal, our next task was to cut a square hole in it, then fit another piece of steel into it with a perfect push-fit so it wouldn't fall back out.

After three months, we were re-housed in the machine shop, where we got to use lathes, milling machines, and shaping machines. It wasn't uncommon for the boys or the instructors to want to get "homers" done—usually a repair job for a car or appliance. On this occasion, Joe Watson, the plating instructor, needed a new washer for a domestic appliance after the old nylon one had split in two. He handed the broken washer to one of the boys and asked if he could make a couple of new ones, just in case it happened again.

George Pollock took the job, carefully turning down a piece of nylon to the required size, boring it out, and parting off three new washers. George would have made a good soldier—he followed instructions precisely. Too precisely, in fact. After making the washers, he took a hacksaw and cut them in half to match the broken sample he'd been given. We laughed about that for weeks.

As an apprentice, you were given a little leatherette book with your name and number, which allowed you to participate in subsidized lunches. When the horn sounded at 12:00 noon, my new best friend Ian Johnston and I would sprint through the Tube and Manifold shop, out into the car park next to the canteen, and leap over a four-foot fence without stopping—just to be first in the queue. Babcock employed 5,000 men, and if you didn't get in early, you'd be in for a long wait.

The meals were basic but filling—perfect for working boys and men. Mondays started with a big plate of vegetable soup, which turned into tomato and vegetable soup on Tuesday, then tomato and rice on Wednesday. By Friday, it was minestrone, served alongside giant plates of steak pie and chips, followed by apple pie with pink custard or tapioca.

After a few months, I was putting on weight fast. Although we tried to keep our own table as apprentices, some of the laborers from the forge would deliberately sit with us, hoping to torment us into handing over our leftovers. A typical conversation went something like:

"What's that you're eating, pal?" "Totties and mince."

"Is it? Because I thought it was a plate of guts."

Some of the boys would push their plates away or just get up and leave. Me? When I was hungry, I could eat a plate of guts. It didn't bother me.

Babcock's was a strongly unionized workplace, with tough conditions but solid provisions for pensions, holiday pay, and medical care. The site had a medical centre and a first aid post near the training school, which was always busy with men coming in with cuts and burns.

One day, we were getting a demonstration on precision drilling from a new young fitting instructor, Archie Murray. He made pilot holes and asked us to get down in line with the drill table to observe. Without thinking, he blew the metal cuttings out of the hole—straight into our faces. A couple of the boys screamed in agony as the shards got into their eyes. They were sent to the first aid post, where a powerful magnet was used to remove the metal.

Working at Babcock's was exciting—it became your whole life, a place where you learned and earned. The site was massive, stretching about a mile long and half a mile wide, with factory units everywhere. The main offices and drawing offices stood at the centre. At the top of Porterfield Road was the header factory and welding research department. On the right of the main gate was the works department for building maintenance, and directly ahead stood the Time Office. Straight on, you'd reach the foundry, the plant works, and the pipe shop. To the left of the Time Office was the main surgery, with the pattern maker's shop behind it, then the forge, the machine shops, the assembly shop, and the steam block area, where industrial and marine boilers were built. Beyond that were the gantry and drum shops, where 8-inch-thick metal drums were rolled into shape using the Floriep Rollers. At the far end of the site stood the high bay and X-ray building. The south side housed the Tube and Manifold bays, the training school, and the clean area, where nuclear boilers for Hartlepool and Heysham Advanced Gas Reactor(AGR) power stations were made.

Babcock's was a hotbed paradise of trade unionists and real socialists. On the corner of French Street (where Mum once saw a man get killed), Willie Dunn, a well-known Communist, would stand handing out copies of the Morning Star. The unions had secured benefits for workers, including a free morning bus service, but compared to management and staff, factory conditions were still tough. The buildings retained their wartime camouflage to avoid German bombs, and their roofs were made of corrugated iron or asbestos sheeting.

After storms, contractors would be called in to repair the damage. One day, a young roofer fell through the roof onto a cast-iron surface table. He died instantly. Death and injury were never far away in Babcock's. Another man, a welder, was crushed dead to a boiler when an end plate broke free from its tack weld and fell back on him. In the training school, two apprentices suffered terrible accidents—one lost two fingers when his hand was pulled into a milling machine, and another lost both thumbs after touching a live transformer. Both eventually returned to work, and we, in our morbid fascination, examined their amputations and imagined their pain. It was during this time that my interest in health and safety took root.

You could get anything in Babcock's a shirt, a suit, household goods, even an engagement ring. The company had arrangements with furniture stores, jewelers, garages, and retailers. All you had to do was visit the secretary of the B&W Club for a stamped voucher to get discounted goods. There were bookies' runners and even men who would teach you math's. Five minutes before the end-of-shift horn, disabled workers were given extra time to reach the buses. For them, socialism wasn't just a philosophy—it was a practical, everyday necessity.

Babcock's was an incredible place, and in the years ahead, I was proud to call myself a Babcock man.

Just before Christmas, Mum told us that Grandpa Joe wasn't well. He was coming over for a bath, something he hadn't done in our house in six years— not since the time he'd "skelped" my ear for sluchttering in my soup. He had prostate cancer, and a hot bath was the only thing that gave him relief. I was given the job of running the bath, and I remember him rubbing his white, stubbly cheeks against mine, full of gratitude. He died a week later from post-operative shock.

At Christmas, the mood at Babcock's changed. Work slowed for some, but layoffs still came.

I don't recall the exact date, but disaster struck when a main boiler drum, supplied by Babcock's to Cockenzie Power Station on the east coast, blew off its end. The Central Electricity Generating Board(CEGB) made B&W pay for the replacement, which devastated Renfrew. Every man, woman, and boy had to take a pay cut, and the political fallout hurt Babcock's markets worldwide. Within a year, more than half the workforce was made redundant. By 1977, Tony Benn Labour Government Minister arrived by helicopter, trying to prevent the total collapse of the company.

CHAPTER 14: VIOLENCE

1968

The Green family was growing larger and older, and the appetites of the children were ravenous as their young bodies demanded more calories. Mum had resorted to filling up the big soup pot with potatoes, sausages, onions, and two Oxo cubes. Boil and simmer for 30 minutes, add some salt and margarine, and you had stovies.

The plates were lined up in order, with the largest for Mum and Dad, gradually getting smaller for the younger children like Anne and Steven. We had plenty of milk, and for supper, we had toast with jam or butter and cups of sweet (two sugars) Brooke Bond tea with full-cream milk. We would get four pints delivered to the doorstep, and at school, we received a half pint to ensure we didn't get rickets.

One of the idiosyncrasies of our family was that we didn't use knives and forks—we used big dinner spoons. Even my Dad used a spoon, which was often amusing as he attempted to balance beef ham on it, only to end up using his hands.

On Sunday nights, Mum would bake a cake or pancakes and cover them in pink, white, or chocolate icing. She used so many eggs that it was a rich, delicious cake—thank you, Mum.

Mum's workload was heavy, but after she was ill, we all tried to help her more. I think it was good for her to know that she had a little army of helpers. Both Charlie and I were also bringing in extra money, and Dad worked hard on construction sites whenever he could. He was a builder's labourer, but it was his other source of income that intrigued me.

On Saturday mornings, Dad would get up, shave, and dress immaculately. He put on new underwear, a white silk striped shirt, a blue silk tie, polished black Oxford shoes, a dark blue double-breasted serge suit, and a long dark blue Crombie coat. He never wore a hat at the weekends. He would meet up with Sammy, who was always dressed the same, and off they went— sometimes by bus, sometimes picked up by car. Occasionally, Dad would return home with blood spatters on his clothes or, on one occasion, with his tie cut off below the knot. At times like these, he was simply not approachable.

One Friday night, I had to go home early because I was working in the shop the next morning. I went to catch the last bus into town from Glenburn. As I waited, Elaine's brother, John, got off the bus as it approached the terminal to turn around two stops away. John and I got talking, and he told me about a fight in Kennedy's pub at the corner of Orchard Street, where two men had cleared the entire bar.

John said it was like an old-fashioned Western saloon brawl, with tables and chairs flying and men being thrown all over the place.

When I got home, I decided to ask Dad if he knew anything about it. He was sitting in his armchair, as usual, rolling a cigarette. There he was, with his tie cut off just below the knot and both hands covered in bloody knuckles.

I asked, "Dad, what happened to you?"

"There was a fight in Kennedy's," he said, lighting his cigarette. "Someone accused me of being a Rangers supporter." Kennedy's was a well-known St Mirren FC bar.

Dad explained that he had cut his tie off and, as he offered it to the accuser, a riot broke out. He and Sammy had ended up clearing the entire pub.

I sighed. "Do you really have to get involved in these fights?"

He exhaled a cloud of smoke and said, "You wouldn't understand—it's good for my blood."

Violence was marbled into our existence in the council schemes. Charlie and I, like my Dad and Sammy, were not afraid of it—we actually enjoyed it. Only a few years later, I found myself crawling around the pavement outside Kennedy's bar, trying to find my brother Stewart's teeth, which had been kicked out of his head.

He had staggered in that night, blood covering his mouth, after being attacked on his way home from a stag party at the Watermill Hotel.

Mum was horrified and immediately sent me out in the early hours of the morning to find the guys who had done it—and to recover his teeth. In the end, it was left to Mr. Copstick, the dentist, to fit two gold posts into Stewart's jaw and cement in two new teeth.

Ferguslie and the other schemes all had their gangs. In our scheme, it was the Little People, who later became the Young Disciple. In Gallowhill, it was the Gallowhill Team. In Renfrew, where I worked, there was Remo, and the nearest Glasgow gang was the Govan Team. There was no way for male teenagers to grow up in that environment without getting into trouble. So, I'll deal with that now.

The first incident involved Charlie and the Young Disciple. The Dee family were at the heart of the gang—violent and unpredictable. One night, when Charlie was about 18, he was making his way home when the YD attacked him. But they got a surprise—Charlie was fast and violent. He bashed a few heads on the pavement and held his own without them laying a finger on him before the police arrived and arrested everyone. Charlie wasn't charged, but they were, and in retaliation, they put a vendetta on him.

Knowing he had to protect himself; Charlie took a large bread knife from the kitchen and tucked it into his belt, hidden under his jacket. If he hadn't, he might have been dead. But it was Mum who noticed.

"Where's my bread knife?" she asked one day.

I had a good idea Charlie had it, but I wasn't about to try and take it from him. Charlie and I had fought before, and it usually ended with blood being spilled—mine, mostly. I still have a scar inside my lip from the time he punched me so hard my tooth went through my bottom lip. I had to go to hospital to get it stitched.

Once, we were fighting, and I was finally getting better of him when Mum came in and broke it up—by hitting me over the head with the metal tubes from the vacuum cleaner. Another time, Charlie had been giving Mum some cheek, and she hurled a brush at him. Just as I walked through the door. Nearly fractured my skull—I still have the mark.

In the end, it was Dad who took the knife off Charlie. I don't know if he and Sammy had words with the Dees, but the vendetta was lifted. At least for a while. Then it was me who got attacked. But I'll come to that in 1971.

Standing at the bus stop near our house was always interesting. I studied the people there—most of them weren't like my family. One handsome man stood out: he wore a leather coat, a black beret, and had a huge handlebar moustache. He carried a big flat square case, and his jeans were stained with different colours of paint. I later learned this was John Byrne, the artist and creator of *The Slab Boys* and the most famous of all Fegs. John lived in Logan Drive and had to walk back into the main scheme to catch a bus, as the earlier buses were always packed with Teddy boys and girls. If you wanted a seat, you had to go closer to the terminus.

On Friday nights, I would put my head out the window to watch for the bus. One time, I had just washed my hair and, wanting a middle parting, tied a towel tightly over my head to dry it into the Steve Marriott (*Small Faces*) pop group of the 60s look. When the bus arrived, I rushed out, jumped on, and sat down—only to realise everyone was grinning at me. I grinned back, oblivious. Then it hit me. I looked like an Arab, complete with towel headdress.

One Saturday evening, after a long shift at the shop, I took a seat upstairs on the bus home—instantly regretting it. The bus was packed with Rangers and Celtic supporters, and the tension was thick.

First, the chanting started. Then the fists. Then the headbutting.

Two seats away, a Celtic supporter suddenly took a knife to the shoulder. He screamed, and in an instant, the bus emptied—everyone, including me, ran for it.

I was only a few hundred yards from home. Just another day at the office in Feegie.

In 1969–1970, more murders happened in Ferguslie than in the New York Bronx.

I was enjoying my work at Babcock's, moving from trade section to trade section. Eventually, I was rehoused into the training school and away from The Dickensian 222 stores. The next section

I was assigned to was the Plating section, where Joe Watson and Frank Findlay were our instructors.

In this section, we had to make two especially useful items. The first was our big toolbox, made from 1/16-inch-thick steel plate. To construct it, we used the big guillotine and bending machines, but what we were all eager to try was gas welding. We practiced extensively on test pieces before finally welding up the ends of our toolboxes, then riveted on handmade handles and clasps for locking. Once finished, we painted them battleship grey and fitted a brass nameplate.

The next item we made was even more important in our Babcock lives—the tea can. Using tin plate and traditional tin craft techniques, we shaped a basic cylindrical holder with a wire handle. We sealed the joints with lead solder, unaware at the time of the health risks associated with lead poisoning. Over the years, the tea can became a trusted companion, developing thick black and brown tannin stains that coated the lead solder. On cold winter mornings, we could always brew up from the ever-ready tea urns in each factory shop. As long as we kept standing, we could drink as much hot, sweet tea as we liked.

Tea breaks in Babcock's in the sixties were unofficial, so we had to be watchful for any superintendents entering the shop. One moment, we'd be enjoying our tea and chits (plain bread sandwiches), and the next, we'd be pretending to work at our benches.

Chits, or "pieces,"(sandwiches) were usually prepared the night before by Mum. She typically used a Milanda plain loaf, spreading margarine on it and adding a single slice of corned beef or cheese. She then halved the piece and wrapped it in the greaseproof bread paper, providing me with one for the morning and another for the afternoon. She also packed a small oval-shaped caddy with a lid on each end—one side filled with loose tea, the other with sugar. In the early days, I also took a small bottle of milk, usually an old whisky flask, but I soon learned that full-fat milk went sour by the afternoon. Eventually, I got used to just having sweet black tea.

We worked hard as apprentices, even though we were still in training. Some of the boys would fall asleep on the bus ride home.

I was lucky—I always had plenty of energy, which I had developed from working in the grocery shops, helping Mum as a young boy, and playing football for five hours at a time.

Dad would often ask, "What was the score?" when we finished playing.

"Forty-four for us and eighteen to them, Dad." "Good, son."

I loved it when either Mum or Dad stood at the back bedroom window, watching me and Charlie play. It usually led to a goal.

After Plating, we moved into the Machine shop, where we learned how to use lathes to turn metal and non-metal materials to different diameters. We used knurling tools to create textured gripping patterns on tool handles. Screw cutting was more challenging, but technology was advancing, and capstan lathes were now being used for multi-function operations, requiring technicians to set them up.

By then, I had completed my first year at Carbrook Street College, and the training department decided I should continue with the Mechanical Technicians course.

At the end of the academic year in June, Babcock held the annual Apprentices' Rally. Parents and friends were invited, and it was an evening of music, prize-giving, food, and soft drinks. With Babcock taking in around 30 apprentices every four months, and with the five-year apprenticeship programme, there were over 500 apprentices, plus their families and friends. It was a fantastic night out. For my first rally, I took Elaine and my mum.

One of my friends, Ian Johnston, was a natural engineer and fitter, just like his older brother, Jim. Both were highly skilled, and each won the craft prize for their respective year. Their prize included a certificate and a £50 voucher for Buck & Hickman in Robertson Street, Glasgow, to buy tools.

During the summer, in the first two weeks of July, everyone went on holiday. A large group from Babcock's went to Blackpool, which was part of Elaine's mum and Dad's annual holiday tradition. I had never been to Blackpool before and loved it. It was packed with people having a great time, and the B&B food was fantastic.

Our group had no young children—it was made up of Elaine's mum and Dad, her Papa John, John, and Cath (Elaine's school friend), who were now engaged, James Junior, and his cousin, Tommy McDowall. Elaine, John, Cath, and I travelled by coach, while the others went by car.

When we arrived at our B&B on York Street, No. 30, we were assigned our rooms. All the boys—John, James, me, and young Tommy McDowall (James's friend)—were put in an upstairs room.

I loved everything about Blackpool. It was colorful, buzzing with life, and full of working-class folk enjoying a well-earned break. The food in the B&B was a l w a y s fantastic, and I was determined to have a brilliant time—and I did.

During the day, we played on the beach or wandered up and down the promenade, soaking in the fun. Elaine's mum and Dad, James and May, were great company—especially Elaine's Dad, who loved swimming. Evenings were spent at the Pleasure Beach or sometimes at the pub. Papa John preferred doing his own thing, but he enjoyed the lively atmosphere and the chance to have a *wee drink* with James or the rest of us.

If there was a show on, we'd stop at Deighton's or Yeats Wine Lodge for pre-theatre drinks—Champagne at 50p a glass—before heading to the ABC to watch Engelbert Humperdinck sing *Please Release Me* or to the Winter Gardens for a comedy farce with Jack Douglas. Despite being well-fed and tanned from the day, we always had a fish supper before bed.

One night, Elaine, John, Cath, and I went to a Bierkeller. An *Oompah* band played while we downed *Steiners* of beer all night. I got so drunk; I punched a hole in the ceiling. The next morning, I was in such a state that I got up early and went for a *shiver* (a freezing dip) on the beach.

Not wanting to go back to the B&B and face the family, I parked myself in a bus shelter. Another dosser was already sleeping there, but when he woke up and saw me, he got up and walked away. That's how bad I looked.

Back then, when it came to drinking, I had no brakes. I drank until I fell over, unable to feel my own cheeks. That usually led to extreme green bile sickness and burst blood vessels in my eyes.

Blackpool 1968

In the evenings, we all went to Dutton's pub for a drink. Elaine had to wear a wig to look old enough to get served. When everyone else went to bed, John and I would sneak back out for a fish supper and a pint of beer. By the end of the holiday, I had put on a stone in weight.

It was a brilliant break for Elaine and me, and we all had a fantastic time.

In September, I started day school at Reid Kerr College and met a new group of apprentices from the Roots car factory. There were about eight of them, including my old school friend from Camphill, Douglas Smith. These boys were called PETs (Production Engineering Technicians) and were also on day release training.

To be honest, I didn't like them much. They were rowdy, often disrupting the class. But beyond that, I had applied to become a PET myself and didn't get a place, which had always puzzled me—especially since I had done so well at the Babcock Construction interview and lived only a quarter of a mile away. Years later, Douglas Smith told me the real reason I hadn't been accepted: I was from Ferguslie, which Roots considered a "risk factor." And "Curse of the Feg"

One day, in one of our workshop classes, one of the Roots boys started throwing little brass grommets at the other lads. One hit me on the head, and it hurt. Without thinking, I got up and warned him: if he did it again, I'd batter his arse in. As soon as I sat back down, I got hit again—this time with about a dozen grommets. I was on him in an instant, landing about ten punches before the other Roots boys pulled me off. I knew they'd try to get back at me after class, but Douglas Smith stepped in, brokering a truce. He told them I was a friend, a good guy, and so on. In any case, I never had any more trouble with the Roots boys after that.

Saturdays were simply great fun. I worked in the shop, and now Elaine had a Saturday job with me. The days flew by. In the evenings, we'd go to the pictures, and in 1968, Paisley had plenty of cinemas to choose from. At Paisley Cross was the La Scala cinema, then there was the Old High Street Cinema, further west was the Regal, and even further was the West End Cinema. Heading east, there was Kelburn, and near the station was the Astoria—commonly known as the Bug Hut. There were also two lesser-known cinemas: the New Alex, next to the Royal Alexandria Infirmary, and another Astoria down the Palladium Pend just off Paisley High St.

Elaine and I usually went to the La Scala, the Regal, or the Kelburn. Occasionally, we'd visit the Old High Street Cinema, which had a fountain and played the Shadows pop group music. I loved the movies then, and I still do—I try to go every week. Back in those days, when the film ended, everyone stood to attention as they played *God Save the Queen*. Before the main feature, we'd get *Pathé News*, and during the interval, we'd have *Kia-Ora* orange juice and vanilla ice cream tubs.

Friday nights at the pictures were a proper night out, and people dressed up for the occasion. I remember standing in queues, watching the different groups: Teddy Boys, girls with beehive hairstyles, and the in-betweeners— Mods and Rockers. The typical Teddy Boy had the DA (Ducks Arse) hairstyle, sideburns, a long, tape-lined jacket, and drainpipe trousers, which were often turned up (since most West of Scotland lads weren't particularly tall). Some wore "bum freezer" jackets with little ornamental belts at the back, usually in wine red. The girls wore patterned knee-length dresses and high heels, though some opted for baseball boots or white dance pumps.

If you look at many of John Byrne's artwork you will see the influence of Teddy boy and girl fashions. (Check out the front cover of this book)

Fashion was in transition. The miniskirt was making its first appearances, as were jeans. For a while, I was a Mod, wearing a three-piece suit with brown brogues and tab-collared shirts—but never a coat. It took another three years before Elaine finally bought me one. Most guys carried a nylon raincoat that folded into a small bag or a brolly, but I mostly just got wet—just like in *Tutti Frutti*.(John Byrne play).

After about a year, Elaine and I started bringing sandwiches and a flask of homemade soup to the cinema. Other movie goers would turn their heads, trying to figure out where the delicious smells were coming from. We always sat in the back row so we could cuddle up and have a snog. And, as always, after the film, *God Save the Queen* would play, and we'd all stand to attention—well, sometimes.

At home, Mum and Dad had bought a new three-piece suite. It was very sixties—green leatherette with soft material cushions, little black legs, and brass footings. That new suite took a pounding from all the kids, and after just a few months, right before Christmas, it collapsed in one corner. The frame had completely shattered. Mum was devastated.

"Oh my God, what are we going to do if we get visitors at New Year?" she cried.

"Don't worry, Maw—I'll get it fixed for you."

Dad's temporary solution? He propped it up with two bricks from one of his building sites.

The next day, I sketched a design for a metal angle frame and leg, complete with drilled holes for fixing it to the damaged frame. During my lunch break, I built the piece and took it home the following day. Once fitted, the couch was as good as new. Mum was delighted.

My repair skills had come a long way with training, and soon, I became the go-to repair man. Whenever something went wrong with the washing machine, I was the one who fixed it.

There was one repair I couldn't fix—the New World 42 gas cooker with a handheld pilot lighter and overhead grill. On the front of the cooker were five hard plastic control knobs, and over the New Year period, someone had burned every single one with the pilot lighter. Mum was furious. It was a brand-new cooker, and she was determined to find out who the culprit was.

Nobody admitted it, and in the end, Cousin Robert Armstrong got the blame. Robert had finally got out of the hospital after the car crash injuries, and everyone was trying to rehabilitate him by being kind and encouraging.

On New Year's Eve (Hogmanay), it was tradition for the first person to enter the house in the new year to be a tall, dark, and handsome man carrying a piece of coal and some black bun cake. Robert was invited for tea (dinner—where in Scotland, lunch was called dinner, and dinner was called tea). At five minutes to midnight, Robert was put out in the cold until the bells rang at midnight. When the time came, he was let back in, threw the coal on the fire, and said, *"Lang may yer lum reek"*—a traditional Scottish wish meaning, "May you always have coal for your fire."

In fairness to Robert, we never found out who actually burned the cooker knobs, but after the accident he'd had the previous year, he wasn't quite himself.

In Scotland, New Year celebrations lasted about a week. You'd bring in the bells at your own house, then spend the next few days visiting all your relatives. It was tradition to take a bottle of whisky to share, along with blackcurrant bun, cherry cake, or shortbread for your relatives' table. Turning up empty-handed was a serious crime—it would fuel gossip for the rest of the year, and you'd be branded a *tight-arsed bastard*.

Granny Isa always had a big pot of soup on the go, made with the end of a Belfast ham, barley mix, onions, and leeks. Second-day soup was always best, but when she made it fresh, I would ask for a *dook* (dip) in the pot. She'd take the *outsider* (the thick, crusty end slice of a loaf) and dip it into the rich, boiling soup for me. Granny always added barley, and by the second day, the soup was so thick you could stand the ladle up in it.

She also made homemade ginger wine, which the women drank instead of alcohol. Every year, she sent a bottle to Mum and Dad. It was strong, with a fiery kick, and the kids would pretend it was making them drunk—though in reality, it just burned our throats.

We didn't have many parties at our house, for several reasons. Mum was an introvert and preferred to be with just us kids. Life had taught her that the outside world was dangerous and full of gossip and people who wanted to interfere, and she didn't trust easily. She also hated relying on anyone. On top of that, money was always tight, and there were far more important things to buy than alcohol for a party; also, those childhood experiences with the Bomb, Bull and Mixer fatality rendered her not to want to travel outside unless it was unavoidable.

A rare party would only happen if people invited themselves over, and when they did, the fun would start. Mum would play along for about 15 minutes before retreating to the kitchen, usually with me and Charlie. The other kids were sent to bed. Meanwhile, the adults—neighbours, Uncle Sammy, and others— would be drinking whisky and *big screw taps* (bottles of McEwan's Pale Ale, which had a stone cork with an orange rubber seal).

Like all kids, I had tried beer and loved the smell of hops. Whisky, on the other hand, made me *groo* (you get the idea—yuck).

One night, I peeked into the living room to see what was happening. Mum's friend, Barbara Strong—who had five kids— had her breast out and was squirting milk on the men. It felt like a totally ridiculous moment for me to step in and ask, *"Does anyone want a cup of tea?"* I never told Mum.

The *real* macho parties were held at my Gran Green's house, where Uncle Sammy, Dad, and other uncles—Matt Tannahill,

Jimmy Burns, and a few of Dad's "associates" (note, I didn't say friends)—gathered.

Dad and Matt Tannahill had history, and it wasn't good. Before Dad was called into the Army, Matt—who was already in the Navy—had been courting Auntie Jenny, Dad's sister. Back then, Matt used to roughly handle and rough up Dad, really hurting him. But when Dad returned from the Army, he was a different man. He had learned how to rough up people himself. When he found out that Matt hadn't been treating Jenny well, he went after him. Matt took second prize in that fight—Dad waited for him in a *close* (a Scottish tenement entryway) in Abercorn Street and made sure he got what was coming.

Matt Tannahill fathered my two cousins, and, like Dad and Uncle Sammy, got involved in the illegal bookmaking business. That was his downfall. He was among a group of men who allegedly kicked a man to death at Paisley Cross. When the trial came, Matt turned *King's Evidence*— meaning he testified against the others in exchange for leniency. The whole group went to jail, narrowly avoiding the death penalty. Though Matt had escaped prison time himself, his card had been marked.

He lived in constant fear of the men he had betrayed. When they got out of jail, Matt disappeared from Scotland altogether. Rumors were that he had fled to Leeds, supposedly because he'd been keeping the funds from a pools syndicate and pocketing the winnings before skipping town.

When these men got together at Gran Green's, the atmosphere was thick with tension. I remember the smells—Brylcreem, whisky, beer, and cigarette smoke. The voices were gruff, aggressive, like sparks falling on dry hay. They argued about war, gambling, and football.

I always had the sense that, if Charlie and I weren't there—or maybe if Granny Isa wasn't in the room—the fists would have flown. But Granny Isa wasn't one to be messed with. When she let loose with her cursing, the room would quiet down. She had been a *mill girl*, and you didn't want to be around when she really got going.

I was beginning to pick up on all the macho stuff around me. I often heard my Dad recite his regimental motto: *Ne Obliviscaris, Sans Peur*—"We do not forget, and without fear." Like most of the Green family men, my Dad didn't get scared. Instead, he became eerily calm and cold in battle.

My Grandad Green's bayonet was notched several times, so I imagine he used it a lot. When he was courting my Gran, one evening she pointed out something in a shop window that she liked. Without hesitation, her *Jeemy*, as she called him, smashed the window, grabbed it for her, and they scarpered into the night.

Checking his war records, I discovered he had spent a lot of time in the *glass house* (military prison) and was frequently on charges for fighting—not surprising for an underage fifteen-year-old drunk on rum who had just fought with the Seaforth Highlanders at the Battle of the Mons in France.

Earlier that year, Elaine, John, Cath, and I had the house at No 84 to ourselves one Friday night. May and James had gone to visit May's mum, Lizzie McMillan, in Ferguslie.

John, now a journeyman cooper, brought back a bottle of bourbon hooch straight from the cask. He handed me half a bottle. *Take it with some Irn-Bru*, he said. So, I did—and drank the lot in about 30 minutes.

I don't know what strength that stuff was, but I was legless. Completely gone. Amusing as it was for everyone else, it became a serious problem when May and James came home. On top of being absolutely paralytic, I had a big love bite on my neck and probably looked as if I'd been drugged and abused.

The others scrambled to cover for me, claiming I had the flu. But May and James weren't fooled. They could smell the alcohol, and I wasn't exactly subtle gripping the bed's headboard and shouting at it to stop spinning. I could hear James and John yelling, but I was too far gone to care.

At weekends, we took trips to the fishing village Dunure on the Ayrshire coast, where we'd have a picnic and play games. It was great to get out in the fresh air and have a laugh. May made amazing sandwiches—chopped pork with sandwich spread—and packed flasks of hot tea.

On the way back, we'd pull into *The Paraffin Lamp Inn* at Lugton so James could have a beer before heading home.

Other times, we'd drive to Rowardennan on Loch Lomond side. James always had us swimming in the loch, which was absolutely freezing. But I didn't mind. Things weren't great for me at home, so it felt good to be accepted by the Keenans.

One Saturday night, I got home from work to find Dad and Sammy well into their drink. Mum sat in the kitchen, muttering under her breath about how she wanted to watch TV but wouldn't go into the living room until Sammy left.

Feeling protective, I decided to play the big man. I marched into the living room and told Sammy it was time to go home. He stood up, puffed out his chest, and, laughing, said, *"How?"*—which, in the west of Scotland, really means *"Why?"*

I squared up to him as he tried to roughly handle me. Dad stayed in his chair, but before things could escalate, Mum stormed in.

"Don't you lay a hand on him!" she snapped.

Sammy immediately let go and, in an instant, was on his way home. *"Sorry, Ellen,"* he muttered as he left.

Mum wasted no time turning on Dad. *"Aye, that's right—just sit there while Sammy roughs up your son."*

Dad said nothing, just turned up the volume on the television. Mum and I went back to the kitchen, had a laugh, and after about half an hour, she finally went in to watch the telly. All was well again, and I got on the bus for Glenburn.

By this time, I had been going with Elaine for a while, and occasionally, I got to stay over until Sunday. It was fantastic. May, her mum, always made the best breakfasts and Sunday teas (dinners).

And what a breakfast it was—two slices of Ayrshire gigot bacon, two fried eggs, two tattie scones, black pudding, and two thick Irish pork sausages, all topped off with a dollop of HP Ideal sauce.

A side plate of pan bread toast with real Danish butter, shaped into a perfect round pat with my own hands. Absolute heaven.

Elaine and I had already made up our minds—we wanted to spend our lives together. We planned to get engaged in the summer of '69.

We spent hours talking about where we'd live, eventually settling on Thornley Park or Potterhill. But we knew we'd need to save for a mortgage deposit, meaning we'd have to be engaged for three years before we could afford a wedding—unless I could bring the date forward by working overtime.

To help with that, I took on another part-time job at J.D. Ure's grocery store on New Street, next to the YMCA. It paid more than my beloved Hays, so I made the switch. I worked alongside Irene Reid, whose Dad worked at Babcock's— not that I knew him yet.

I only lasted a few months at Ure's, though. Soon, I was getting overtime at Babcock's, and that took priority.

CHAPTER 15:
SERVING TIME

1969

I should have left the training school in September, but the EITB (Engineering Industry Training Board) had introduced a new modular training system. Previously, apprentices had to serve four years, but under the new system, they could complete additional modules to qualify as either a Fitter/Turner or a Fitter/Welder. Initially, the unions resisted this change due to the strong demarcation within Babcock's, but eventually, it was implemented. This worked in my favour, as it meant that once I completed the H1 and H3 fitting modules, I would be a journeyman and eligible for full pay. Apprentices only received a portion of the full rate, depending on how many years they had served.

At Babcock's, all workers were paid in cash, handed out in white pay packets that were prepared in a way that allowed us to count our money. If you opened your pay packet and found it was short, there was no way to take it back—tough luck. At holiday time, we received two extra weeks' pay, which was great if you wanted to go on holiday or buy new clothes. I had agreed with Mum that I would start saving, but I would still give her my keep money, which in 1969 was £7 and 10 shillings. I got to keep my shop money and any overtime earnings so I could save to get married, which left me with around £7 for myself.

I had an account with Jacksons, the tailors on Paisley High Street, where I would order suits designed to my own specifications. I did the same with Frank Carty's men's fashion shop, where they made custom shirts for my design. One of my suits was a faint pinstripe in dark green with the following specifications:

Single-breasted

12-inch side vents

Handkerchief pocket

Two side pockets with flaps at a slight angle

One ticket pocket

Quarter-round front finish

Six sleeve buttons (openable)

Pale blue silk lining

Standard lapels with a buttonhole on the left-hand side

Trousers: extra-high waistband (non-hipster), silk lining to the knee, zip fasteners, no turn-ups, and French seams on the side leg.

I became so skilled at designing suits that I started doing it for the other boys.

After training school, apprentices were temporarily placed in the "Boys' Corner" within the Assembly Shop. The shop instructor, Campbell Reid, was not particularly popular, and we even had a little poem about him:

> *"Dae ye see Campbell Reid?*
>
> *Dae ye see his heid?*
>
> *Dae ye see his hair?*
>
> *Aye, there is fuck all there."*

Once in the shops, all I wanted was to get into a squad that made money. So, it was agonizing having to do repetitive, menial tasks—filing thousands of bushes or removing burrs from plates by filing or grinding.

After three months, I was finally moved to Jimmy McGinley's soot-blower squad. The soot blowers were large, elbow-shaped cylindrical castings designed to hold soot-blowing jets for coal power stations. They weighed about a ton and had to be marked for drilling before the journeymen fitted the plates. My job was to mark them off using a template. I would paint the rim with yellow, spirit-based paint that had quite a pleasant smell. Then, I would take the template, scribe the holes, and use a steel centre punch to mark each hole at the north, south, east, and west positions. The next step was to get the slinger to lift the job and send it to the drillers at the other end of the bay.

There were some fantastic men at Babcock's, but we had to get used to a bit of rough horseplay. One day, the crane man asked if I was hungry and wanted an extra piece (sandwich). Apprentices were always hungry, so I eagerly said, "Aye!" He threw down a parcel that looked just like a piece parcel— only when I opened it, it was full of shite.

Another classic prank involved the unofficial tea breaks. One of the men, Alec Coulter, asked what I had on my sandwich. "Corned beef," I replied. He smirked and said, "Are you sure?" "Aye," I said. "How much would you bet on it?" That's when I realised they had tampered with my sandwich. When I opened it up, a dead rat was staring back at me.

Jimmy took me aside and told me not to get too friendly with the men. He then asked which day I went to day school. "Wednesday," I replied. "Then on Tuesdays, you study," he said. He pointed to the template room, a rough metal cage, and told me there was a desk inside. "If you get stuck with math's or anything, see me—or that guy up there at the pantograph burner in the brown overalls. He's a genius."

Jimmy had a reputation for looking after his boys, and apart from being a Babcock man, I was now a McGinley boy. This went on for a few weeks, but I still wasn't getting any overtime. I asked another apprentice my age, who was getting overtime, "Why am I not getting any OT?"

"It's because you're a Tim (Catholic), mate," he replied.

Then he pointed across the bay. "Isn't that your cousin John Green over there?"

"Aye," I said. John was a technical apprentice working in the next bay. He was actually a distant cousin with us sharing the same great great grandfather

"He was here for a few weeks. He went to St Mirren's Academy, so he's a Catholic. I guess Jimmy thinks he's your cousin, so you must be Tim as well."

I wasn't having that, so I went up to Jimmy to protest.

"Hey, Jimmy, I went to Camphill, not the Academy."

Jimmy stepped back and said, "Okay, so what was yer school motto?" "Onwards and Upwards," I replied.

"Very good, son," he said, putting his arm on my shoulder and pointing over at John. "Is he not your cousin, then?"

"Aye, he is a distant cousin but that disnae make me a Catholic."

"Okay, fair enough, son. I'm very glad you told me that," Jimmy said.

"So, any chance of some OT, Jimmy?"

"Aye, you're oot Saturday morning and Sunday all day."

I had to get used to this partisan way of life in the west of Scotland, where Catholic-Protestant divides, and the secret order of the Masons played a big role. But at that point, all I cared about was making money, and that's exactly what I did.

After three months with the soot-blower squad, I got a transfer to the Forge— the shortest transfer ever. Before I left, Jimmy advised me to take my tools home, saying, "All you'll need there is a hammer, a ruler, a centre punch, and a file. The older men and apprentices will steal your tools, so take them home." I took his advice.

The forge was incredibly industrial, with powerful machines hammering red-hot blanks into shape. The noise and the heat hit you like a wall as soon as you stepped inside the door. The men in the forge and the foundry got an extra fifteen minutes at the end of their shift to clean up. After my first day, I went to see Mr. Gibb, the shower room attendant.

"Can I have my soap and towel, please?" "Whit's yer name, son?"

"James Green."

He checked his list and shook his head. "Your name's not on my list, so no can do."

I started to protest, but an older man grabbed my arm—nicely, but firmly— and said, "Listen, son, you're not too dirty. We're all black, so unless you want to be picking the soap up in there, I'd give it a miss."

It took me a second to realise what he meant, but I quickly decided that this fair-skinned boy with long blond hair wasn't taking any chances. I was more than happy to go home dirty.

Luckily, salvation came quickly. Within a few days, I got a note from the training school that I was needed in the pipe shop. My shift in the forge had been short-lived.

I got one of my apprentice brothers, Ronnie Syme—who had been in my class at Camphill—to help me carry my toolbox over to the pipe shop.

The squad there was full of characters. My journeyman was Bobby Porter, and others included Curly Simpson and Freddie Allan, a fourth-year apprentice. Freddie and I teamed up because our job was piecework. The pipe shop was working on the Peterhead pipe panels for a new power station. This involved bending huge lengths of steel pipes at different angles so they could be connected on-site.

Our job was to jack the pipes together on a large surface table, insert steel blocks, and lay welding fillet strips. The welders would then tack them in place and start the first weld run. Once that was done, Freddie and I would sling the panels—now about ten pipes wide—and signal to the craneman to turn them so they could be welded on the other side. The air was thick with smoke and paint fumes as the painters covered the pipes in red lead paint.

When we weren't doing that, we had to manufacture number plates for each pipe section in the yard. Each pipe had its number painted on by the inspectors, so we couldn't go wrong. We just had to cut the plates using the guillotine, punch the numbers in with metal type stamps, then go out into the yard and tack-weld them onto the pipes.

After a few days, I said to Freddie, "We could save some time here. The pipe codes all have the same first six numbers."

So, we came up with a system: we'd get a hundred plates at a time. Freddie would stamp all the first numbers, and I'd follow up with the next. We'd keep going like that until we had the first part done, then check the drawings for the rest of the number and punch them in. This way, we moved faster, got the plates fitted quicker, and booked them up as piecework.

Freddie and I were nearly doubling our wages every week.

It was a great squad, and every time I did something right or did someone a favour, big Curly would kiss me on the cheek—for fun, of course.

Freddie and I were totally into the music scene, still trying to keep the Beatles alive while Motown was taking over. Freddie was tall with long, lanky hair that he refused to cut. He was told he'd never get a job in the machine shop unless he did. Fred just shrugged and said, "Fine by me." He was a full-on hippy—but strangely enough, he absolutely loved John Wayne. He'd mimic the Duke all day, and sometimes, when walking through doorways, he'd turn sideways to exaggerate John Wayne's broad shoulders. The rest of the men would be in stitches laughing.

I learned that despite the hard work and the Dickensian surroundings, most of the men were just big kids. They made fun wherever they could, keeping things light to get through the day.

Freddie was fascinated by Bobby Porter. He was always trying to get bits of information out of him, and Bobby—sometimes willingly—would supply it. Their conversations were pure magic.

One Monday morning, Freddie asked, "Did you have a good weekend, Bobby?"

"Aye, son, when we got a new carpet the wife had me take an eighth part off the door."

Freddie's ears perked up immediately. The term "eighth part" was pure engineering jargon.

"Did you say she told you to take an eighth part off?" "Aye, that's right, that's what she said."

"She did not just say, 'You'll need to take a bit off the door, Bobby'?"

"Naw, she said 'an eighth part.'"

Freddie's eyes widened. "Is your wife a fitter, Bobby?" "Naw, she's a turner in Polar Engines in Govan."

We nearly peed ourselves laughing.

Bobby had a pipe in his mouth at all times, just like Popeye. He had smoked it for so long that it had worn an arch-shaped groove into his dentures. He also had a permanently misaligned eye—one looking up at all times like Marty Feldman. But the thing that really got us curious was the horseshoe-shaped scar on his forehead.

One day, Freddie asked, "How did that happen, Bobby?"

Bobby's face darkened. "I don't want to talk about it, son, if that's okay?"

Freddie backed off, but now we were all desperate to know what had happened to Bobby that it was so bad he could not even talk about it. So, we asked Curly.

Turns out, about ten years earlier, Bobby had been walking under a load of pipes when one slipped and came crashing down on his head. The reason is his eyes were misaligned. Ever since that day, he had always been checking—just in case another pipe was on its way down.

The running joke was that while Bobby was lying on the ground, dazed and bleeding, he asked one of the Paisley men smokers for a cigarette. The guy just looked at him and said, "Where's your jacket?"

The supervisor of our squad in the pipe shop was Alec Smith. Alec fancied himself to be a really tough guy and was always talking about fighting. He wore a brown shop coat, and his neatly trimmed moustache was the exact same shade as the coat. He also wanted to be one of the boys, so he had come over and just stand around, hanging out with me and Freddie for hours.

That was not ideal when you were on piece work.

Freddie, exasperated, would mutter under his breath, "I wish he would fuck off so we can curse like fuck and act like fiends, for once. Just let me drop my hippy halo."

I should note for the reader that most of the men from Scotland and in particular the West of Scotland come in various shapes, forms, and personalities however at their core there is a hard nut like an avocado. Formed over the millennia in battles with other tribes, the Romans, Vikings, English, Germans, and Japanese who were all defeated. They are always ready.

One Thursday night, just before clocking out, the crane operator complained to Alec about the pigeons.

"They're making a right mess near my cab," he grumbled. "Bird shite everywhere."

Babcock's was either a paradise or a hellhole for wild animals—depending on whether you were a cat or a pigeon.

Next to the main factory was the BOCM (British Oil and Cake Mills), which provided a constant food source for the pigeons. Grain lorries spilled their loads, and the pigeons feasted. There were never any dogs in Babcock's, but the place was crawling with cats.

Most of the men liked having a cat around. They'd feed them and leave out water, which also helped keep the pigeons at bay.

But not everyone liked them. Some men hated the smell of cat piss, and a few even despised the cats themselves.

It wasn't unusual for those men to grab a cat and throw it, alive, into the induction furnaces.

The next day, Alec brought in his 0.22 air rifle and wandered around the pipe shop, taking shots at the pigeons. By the end of the shift, the crane man came down and said, "There's a pigeon up there, wounded. Someone should put it out of its misery."

Freddie and I, ever willing to take on a mission, decided to deal with it. The problem was, the bird was perched high on the crane gantry, completely out of reach. Thinking ourselves inventively, we sharpened welding rods into spears and tried to skewer the poor creature. For good measure, Freddie decided to bludgeon it with heavy nuts and bolts. By the time we were done, there was absolutely no doubt in our minds—the bird was dead.

Satisfied, we went home and had a nice weekend.

Monday morning, we walked into the bay, and there, lying on the surface table—still alive—was the pigeon. It looked more like a porcupine than a bird, with welding rods still embedded in its tiny carcass. A lot of big men were not happy about this, and Freddie and I were gutted. The poor thing had suffered all weekend.

Curly McCann took one look, lifted the bird up, yanked out the rods, and threw it into the furnace. It burst into flames instantly.

For the rest of the day, Freddie and I stayed out in the yard, trying to avoid the dirty looks. We had officially been labeled a pair of cruel cunts.

It was winter, and it was always nice to be in from the cold. That day, I caught a rumor wind through the jungle wire that Ronnie Syme had been arguing with one of the welders, and now it was a 'square go' (fight) at lunchtime in the pipework yard.

Disputes were sometimes settled this way. I had only seen one proper fight before, and it had been shockingly fast and brutal fists flying, headbutts landing, blood everywhere. Eventually, the vanquished would raise his hand in surrender.

The word was that the welder Ronnie was up against was an amateur boxer, meaning Ronnie was in for a pasting. Ronnie and I had been mates since Camphill, so I left the pipe shop to try and find him.

No one knew where he was.

Turns out, instead of going to the yard, they'd gone to the old railway line at the back of the factory site, near the River Cart. Ronnie was a tough kid with a fast temper, but toughness didn't matter much when the welder hit him three times in the right spot. It was over before it had even begun.

By now, I was eighteen, and there was one piece of business I had to attend to—voting in the general election.

I had no clue who to vote for, so I asked my Dad.

"There's only one party to vote for," he said. "The party of the people. Vote Labour."

So, I did. We lost.

Ted Heath became Prime Minister in June. The next order of business: learning to drive.

I enrolled in the Able School of Motoring in Wellmeadow Street, Paisley. They used Hillman Imps, and lessons cost ten shillings for an hour.

I failed my first test because I couldn't reverse properly. On my second attempt, the car broke down, and the test was abandoned.

This happened on St Mirren Brae—on a Friday afternoon, the busiest time of the week. The driving examiner, clearly fed up, took the car keys, hopped on a bus back to the test center, and left me sitting in the passenger seat.

I was running out of money. That's when Elaine's Dad, Jimmy Keenan, stepped in to help.

Jimmy was a long-distance lorry driver. His teaching style was… robust. But he got me ready.

For my third test, I used Jimmy's old Ford Prefect. It was pouring rain with a howling gale.

My first Car the Ford Prefect

Of course, this presented some problems.

First, halfway through the test, the L-plate blew off and flew over the top of the car. Without thinking, I did a full stop, jumped out, chased it up the road, re-fixed it to the car, and carried on without saying a word to the tester— who, by the way, looked like he'd been carved from stone.

Then came the hand signal portion of the test.

The Ford Prefect had a slight issue—the driver's window winder was broken. Jimmy had wedged it up using a little yellow rubber stopper. When I went to do my hand signals, I pulled out the wedge. The window dropped straight into the door frame, and the horizontal rain came blasting in, drenching me— and more importantly, splashing the stone-faced examiner.

I kept following his instructions, soaked to the bone. He never asked me to put the window back up, so I didn't. By the time we returned to the test station, I was sure I'd failed.

I didn't.

He passed me—with a big smile.

I reckon he had a few beers over that story with the other examiners later that night.

Being able to drive was fantastic—it opened up a whole new world of travel beyond the bus or train. In Paisley, several bus companies operated, the biggest being Western SMT, based in Gordon Street. Their buses were London red with gold lettering, always manned by a driver and a ticket collector—usually a woman, the "Clippie," or occasionally a gay man. There was a little trick people used: when buying a ticket, you'd press Clippie's hand, and she'd give you a cheaper fare without issuing a ticket. Of course, this was risky if an inspector got on the bus, but it never happened to me, and it was common practice.

At that time there was a quirky system with bus tickets where if you got a ticket that's numbers added up to 21 you could pass it to a girl or boy as a sign that you wanted to date them.

Winters on the buses were brutal. Diesel fumes built up as passengers shut the windows to keep out the cold, and upstairs, where smoking was allowed, nicotine-saturated condensation dripped down the windows and walls. Looking back, I wonder how many people perished due to passive smoking in those days.

Around this time, I realized things weren't right at home. Mum and Dad were obviously going through a rough patch. One night, they had a huge, noisy row, and suddenly, I heard Mum screaming. I ran into their bedroom and saw Dad lying on the bed, turning blue. He had been drinking and was worse for wear, and during the argument, Mum had pulled his tie so tight that he couldn't breathe—and now she couldn't get it loose. I grabbed a kitchen knife and cut the tie. If I hadn't, he would have died.

Mum was an Armstrong, and she was well named—those arms could tear a limb off, if necessary.

Not long after, Dad and I had our own fight.

One Saturday after work, I came home to find Mum upset—she and Dad had been arguing again. I had always been protective of Mum; she was a fantastic parent. But Dad and I had been heading for a clash, and that night was it. He'd been drinking, and I confronted him about how he treated her. In fairness to Dad, he really did love Mum, but it was my perception at that time, especially as a mummy's boy fueled with fresh testosterone and adrenaline like the young lion taking on the old one I was in for a surprise.

He got up from his chair and said if I didn't like living in his house, I should leave.

We argued in the hallway. He got too close. I headbutted him.

I've always been ashamed of that, even though I never saw the uppercut that knocked me clean out.

When I came to, I grabbed my small sports bag—the one I used for my college books—threw in some clothes and left. I wouldn't return for three years.

I know Mum and my siblings were upset, but I stayed connected as best I could and continued sending my wages home.

Ian Johnston's Dad had passed away not long before, and his brother Jim had just married Maureen, one of the Babcock office girls. That meant there was a spare bed in Ian's room, so I stayed with him and his mum for about two years. After that, I moved in with the Keenans, where I slept on the floor.

By September, I had done my six months in the pipe shop when I was called to the training department to find out my next shift.

Jimmy Connell called me in and asked me to take a seat. Jimmy was a nice man—always keen to talk to the apprentices, learn more about their work and lives.

But he seemed to like me. He often told me about his own life, about his disabled wife. Life must have been hard for him.

That day, he told me that both he and Mr. Higgins were pleased with my progress. They had received good reports about my work and college performance. I wasn't the best, but I was the best of a bad lot.

Then he hit me with the news: I had been assigned a shift at Paisley Technical College (PTC) for a full year. Only the best apprentices got that shift.

I thanked Jimmy, told him I wouldn't let him down, and walked back to the pipe shop with a grin on my face.

"You're a jammy bastard," Freddie said. "That's the best shift ever."

Curly gave me a big, slobbering kiss. Bobby just drew hard on his pipe and smiled.

As I was about to leave, Bobby called me back.

"Oh, by the way," he said. "You're getting the Apprentice of the Year award for works ability. You'll get your prize at the Rally in June—£50 worth of tools from Buck & Hickman in Robertson Street, Glasgow."

Ya beauty.

CHAPTER 16:
COLLEGE BOY

1970

Some of my apprentice brothers had already passed their tests and had cars. Ian Johnstone had a pale blue Vauxhall Viva saloon, and it was great to get a lift from him straight to Glenburn, where he would drop me off at Elaine's house. Ian also helped me get my toolbox up to Paisley Technical College (PTC), and at that time, he was like a brother to me and that is how it remained. Ian and Jim Johnston's Dad who had not long passed away, and both lads were supporting their mum. They were diligent in their trade, which is why they always won the craft prizes.

When I arrived at PTC, I was given a warm welcome by Alec White, the chief mechanical technician. He led a team of technicians, including Davey Clonie, John McLean, Harry Stenhouse, Les Edington, Duncan Fraser, Stan Low, and Jimmy Minto, the labourer. They were a great bunch of men, and the work at PTC was remarkably interesting. They encouraged me towards becoming a technician rather than just a fitter.

There was a clear hierarchy in the team—Alec was at the top, reporting to Professor John Andrews, the head of the Mechanical Engineering Faculty. John McLean was second in command, having narrowly missed out on the chief's job to Alec. The tension between them was still evident every time they met. My role was straightforward—I reported to whoever needed me. In matters of welfare, I could always speak to the chief, but for day-to-day arrangements, I was told to stay close to Jimmy Minto.

Over the following weeks, I worked on some of the most advanced technology of the time, including wind tunnels and acoustic chambers. The acoustic chamber was fascinating—completely soundproof, with deep synthetic foam cones on the walls, ceiling, and floor to absorb all noise. It was used to calibrate and test microphones. Duncan Fraser once let me experience it with the door shut and the lights off. Deprived of both sound and sight, I found it deeply unsettling and asked to be let out almost immediately.

The technicians were also building and testing explosion devices, and I assisted them. One project was particularly intriguing, carried out in a remote basement of the old college building, which the technicians jokingly called the 'Tea House of the August Moon.' Two Egyptian PhD students, Mr. Zaid and Mr Badawi, were leading the research. The rig consisted of a thick steel cylinder with a trigger mechanism that fired metal blanks onto a base plate. Carbon rod sensors at both the nozzle and base plate measured velocity before impact. In hindsight, it was effectively a ballistic missile testing device, researched and funded by two Egyptians. For me, it was great fun loading it up and analyzing the deformation of different materials, though I often wonder what they did with that information when they returned to Cairo.

The college also had the MACDATA centre, which developed automation solutions for industry. I worked on several projects, including a machine that applied Formica edging to kitchen worktops. I was attached to the welding development team led by Dr Andrew McEwan, brother of Bill McEwan, the B&W welding instructor. They were experimenting with sintered metals and metal spraying, and I was getting hands-on experience with cutting-edge technology.

PTC also ran courses for the weaving and thread-making industries, as Paisley was the global center for thread production at the Anchor and Ferguslie Mills. During exam season, I was once asked to invigilate an exam for five minutes while the official invigilator went to the toilet. One of the examinees was Hector Galbraith, my next-door neighbour from Feegie. He had always seemed aloof, never playing with the local kids. His face was incredulous when I was introduced as the temporary invigilator, but neither of us said a word. I found out later that Hector and four friends went winter climbing in the Scottish Highlands. An avalanche struck, and he was the sole survivor. I don't recall ever seeing him again after that.

John McLean was a highly capable and handsome engineer, and if I'd had a choice, I'd have preferred him as chief over Alec.

However, the Masonic hand tipped the scales in Alec's favour. John sometimes worked private jobs in his own time and would ask me to assist him. He always shared the pay, which was great.

It was Jimmy Minto who led me into damnation—he introduced me to gambling. Well into his sixties, Jimmy should have been retired. He always wore an old, greasy working man's cap and walked with the stiffness of age. We would sit in a corner of the boiler house, picking out horses from the Daily Record, and I would run out at lunchtime to place our bets. I'd inherited a love of gambling from my Dad and grandad, and I got a real buzz from the races, especially when we had money at stake. Surprisingly, Jimmy and I regularly picked winners and made a few quid.

John McLean disapproved, accusing Jimmy of teaching me bad habits. He proposed a test—Jimmy, and I would pick two winners, and he would finance the bet. If it won, we could keep the money; if it lost, we would owe him the betting stake. Jimmy and I never bet more than £2, but John insisted on putting down a tenner. We chose Red Teal and Red Truck, what he called a 'mug double.' I placed the bet, handing the ticket to Jimmy while Harry Stenhouse held onto our £2 and John's £10.

Jimmy asked me what my nom-de-plume was, and I advised him to use his which was MINTY. I did not want to extrapolate from my grandfather's and father's nom de plumes Punty, Bunty and C***ty.

To everyone's amusement—except John's—Red Teal won at 4-1, and Red Truck at 14-1. Since it was a straight double, we won £600, plus John's tenner and our £2. Jimmy and I were ecstatic, and the technicians had a good laugh. I suggested giving John his money back, but Jimmy scoffed, 'Fuck off—he was trying to make us look daft.'

The next day at tea break, Jimmy counted out the winnings in slow, deliberate twenty-pound notes. 'One for me, one for Cloth Ears'— my nickname at PTC— 'and oh... none for John.' He continued until I had a pile of £300, handed me a pound note, and left a tenner for John. The tenner sat untouched on the table for weeks before it was eventually placed in the apprentices' box just before I returned to Babcock's.

When we weren't picking horses, Jimmy and I would blether away in the heat of the boiler room. He'd tell me stories about his life, and I'd often ask him about the worst thing that had ever happened to him, hoping he'd share a war story.

"Ach, that's easy," he said. "It was when I was put in jail for breach of the peace. I ended up in a cell in Paisley jail, and the police roughed me up. I'd been there for ten hours without anything to eat or drink, no covers, no pillow—just a piss-and a blood-stained mattress."

As he spoke, I imagined the grim scene inside old Paisley Gaol(Jail). He went on,

"This big, ugly sergeant kept telling me I was scum, then eventually sent in a young newcomer with a giant outsider (end of loaf) piece of bread covered in jam—it was mouldy and thick as fuck—and a cup of boiling tea with no milk or sugar."

I asked, "Did you eat that mouldy piece?"

"Naw," said Jimmy, grinning with his toothless smile. "I used it as a pillow and fell asleep."

That was Jimmy. He told story after story, and was always light-hearted, never anything too serious. Yet, as it turned out, he was a war hero. He had every right to hobble about, given that his legs had been riddled with Japanese machine-gun fire—and he still managed to escape capture.

One day, Davy Clonie went home for lunch on Glasgow Road in Paisley when he spotted a man in his car. Without hesitation, he pulled a big shifting spanner from his boiler suit leg and knocked the guy out cold. The man ended up in hospital, and Davy was charged—but the charges were later dropped.

Working at the "Tec," as it was called, was remarkably interesting. It had a reputation for being at the cutting edge of science, and one of its leading fields was lasers. I was assigned to a PhD student named Bill Fagan. When I entered his test lab, I was amazed. A green laser beam bounced around precision mirrors, and he was producing holograms of 3D chess tables. I never failed to get excited about new technology, and it wasn't long before I landed a high-tech job myself.

Bill went on to become a major force in laser technology and was better known in later years as Professor Dr Bill Fagan.

Chess Board Hologram

I was a driver now, and Elaine's Dad was great—he lent us the car to get back and forth for family visits. At weekends, we could take it for a run to the coast, provided we took Elaine's little brother, James, with us. Having the car was brilliant—until I bumped into another car and dented the wing. I took it back to my place, hammered it out with basic tools, rubbed it down, primed it, and sprayed it so it looked brand new. Jimmy never knew, and we carried on getting the car.

One night in December, we were driving back from Auntie Isobel's house in Annan Drive Foxbar. Just as we passed Stanley Green School, the car spun round, facing the opposite direction. Luckily, there were no other cars around. We learned quickly about black ice that night.

During this time, Elaine and I would go out on Sunday evenings to some of the local pubs. One night, we went to the Bungalow Bar at the bottom of Renfrew Road, near Reid Kerr College. Just days earlier, my brother Charlie had been attacked by a gang from Glenburn—the Glenburn Team. One of their leaders was Russell Pollock, who I'd gone to school with.

Rusty Pollock saw himself as a hard man. I remembered him fighting my old school pal, Kenny Gibb, for nearly an hour one day after school in 1966. We were sitting in the corner when Rusty and his gang walked in. He and I should really have been friends, as we both knew Ian Johnston, but that wasn't how things were. I got up and had a quiet word with him. I knew if I started a fight inside, it would turn into a riot, so I invited him outside for a private chat.

I challenged him to a one-on-one after work in the alley behind Kilpatrick's offices in Paisley on Monday night. I told him to leave his pals out of it. He agreed. He thought I was in the Young Disciples, a Ferguslie gang, or the Little People from the same area a one-on-one would save a gang war. In truth, I'd never been in a gang, though gang culture was rife in the '60s and 70s.

Rusty never showed up. I heard a few years later that he'd got cancer and died.

Young couples need places to go, or they end up walking the streets. When John and Cath got married, we'd visit them often—they were great fun. Cath Gordon had gone to St Margaret's Convent School with Elaine, and they were best friends. John and I got on well too. He was always into making things and loved history. I helped him build a scale model of the Battle of Waterloo, repair the plastering in their flat, and—once, after a few beers—paint his outside windows while hanging off the roof.

Elaine my childhood sweetheart at St Margaret's Convent Paisley

We also tried our hand at home brewing. Neither of us knew much about beer-making, so we worked from an old instruction book from Paisley Library. We took a door off a cupboard to grist the malt, sparged the hops— whatever that meant—then filled the demijohns and fitted fermentation locks. We left it to ferment for a month. John added Camden tablets to clarify it, and when the time came, we split the six bottles each.

I took my bottles home and stashed them behind the headboard of my bed, then forgot about them for months.

One Sunday night, my Dad said he really fancied a pint (beer). I remembered the home brew and asked if he'd like to try it. He was well up for it. At that time, the Yuletide Ale was completely clear and extraordinarily strong. A hard cake of sediment had formed at the bottom, but as long as you poured carefully, it was fine.

I poured Dad a full pint.

"Jesus," he said, taking a sip. "That's bloody good stuff, son."

I decided to try one myself. It was strong—like Newcastle Brown Ale. We both got legless, and the six bottles were no more.

Just before the July break at Babcock's, the big event for apprentices—the Apprentices Rally—took place. The managing director usually gave a speech, and you could bring your mum and Dad. It was a good night out with live music, and prizes were awarded for academic achievement and works ability.

Over the four years I served my time, I won the works ability prize in 1970 and the scholastic attainment prize in 1969. Ian and Jim Johnston usually won the craft prize, which was £50 worth of tools, whereas scholastic attainment was £50 worth of books.

Mum and Dad both came, and afterwards, we went to the Cross Keys Bar at the bottom of Porterfield for a celebratory drink.

CHAPTER 17:
ENGAGEMENT

1971

I was making good progress at PCT, and Elaine and I received a line (voucher) from Babcock's to get engaged. So, we took the train from Gilmour Street to Glasgow and presented ourselves at Hamilton and Laidlaw in St Enoch Square. Climbing to the first floor past the old mesh elevator, we found a long queue of couples, all eager to buy engagement or wedding rings. I was relieved to finally get the ring, as we had been searching in shops for weeks, and I was going diamond blind. In the end, Elaine chose a sapphire and diamond cluster ring, similar to the Lady Diana ring but smaller.

We held an engagement party at Elaine's mum and Dad's house. John and I were well aware that, after a few drinks, both Dads had the potential to clash. So, we agreed that if trouble arose, John would handle his Dad, and I would deal with mine. Elaine's Papa had served as a soldier in the Argylls like my Dad, which was a useful connection. In the end, the night went smoothly—they reminisced about the war, and we eventually got a taxi to take Mum and Dad home to Feegie.

That was when the fun started, as Elaine came home with us to stay over. In the taxi, Dad decided he wasn't going to pay the driver because, according to him, the man was a bad driver. By the time we reached our house, I was sure the taxi driver was ready to call for backup. Dad got out of the car, and I paid the fare. As the evening wore on, he became more drunk—I suspected he had more to drink once he got home. He wasn't aggressive, but, unlike his usual self, he wanted to chat.

Elaine and I were sitting in the living room on the iron-legged couch when Dad excused himself to go to the toilet. Five minutes later, he came back into the room—in a state of undress. It was amusing. I had to take him to bed, where he promptly passed out.

weeks later, Dad was working on a building site in Glasgow when he fell off the scaffolding, fracturing two vertebrae in his spine. He was taken to the Western Infirmary just off Byres Road. Mum was in a state, so Elaine's Dad kindly let us borrow the car to take her to visit Dad. We had no idea what to expect when we arrived.

Dad lay flat on his back, conscious but covered in heavy grazing on his head and arms. He couldn't move due to the neck brace, so he asked me to check his body for injuries. I lifted the cover and saw some nasty bruises and grazes on his sides and legs, but what struck me most was that he had an incredibly athletic body.

He remained in hospital for a few weeks before we got him home. On one visiting night, Dad asked me to bring him some whisky, so I got him two miniatures. Uncle Sammy wanted to visit too, so I took him along with the rest of the family. When we reached Dad's bedside, I asked Sammy to pass him one of the miniatures— only for Sammy to decide to drink it himself! It was hilarious watching Dad chisel him, especially as Sammy had emptied the bottle with a big grin.

The next night, the matron was waiting for us with a frosty expression.

"You're the culprit giving him drink," she declared.

Apparently, it had shown up in his blood test and although I suspect she simply smelt it on his breath. Once she was gone, I passed Dad another couple of miniatures.

"God bless ye, son," he whispered.

When he was discharged, Charlie and I set up a bed for him in the living room, and whenever he needed the toilet, we carried him back and forth. Eventually, he healed, but he was off work for about a year.

Meanwhile, my shift at PCT was coming to an end. I was making some extra money on the side by doing planning permission drawings for friends and family, using linen and Rapido-graph draughtsman pens in the PCT drawing rooms after work. I wasn't sure about my next career step, but I knew it had to be something that made me money. I'd spent years working hard and giving most of my wages to the family, but now, it was time to focus on me and Elaine.

I was also preparing to become a draftsman—a staff job with good prospects. However, I had an opportunity to complete a four-year apprenticeship with the module system to become a journeyman, whereas draftsmen had to undertake a five-year apprenticeship approved by the DATA Union.

Then, I got another call from Jimmy Connell at the training school. My shift at PCT was ending, and he was transferring me back to the boys' corner, which had been relocated to the structural bay, noisy and dangerous section.

In the evenings, Elaine and I went for walks, and at weekends, we tried to go to the cinema in Paisley, where we would choose from the many cinemas as mentioned above.

We took the bus to Glenburn from the bottom of St Mirren Brae, praying that the Young Disciple team (gang) wouldn't make an appearance or that the Govan Team wouldn't pay us a visit. When we reached 84 Glenburn Road, we'd stop on the first-floor landing for a final cuddle—until Elaine's mum rattled the milk bottles, her signal for Elaine to come inside.

I'd then sprint to catch the last bus from the Glenburn terminus. At the next stop, Kenny Gibb would get on—he had been out with his girlfriend, Sheila. Kenny and I had known each other since primary school and were good pals, having played in the school team together.

We usually missed the last bus to Feegie, so we walked home together in hail, rain, snow, or moonlight, singing Motown songs like "This Old Heart of Mine."

One night, we walked along the High Street past the Regal Cinema and turned right into Well Street when a man emerged from a close.

"Got a cigarette or some change?" he asked.

"Sorry, pal, we don't smoke, and we're skint—we've nae bus fare," I replied.

Suddenly, he pulled out a huge sword from his coat.

"Are you sure about that, boy?"

Now, Kenny and I were both fit—especially Kenny, who played amateur football for the junior amateur team Glentyan Thistle. But I swear to God, that night, I outran him, my knees pumping up to my chin.

The guy with the sword gave up pretty quickly.

Mum hadn't been keeping too well, and it was clear she was more than just a little worn out by life in Feegie. She had been trying for a council house exchange for years, but we never had enough points to qualify for one, even though nine people were living in a three-bedroom house—five of whom could be classed as adults.

Luck was about to change for Mum and Dad. They had applied for a new house in Gallowhill, on the east side of Paisley, near my work in Renfrew. The council had built a block of new Wimpey houses on the grounds of the old prefabs, which had now been demolished. Elaine and I took Mum and Dad to see the houses, and she was so excited at the thought of getting one. But it would prove more difficult than she thought.

The council had a points system, ranking applicants based on family size, years on the waiting list, and other factors. At her interview, Mum explained that she had seven children, ranging from nine to 21 years old, and had been waiting for a bigger house for ten years. She described how three boys shared a tiny room, while three girls shared another with their younger brother, Steven.

The official told her there were two problems: first, she wasn't at the top of the list, and second, none of the new houses had four bedrooms. Mum was heartbroken. The thought of missing out on one of these homes was too much, and she grew tearful.

By chance, my cousin Robert Armstrong was visiting us with his fiancée, Jane Allison, whose mother was Labour councilor Nancy Allison. Jane was sympathetic and, when she got home, told her mother about Robert's aunt Ellen's plight.

Whatever Nancy Allison did, it worked. Within days, Mum had the keys to No. 13 David Way, a new house in Gallowhill—the last house available because nobody wanted "unlucky" number

13. But for Mum, whose birthday was the 13th of December, thirteen had always been lucky.

The problem was that it was a brand-new house, which meant new carpets, curtains, and furnishings. The only person with any money was me. I handed over most of my savings so Mum could get a carpet and curtains. I'd never seen her so happy as the day we left 94 Ferguslie Park Avenue.

A huge removal van came, and we loaded up what little furniture we had, along with our family cat called Puss. Some of the kids got to travel in the van with her. As we pulled out of Feegie, families stood outside our house, watching. Some of the older women were crying, and many of the little children looked lost and dirty.

None of us ever returned to Feegie. But Puss did.

She disappeared soon after we moved and was never seen again, despite our best efforts.

Goodbye, Feegie and farewell Puss.

CHAPTER 18: JOURNEYMAN

It was springtime, and my younger brother Stewart and I decided to go into Paisley to get him measured for a suit. Our troubles with the Young Disciples were not over. Stewart and I had been in Lang's Pub on Moss Street for his first pint of Guinness before heading off to get him measured. He was only sixteen but already a good four inches taller than me and easily looked eighteen.

After the pub, we made a quick stop at the toilets in Dunn Square at Paisley Cross. The Disciples followed us in from both entrances and set upon us. All I could do was hit the biggest guy as hard as I could, knocking out his front teeth in the process, I put a big hole in my knuckles. I was soon on the floor, curled into a ball, covering my head with both arms. It felt like forever as they kicked and punched me until I lost consciousness. Eventually, Stewart helped me up. I could barely see through the blood running into my eyes and was dizzy from the beating. Surprisingly, Stewart was fine. It was me they were after.

We got on a bus to the Royal Alexandra Infirmary (RAI), where they patched me up. When my Dad saw me, I was covered in bruises, with two black eyes, and a head kick had left me with a misshapen jaw. My hand was bandaged, and as I lay on the couch, he asked who had done it. Without waiting for an answer, he said it had to be the same gang that had knocked Stewart's teeth out—the Young Disciples, led by Wee Kelly.

I don't know what Dad and Sammy did, but we were never troubled by the Young Disciples again.

I had only five months left, and if I could get a good shift, my time would be served. When I arrived at the boys' corner, Campbell Reid was waiting. Most of the boys just wanted out of the corner and into proper work, so they were waiting for a shift into the main squads—but first came the trial by ordeal. The work was supervised by senior engineers or journeymen, but to secure a good shift, you had to complete a difficult assembly for a client, which would then be subject to full quality inspection.

The job I got was an ash pan activator—a huge casting assembly with a gearbox, shafts, and blades to remove coal ash in power stations. It weighed about ten tons and had fifty heavy cast iron wear plates that had to be fitted by drilling and tapping threads through the casting. A heavy, round machined section had to be lifted into place to complete the seals. Campbell knew it was a big task for any apprentice, but he told me that if I did a good job, he would get me a good shift out of the corner.

I have never worked so hard in my life. It took me three months to complete, and I was up against my deadline. One of the boys assigned to help me was a technical apprentice, Willie Vale. He was a great guy to work with—an interesting bloke and a keen motorbike enthusiast. Sometimes, we'd meet up in the Afton Bar in Paisley for a pint.

One Friday, we had a drink together after work as usual. By Monday morning, the corner was eerily quiet. Willie had been found dead in his lock-up from monoxide poisoning. He must have had a few too many, gone up to his lock- up in Gallowhill, set the engine running on the test stand, and fell asleep with the door shut and the engine fumes. His funeral was incredibly sad, and it stuck with me for a long time that I had been the last person to talk to him.

That Friday, Campbell came up to me with a letter.

"You're one lucky bastard, Green. Have a look."

I had been allocated to the Engineering Research Station on High Street in Renfrew as a research rig operator technician. It was great on so many levels—staff position, white boiler suit, interesting work with site visits that paid well, and plenty of opportunities for promotion and overtime. I left the boys' corner and never looked back.

I was to report to Drew Dempster, Scientific Officer (SO) in charge of metrology and leak detection. I got the shift because Danny Boag, a newly qualified journeyman a year older than me, had decided to go to sea as a junior engineer. He left, and I never saw him again.

Working with Drew was almost magical—he was flamboyant, educated, and full of experience. I knew I could learn so much from him, and I absorbed every word. He taught me how to learn properly—how to read and write effectively. He was up to date with advanced equipment, using Mass Spectrometers and Quadrupole Gas Analyzers. He trained me on operating these machines but also their history, telling me that the first Mass Spectrometers were used in the Manhattan Project to create the first atomic bomb. I also trained in stripping and rebuilding them.

My Mentor Drew Dempster MBE

We used liquid nitrogen to cool down the diffusion pumps, which were essential for producing the high vacuum the instruments needed to work properly. He taught me about Pirelli and Pirani vacuum gauges and how to measure small laminar flow rates in Torr-liters per second. I felt like a real scientist. I had completed my City and Guilds technician's course in engineering, which was good enough for the job, but most of the men at the research centre were first-class Honors graduates or PhDs.

The technician squad was made up of ex-seagoing engineers, some of whom specialized in metal spraying, strain gauge work, or thermocouples. The Babcock Research Centre was like a mini university, and I fitted right in.

The campus was laid out with a main building, offices on the top floor, and laboratories on the ground floor. As you entered the reception, you were greeted by the beautiful Sheena. Back then, I was only twenty-one, and any woman who wore makeup was beautiful to me—not to take anything away from Sheena, who was genuinely attractive. A staircase led directly up to the offices above, while a double door led to the lab areas. Beyond that door was a dark corridor, with another staircase on the left leading to the research library.

The library had one assistant, Helen, and the chief librarian was the famous Dr John Thom.

Over the months, I got to know Dr Thom very well. He took an interest in my education and asked about my qualifications. When I told him I only had my City and Guilds certificate, he beamed from ear to ear.

"Come and see me tomorrow," he said.

The next day, he showed me a velvet case, about the size of a small tea plate, with a blue velvet covering. When I opened it, I saw a large gold medal emblazoned with the City and Guilds crest. On the other side was an inscription:

To John Thom PhD for creating the first enthalpy-entropy steam tables.

It was a special moment for me because Dr Thom and Drew saw something in me that I hadn't recognized and that was potential. I felt reinvigorated in my studies and realised that many people fail simply because they don't apply themselves. Drew would say, "You need to be in the game," and "It's all part of the act."

Looking back, I can see that I hero-worshipped Drew, but I also respected him for taking the time to develop me. He quickly crushed any laziness in me, whether through a sharp-tongued remark or by letting me witness his explosive side when others messed up. It was all deliberate part of the act, his act, as he would repeat. It taught me how to lead men, motivate them, and earn respect.

One of the first projects we worked on was the Advanced Gass Reactor (AGR) test programme for the pod boilers being built for Hartlepool and Heysham nuclear power stations. My job was to build the equipment to create a vacuum in the pipework of the pods and then spray the external area with helium, which would enter any cracks or porosity in the metal. The mass spectrometer would then detect the leaks, triggering an audible alarm.

For weeks, we carried out the tests without finding a single leak. We had reference leaks built into the system, so we knew we could detect even the smallest faults. These pod boilers were highly sophisticated pieces of engineering, made of austenitic steel, and designed to withstand high- pressure superheated steam to drive the turbine generators.

Jim Green testing the AGR Pod Boiler with a Mass Spectrometer

The production schedule was tight, so I often worked through the night and for three days straight with little sleep. We eventually modified the test method, enclosing the entire assembly in a polythene envelope and injecting helium inside, letting it saturate for an hour. If no signal was detected, we would test the reference leak; if that triggered a signal, the test was signed off by the CEGB inspector.

Each pod consisted of rows of finned stainless-steel tubes, ranging from two rows around the inner drum to 18 on the outer row. Five months into testing, on row 13, we found our first leak—a four-inch laminated lateral crack caused by a carbon inclusion during the extrusion process. The CEGB inspectors were busy fussing over it, bringing in engineers to cut out the faulty section, while Drew patted me on the head for finally finding a leak. He was delighted because this discovery virtually guaranteed his promotion to SO5 and secured years of work for our section.

Up until then, Drew had always called me "Tiger," but after this, I was promoted to "Killer."

It was common for men working together to use nicknames rather than real names. Drew was always "Double D," derived from A. D. Dempster. One of the laborers was called "Feets" because he limped, while Old Davy was "Chattanooga" because he constantly sang the first verse of the famous song. My best friend, Ian Johnson, worked at a blinding pace, earning him the nickname "Zoom-Zoom."

With secure work and money building up, Elaine and I set our wedding date for 22 July 1972.

Before that, however, Drew took me on an adventure to Dounreay Nuclear Power Station in the north of Scotland.

It took a couple of days to prepare the equipment. We hired a Transit van, loaded it up on Sunday, and set off on the Monday. I was driving, as Drew was still taking lessons and couldn't yet drive. He had just been promoted to Scientific Officer 5, with the promise of a Group Leader position if he continued his good work on the nuclear testing programme.

During the long drive, Drew talked to me about subjective political language, explaining how words like "massive" mean nothing unless quantified. He was an active Tory and staunchly anti-trade union.

We took the ferry at Ballachulish, just north of Oban, then continued through Inverness. Entering Sutherland, we stopped for the night at the Dornoch Castle Hotel. After a good meal, the drinking began. I turned in after two drinks, but for Drew, which was just the start. He confided in me that once he started on gin and tonics, he couldn't stop and feared he was a candidate for alcoholism.

By morning, he was as fresh as ever, and we resumed our journey north along the coast towards Dunnet Head and Dounreay. Through the rain, we glimpsed the ominous sight of the old Dragon reactor—a giant golf ball looming on the horizon.

At the site gates, the MOD police stopped and searched us thoroughly. We had already completed disclosure forms, but site entry required signing the Official Secrets Act(OSA).

Once inside, we met the Senior Site Engineer, who took Drew aside for a meeting while I unloaded the equipment. He was gone for what felt like an eternity before returning and directing me to test some tube circuits on a large circular plate a few levels up in the building.

I asked him where the reactor was, and he casually replied that we were standing on top of it. We were, in fact, on the main tube sheet above the reactor, which had been deactivated. What I didn't know was that radioactive material had leaked into the cooling waters of the Fast Breeder Reactor and that a missing fuel rod—V55—had been causing serious concerns. The rod was never found.

After two days of testing, we did find leaks, but neither Drew nor I ever discussed it. Even years later, when I asked him about it, he refused to say a word.

Each evening, we returned to the Dunnet Head Hotel, perched on the red sandstone promontory at Scotland's northern tip—one of the wettest, windiest places in the UK. On the way home, we stayed at the Dornoch Castle Hotel again, where Drew once more relieved them of their gin and tonics.

That trip changed me. A new steel entered my soul. I was about to get married, and I knew I had to be fully "in the game."

CHAPTER 19: WEDDING

1972

I started the year by working as many hours as I could, especially in the Clean Area of Babcock's main factory, where they were building the AGR pod boilers. One Tuesday night, after finishing work, I decided to take a shortcut through a hole in the fence towards Paisley Road in Renfrew, where the bus stop was at the corner of Cockles Loan. I had to walk diagonally from where I entered the main road to the bus stop. As I crossed the road, I saw a woman hugging her son, who was wearing a Cub Scout uniform. Just as I reached the halfway point, I heard a bang and the squeal of brakes. A speeding car had hit the boy, killing him instantly. It took me a long time to get that image out of my head—not the best preparation for marriage.

Before the wedding, Elaine and I weren't getting on well, with faults on both sides. However, in April, we took a weekend break at the Caledonian Hotel in Ayr, which helped to heal things. We also placed a bet on the Grand National and won a lot of money. After seriously questioning whether to go through with the wedding, we decided to proceed—for better or worse.

One Sunday night, Elaine and I went to the Tappit Hen pub, part of the Brabloch Hotel in Gallowhill, Paisley, opposite Reid Kerr College. We were sitting with another couple when the Govan Team, the notorious Glasgow gang, decided to pay a visit. They were looking for trouble, and when they got to our table, they picked a fight with Peter Robertson, who was sitting with us. One of them split Peter's head open with a pint mug, and they tried to stab me with the jagged remains of the glass tankard. I blocked it with the back of my left hand, which was ripped open, and the glass slightly punctured my shirt and punctured my stomach. A general melee followed, and Peter and I ended up in the back of the owner's new Jaguar, bleeding all over his seats and on our way to the hospital emergency dept. That was the end of our visits to the Tappit Hen.

Back at my parents' house, my Dad was going through rehabilitation and had been sent to study at Barmulloch College in North Glasgow. There was a shift in attitude at home, and a few weeks before my wedding, my mum asked me to return after three years away.

I remember walking slowly into the living room, where Dad was in his usual seat. I said hello. He replied, "Hello." And that was it.

David Way gave my mum and Dad a new lease of life, as it did for all the kids. Its front door was right next to the Gallowhill Public Bowling Green, and all the neighbours were very friendly. But I was leaving soon to get married.

Within a week, we had problems—clothes disappearing from the washing line—and one night, the local gang, the Gallowhill Team, had a go at me as I walked home from Glenburn. About ten of them were hanging around outside the Gallowhill chip shop and decided they wanted my blue duffle coat. I was ready to run but decided to fight, as I was better prepared this time. I pulled on my leather gloves—teeth can make an awful mess of your knuckles. Like most bullies, they backed off, though I may not have been so lucky if some older men hadn't just come out of the chippy and chased them away. After that, until I left Gallowhill, I always took the Arkleston route home avoiding the main housing scheme and the chip shop.

In April, Charlie and Christine got married, with their reception at the Masonic Halls in Paisley's west end.

Earlier that year, Dad completed his course at Barmulloch College and earned his certificates. He landed a job as a store man with Chivas Brothers, just a five-minute walk from our house in Gallowhill. It was perfectly light work, which would save his back, and at 46, he could still build up a good pension. But the job only lasted a few months, apparently, Uncle Sammy was working at Chivas for Hugh Allan & Son Builders. One day, the shop floor employees held a meeting in the lorry park due to a workers' dispute. Dad took the opportunity to relieve the lorry of a bottle from one of the cases of whisky—and share it with Sammy. That was the end of his career at Chivas.

In April and May, we were frantic, trying to find a place to live. We put in several offers but lost out. One night, we were sitting with Elaine's parents when her Dad suggested we stay with them. It was a generous offer, but I was more determined than ever to find our own place. Then, just a month before the wedding, our offer was accepted for a luxury flat at 129a Meikleriggs Drive.

Elaine and I were ecstatic. We could hardly contain ourselves. We borrowed her Dad's Ford Prefect and drove to the flat, where we sat outside, staring up at the windows. David and Mari Beck, who lived there, were newly married and expecting a baby, so they were moving to nearby Elderslie. They spotted us and invited us in, which was both embarrassing and wonderful. The flat smelled of Tweed perfume. We had a home at last.

At that time, I didn't get on with either my Dad or Elaine's, and I suppose I'll never fully understand why. I've always considered myself a fair person— perhaps even too kind—but I think that generation was shaped by the war. At 18, they were sent to kill or be killed, while aside from a few street fights, I had led a relatively charmed life.

Our next challenge was the Church and religion. I was a Protestant; Elaine was a confirmed, convent-educated Catholic. I was invited to St Peter's Chapel House in Glenburn, Elaine's local church, where we met Father Kelly. He asked me if I'd consider becoming a Catholic and, respectfully, if he or Elaine would consider being a Protestant. Eventually, he proposed that we seek a dispensation from Rome to marry in Paisley Abbey, provided we agreed to raise our children as Catholics. That never happened, as I'll explain later however we did the dispensation from Rome on parchment embossed with the Crossed Keys of St Peter.

We had planned to get married in Paisley Abbey, my local church, where I was a member. I had been attending regularly and had become friendly with the minister, Reverend James D. Ross, who had baptized me as an adult earlier that year. However, as the wedding approached, we were told that Rev. Ross was unwell, and his deputy, Mr Sneddon, would conduct the ceremony instead.

The weather was a bit overcast on the day, but the Abbey was packed. Elaine's parents had spared no expense, hosting a reception for over a hundred guests at the Town Hall opposite the Abbey. My Dad had also provided a free bar all night for everyone.

Elaine looked stunning in her wedding dress, while I wore a grey morning suit with a top hat.

Our Wedding Day

After the speeches and dancing, we changed into our going-away outfits—Elaine in a blue dress, and me in a grey suit with an open-neck shirt.

We spent our first night at the Excelsior Hotel at Glasgow Airport, leaving a trail of confetti wherever we walked.

My Dad had given us a bottle of champagne for our room, and we drank half before I attempted—rather unsuccessfully—to recork it.

In the middle of the night, the cork popped again, scaring us half to death. He also gave me two bottles of Glen Grant malt whisky an 8-year-old and a 10-year-old. He explained to me that if our marriage did not work out we should share the 8-year-old one and if we had a son we should share the 10-year-old one.

The next morning, we went to the breakfast room, convinced that everyone was staring at us. In reality, they probably weren't—it was just newlywed embarrassment. I had hired a white Ford Escort from Hertz, and soon we were on our way south to Blackpool.

Our hotel was opposite Central Pier, and I remember sitting at the window, watching the crowds heading to the theatre. The next day, we continued to Birmingham, staying in a fancy hotel and visiting my old haunts in Edgbaston before moving on to Basildon via the North Circular Road.

Elaine's best friend, Marjorie, had married John Waters just a week before, and she had also been Elaine's maid of honour. We had agreed to visit them in their new house in Basildon.

John and Marjorie were such great friends that, having spent their first week of marriage without a bed, they insisted we take their brand-new one when we arrived. I'm not sure I could have done the same, so we owed them big time for that one.

We spent the next few days visiting Hendon-on-the-Hill, Canvey Island, and attending a party in Southend, where some of John's new work colleagues lived. Eventually, we left John and Marjorie to settle into their new lives and travelled north to the Lake District, where I had booked us into the Beech Hill Hotel in Bowness-on-Windermere.

This was where I made my first mistake as a married man. The day before we were due to return to Scotland, I needed my shirt washed and ironed. Playfully, I tossed it to Elaine and asked her to sort it out. The shirt came flying back with a firm, "I don't do ironing."

A terrible silence descended, and at that moment, the honeymoon was over.

Back at our new flat in Meikleriggs, life was simple but wonderful. We had only a cooker and a bed—no other furniture. After my first day back at work, I came home to find that Elaine had made me a lovely dinner, served on top of a cardboard egg crate.

Within a few weeks, we had a new three-piece suite and finally opened all our wedding presents.

It was a great place to live, with underfloor heating that was lovely to lie on—until the first electricity bill arrived, giving me a shock (pardon the pun). I had a genius idea to bypass the meter and nearly blew myself up. After the first meter reading, Scottish Power sealed it all up.

During the second week of married life, I went to work half-asleep (I wonder why) and entered the engineers' bothy in the Research Station, as usual, for my morning cup of hot, sweet tea. Unfortunately, I caught the mug on a button on my overalls sleeve and sent the entire contents spilling onto my lap—scalding my most vital parts.

I was in agony. My friend and colleague, Ronnie Syme, grabbed an old, dirty wet mop and slapped it onto the scalded member in an attempt to relieve the pain. There I stood, trousers at my ankles, while Ronnie held the mop against me.

I was promptly sent to the main first-aid centre at Babcock's works in Renfrew, where I was met with full, smiling sympathy. There isn't much you can do for a blistered penis other than throw cold water on it. It took a few weeks to heal for obvious reasons, though I'm sure Elaine was secretly grateful for the rest from her enthusiastic new husband. When I returned to work, the jokes about "five-skins" and "hot rods" were relentless—men can be cruel.

Despite this, I was so happy to be married and living with Elaine. It felt fantastic, and we noticed a big change in our parents, who became far more welcoming and supportive. It was a special time—good jobs, no children, and completely in love.

Buying our first Christmas tree felt magical. We dressed well, enjoyed evenings together, and Elaine's Dad even gave us his car. That was brilliant— until we blew the engine.

I took a site job for a few weeks at Lithgow's Yard in Port Glasgow, where they were building the oil tanker Naes Scotsman on the Clyde. My role was to test the boiler for low moisture content before it was fired up. Initially, I worked with Tommy Jomes, who lived in Port Glasgow, and later assisted Bobby Marshall, one of the engineering foremen.

Bob—Boaby, as we called him—was great fun. He taught me proper engineering practice and had an endless supply of stories. One day, after setting up our test equipment to pump for a few hours, Bob suggested we take a break.

We drove to the nearest off-licence, where Bob bought a full bottle of Four Crown wine. Then we headed for the benches on Gourock Esplanade, looking out over the Clyde towards Rothesay and the Highlands.

Bob took a long swig and handed me the bottle. The burn of the wine spread through me, and soon, I was in another world as Bob recounted his seafaring adventures. He had been a marine engineer and held his Chief Engineer's ticket.

"Before a cruise ship even passed the notable island in the river Clyde "Ailsa Craig," he declared with a grin, "some of the crews were already in bed with the women passengers. There's something about the sea, sailors, and women, son."

He raised the bottle again with a wry and knowing smile.

As Christmas approached, Drew inveigled me into a favour for John Neilston School, where his daughters were fee-paying pupils. We had to collect a huge Chinese dragon costume from St John's Church in Paisley and deliver it to the school. The best way to carry it was for me to wear the dragon's head while Drew took the body.

The sight of us—me in the dragon's head, Drew trailing behind—caused plenty of amusement among staff and pupils. With Drew, you never knew what was coming next.

That first Christmas, Elaine and I attended the Babcock Research Dinner Dance, dressed for show—Elaine in a stunning ballgown, me in a dinner suit for the first time. Earlier that day, Drew had me fill hundreds of balloons with helium to decorate the ballroom.

Later, as the drinks flowed, guests inhaled the helium, filling the room with high-pitched, squeaky voices.

Large red candles adorned every table. We kept one for our flat, using it to create a romantic atmosphere.(I think Jamie was conceived that night) (Sorry Jamie you know your mum loves candles)

We soon got to know our neighbours at 129 Meikleriggs Drive. Fiona, an air hostess, lived in the flat next to us. At first, we thought she lived with her mother—until we realised that the "mother" was actually Fiona without makeup. The transformation before her flight was miraculous.

Below us lived Charles and Katrina, a lovely young couple who kept the whole building buzzing with Rod Stewart tracks. In the other downstairs flat was an older couple Elaine befriended.

Across the road were Bill and Barbara Baillie and their three kids. It was heartwarming to watch their daily routines—coming and going, laughing, arguing, and gardening.

That Christmas, we bought a full-sized tree, decorating it with colorful lights. As newlyweds, life was bliss—our own place, no major responsibilities, and both of us working to build our future.

It was a special time, and we loved every moment of it.

CHAPTER 20:
STARTING A FAMILY

1973

In the spring of 73, Elaine told me she was pregnant, and we were both delighted at the prospect of starting a family. At just 22, we were young, but for our generation—the baby boomers—this was perfectly normal. Elaine was extremely strict about her health, even refusing to eat her favourite food, potatoes, due to concerns about the risk of Rubella affecting the baby.

At work, I became more switched on and was promoted to Rig Operator 2, which came with a welcome salary increase. The personnel manager at the research station, Bill Burnside, had a small ceremony for pay rises. He would personally hand you a ticket with your updated details, which felt quite official. Like many of the senior managers at the research facility, Bill was ex-RAF, and their gentlemanly manners and structured approach, looking back this was a positive influence on me.

I was studying engineering for an Ordinary National Certificate, with Babcock's sending me to day-release classes at Carbrook Street School every Wednesday. The rest of the working week, I kept close to Mum by having lunch at her house in David Way, Gallowhill. The problem was, Mum was determined to feed me up. When I got married, I weighed just 10 stone 2 pounds, but between Elaine's generous fry-ups and Mum's hearty lunches, I quickly gained weight. A typical lunch at Mum's consisted of:

A bowl of thick Scotch broth with bread Two crusty rolls with beef burgers, one Scottish snowball two eggs mashed up in a cup with butter.

On top of that, Elaine made me sandwiches to take to work. Within a year of marriage, my weight had jumped to over 12 stone. One afternoon, after one of these heavy lunches, I dozed off and woke up an hour late for work. Mum said I looked so peaceful that she hadn't the heart to wake me. Eventually, I cut back on the food but still visited Mum once or twice a week.

As Elaine's due date approached, she became huge, and we went into debt to buy a Super 8 cine camera and projector—it's wonderful to still have those old films. We bought a baby crib in preparation, and in the early hours of 17th August 1973, Elaine's waters broke. I went into a complete panic, and while pulling on my trousers, I somehow managed to put both legs down one side and fell over in the bedroom.

It was a frosty morning when we arrived at Paisley Maternity Hospital. Our son, Jamie, was born very quickly after we got to the birth unit. I will never forget the love in Elaine's eyes, and when I held him for the first time, my heart melted. On the way out of the hospital, in my euphoric state, I picked up a small, perfectly square stone, thinking it was a special keepsake for Jamie. The next day, I found more of these little stones and laughed at my own sentimentality when I realised they were just terrazzo pieces from the newly built hospital.

Life quickly became all about Jamie. We bought a new car, took pictures of every milestone, and both sets of grandparents were delighted. I still remember the wonder in his eyes when he saw our Christmas tree for the first time. Elaine adores Christmas, whereas I'm a bit of a Grinch. That year, money was tight—Elaine had to give up work, and I took on extra overtime to keep us afloat—but we were incredibly happy.

That Christmas was also Elaine's parents' silver wedding anniversary, which she planned as a total surprise. We hired the local Scout Hall near Morar Drive in Foxbar Paisley, just a mile from our flat in Meikleriggs. We invited the whole family, pretending it was just a dinner dance. It was a fantastic night, and a great time was had by all.

CHAPTER 21:
DEATH AND DYING

1974

I do not know the exact reason why I have no real memory of loved ones who have passed away. Perhaps it is a trick of my emotional brain, but unless I look it up, I still do not remember dates or even the years of their deaths.

Around this time, we lost Elaine's Papa and my grandmother, Nellie, affectionately known as "Granniemaw."

Elaine's Papa had been growing weaker, suffering from blackouts and a sore on his only foot that refused to heal. His other foot had been amputated during the First World War after he was blown up during the Salonica campaign in the Dardanelles. He had developed frostbite, and the old wound had come back to haunt him.

John Keenan was a gentleman and a devout Catholic, attending chapel every Sunday. He lived in a room just inside the door of the first-floor flat at 84 Glenburn Road, where Elaine's family had lived for about 15 years. From the age of 15 until I was 22, I was fortunate enough to speak with him about his soldiering and working life. Elaine's older brother, John, and I would sit with him in the kitchen on Saturday mornings, soaking up every detail.

He told stories of how he "bought his ticket" when his foot was blown off, crawling back to safety from no man's land, where he met his pal Billy Wilson from Renfrew. Billy was on his way back up to the front line after losing an eye. In the following days, gangrene set into John's wounds, and several operations left him with his leg amputated at the knee.

He also shared how, when his clothes and cape became infested with lice, he would place them on an anthill and let the ants eat the lice. Eventually, he was brought home to recuperate on the Isle of Skye. When he returned to Paisley, he was cared for at Erskine Hospital for veterans and by his devoted wife.

After the war, he had an artificial leg and returned to work as an inspector at Babcock's, leaving behind his original trade as a saw doctor. He and his wife had four children: John, twins May and James, and their youngest daughter, Sadie, who sadly passed away at the age of 10. He later lost his wife during the Second World War, while both his sons served in the Navy.

At night, we could hear him chatting away to his loved ones on the other side. He loved his food and worked into his seventies. In the end, he was sent to the Mearns Hospital in East Renfrewshire. I remember him saying, "If there is a heaven Jim, it must be a terribly busy place." He died that week, back in his bedroom.

Ellen Lowe, my grandmother—my mother absolutely adored her. She was a redhead who played the piano and had four sisters and two brothers. One of her brothers, Alfie, was killed in the First World War, while the other lost a leg but survived.

She worked as a servant in Govan, Glasgow. According to my mother, the gentleman she worked for was an artist and as mentioned earlier who allegedly painted her portrait, which was later displayed in the Kelvin Art Gallery in Glasgow. Her family, the Lowes, lived in Craigton.

Albert Lowe, her husband, was a Londoner and the manager of the local brush factory. The Loewe's (Jewish family) had been pogromed from London during the Cable St Riots, so Albert Anglicized the name. She was 12 years older than my grandfather, Joe Armstrong, when they married. He had served in the Highland Light Infantry during the war. They had three daughters—Alice, Margaret, and my mother, Ellen— and two sons, Joe and Robert. They lived in Leigh Park, New Sneddon Street, opposite Carlisle Quay in Paisley, where the first American troops came ashore during the war.

Grandpa Joe had plenty of character, especially after a drink, when he would pretend to be Al Jolson. He worked as a radial arm driller at Whites Engineering Company in Abercorn St until he retired in 1970. As a younger man, he was a professional footballer, playing for St Mirren under the nickname "Ironsides." He passed away in 1972, as I mentioned earlier.

Before she died, Granniemaw had laid out all her books, money, and affairs on her kitchen table. She passed away sitting at that very table in her single room flat at 77 Abercorn Street, Paisley. The whole family was grief- stricken, and my mother never truly got over it.

Now that we had Jamie, we needed a new car. My overtime working on the AGR pod boilers was good, and one of the guys in the Research Station drawing office was selling a Ford Corsair V4. So, I bought my first car. We fitted a car seat for Jamie, and we were off. Not everyone had a car in those days, and the roads were quiet. Like most young men, I drove too fast and soon got a speeding ticket. I also crashed into a wall at the Research Station.

Being an engineer had its benefits—I was able to cut off the damaged wing and headlights and replace them at a fraction of the garage costs.

My old school pal Ronnie Syme married Anne and moved to Meikleriggs Drive, next door to our flat. This was great because Ronnie had also got a shift at the Research Station, so we could travel together in my car, and he chipped in for petrol.

Ronnie and I fitness trained together at Moorpark Recreation Club, which was subsidized by Babcock's. He focused on heavy weights, while I concentrated on track and field. One cold winter's night, after a tough session, Ronnie struggled to button his shirt and sneezed so hard that a neck button pinged off and hit the windscreen. He was starting to look like the Hulk—quite a transformation from his school days, when he had been considered quite small.

I think the heavy training took its toll. Within ten years, Ronnie developed a heart condition, suffered three heart attacks, and had to retire at fifty. He eventually passed away in 2011.

By then, I was part of a five-man team testing pod boilers for leaks. I was promoted to RO3,(Rig Operator grade 3) which meant a bit more money, and I worked with Tommy Jomes, Charlie Kay, Wee Alfie, Drew, and the latest recruit, Brian Cameron.

At home life was perfect as we were so in love and had our whole lives ahead to continue building our family and life.

*Fashionistas 1974 at a wedding in St Mirrin's Cathedral Paisley
(Brian and Dorothy Cameron)*

Many nights, we worked overtime in the Clean Area, making extra money. I would then drive him home to his dear wife, Stella, and their teenage son, David. Charlie loved when I put the radio on—he would sing along to Billy Ocean's "I Can Help."

Charlie Kay was ex-RAF and had worked at the Research Station for over twenty years, back when it was Kings Aircraft Company, next to the now- demolished Renfrew Airport. He was in his fifties, carefully dyed his hair and moustache, and was a real gentleman—never swore, only ever using "FnB" in place of real swear words, and he would never use the C-word.

Charlie always lamented his father's early passing, having dropped dead the very week he retired. In 1990, David phoned me to say that Charlie was terminally ill with asbestosis. He wanted me to be privy to the autopsy because he feared that Tommy and I might also have been exposed. David was clearly distressed.

Sadly, his call came the night before Elaine, and I were due to travel to America for a three-week holiday. I told him I would visit Charlie as soon as I got back. But when I returned, he was already gone.

The autopsy confirmed that Charlie had mesothelioma, not from asbestos but from beryllium dust, which he had been exposed to in the 1960s while working in the Beryllium Lab at the B&W Research Station. David told me that, in the end, Charlie had drowned in his own blood.

This prompted me to get tested. I remembered how, when we worked on the High-Temperature Steam Rig, we used asbestos rope to lag the test cans. I had always worn a double-thick Martindale mask, but Charlie's never fitted properly because of his moustache. That moustache had cost him his life.

The Research Station was full of hazards, including dangerous chemicals, radioactive isotopes, high pressures, and an extremely dangerous sodium rig. In the past, this facility had machined Magnox cans and worked with beryllium, with most of the waste never leaving the site. In 2004, the managers then contacted me to identify the locations where the waste had been buried, as they were planning to sell the site to developers for new housing. I'll come back to this later.

Tommy Jomes was a God-fearing Catholic from Port Glasgow, about forty years old, and a heavy smoker—a habit he'd picked up during his time in the Merchant Navy as an engineer. He was a nice man who loved a daily bet on the horses. Unconsciously loud, he often let his passing remarks be heard, much to the amusement of the squad.

His ears worked especially well when Ronnie and I were making up an order for condoms from the little rubber shop for gents in Paisley town centre.

Tommy was always gently enquiring about our sex lives, which we grossly exaggerated for a laugh. We were genuinely saddened when, at forty, he admitted he'd never had the courage to partake in oral sex. It was my turn to go to the shop, and Ronnie asked me to get a 12-pack of Black Shadow Durex. Tommy piped up, "What's Black Shadow?" Ronnie explained they were black-coloured condoms. "Get me a packet, boys!" he said, his excitement uncontained. I had never seen a man so enthusiastic about condoms in my life. Sometimes, he would turn up at my door on weekends to see if I had any spare.

After Charlie Kay died, Tommy declined to hear the autopsy results and refused to talk about it. We lost touch after that.

Wee Alfie was a completely mental fantasist. He would boast about owning a collection of 1,000 ties. Useless at his job, he lived for the weekends when he'd taken his camera with a telescopic lens to Glasgow Airport to photograph aircraft and some of the passengers. This pastime came to an abrupt halt when he was caught taking pictures of ladies bending over and was promptly expelled from the airport. Not long after, Alfie died of a heart attack.

Brian Cameron joined the squad through a relative—one of the inspectors at Babcock's main factory who knew Drew. Brian and I were the same age and got on well; we just had a good laugh. Clever but manipulative, he had no problem taking liberties with those who weren't as well-read. He was also a complete sociopath. He constantly annoyed Drew and the other men, and after work, when we went out with some family members, he never failed to get up their noses.

Eventually, he joined the Territorial Army and took his officer's commission at Sandhurst. During training, we'd often finish up with a Chinese takeaway at the officers' mess at the Royal Engineers Field Squadron Depot in Paisley High Street. This usually ended with Brian and me getting drunk and fencing with regimental cutlasses.

He was keen on me to sign up, but after speaking to the recruiting sergeant, I decided it wasn't for me.

Brian had already flunked his first year at university and was about to lose his job at the Research Station—Drew had had enough of him. His other problem was that his girlfriend, Doris, was now pregnant.

At that time, I knew there was more to life than Babcock's. If I wanted to move forward, I needed better qualifications and a degree. I found a new course at Paisley College (now the University of the West of Scotland): a BSc in Engineering with Marketing. Both Brian and I had separate interviews with Professor Neil Hood, who warned me that, with a job and a family, taking the course would put us in a very restricted financial situation.

In the end, I opted out, and Brian opted in. He got married, and their daughter was born. Brian never forgave me, but it was the right decision—as events would later prove.

CHAPTER 22:
TIME TO MOVE.

1975

Early in the year, Elaine told me she was pregnant again and as before, we were delighted. When we shared the news, everyone would say, "You'll be hoping for a wee girl this time—then you'll have the gentleman's family!" (one boy, one girl).

Elaine became huge in no time and suffered from morning sickness. Sometimes, she would ask me for tea and a biscuit just so she could be sick.

The flat was now far too small for us, so we started looking for something bigger in the area. We found a house at No. 15 Tantallon Drive, just around the corner. It was a John Lawrence semi-detached with three bedrooms, a garage, and a driveway. The neighbours were great, so I put in an offer of £12,950, hoping we'd get more than the £4,700 we had paid for our flat. In the end, we sold the flat for £10,400, which meant we could put down a good deposit and still have a low mortgage. The flat had been costing us £30 a month, while our new mortgage was £108.

We moved in April. I ripped out the old fireplace, and we had central heating installed. Jimmy Boyle, my Dad's stonemason friend, built us a new fireplace in Fifestone, and I fitted mahogany-effect mantelpieces to the split-level masterpiece.

That summer, we had BBQs, and Jamie, now walking, followed me everywhere. Once, while I was painting the porch roof, he climbed out of the bedroom window to join me—completely fearlessly to the consternation of the neighbours.

Weekends were wonderful when I wasn't working. We'd pack up the car and go for picnics, sometimes to Inveraray, Ayr, Irvine, Loch Lomond, or Balloch.

On the 13th of September, Elaine gave birth to Jennifer Elaine—a beautiful red-haired girl—and my heart melted all over again.

Our new home came with fantastic neighbours. Jimmy and Nancy Kennovin, both keen bikers, lived next door. Jimmy once told me he could judge a man by the way he rode a bicycle. I laughed my head off, but I'm sure he meant it.

That first summer, Jimmy was always out digging and planting, and when the time was right, he would hand in fresh tomatoes and lettuce to Elaine. He was a college lecturer, and Nancy worked as a medical administrator. They had three children—Gordon, Donald, and Jeannette—who were a bit older than us but great company. Donald drove us mad practicing his tuba for the school band, Gordon was always off skiing or hiking, and Jeannette loved peeking into the pram when Jennifer finally arrived.

On the other side, there was an older couple who moved to New Zealand shortly after we arrived. Their replacements, Jim and Betty were lovely. They had two daughters, Elaine and Alison. Jim was an upholsterer and an ex-professional footballer for Greenock Morton FC. Betty, a house-proud woman, never let Jim smoke in the house—he was relegated to the garage for that. They were devout Christians and spent a lot of time trying to get me into their church.

Now, with two kids, a mortgage, and bills to pay, I had only a basic manager's salary with no overtime. Things got tight as winter approached, and we had to keep the heating on for the children.

My heart pounded as I walked into Bill Burnside's office, adrenaline surging. I explained that we had another mouth to feed, and things were tight. Bill was sympathetic and said he'd see what he could do. A week later, he promoted me to Rig Operator Technician 3, recognizing that I had a lot of responsibility, and my work was good. I also continued studying for my Ordinary National Certificate in Engineering.

Even with the raise, that winter was tough. Elaine got her mum to watch the kids while she worked the Christmas post to earn extra money. I hated that she had to do it, but she was a fighter—petite but formidable, and an incredible mother.

I tried to help, but I wasn't very hands-on with the kids. I saw myself as the provider, and that's what I focused on. Still, it wasn't easy. We had to cut back cancelling the phone, returning the rented TV. One month, we had just £40 for food for the four of us. I don't know how Elaine managed, but we got through it— eating a lot of beans, eggs, and chips. She also made sausage rolls and bridies for the freezer, stretching every penny.

Around this time, we heard that my uncle Matt Tannahill had returned from exile in Leeds. I say "exile" because of the circumstances under which he left as discussed above.

I barely knew him. As children, he'd sometimes visit our house in Ferguslie, always bringing a big jar of pick 'n' mix from Polly Brown's shop on Causeyside. He once gave me half a crown, which I'd never forgot.

One evening, Dad asked me to come with him to visit Matt. He'd heard Matt was ill.

On the way, Dad told me the truth about my uncle mentioned earlier in this book.

I asked Dad why we were even bothering with this man now.

He replied, "I have a message for him."

Most of the men who had wanted to kill Matt were dead. The few still alive were too old to care. They'd heard he was dying and decided that the one who had truly suffered was his wife Jenni.

Aunt Jenni's house was at No. 1 Motehill Road in Gallowhill, just a five- minute walk from Dad's place in David Way. When we arrived, she was pleased to see us and led us to the bedroom where Matt lay. He and Dad talked. Dad passed on the message. Matt dismissed it. "I'm already done," he said.

In reality, he lived another year.

He was even invited to our wedding and Mum and Dad's silver wedding anniversary at the Silver Thread Hotel, near the Anchor Muir—the very place where his troubles had started.

CHAPTER 23:
MASTER OF WORKS

1976

In '75, Drew was clearly not getting on with his wife, and rumor had it he was secretly dating Eva Dempster (no relation). He was also drinking heavily, and I noticed a change in his moods.

One particular weekend, he approached me and asked if I still did car repairs. I said yes. At lunchtime, he took me to a garage in Ralston, where he showed me a damaged car and asked if it could be fixed. I told him it would take about a week. The car belonged to Eva.

Around that time, considering Drew's changing disposition, I had applied for the job of Master of Works (Works Engineer in Scotland). Drew said he'd let me know if I got an interview and, in the meantime, suggested I work on Eva's car. Every day, I brought in a change of clothes just in case I was called in by Bill Burnside the Personnel Manager.

After a week, I stopped bringing a change of clothes. I was rolling around in the mud under Eva's car when Drew appeared.

"You'd better get tidied up—Burnside is interviewing you in an hour."

Drew made a personal sacrifice here. I knew I was one of his star players, but he also knew I had to take my chance. When Burnside interviewed me, I was still dirty and disheveled. He asked me what I knew about building works, and I waffled on about bricks and cement, mentioning that I had already drawn up plans on linen and successfully submitted them to the local council for a friend—Elaine's uncle Tommy.

Burnside said he'd let me know in due time and reminded me that this was a managerial position, meaning no overtime pay.

A few days later, I got the call—I had the job. With over 60 direct-line staff, I was given an EO (Experimental Officer) grading—a very British research system. Bill called me to his office and advised me of two things: first, I was on a six-month trial since I had no prior experience, and second, as the new Health and Safety at Work Act 1974 was in place, I would also serve as the site's Safety Officer.

One of my last jobs with Drew's team was a trip to Hartlepool to conduct further tests on the first pod boilers, which had been transported from Renfrew to the nuclear power station site near Billingham. Part of this trip was to assess the site and plan the operation. The day of the assessment, I was at college, so Drew took Charlie Kay and Tommy James.

By this point, Drew had finally learned to drive and had a hire car for the trip. The problem was, he drove like a lunatic. Charlie and Tommy were terrified, swearing they'd never travel with him again.

When it came time for the actual testing, I took Charlie in a transit van, driving slowly to his great relief. After setting up the site and getting our vacuum pumps running, we had to wait. Charlie and I retired to the Billingham Arms Hotel, had a few beers, and relaxed. He was great company. The next morning, we had full English breakfasts before starting work. After a week, we returned to Renfrew, mission successful.

I had also completed my ONC and had started the HNC course at Glasgow Technical College (now Caledonian University).

I was always the one who organised nights out for the men at the Research Station. Around September, we had "Chattanooga's" retirement do. The men wanted a "smoker night"—which meant strippers—so I called an agency on the east coast that agreed to supply the entertainment. I booked Friars Hall in Paisley.

Being a hopeful entrepreneur, I printed 100 tickets at £5 each, which included a free buffet, a band, and a comedian to compere the night. Expecting a moderate turnout, I was caught off guard when demand soared, forcing me to print another 100—the venue's capacity.

The night was a roaring success, and I got plenty of pats on the back. Some of the younger lads had never seen a pair of tits before, so I reckon I made a lot of happy boys.

A few weeks later, Elaine and I had dinner with my brother and his wife. Over the meal, he casually asked why he hadn't been invited to the 'smoker' night out. I tried to make excuses—claiming it was for employees only—but the damage was done. The word 'smoker' had already slipped out. I tapped his leg under the table, hoping he'd let it go.

Elaine said nothing. We went to bed as normal.

Just as I was drifting into a peaceful sleep, she pounced—absolutely livid. I ended up on the floor, tangled in blankets, as she continued to pound me. I hid under the bedclothes until she calmed down. I tried to feign incredulity, disguising my amusement, but she wasn't having any of it. It took days before she spoke to me again.

In the end, I made a handsome profit from the event, which went into the kitty for the next night out.

The lads wanted another smoker, so I booked the Silver Thread Hotel and printed another 200 tickets. The event sold out again.

I organised everything—the stripper, two go-go dancers, a compere, a band, a raffle, and a free first drink.

The night kicked off at 7:00 p.m., with the main event scheduled for 9:00

p.m. I wore a dinner suit, making me easily identifiable.

By 9:30, the stripper and her pimp still hadn't arrived, and the lads were getting drunker, singing "Why are we waiting?" Big Curly McCann approached me outside.

"Don't you worry, Jimmy. If they don't turn up, you're on next." He meant it.

Eventually, they arrived, and the show got underway. When the bra finally came off, the men went wild—some of the female bar staff seemed equally intrigued. The hotel manageress was making a fortune on drinks and food, but she pulled me aside.

"The police are at reception. We've had a complaint."

Thinking fast, I got the comedian to takeover and hid the stripper and dancers in the kitchen.

By some stroke of luck, we got away with it. Once the police left, the party resumed, and a good time was had by all.

At the end of the night, I went to pay the pimp. He complained that the men had stolen the bra and panties as souvenirs and wanted compensation—plus a few drinks for his girls. I obliged and gave him more cash. Then he offered me "a good time" with the girls for another £50.

It's a sleazy world, and profitable for some. But I declined (honest).

That was my last smoker. I left it as a happy legacy for the Babcock boys.

It was also during this time that I read my first Wilbur Smith novel "When the Lion Feeds" This book took me on a journey of imagination where in reality I was living in a very real west of Scotland life as an engineer and in my mind with this book I was transported to the wild South African landscape and the trial and tribulations of Sean Courtney. I went on to read all of Wilbur's books.

As the year ended, I filled my last balloons with helium for Drew. We chatted about the future. I was sad to leave Drew's squad, but moving on was never an issue for me. I was always ready to "paint my wagon," as the song goes—

"Hell is in hello, and heaven is in goodbye forever. It's time for me to go," as Lee Marvin sang it (Paint Your Wagon).

The young Master of Works

CHAPTER 24:
BAPTISM OF FIRE

1977

I was still on holiday on the 4th of January and due to take up my position as the new Safety Officer/Master of Works at the Research Station when I got a call from Drew.

"You better get in here quick, son. There's been an explosion."

About 500 yards north of the Research Station, across a flat wasteland, was a container depot stacked high with fertilizers. The depot had ignited, causing a massive explosion that completely destroyed it and inflicted serious damage on the Research Station. Fortunately, the explosion had occurred in the early hours of the morning, but there had been a fatality at the depot. One of our men, who had come in early, had been blown off his feet and suffered a back injury.

When I arrived at the gatehouse, the area was swarming with news crews, their cameras pointed at the chaos. The police had cordoned off the entire Research area, following the emergency contingency plan in place for such a high-hazard site. The only problem was—I had no clue what to do. As Master of Works and Safety Officer, I should have been the one at the centre of the emergency.

Luckily for me, during this baptism of fire, a team of older, experienced men—who had lived through the war—had already taken control. They were led by the formidable Bill Urquhart. He wasted no time.

"Set up a logbook," he ordered. "Don't talk to the press. Pull together an assessment team from those arriving."

We allocated key individuals to different high-risk areas to advise the fire crews on known dangers. I arranged for all essential services to be cut off at the main valves and switch rooms. The damage was extensive to windows at the back elevation had been blown out, and in the chemical lab, roof lights had caved in, sending debris crashing into work areas. Among the stored chemicals was liquid bromine, and spilled mercury releasing hazardous fumes.

That day changed me. From then on, I resolved always to be prepared and "be in the game" and to "know all the moves" I developed a thirst for knowledge, and though it took a few years, I gained a deep social conscience about health and safety. Some people say goodbye to their loved ones in the morning and never come home. I had seen it happen.

My father had fractured his spine in a fall from scaffolding, and I had carried him back and forth to the toilet. I had witnessed other horrific accidents—a friend lost half his hand in a milling machine, an apprentice electrician blew off both thumbs on a transformer, and a young roofer fell 60 feet through an asbestos roof, dying instantly. In the training school, a high-speed grinder exploded, sending fragments flying—one boy escaped with only cuts and bruises, but it could have been far worse.

Then there was the welder in the assembly shop. He had been tacking a boiler endplate onto a drum section (outside ring of a boiler) when it gave way, pinning his head against the drum behind him. He was killed instantly.

I became acutely aware that injury and death were always just around the corner.

I learned more about safety, risk, emergency management, and people in those days than any book or lecture could ever teach. The lessons I absorbed that day set me on a path that would define my career.

Once I settled into my new role, Bill Burnside advised me to find a suitable safety qualification. I was already studying for my Higher National Certificate (HNC) in Engineering, having completed my ONC. I found a five-day diploma in Safety Management with the British Safety Council, but when I showed it to Bill, he laughed.

"That's basic," he said. "Not credible."

Instead, he booked me on a two-year IISO(Institution of Industrial Safety Officers) course at Glasgow College of Building—a professional qualification. Those old boys were giving me a chance to better myself, and I took it.

My new job put me in charge of those 60 tradesmen and staff—joiners, painters, plumbers, cleaners, security, and the company garage. One member of my team was the well-known Bob Leyden, my second-in-command. He was recovering from a heart attack and had lost a lot of weight. Every lunchtime, he would eat a whole grapefruit before going for a walk.

I genuinely liked Bob, but we had our moments. One day, during a disagreement, he called me "boy." That was a mistake. I gave him a blast he hadn't expected, and he stayed quiet for the rest of the day. In fairness, he was just testing my boundaries. At 26, I was on edge—I was managing 60 hardened men, all older than me. I needed their respect, and the opportunity to earn it came quickly.

During the summer holidays in July, two security guards decided to throw a party after hours on a Friday night. I got a call from Ian Crawford, head of the Mechanical Service Department.

"We've got a personnel problem," he said.

At the gatehouse, Ian was in control, while one security guard lay drunk on the floor. His replacement was nowhere to be found. I called a taxi to take the drunken man home and left Ian at the gatehouse. Then I walked down the High Street in Renfrew to the 19th Hole, a local pub, and found the missing guard—pissed.

"Don't come to work," I told him.

Back at the gatehouse, I phoned an off-duty guard to come in as backup.

On Monday, the two offenders faced a disciplinary hearing. Their shop steward, Alec Spiers, appealed for leniency, citing their 60 years of combined service. Bill Burnside asked for their explanation, but they had no real defense—except to accuse me of making things look worse by calling a taxi, as if I were pushing for constructive dismissal.

Bill turned to me.

"It's your call, Jim."

I had no sympathy for them. Knowing how dangerous our premises were, I couldn't afford to be lenient. If I let this slide, I'd continue to have problems and would never earn the respect of my team.

"They have to go," I said.

Bill checked if I was certain. I was.

When the guards were brought back in, one of them—Joe—went berserk. It took Alec and another guard to restrain him.

A few days later, I noticed a shift in behavior towards me. The men stopped calling me Jim. I was now Mr Green.

When I told my father what had happened, he thought I had been too harsh. But when I explained that it had been me or them, he just smiled. My father was not a man of many words.

I had several projects on my plate, including plans for a new building near the old joiners' workshop on the northern boundary. When I mentioned it to Bill, he frowned.

"Leave that ground alone," he said.

When I asked why, he told me they had buried some radioactive waste there under a concrete slab.

Years later, when the site was being sold, I was called back to point out the location. A specialist team had to be brought in to purify the ground.

Overseeing the garage had its benefits. Firstly, I had access to the pool cars, and secondly, I got first choice when disposing of old ones. The garage was run by chief mechanic Jake Cameron, who was simply great to have around. Jake had a colorful past—he was one of the original "Cheeky 40" Glasgow gangs based around the old docks on the south side of the city centre. The "Cheeky 40" were a razor gang in the mould of the "Peaky Blinders"

Whenever I needed a car, I just had to slide the windowpane in my office, and Jake, who sat in his own office, would take the order. By lunchtime, I'd be presented with a freshly washed and polished Ford Granada GXL—a flying machine. It was a great perk, but one or two of the non-driving managers complained that it wasn't fair that I had a company car.

Bill called me up, wanting an explanation for why I was taking cars out, especially at weekends. I told him my operation ran 24/7, 365 days a year, and he could either let me use the cars or pay for mileage and taxis out of hours.

Bill produced a better idea. In the carpool, there was a four-year-old Vauxhall Viva estate car getting ready for sale, and he offered it to me at a knockdown price. I could also claim mileage on it. As it happened, Jake had practically rebuilt this car with his routine maintenance budget, so for £200, I had my own pristine car.

Another perk was taking possession of new cars for senior managers. That summer, George Reising, the Research Director, had been supplied with a new Chrysler Alpine in white. I was the first to sit in it after the delivery driver handed over the keys. The first thing I did was ask when he'd set out so I could check he hadn't been speeding during the running-in period. The car was fine. I took it for a quick drive around the block before passing it on to Jake for a final mechanics check. Somewhere in my head, I made a note— I'd get a new car like that one day. Never underestimate the power of a car on a young man.

The Ford Corsair was becoming a liability, so I scrapped it.

Another benefit was that, at weekends, I could take Jamie to work with me. He loved sitting in the big green company lorry, pretending he was driving it.

One morning, on my way to work, I was motoring downhill towards Morar Drive in Paisley, just a few hundred yards from my house, when a young beagle dog ran under my wheels. Its owner, a young woman, stood frozen in horror, along with about a dozen people at the nearby bus stop. The dog was trapped under my front wheel, squealing in agony. The woman was in a terrible state but kept apologizing for not having it on a lead. I backed the car off to free the dog, then grabbed an old blanket from the boot. We wrapped it up and placed it in the back of my car, where the boot was lined with neoprene.

We drove about a mile to the vet, and I gave the woman my phone number so she could update me. Looking at the injuries, I was certain the dog would be put down.

When I got to work, I drove straight to the garage and asked Jake if he could clean out the mess. Blood and fur covered the boot. I explained what had happened, and Jake just smiled. "Well, this is different," he said.

That evening, the woman phoned to say the dog had a broken leg and extensive lacerations but was expected to survive.

Around this time, I noticed Elaine seemed a bit stressed. When I asked what was wrong, she said she'd found a lump in her breast. She saw the doctor and was soon scheduled for surgery. We were both terrified—for the first time, we had to face the possibility that things might not work out.

Donald McArthur, Elaine's doctor, was a rough rugby-type man but treated her with great kindness. Aware of our anxieties, he arranged for a swift procedure at the Western Infirmary in Glasgow. I remember being with her the night before the operation, focusing on her beautiful face and hair, wondering how I'd manage if the worst happened—how I would manage to raise two small children on my own.

I was by her side in the recovery room the next day when I got to tell her the good news: the lump was a benign cyst. She smiled and drifted back to sleep. After that, my love for her deepened, and I made up my mind to give her and our children the best life possible.

That summer, as usual, we went to Blackpool for our holiday. In the evenings, Elaine's mum and Dad watched the kids while the twenty- somethings went into town.

After the holidays, I returned to work. I was having tea with Bob Leyden when one of my laborers, Brian Gentle, reported a problem.

Bob Patrick, one of the older members of my team, was lying drunk as a skunk behind one of the boilers near my office—still drinking his can of Super Lager when I approached. It hadn't been long since the incident with the security guards, and even though he was drunk, Bob knew he was in trouble.

I took the other cans he had stashed away and gently removed the one from his hand. He started to cry.

I asked him what the problem was, and he told me that both his wife and daughter were ill and in hospital. He was living alone and struggling to cope. He also pointed to his leg, saying it was sore. I asked him to roll up his boiler suit, and his leg was badly ulcerated. I decided not to discipline him and instead arranged for one of our drivers to take him home. I told him to take a couple of days off to see to his leg and his family.

When he returned to work, he was very apologetic. He told me his daughter was out of danger and that his wife would be home in a week. I never regretted that decision. I had been extremely tough on the security guards— and for good reason—but with Bob Kilpatrick, I had good reason to be sympathetic.

When someone who is normally reliable starts struggling, you need to assess what's really going on. If I had sacked Bob, all his other problems would have worsened, with potentially terrible consequences, and I wouldn't have wanted that on my conscience. I never had another problem with Bob, and the rest of the men respected what I had done. They knew I was firm but fair.

During this time, my brother Charlie had emigrated to Iran, where he worked in the local Blood Transfusion Services labs in Tehran. He had a nice apartment with a pool and was enjoying a good standard of living. However, the revolution was approaching, and Charlie managed to get Christine and the children back to the UK. I stayed in touch with him via the Research Station's fax machine. It became clear he was in danger. Eventually, armed revolutionaries rounded him up in the lab, along with several other Western staff. Only the demands of the lab chief saved them from execution. An American agent, who lived in the same apartment block, managed to get Charlie out via Kuwait. Thankfully, they all made it home, but they had lost everything, including their bank accounts.

One of my projects involved building a new LPG facility for testing gas boilers. I had sourced two LPG tanks from Northern Ireland, which were ideal for the job. However, the proposed site was close to domestic properties on the north side of our boundaries, so the Health and Safety Executive (HSE) took an interest. The research engineer had suggested filling the tanks with carbon balls, each about the size of a golf ball. The HSE completely rejected the idea, stating that it would have created the biggest grape-shot bomb in history. Eventually, we installed smaller tanks successfully—but not without incident.

It was the evening of the "Daft Friday Ball" at Glasgow University, and I was already dressed up like a penguin for the event when I received a call. An LPG Road tanker had arrived to pump liquid gas into the tanks but had gone into a ditch on site and was leaning dangerously. When I arrived, I saw that the tanker was badly tilted—if it moved another foot, it would puncture its tank on a steel post sunk into the concrete base. The driver had tried to drive out, but his wheels just spun, burying the back end deeper and making it even more precarious.

I called the emergency services and had the entire area evacuated. The fire brigade officer assessed the situation and consulted with me. The firefighters quickly provided wooden props to stabilize the tanker, preventing it from tipping further. Then they used a heavy nylon rope and one of the fire tenders to pull the tanker out of the hole.

I arrived a little late for the university dinner, but a few beers were very welcome before I could finally relax.

In November, I came home from work to find Elaine had been crying. When I asked what was wrong, she told me she was pregnant again. I hugged her and said, "That's great! Why are you crying? It's not as if you haven't been pregnant before." She replied, "That's why I'm crying." We hugged, then laughed. To be fair, Elaine is very petite, and all our babies had been quite big. Each time, she had to be cut, or she would have torn, and the healing process was always long. But within a few days, she got on with it and prepared to grow huge again through the first half of 1978.

Once again, I climbed the stairs to Bill Burnside's office with a heavy beating heart. Bill was always welcoming, and I instinctively knew he liked me. I was doing well along with my safety studies and due to pass my Higher National Certificate in Engineering in '78. As my direct boss, he knew I was doing a good job. He smiled and said he'd heard we had another baby on the way. He had no hesitation in making me Group Leader—the highest grade he could give me—which came with a good salary increase.

There was a lot of jealousy over my promotion, as my career had progressed faster than that of many PhD and First-Class Honours researchers. Bill asked what I wanted to study next, as he was responsible for my development. I told him I wanted to study management, and he agreed, asking me to research some courses.

Most weekends, I would go out for a beer with my friend and namesake, Jim Green #2. Jim was married to Susan Elliot, who was Marjorie Elliot's sister and Elaine's best friend. Jim had more charm than any man had a right to, and I really enjoyed his company. In fact, we were distantly related—but that's a story for another time.

The author with his name sake the other Jim Green #2

One evening, we talked about what it took to be successful. We agreed on one thing: a good education. I had realised that senior managers and directors spoke a language of management that we needed to learn. Jim agreed.

At the time, I bought the Glasgow Herald during the week and the Sunday Times at the weekend. The Sunday Times was packed with information, and its magazine section was excellent—it usually took Elaine and me all week to get through it.

Not long after, I saw an advert for an MBA (Master of Business Administration). At the first opportunity, I arranged an appointment with David Boddy from University of Glasgow Business School who was responsible for admissions. After our chat, he acknowledged that my HNC was a strong qualification but explained that they were looking for graduates with at least a good second-class honours degree. However, he gave me hope—if I completed a Postgraduate Diploma in Management Studies (DMS) with a good mark, he would let me in. Undaunted, I remember my determination when I left the Business School at Bute Gardens.

Bill Burnside thought it was an excellent idea and made provision for it in his 1978 budget. I spoke to Jim #2, and he agreed to do the course as well. The only problem was that it was a three-year, part-time programme with a lot of work involved.

At Christmas, I got the works joiner to build a playhouse for the kids in the garden. Bob Leyden hand-painted it, complete with roof tiles and a chimney. Elaine made curtains for it, and we added hand-painted daffodils. The kids loved it.

CHAPTER 25:
WHISKY GALORE

1978

Working and studying became my life, and at weekends, Elaine and I took the kids out in our new car. Jamie was attending nursery as he would soon be starting school, and Elaine had bought a buggy pram that could accommodate both a toddler and a baby in preparation for our new arrival.

We reorganized the house so that Jamie and Jenni shared the children's bedroom, while I used the box room as a study. I bought a cheap desk, chair, and a flatpack bookcase from MFI and assembled them.

By April, it was time for my final HNC exams. I had been worrying about them, particularly the Math's paper, as I had barely managed to pass it for the ONC. However, an unexpected incident ended up helping me in a superordinate way.

It happened when I found myself in court, charged with dangerous driving. After having lunch at Mum's, I was on my way back to the research station, turning into the High Street in Renfrew just below the Town Hall clock tower. A motorbike with a passenger came speeding through a pedestrian crossing while people were still on it, and I hit the bike side-on, throwing both riders onto the road. It was a low-impact collision, and they both got up unharmed, but the female passenger was furious. I immediately asked if they were okay, but they were both incoherent. I then spoke to the witnesses on the crossing and took their contact details before reporting the incident to the police and heading back to work.

I had almost forgotten about it when, months later, a summons to court arrived. The hearing was scheduled for May—the same day as my HNC Math's exam. I showed the letter to my lecturer, who arranged for me to sit the exam the day before or after. In the end, I had to take it the following day to avoid any risk of cheating.

On the morning of my court appearance, I arrived well prepared. I had contacted each witness and obtained signed statements, and I had also drawn up a diagram of the accident scene to present to the judge. My witnesses were called to testify, and one of them stated that the motorbike had nearly hit him at the crossing. The woman, however, was still livid and sneered at me throughout the proceedings. Despite her hostility, I was fully exonerated, and the judge even commended me on my presentation. It turned out to be an excellent training ground, as I would need court skills later in my career.

Realizing that I still had time, I rushed to Glasgow Tech, where the exam was already in progress. Waiting nearby, I managed to catch one of my classmates, who gave me a copy of the Math's paper. I then drove to my friend Brian—an absolute sociopath but brilliant at Math's. We went through the paper several times until I had all the solutions memorized.

The next morning, I sat the exam, confident that I had passed. Two weeks later, I was told to phone in for my results. When I called, the administrator checked my details and then informed me that I had failed.

"You must be mistaken," I said, but she insisted.

Determined to see my marked paper, I jumped into my car and sped to the Tech, parking haphazardly at the front of the building. Storming through the corridors, I found my Math's lecturer, Frank Dornan, and grabbed his arm.

"Frank, I've just been told I failed my Math's exam—In need to see my paper!"

"Calm down, Jim. You passed. They must have made a mistake."

Eventually, we went back to the administrator, who pulled the failed paper— only to discover it belonged to my distant cousin, Jim Green, who was on the HNC Civil course.

Now, I am well aware that what I did was cheating. But I did put a lot of thought into it, and sometimes in life, you must do not what is right, but what is necessary.

After the summer, we prepared for the new baby by reorganizing the rooms once again. This time, we created separate boys' and girls' rooms, and my study was relegated to the attic. I gained access via a cupboard in our main bedroom, using a staircase built as a favour by Malcolm, one of the Babcock joiners.

On 22nd July—our wedding anniversary—Elaine gave birth to a beautiful little girl, Emma Louise. Our children's names were classically British and straight out of the Sloane Ranger Handbook: Jamie, Jennifer, and Emma. In those days, we were aspirational, particularly for children. I can't recall having a nickname for Jamie, but we did call Jennifer "Pie" and Emma "Caboobie." Elaine had always loved the name Jamie, after the character played by Barry Evans in the film Here We Go Round the Mulberry Bush.

The year we got married, in 1972, Elaine and I had purchased a Super 8 cine camera to document our lives. On the day we went to collect Emma, I filmed the entire journey—from our house to the hospital, picking up Emma, and driving back home, where Elaine's mum was waiting.

Over the years, we took countless photos and videos, and even now, it brings us joy to look back and see everything in colour.

In my role as Master of Works at Babcock's, I dealt with many contractors, but one company stood out—Hugh Allan and Son Ltd., a well-known Paisley building firm. Their contracts were run by Bertie Baxendale, a former soldier who bore a striking resemblance to Field Marshal Montgomery.

Bertie often dropped by at break time with a packet of shortbread and was always good company. It was fascinating to sit and listen to him and Bob Leyden reminiscing about the war. Bertie had been one of the Desert Rats, giving Rommel a run for his money, while Bob had served with the King's Own Scottish Borderers (Kosbies). He had been at Dunkirk, surviving the evacuation, and later found himself helping with emergency services in London after the Blitz.

"Dunkirk was bad," Bob once told me, "But after seeing London, morale was rock bottom."

He had also fought at Arnhem, where his battalion suffered 90% losses. It hadn't been a good war for Bob, and I could see why he still carried a lot of anger. I felt guilty about the time he had called me "Boy."

Bob and I became close friends, taking daily lunchtime walks in the fresh air. I learned a lot from men like him and Bertie and was saddened to hear that both passed away not long after retiring.

During my time as Master of Works, I developed my skills as a manager and oversaw numerous projects, from building roads and culverts to designing new structures and improving my drafting abilities. At one point, I seriously considered shifting to construction and leaving engineering behind. But as it turned out, change was coming anyway.

Just after Emma was born, I saw an advert in the Glasgow Herald for a Health and Safety Officer position at Long John International Ltd, a whisky company based in Glasgow. I applied and was invited for an interview at their plush offices in Farnborough House on Bothwell Street in Glasgow.

All I had known in my full-time working life was Babcock's, with its austere engineering workshops, buildings, and yards. The Research Station offices were functional, but the Long John offices were sensational. Every office was carpeted, with yellow doors, and the reception area looked like something out of a Hollywood film set.

I was interviewed by Bill Christie and his assistant, David. A week later, I received a letter confirming my appointment and salary. It was a significant step up for me. They also confirmed that I could complete my safety studies and continue the DMS course I had just started in September.

As usual, my heart pounded as I climbed the stairs to Bill Burnside's office. I smiled as I entered, and without prompting, Bill said, "No more rises, Jim." I pulled out the job offer letter apologetically—

Bill had been more than good for me. When he read the letter, he simply looked at me and said, "Well done." He admitted he couldn't compete with the offer, as I had already taken promotions to their limit.

He also knew that even if he had been able to make a counter offer, I would likely have been back within a year, looking for more.

It was sad to leave Babcock's and all my friends behind, but I stayed in regular contact, especially with Drew, Ronnie, and Ian. My wagon was painted, and I was off on a new adventure.

On the Sunday night before my first day at Long John, Elaine and I decided to make homemade wine. The recipe was called "Barp" and was made from bananas and pears. We squeezed the murky liquid into a large demijohn, sealing it with a fermentation trap.

I had bought two new suits, shoes, shirts, ties, and socks, ready to make a good first impression. But when I stepped into the kitchen the next morning, I slipped on the slimy Barp mix, which had exploded from the demijohn overnight, splattering the walls and floor. Not the best start to the day—but I still managed to get to work on time.

I was given an induction, shown my office, and introduced to everyone.

I was based in the Staff Engineer's office with two colleagues: Dick Baker and Davy Hall. Dick, a highly intelligent and entertaining graduate chemical engineer in his forties, was always active, playing hockey in his spare time. Davy, the Staff Engineer in his fifties, was so laid-back he was almost unconscious. A few days in, he confided that he had suffered a heart attack, which explained his relaxed approach.

Dick occasionally took me to the Bon Accord pub for a liquid lunch. One day, he bought me a pint of Old Peculiar, an extraordinarily strong ale, followed by another drink that left my cheeks numb. After that, I decided against any more pub lunches with Dick.

The offices were split into two areas: the corporate side, where I was based, and the commercial operations and administration side. To my right was the personnel office, home to Bill, David, and Sandy. To my left was the typing pool, staffed by three dedicated secretaries for each director.

The directors—Bill Rankin, Duncan Grieg, David Heilbronn, and Alistair Moncrieff—insisted on being addressed as "Mr." The company was steeped in hierarchy, even down to the toilets. Directors had a private suite with changing rooms. Managers had a separate toilet on the main landing, accessible by key. Other staff had a toilet next to the managers'—but without a key.

I settled in quickly and soon embarked on my first tour of duty, which involved visiting various company locations:

Westhorn Bottling Plant, Glasgow Strathclyde Distillery, Glasgow Plymouth Gin Distillery, Plymouth Tormore Distillery, Speyside Glenugie Distillery, Aberdeenshire Laphroaig Distillery, Isle of Islay

Ballindalloch Feed Products, Speyside

Long John HQ, Queen Anne's Gate, London

My brief was to visit each location once a month and report to Mr Grieg. For my first tour, I used the family car and claimed mileage at 4p per mile. After my first month, Bill approved my expenses. The next day, Mr Grieg's secretary, Debbie, informed me that he wanted to see me.

I had only met Duncan Grieg once before, during my introduction as his new safety advisor. This time, I was led into his cigar-smoke-filled office, where he sat behind an ornate desk, puffing on an excessively large cigar.

He pointed to my expense summary and asked, "Is this yours?" "Yes," I replied.

"Did you have to finance this from your pocket?"

"Yes."

"Well, that's not good enough—we need to fix this."

He told me he had spoken to Bill and made arrangements. Without elaborating, he simply told me to see Bill and added, "Keep up the good work."

When I met Bill, he explained that I would be getting a company car and a corporate American Express card. "The problem," he said, "is that the grading we gave you doesn't technically support such benefits." He warned that I would be taxed on them but assured me that, since I needed them for the job, they were increasing my salary to compensate.

And with that, I had my first taste of corporate life.

This marked a meteoric change in my life. Elaine could now use the old car for herself and the kids, while I could travel business class on my Amex card. My salary had also seen a huge hike—doubling since I left Babcock's. I had to pinch myself to stop grinning.

As I was about to leave Bill's office, he mentioned one more thing: I needed to choose a car from a list of fleet vehicles. That decision was easy—on the list was a Chrysler Alpine.

Looking back, this was a fantastic job for a young man. A good salary, company car, fringe benefits, and the opportunity to work in Scotland's national industry while travelling around the UK every month. On top of that, my studies were being paid for. It truly was the best job ever.

The first locations I visited were in Glasgow, starting with Strathclyde Distillery in the Gorbals. The site was run by Manager Mike Trotter and his team. Their job was to produce millions of litres of new grain whisky for casks at the Westhorn Bottling Plant, along with rectified spirit for Plymouth Gin. The distillery also had a dark grains plant producing cattle feed pellets as a by-product. Grain lorries supplied the raw materials, which were mashed and mixed with yeast. After fermentation, the liquid was distilled and tanked for storage in bonded warehouses. Each stage of the process had its own distinct aroma—the spirit house smelled of alcohol, the mash tuns of soup, the dark grains plant like freshly baked bread, while the fermentation tanks gave off fizzy CO_2 fumes.

This was a high-risk environment, so I had plenty of work cut out for me.

Next, I visited the bottling operation at Westhorn, located in Glasgow's east end near Celtic Park. The vast 100-acre site sat on a natural oxbow lake on the River Clyde. A few years before I arrived, a massive warehouse fire had broken out. In an unusual move, the fire brigade let it burn rather than attempt to extinguish it. This decision was made due to the tragic Cheapside disaster of 1960, in which 19 firefighters lost their lives. With 19 warehouses on site holding 400,000 barrels—worth £2 billion after revenue—it was paramount that such a catastrophe never happened again. My job title now included Fire Officer.

A new warehouse was under construction, incorporating state-of-the-art technology. I was appointed to the Site Project Team as Safety and Fire Adviser, alongside my other responsibilities.

The site was managed by General Manager Charlie Smith, supported by his leadership team:

Ronnie Jackson (Deputy GM) David Mac (Bottling Operations) Jimmy James (Bottling Engineering) David Fernie (Plant Engineering) Jack Andrews (Security)

Hugh White (Quality Control & Laboratories) Angus Wighton (Planning)

David Hudson (Packaging)   Heather Wolstenholme (Logistics)

Phil Gerrard (Transport & Warehousing)

There were around 300 employees in total, and like all bonded sites, it was policed by HM Customs & Excise—everywhere except the offices.

Although I spent considerable time at other locations, my fate and future would ultimately be shaped at Westhorn. But I'll leave that part of my story for later.

My first trip north took me to Tormore Distillery in Speyside. As I approached, I was struck by the magnificent building emerging from the hillside, overlooking the mighty River Spey. Opened in 1958, Tormore was one of Scotland's youngest distilleries. Designed by Sir Albert Richardson, it was built from granite and featured Austrian bells that chimed every 15 minutes. A row of distillery workers' houses, built in a similar style, lined the site. In front of the property, two curling rinks sat amidst hedges trimmed to resemble whisky stills.

Tormore was run by Adam Johns, who lived locally with his wife, though they had the option of staying in the distillery's tied house on-site. John was a capable manager but plagued by bad decisions and sheer bad luck. His assistant, Ross Collins eventually succeeded him. Ross and his wife, Rose, lived in one of the tied houses. On one of my visits, I asked about a small engineering plant across the road. Ross bluntly replied, "Shite." He was nothing if not direct, and I was pleased when he later took over as manager.

I usually combined my visits to Tormore with a trip to Glenugie, about 70 miles away near Peterhead's fishing port. My accommodation was either Dowans House in Aberlour or Blairfindy Hunting Lodge near Glenlivet Distillery.

Blairfindy gave me two unforgettable memories. In the winter of 1980, I got snowed in for three days. Duncan the Long John MD phoned to say that if I remained trapped any longer, he'd send a helicopter to fetch me—and he meant it. Truthfully, 'trapped' was an exaggeration. It was more like an unexpected winter holiday. I had my study books with me but spent most of the time sitting by a roaring log fire, sipping Glenlivet or Tormore, and enjoying conversations with the local gamekeeper and a team of exceptionally attractive air hostesses who had been also stranded on their way to Aberdeen airport.

In late spring, I brought Elaine with me. The landscape was breathtaking, with stunning views of the mighty Spey River, teeming with salmon.

After Tormore, I would drive a few miles to Ballindalloch Feed Products, where the dark grains from whisky production were dried and processed into cattle feed pellets. This factory was under Duncan Grieg's supervision, and he asked me to carry out monthly inspections and submit reports.

From there, I'd travel to Glenugie Distillery on the outskirts of Peterhead, where I was always greeted by the legendary Sandy Auchinachie and his right-hand man, Bill Bain. Glenugie was one of Scotland's oldest distilleries, though it had a turbulent history of closures and reopening's. It eventually shut its doors for good in 1983, so I was fortunate to witness it in full operation under Sandy's management before he retired to his holiday home on Skye.

Bill Bain and his wife were exceptionally kind to me, often inviting me to dinner at their tied cottage beside the distillery. They recounted tales of Johnny Ramensky, the notorious safe breaker who repeatedly escaped from Peterhead Prison next door. Locals would shelter him at the distillery, hiding him from the police. Ramensky was a wartime hero, briefly released to assist the Allies with his safe-cracking skills, but after the war, he returned to his old ways and ended up back behind bars.

On my final visit to Glenugie, I was driving south towards Aberdeen near Ellon when a lorry kicked up a stone, shattering my Chrysler Alpine's windscreen. At 70 mph, I had mere seconds to react as the glass blew inwards. Fortunately, a garage specializing in windscreen repairs was just a few hundred yards down the road. Within hours, I was back on my way— only a few minor cuts on my hands and face to show for it.

I next travelled back to Glasgow for a few days to write up reports and visit the bottling plant and distillery, familiarizing myself further with the operations. I attended the Safety Committee at Strathclyde Distillery and the morning meeting at Westhorn on a Friday. On these occasions, Chic Smith— known to all simply as Chic—was like Caesar; his managers were afraid of him. Of course, there was a reason for this, which I would only discover much later.

My next trip was to Laphroaig Distillery on Islay. I drove north to Kennacraig, where I boarded the Caledonian MacBrayne ferry to Port Ellen or sometimes Port Askaig—always a brisk crossing, taking just over two hours.

Islay is a fascinating place with some remarkable statistics. It has the highest income per capita in the UK, yet also the highest rates of illegitimacy and alcoholism. The island was frequently visited by Margaret Thatcher, a friend of Lord Margadale, Chairperson of the 1922 Committee, and had once served as a romantic retreat for Victoria and Albert.

Islay is also home to several other famous distilleries—Bowmore, Lagavulin, Ardbeg, Bruichladdich, Bunnahabhain, and Caol Ila— each with its own history and a fierce rivalry, particularly between Laphroaig and Lagavulin. As I stepped into the reception area of

Laphroaig, tucked away at the side of a warehouse, it felt like stepping back in time. My eyes were immediately drawn to whisky bottles containing dead adders suspended in the liquid. The place still seemed haunted by the spirit of Bessie Williamson, the distillery's one-time owner and a legend in her own right. The receptionist, cut from a similar mould, greeted me dryly: "We've been expecting you, Mr Green."

The manager, Dennis, was one of the nicest men I had ever met—exceptionally well-educated and a master brewer. After inspecting this remarkable distillery, with its peat kiln and malting floors, I retired to either the White Hart or the Machrie Hotel.

I got to know Dennis well, and he confided in me about his marital troubles. His wife struggled with island life and had tried to liven things up by having an affair with the local air traffic controller—an affair that ended with Dennis chasing him with a shotgun. The whole thing had made the papers, and Dennis was still deeply upset. Eventually, Duncan our MD arranged a settlement that put an end to both the marriage and Dennis's despair.

During the summer months, Islay hosted an annual fire team competition, which I monitored for the Laphroaig team. Each distillery, along with a team from RAF Machrihanish, competed across several events for some rather attractive silverware. Two of the key events were the fire pump challenge and the boiler suit event.

Remote locations like Laphroaig did not benefit from a high-pressure mains water system, so they relied on sea pumps. The competition was simple: the team that could get their pumps up and running first, with hoses in the sea and water spraying into the air, won. Of course, there was always a bit of gamesmanship beforehand, with rivals tampering with each other's pumps.

The boiler suit event was even more amusing. A competitor would lie down on a metal bed in a field, waiting for a bell to ring—signalling a fire—before leaping up, pulling on a boiler suit and wellies, and rolling out a fire hose. The event was always held on a Saturday, by which time most of the men were already drunk, making it all the more entertaining.

After the competition, a ceilidh was held in the local hall, where the trophies were presented, promptly filled with whisky, and consumed over a night of music and dancing. I always got drunk on Islay—you should try it.

On other occasions, Dennis took me to visit his friends in Port Ellen, Tom Simpson, and his wife, where we enjoyed great food and music. He also took me to other distilleries, including Bowmore, and to the famous Islay cheese factory, renowned for its so-called aphrodisiac cheese.

One night, after a particularly good ceilidh about 2:00am, I stumbled back to the Machrie Hotel, desperate for bed. As I walked through the reception area, past the bar, a booming voice called out: "Mr Green, come and join me for a wee dram." It was the famous Dr Archie. How could I refuse?

The next day, I had to fly back to Glasgow on a Loganair 14-seater Bandolero. Dennis drove me to the airport, which was little more than a basic strip of tarmac on the beach. My body was in shock from the alcohol, the noise, the lack of sleep, and impending air sickness. I passed out on the flight, only to be woken in Glasgow by Diane Welsh, one of my mum's neighbours from David Way in Gallowhill, who happened to be a Loganair ground hostess. When I got home, Elaine assumed I had some kind of virus and put me straight to bed.

The water on Islay is brackish—so much so that it looks like tea coming out of the tap. I tried to blame my condition on that, though, of course, the only liquids I had actually consumed were the Islay malts.

Back home, things were getting busier. Elaine had her hands full with three kids to look after. Jamie had started school at Brediland Primary, just across the road from our house, while Elaine carted Jennifer and Emma around in a two-seater buggy—one of its wheels held together with a metal pin and some glue after I failed to find a proper replacement. The wheel gave a little bump with every revolution, which was quite amusing.

It was around this time that Elaine took Jennifer to the baby classes at the Helen Young School of Dancing in New Street,

Paisley. That day would prove to be a pivotal moment in Jennifer's life.

In the summer, we borrowed a tent from our neighbour, Jim Kennovin, packed up the car, and headed north to Dornoch, to a campsite called Granny's Heilan Hame. Nestled among the white sand dunes of the Dornoch Firth, the site was close to a private airfield.

We pitched the tent quickly and set off to explore the beach and dunes. Jamie loved it, so I bought him a little notebook to document his discoveries. He came back with a drawing of a small moth, which we later identified as a Six-spot Burnet moth. That moment sparked his lifelong interest in nature.

In the evenings, we made toast on a small gas stove, tucked the children into their sleeping bags—faces glowing from the fresh air—then climbed into the car, where I had rigged up a small portable television to the battery so Elaine could watch Coronation Street.

On our first morning, as I stretched outside the tent, I spotted a large delta- wing aircraft making an unusual dive across the firth. Moments later, a huge bang boomed through the sky before it swooped back up. Elaine and the kids jumped in fright. I quickly realised that our campsite was only a few miles from RAF Tain's bomb test range.

Over the next few days, we travelled further north into Sutherland, visiting Dunrobin Castle—well, at least the grounds, as the entrance fees were too expensive for a family. On other days, we visited Lairg and then continued up to John O' Groats the northern tip of the mainland.

On the second day, a German family arrived and started pitching their tent next to ours. Seeing them struggle against the strong wind, I decided to help, as I was making good progress with my own tent. I thought the German man was saying, "Thanks, but I can manage this myself," when, in fact, he was pointing out that I was putting his tent up inside out. Realizing my mistake, I backed off with a cheesy smile and left him to it.

It was a fantastic holiday, but on the day we were due to leave, a torrential downpour hit. I reversed the car up to the awning, got Elaine and the kids inside so they stayed dry, then loaded the car with our belongings. Once everything was packed, I stripped off my dry clothes—except for my shorts—and put them in the car. Then, braving the downpour, I took the tent down, squeezed it into the boot, and we were off home.

After the holiday, it was straight back to work. This time, I had to travel south to the Plymouth Gin distillery on Blackfriars Street. It was a long journey, so I left early in the morning and arrived at the Mayflower Hotel around 5 p.m. My room had a sea view, and as I stood on the veranda overlooking Plymouth Hoe, I watched a replica of the Mayflower sail past. On another occasion, I saw the Ark Royal with its full complement on deck—quite a sight.

The next morning, I met up with Bert Roberts, the distillery manager, and his Master of Wines, Desmond Payne. The distillery, housed in one of Plymouth's oldest buildings, had a unique history. The vaulted rectory roof was where the Pilgrim Fathers had their last supper before setting sail on the Mayflower. Bert was preparing for retirement and had handed most of the operational duties over to Desmond.

Bert's office was something to behold. A collection of ties was arranged like a giant dartboard, and the walls were covered with shields from nearly every ship and submarine in the Royal Navy. Plymouth Gin was the Navy's gin of choice, and visiting sailors received the full PR treatment from the distillery.

Leaving Bert to his office, Desmond took me to his brewing lab and explained that Plymouth Gin had a secret recipe. Gin, he told me, was simply double- rectified amyl-alcohol blended with juniper berries, dried lemon peel, and a few undisclosed ingredients. He demonstrated the difference between Samovar and Vladivar vodka by taking a pipette with just a few millilitres of essence. Adding five drops to a 50,000-litre vat turned it into Samovar vodka—ten drops, and it became Vladivar. He also revealed that the only difference between Plymouth Gin and Seagram's Gin was a few drops of apple essence.

Next, he took me to the bottling operation, housed upstairs in one of their warehouses. The production line was run by about a dozen women, with one forklift driver and one engineer. Everything was semi-automatic. One major logistical challenge was transporting the raw spirit from Glasgow to Plymouth by tanker.

That evening, Desmond took me to a restaurant near the naval base. While I had suspected he was gay, the confirmation came when a group of young men from the French Navy walked in, dressed in full uniform—striped jumpers and berets with red pompoms. Dennis lit up, chatting them up enthusiastically, though with little success. He seemed delighted just to be in their company, so I was happy for him. Later, he took me to the One O'clock Club in the Moat House Hotel. I had one drink before leaving Dennis to enjoy the rest of his evening.

The next day, I drove towards London, heading for Long John HQ at Queen Anne's Gate. At the entrance, I was met by Ron Lacy, the office manager— a true Londoner. The offices had an old-world charm, like stepping back a hundred years. Most of the desks had table lamps with fringed edges, and at the top of the Edwardian terraced mansion was a room called the "Crow's Nest," used for entertaining. It was filled with Lord Nelson memorabilia, as the building had once been the home of his mistress, Emma Hamilton. The whole place had an upstairs-downstairs feel.

Over the next few years, I ensured that this historic house never burned down. While I knew the lamps were a fire hazard, I let aesthetics, culture, and charm take precedence over strict safety regulations.

As if life weren't busy enough, I took up squash around this time. I quickly realised I wasn't particularly good at it, and when I heard that world champion players were dying of heart attacks, I gave it up. I was never especially sporty—I had played a bit of football and done some cycling—but I did take up marathon running, which I found surprisingly addictive. However, that would have to wait until 1980.

At the end of the year, the company Christmas Ball was held at the Central Hotel. It was a grand and lavish affair, a formal dinner requiring me to buy a dinner suit, while Elaine got a new ball gown.

1979

I settled into a routine, travelling between different locations and compiling my reports. Duncan the Long John MD was extremely pleased with my performance, as the number of accidents and incidents had significantly decreased.

One ongoing issue, however, was the accident rate at Strathclyde distillery. One engineer, Jim Chapman, was responsible for 10% of all accidents in a company of over 1,000 employees. I interviewed him and reviewed his training, tasks, PPE, and accident history. While most incidents were minor, they had potentially serious consequences. The distillery had already suffered a fatality years earlier when Bill Bain was still a junior employee with Long John before his transfer to Glenugie.

After interviewing Jim Chapman, I arranged for him to attend a week-long Health and Safety training course and updated all his PPE. Two weeks after his return, I got the call—he was back in hospital receiving treatment for an eye injury. Fortunately, it was minor. He explained that while welding overhead, a spark had bounced into his visor from behind and settled on his glasses inside the helmet, burning his upper lid.

Some people are accident-prone, and sometimes there are good reasons for it—fatigue or dissatisfaction with their job, for instance. We discussed this, and to be fair to Jim, he did take on many of the more hazardous tasks on-site as an engineer and welder. Overtime, his accidents became less frequent, and I believe simply monitoring him had an effect. Observing behaviour changes behaviour—it's called the "Hawthorne Effect."

At the time, I was studying for my DMS at Glasgow College and particularly enjoying my first-year psychology studies. My namesake, Jim Green #2, had also joined the course. The subjects were quite dry—accountancy and economics were nowhere near as engaging as marketing and psychology. Our lecturer, Stan Lees, was entertaining, and both Jim and I absorbed this new knowledge eagerly. I started reading Warren Bennis on leadership, Mintzberg on organization studies, and Kotler on marketing. I suppose Jim and I were classic BYMBOs—"bright young men being obvious"—though we didn't realise it at the time.

We had company cars, dressed in pinstripe suits with white shirts, silk ties, handkerchiefs, cufflinks, and, of course, black socks. Not only were we learning, but we were also applying what we learned at work. I became particularly interested in analyzing workplace metrics and the behavioral effects on individuals and groups. We weren't highly intelligent in the academic sense—true academics remain skeptical and dive deeper into research. We, on the other hand, wanted to apply what we learned, and we did.

Once a year, we attended summer school at various locations with our lecturers. On one occasion, we spent a long weekend at the Park Hotel in Kilmarnock. There was a guest speaker from Rolls-Royce, plenty of business games, and, after dinner, the inevitable small groups forming around the three girls in our class, each hoping for an invite for coffee in the bedroom. The unwritten rule was simple—what happened at summer school stayed at summer school.

The lecturers were great fun, and we formed lasting friendships with many of them. Jim got on particularly well with Norrie Train, who taught organizational subjects, while I clicked with Dick Weaver from Strathclyde Business School. The coursework was demanding, and in those days, there were no laptops or Google—it was just a hard slog through library books.

I remember visiting the college library one day and chatting with the man checking out books. He was in his 30s and didn't seem particularly happy. When I asked him what was wrong, he said he was bored. "How can you be bored surrounded by all this information?" I asked. His response shocked me—"I can't read." How cruel, I thought. I have always felt privileged to have had a good education, but I've also been acutely aware that many fall through the cracks due to circumstances beyond their control. It could easily have been me, were it not for luck and circumstance.

One day at work, I got a call that a contractor erecting steel at Laphroaig had been hit on the head with a steel bracket. He had been airlifted to the Southern General Hospital's neurosurgical unit in Glasgow. Expecting the worst— serious head trauma, brain damage—I arrived to find him sitting up in bed, laughing. He had a bad cut and a fractured skull, but he was otherwise fine. He felt he had let the side down because he hadn't been wearing his safety helmet. He made a full recovery.

Looking back, many employees blamed themselves for workplace injuries and avoided reporting incidents for fear of losing their jobs. In reality, most accidents stemmed from failures in the Safety Management System. If we had enforced a compulsory hard hat policy at Laphroaig, he might have avoided the injury altogether.

In the summer of 1979, my sister Caroline got married . My parents were strongly against the marriage—her husband was unstable—but it went ahead regardless.

The reception was at the Burnside Hotel in Johnstone. After meeting her husband's parents, I could see why he was the way he was. I had only met the groom once before when he and Caroline came to announce their engagement. I offered them a celebratory drink, and his eyes lit up. It didn't take him long to demolish what was left of my vodka supply. When I offered him some hooch I had distilled, he knocked it back with delight. Right then, I knew there was a problem with him and alcohol.

Their marriage didn't last long. They moved to Corby, near where my brother Stewart and his wife Margaret had settled. He was a trainee chemist, and Caroline, a strong swimmer, took a job at the local swimming pool. But his drinking spiraled out of control, and he became violent. When Caroline slipped at work and damaged her hip socket, she returned home, a shadow of her former self. It took my parents sometime to help her heal. Thankfully, she made a full recovery and in time became a triple graduate.

My sister Caroline's Graduation and me University of Glasgow

Meanwhile, Emma was beginning to walk. She was such a lovely baby—her hair was now more strawberry-blonde than Jennifer's. She was sweet-natured and clung to Elaine constantly.

We decided to go camping again, this time to the Gareloch north of Ullapool. Jimmy Kennovin lent us his little blue box trailer, which made packing much easier, leaving more space for the three kids in the back seat. We set off for Sands Caravan and Camping Site, just opposite Gruinard Island. Nobody told us it was still contaminated with Anthrax.

After a couple of days, our tent was covered in flying beetles, and I developed a strange boil inside my mouth. That was enough—we packed up and headed south to the Isle of Skye. The weather was dreadful, raining non-stop. We ended up taking the kids to the swimming pool in Portree just to stay entertained. We decided that if we ever went camping again, it would be somewhere warm.

That Christmas was wonderful. Jamie got his first bike but threw a tantrum when he struggled to pedal in the driveway. Elaine always made the best of every occasion. Even though money was tight, she found ways to give the kids memorable birthdays, Easter, Halloween, Guy Fawkes Night, and Christmas. Her cooking had improved considerably since we first got married. She had a book titled 50 Ways to Cook Mince and made a fantastic sweet-and-sour dessert with marshmallows, cream, coconut, and pineapple.

On weekends, Elaine's parents watched the kids so we could enjoy a Saturday night out. This usually meant going to John and Marjorie's or Jim and Susan's for a themed dinner party. We had French nights, Italian nights, and so on, taking turns hosting every third Saturday. John would play his guitar, and Jim would charm us all with his stories.

John, a keen marathon runner and talented musician, had moved back to Scotland with Marjorie, settling in Pennyburn, Kilwinning. He had graduated from Paisley College in Land Economics and secured a job as a surveyor with the Irvine Development Corporation. Marjorie was also pregnant at the time.

It was a fun, busy period in our lives as we balanced work and family, navigating all the challenges and joys that came with it.

Jim and I had become good friends, attending DMS classes in the evenings and at weekends. Afterwards, we would often head to the Balnagowan pub in Paisley, or on Sunday nights, if we were working on coursework together, we'd walk up to Friars Hall (the scene of my earlier misdeeds) for brandy and a cigar.

We spent a lot of time discussing work and business. Jim was now with Sperry Univac and becoming more involved in sales, while I continued to enjoy both my job and my studies.

At Christmas, I was invited to the Long John Bottling Plant works party by Charlie Smith. The event was held at the County Inn in Cambuslang, and Charlie asked me to withdraw £200 from petty cash to buy drinks for the staff and workers. All the managers were expected to do the same, mingling and ensuring the money was spent.

It turned out to be a wild night. The alcohol flowed freely, and these folks could certainly drink. As the evening progressed, I was relieved Elaine hadn't come along—by the later hours, the women became quite outrageous. I soon understood why most managers left after the speeches, rarely staying beyond 9:00 p.m. The raffle prizes were impressive, including holidays, luggage sets, and even washing machines from the nearby Hoover factory.

One of the nicer traditions at the bottling plant was the Christmas party for employees' children. Elaine and I took Jamie and Jennifer, who had a great time and received good presents from Santa—played by John Kilbride, the Production Manager. I got on well with John, an ex-Rolls Royce engineer with strong managerial skills. He had previously worked as a consultant for PA Consulting and spent time with Rolls Royce in America. He lived in East Kilbride with his wife, Jessie, and their two daughters.

John could be highly amusing, but alcohol brought out an unpleasant side to him—something that would ultimately lead to his downfall five years later. He was a fervent Rangers supporter, often claiming he was on an IRA death list due to being a Rangers shareholder. His hatred of Catholics always baffled me, given his intelligence. He was also a bully, particularly towards women, and I witnessed him reduce more than one to tears.

I only visited Westhorn Bottling Operation once a week for site inspections and the morning meeting, addressing any issues with Charles Smith or Ronnie Jackson before leaving.

At Strathclyde Distillery, they hosted a Christmas party for all the Long John pensioners, organised by Mike Trotter and his team: Bob Dunning (Administration Manager), Jack Trotter (Engineering Manager), David Ruffle (Lab Manager), and his shift leaders, Danny O'Donnell and Bob Alexander. Mike was a true professional—a gentleman who ran the plant like a Swiss watch.

CHAPTER 26:
GRANNY ISA LEAVES A HOLE
IN MY HEART.

1980

In February, during deep winter, I received a call from Mum to say that Granny Isa had been taken into hospital with a heart problem. I went to visit her that evening, and she was so glad to see me.

I loved this granny more than I can say—because I knew, without doubt, that she loved me. She showed me it every time we were together. Now, as an older man with grandchildren of my own, I truly understood her love and the many ways she tried to help me.

She wasn't in bed but sat beside it. She looked pale, almost grey, yet she was still cheerful when she saw me. I stayed with her for some time until the visitor's bell rang, then gave her a hug and a kiss before leaving.

When I reached my car, I turned to see her at the window, blowing kisses to me. She passed away just after I left.

Dad had the painful task of going around the family to tell them, and I went with him. As the eldest son, he knew that one day, when he was gone, this duty would fall to me.

Even as I write this, I am still heartbroken. I miss her as much as ever, and there remains a big hole in my heart.

Granny Isa

CHAPTER 27:
WORK REST AND PLAY

It's amazing to think that in 1980, there were no laptops or mobile phones, yet businesses managed perfectly well without them. Back then, typists produced letters, reports, and other documents from handwritten drafts. When Jim#2 and I worked on coursework, I would take notes and then try to construct a coherent narrative for the piece. Jim would photocopy texts from several books, cut them into relevant sections, and piece together his reports and assignments—an early form of cutting and pasting.

Meanwhile, in America, IBM was working on its first PC, set to launch the following year. Marketing as a business concept was beginning to take hold, and advertising campaigns were changing the landscape. Benson & Hedges used such striking artistic imagery that they didn't even need to include their name on billboards—everyone knew it was B&H. Smirnoff Vodka boosted its market share to 40% through clever advertising, while Homepride Flour's bowler-hat-wearing flour graders became a hugely effective campaign. I mention this because, at the time, my interests were shifting towards business management and the power of strategic thinking—perhaps as a reaction to my studies.

That summer, the DMS class held a residential weekend in Dunoon. Jim and I took the ferry from Port Glasgow, then drove along the coast to the Glenburn Hotel. The weekend was packed with guest lecturers and business games, and it was clear that our class size had shrunk considerably since the first intake. Our lecturer, Stan Lees, had warned early on that if students treated the DMS like a hobby—choosing it over something like photography or guitar lessons—they wouldn't last. The first-year exams had already eliminated 20% of the original 44 students.

That summer was also special for my family, as my sister Anne married the love of her life, Gordon, at the Church of Scotland in Underwood Road, Paisley. Jennifer was the flower girl. After the ceremony, a coach took us to the MacDonald Hotel in Giffnock for the reception. Anne and Gordon made a wonderful couple, and Gordon was a fantastic brother-in-law to both Elaine and me. As life moved on, we stayed in close touch, and they became invaluable babysitters for us.

1981

In April 1981, a fire broke out at Tormore Distillery, and I was sent to investigate on behalf of the directors at Long John. Fortunately, the fire was contained in an outbuilding used for storage. My investigation confirmed it was caused by faulty electrical wiring. I stayed for a couple of days at the Blair Findy Lodge while I wrote up my report. The lodge was run by a mother and daughter—one retired, the other a supply teacher. It was a wonderful place to stay, with a help-yourself bar and sensational food.

A few months later, when I returned, I brought Elaine with me. Thanks to my in-laws watching the children, we had some rare quality time together. I can still picture waking up on a summer morning to the sound of birds in the Lodge gardens, looking out over the stunning view of Speyside, then sitting down to a hearty full Scottish breakfast before setting off towards Peterhead Distillery—100 miles away through the Whisky Triangle—before making our way back to Glasgow via Perth.

Each month, I did a grand tour, starting in Glasgow and heading west to Kennacraig, where I caught the ferry to Islay. Depending on the route, I would disembark at either Port Ellen or Port Askaig before making my way to Laphroaig Distillery for a couple of days. There, I carried out inspections and often delivered training sessions to the operators. I was invariably hungover by the time I caught the ferry back.

One particularly cold winter morning, I set sail at 08:00. The sea was rough, and at one point, a huge wave crashed over the deck, drenching me from head to toe and filling my pockets with sea water. I spent the next few hours inside the ferry, trying to dry off.

Back on dry land, I would travel to Tormore Distillery on Speyside, a five- hour drive along the A85 via Loch Awe—some of Scotland's most breathtaking countryside. I was always warmly welcomed there, working with managers Adam and Ross. From there, I moved on to Peterhead's Glenugie Distillery.

The next stage of the tour took me south to Plymouth Distillery, where I met up with Bert Roberts, the distillery manager, and Desmond Payne, the chief brewer and a master of wines and spirits. From there, I travelled to London to inspect the company's headquarters at Queen Anne's Gate, meeting with Ron Macey before finally returning to Glasgow. That marked the end of my monthly circuit.

At home, Elaine and I were fortunate to have her mum and Dad as keen babysitters. This meant we could enjoy a Saturday night at the cinema now and then. The most memorable film we saw that year was Gregory's Girl, starring Clare Grogan, Gordon John Sinclair, and Dee Hepburn.

1982

The start of 1982 was much the same as the previous year. I continued travelling across the country in my role as Safety and Fire Advisor, and I was now in my final year of the DMS at Glasgow College.

I had decided to learn more about the packaging industry, so I booked a course run by the Institute of Packaging. It was a week-long programme held in East Grinstead, Mid Sussex. However, one big cloud loomed on the horizon—the Falklands War. My father-in-law, James, had been winding up my brother-in-law and me, insisting this was it—that our call-up was imminent. I never seriously thought it was possible until we started hearing news bulletins from Brian Hanrahan on the BBC news, making it clear we were suffering casualties.

It was difficult to concentrate on the course, and in the evenings, we would retire to The Swan pub, where we had a good drink every night. One afternoon, a couple of delegates and I took a walk through the grounds of the training centre, which were part of an old hospital where WWII burn victims had been treated. As we wandered, a squadron of jet fighters suddenly buzzed us, flying exceptionally low. It startled us, making the war feel much closer than before.

On Thursday night, we all got pissed on draught beer and had a big sing- song before heading off the next morning to our respective homes across the UK. I was so hungover I shouldn't have been driving. As I pressed north through London, I had to stop every few miles—either to be sick or rush to the toilet. By the time I reached Charnock Richard, I had to pull over for a sleep. I was relieved to get home safely and even more relieved that we won the war—or the "conflict," as it was officially declared at the time.

After such a wet holiday the previous year, Elaine found a camping trip in the South of France, run by a travel company called Euroscot. They were based in Kilbirnie, so we went to get booked up one Saturday and paid £400 for a two-week holiday. In July, we boarded the coach and set off towards Dover. The kids were so excited, though the journey was long. Both Elaine and I wore jeans at first but soon changed into shorts as we headed south. The bus was air-conditioned, and under the circumstances, the kids behaved brilliantly. When we stepped off in Lyon for a stretch, the heat hit us—it was sweltering, even at 6am. I grabbed breakfast for us all, and soon we were back on the road.

As we reached the Giens Peninsula, we saw the deep blue Mediterranean and the little island of Porquerolles. Passing through Hyères, we finally arrived at the Clair de Lune campsite. The heat hit us again, as did the relief of getting off the coach at last. Our ready-made tent was on a terrace up a short hill. We settled in quickly, and I headed to the camp shop for some bread while Elaine made a meal. The kids were desperate to get to the beach, which was only a few hundred yards away.

As I emerged from the tent, still adjusting to the holiday, I turned my head and caught sight of a young topless woman. I had forgotten that the French enjoy the freedom of going naked on the beach. Turning to Elaine, who had also noticed, I joked that this might be a good holiday after all. She shot back, "I'm watching you, Sunny Jim."

The beach was fantastic. The kids loved the water—Emma was just a toddler, but Jamie and Jennifer were like fish. As we walked along the shore, noticing the topless sunbathers, I told Elaine that if she was going to go topless, she should do it now to avoid tan lines. She didn't need much persuasion and soon embraced the naked freedom. I bought a large inflatable ring for the kids, which they played with for hours, making new friends along the way.

Elaine was extremely careful with sunblock, as our kids are very fair- skinned—especially the girls, who are both redheads. On the second day, the campsite had organised play leaders, and Jamie and Jennifer were happy to join in. When Jenni left, she had her sunblock on and was wearing a white T-shirt. When she returned, the shirt was gone, and she had got burned. As she got older, the burn scar changed, and now she has to have it regularly checked.

On the third day, I was swimming with the kids, who were playing with a friend in the inflatable ring. I noticed they were drifting further out to sea, so I swam after them. As I grabbed the ring, it suddenly burst. I could just touch the seabed with my toes, but the kids would struggle in the deep water. Grabbing the torn ring, I managed to pull them safely to shore, feeling an immense sense of relief.

In the evenings, once the kids were in bed, we socialized with John—an older man in his seventies—and his two girlfriends. He was quite the character. We sat around a plastic table, drinking brandy and wine, listening to French families playing the accordion. One night, John asked, "Do you know anything about insect bites?" He rolled up his sleeve to reveal a massive, golf-ball-sized lump near his elbow. "Jesus, Gus, that needs a doctor," I told him.

The next day, John had to go to hospital to have it removed.

During day trips, we explored the market in Hyères and, on Bastille Day, watched fireworks from La Tour Fondue, overlooking the Île de Porquerolles. On the mile-long walk back to camp, I carried Emma on my shoulders. As we passed a tree, I tugged on what I thought was a hanging belt—only to realise, to my horror, that it was a snake.

A trip to the local supermarché led to another mishap. I accidentally bought horsemeat instead of beef. When Emma found out, she was sick all over the supermarket floor.

It was a great holiday, but eventually, it was time to head home. We boarded the coach, and many passengers had taken advantage of the ridiculously cheap wine. Some had even bought flagons from the local wineries. We stopped briefly in Lyon and had a longer break in Paris, where Elaine was determined to see the Eiffel Tower and the Arc de Triomphe. By this point, she was best friends with John's two girlfriends, and they trailed after her at high speed as she squeezed the sightseeing into under an hour. The poor old ladies were utterly exhausted when they returned to the coach.

Before we reached the ferry at Dover, the bus driver warned us about customs allowances. Those with flagons of wine were in trouble. He told them they either had to leave the wine in France or drink it. Not a single drop was left behind. As a result, some very pissed holidaymakers returned to the UK. Fortunately, it was night-time, so most of them snored their way home.

A few weeks later, John and his girlfriend's came to visit us. It was genuinely lovely to see them again.

CHAPTER 28:
ORGANISED CRIME

On my first day back at work, I took a break from the office and walked down Bothwell Street, past Central Station, and finished up in Buchanan Street. I went into Frasers for a browse, and as I was walking through the shoe section, I noticed a pair of silver-buckled shoes for a little girl. They were about £80, which was quite expensive for children's shoes, but I had to have them for Jenni. I have never been particularly prudent with money, often acting on impulse, so I bought them without hesitation. I did the same with a G Plan dining table and chairs. Elaine and I have reasonable taste, and we tend to complement each other in our choices, but I generally prefer Elaine to take the lead—she has much better judgement than I do when it comes to home furnishings and design.

After browsing, I sat on one of the black marble stones in Buchanan Street and reflected on our French holiday. However, things were about to change—a new chapter in my life was beginning.

Back at the office, Duncan Grieg's secretary, Anne Livingston, told me he was looking for me and that I should go straight to his office. When I stepped into the cigar-smoke-filled room, he was forthright. "Have a seat," he said. He explained that Jack Andrews, the head of security at Westhorn Bottling Plant, was seriously ill with cancer and would not be returning to work. In the meantime, he needed me to manage security operations until a replacement could be found. I was to report to Charles Smith, the Westhorn General Manager, and combine the role with my existing Safety and Fire duties, cutting back on travel to accommodate both roles. He reassured me that he was pleased with my work and that I had a promising career ahead.

The next morning, I drove straight to Westhorn, located on London Road in Glasgow's East End, near Celtic Football Club at Parkhead.

I sat across from Charles Smith as he launched into a lecture. He told me that he saw me as a 'black and white' man in a world that was largely grey. He made it clear that he did not want me reporting any issues to the directors without informing him first. Then, unexpectedly, he got up, locked the office door, and returned to his seat.

He looked me in the eye. "Do you like guns?"

I told him I had no experience with them. He then revealed that he was president of a gun club, pulled open a desk drawer, and took out a canvas holster containing a handgun. He handed it to me, inviting me to feel its weight. Stupidly, I covered it in fingerprints as I examined it.

Charles invited me to join his gun club, and I said I'd think about it. He then handed me two-gun club magazines. My knees were beginning to feel like jelly when he walked over to a cupboard, opened it, and revealed boxes of ammunition—2,000 rounds, he declared. He then handed me a heavy metal box containing about 20 high-caliber bullets. "Look closely," he said, pointing to the tips. They were hollowed out.

"These are dum-dums," he said. "Banned by the Geneva Convention. They'd take your head clean off."

Then, as if the conversation had taken a perfectly normal turn, he asked,

"Would you like a cup of tea?"

My hands were shaking as I declined.

Next, he produced a cardboard box filled with keys. Jack Andrews, he explained, had been trying to match them to locks on-site, and I was to continue this as an ongoing project. He assigned Alan Addison, the senior security officer, to help me familiarize myself with my new responsibilities.

Whisky premises are bonded under strict regulations by Her Majesty's Customs and Excise (HMCE). Officers range in grade, with Watchers and Collectors being the most senior ranks. Whisky can only leave the premises once records are in place and duties are paid—a process with no room for error.

Allan Addison introduced me to the security team, all retired Glasgow police officers, and took me to the kennels, where we had four police-trained Alsatians. As I entered the security building, a huge Alsatian suddenly leapt at me, only to be yanked back hard by its leash, which had been tethered to a floor hook. My new team had set it up as a joke. They struggled to conceal their childish glee, but I was not amused. I was, however, beginning to get a feel for the nature of this new environment.

Upstairs, I was shown into Jack Andrews' office, a large space overlooking the warehouses and barrel park. I set up a coffee percolator and sifted through Jack's cupboard, boxing up his personal effects. Smith had already told me that Jack wouldn't be returning—his cancer was terminal. In his locker, I found two uniforms: one for an Inspector of Police and another for a senior industrial security officer, complete with a cap bearing silver braided insignia. I vowed I would never wear that uniform.

From day one, it was clear something wasn't right at Westhorn. Addison was tracking my every move and reporting back to Smith. The best I could do was manage security operations and document my progress.

That summer, I received a message from the local CID: a wages heist was being planned at Westhorn bottling operation at 1780 London Road. At the time, most wages were paid in cash, meaning a weekly haul of £150,000 was up for grabs. Police intelligence was solid, so a covert operation was put in place.

The wages arrived in bulk cash and were sorted in a secure room within the security building next to my office—also home to the site's radio base station. Several armed officers were stationed throughout the factory, disguised as workers.

The expected entry point was via St Peter's Cemetery on the factory boundary, where an internal road led up to a vulnerable section of the security building's perimeter. A vehicle could easily ram through the wall.

We expected the heist at 14:00. Tension was palpable among the wages staff; the Police assured them they were perfectly safe. The wait dragged on until 14:30, when word came through—the heist had already taken place offsite, at Bridgeton Cross, about a mile away. The robbers made off with the entire £150,000 payroll. The G4 wages van was later found burned out, along with a getaway car abandoned a few streets away.

Clearly, the criminals had been tipped off.

It took G4 three hours to prepare replacement wages. Under armed police guard, the workers were finally paid in the Westhorn canteen.

As the days passed, I found it harder to sleep at night. I was now constantly carrying a site radio—call sign 'Westhorn 1'—even at home, where I listened to routine updates from the officers.

Over the next few months, I became increasingly aware that something was seriously wrong at the site. Criminal forces were at play, and Smith was at the centre of it all, running an internal organization built around his nefarious activities. His right-hand man, Ronnie Jackson, was in his 50s like Smith and had worked for him for twenty years. Smith had ensured that Ronnie was promoted well beyond his capabilities. Next in line was David McClum, the bottling manager, a man in his thirties who controlled the bottling and packaging of around 50,000 cases of whisky each week. Then there was Jimmy James, the bottling engineer—another who had risen arguably far above his competence. Crucially, he had a direct link to Glasgow's gangland via his cousin, the notorious Arthur Simpson.

At morning meetings, these men spoke in code and openly flaunted wads of cash. They dressed in the finest suits and carried themselves like gangsters. As a young man, I was not seen as a threat, and from time to time, they let their guard down. My orders from Duncan Grieg were simple—support operations until a replacement was found.

However, after six months, no replacement had materialized, and instead, I received news that I was getting a new boss.

Jim O'Neil was already a director in Whitworth's retail division. His Irish family was moving to Glasgow so he could take on the role of Director of Personnel for Long John International Limited. An accomplished professional, educated at Queen's University

Belfast, he had a no-nonsense, direct approach. I liked him immediately. In our first meeting, he asked me for a full briefing on what was happening across the sites, particularly at Westhorn.

Over the next few weeks, he spent more time with me, and I soon realised Jim was on a mission. He had bought a house on Terregles Avenue in Glasgow's affluent Pollokshields area and asked if I could use my Master of Works skills to help get it ready. I arranged for contractors to install a new kitchen and double glazing—all at company expense. One day, a lorry arrived carrying a team of gardeners and landscaping equipment. To my surprise, they were the same contractors from Westhorn. Jim had no idea— this was the result of a casual remark he had made to Smith about the garden being in a state. Smith, always keen to keep people "in his pocket," had taken care of it without being asked.

Once Jim's family had settled in, he invited me to dinner. That evening, he revealed his true purpose.

Whitworth's directors had received intelligence that serious criminal activities were taking place at Westhorn, led by Smith. The scheme was not just about skimming off whisky to sell on the black market. The gang was bartering stolen whisky with British military personnel in the Scottish Borders for bullets and weapons, which were then supplied to the UDA in Northern Ireland. MI5 and MI6 were already involved, along with a senior investigation by HM Customs & Excise.

Now, careful monitoring was required, and Jim asked me to support the investigation—strictly confidential, of course. Effectively, he was asking me to become an industrial spy.

The risks were obvious. After six weeks of observation, their operation became clear. They had two major methods of siphoning off whisky for illegal sale.

The first was relatively minor, involving the test lab next to the security building. The site logbooks showed that the gang of four was regularly active there over weekends. Every barrel of whisky had to pass strict quality control tests, which meant drawing off a one-pint sample from each cask. While one pint per cask seemed insignificant, with 50,000 cases processed per week, this amounted to around 2,000 full-strength samples—equal to 4,000 standard 40% ABV bottles. That added up to roughly 300 cases per week, sold on the black market at £60 per case, generating £18,000 weekly. While this didn't happen every single week, it was frequent enough that an average of 200 cases per week could be moved, bringing in clear profits of at least £500,000 a year.

The second scam was far more sophisticated, exploiting the 2% process loss allowance permitted by HM Customs & Excise at each stage of production.

Whisky could "legitimately" go missing (The Angels Share) at several points: from cask to disgorging tanks, from tanks to bottling vats, from vats to filling machines, and finally, from filling machines to cased goods. Smith ensured that even the C&E inspectors received a free case every Friday night to keep them complacent.(It was more like the Devils Share)

After each bottling run, leftover whisky in the vats and tanks should have been returned to bulk storage. Instead, a quick calculation determined how much could be rebottled within the allowed loss margin without raising suspicion. If 500 litres remained, it would be bottled under the same rotation numbers as the original batch, creating 666 extra cases with a secret mark. External stock controllers never noticed—they only checked the numbers on file. The surplus cases never stayed long in the warehouse; Smith moved them out over the weekend.

In practical terms, this amounted to one container load per week—1,000 cases, each worth £60. That meant £60,000 per week or £3 million per year.

Smith lived well on the proceeds: a comfortable house in a leafy suburb, a boat, and a mistress. Ronnie Jackson's relatives benefited through the licensed trade, while Jimmy James had the criminal underworld at his disposal. Even allowing for disruptions, this was a massive operation.

They might have continued indefinitely had they not tied up with the UDA and Arthur Simpson. But serious crime at this level demands serious connections—money, guns, and explosives.

As this all unfolded before me, I realised how deep I was in. I had been naïve, but now, I was afraid for my life.

O'Neil wanted a daily briefing and took the meetings off-site as often as possible. Eventually, it came down to me producing evidence that went back as far as possible so the activities could be properly quantified. However, this was going to be self-defeating for Whitworth PLC, as all the duty on the lost whisky would have to be repaid to the Crown. I knew that if I asked for all the diaries, Addison would let Smith know, and I would be in danger. I didn't even know if the logbooks existed.

Around this time, Smith was becoming aware that he was under scrutiny. One afternoon, he invited me for tea. I noticed he had two phones in his office, one of which was concealed inside a low-level cupboard. The plant at Westhorn was serviced by Sutcliffe's, the industrial catering company, so he called them and asked for tea for two in his office as soon as possible. It didn't take long for the tea and sandwiches to arrive. He closed the door and locked it, and my heart pounded with adrenaline.

He was very friendly, and I knew this was a cat-and-mouse game. Taking a large bite of a cream and jam scone, crumbs rolled down his tie. Then he reached for his drawer, and I was shitting myself.

"Help yourself, Jim. Have some tea and sandwiches."

As I approached his desk, he took out an envelope and placed it in front of me. For a moment, I thought he was about to bribe me. My cup rattled on its saucer as I tried to control my worst fears, and I took a token bite of a small salmon sandwich.

"Have a look at the contents, Jim."

Cautiously, I pulled out about half a dozen black-and-white photographs. They showed a man hanging dead from a tree in the grounds of Westhorn from different angles. Another showed a man whose head had been crushed by a barrel, his skull shattered, brains spilled out. It took everything in me not to heave. I gently pushed them back into the envelope, meeting Smith's gaze—he was boring into me, right through to my soul.

"That's a bit graphic," I said, trying to sound unfazed. "I wish you hadn't shown me without warning."

He let out a big belly laugh.

"Lesson number one, Jim, we are surrounded by death. Who knows? Maybe it'll be me next. Or you. You should know that as our resident safety and security man."

I was being toyed with, intimidated. But I had one advantage—Smith believed there was already a mole on-site. He suspected the transport manager, Phil Judd, a cocky Englishman forced on Westhorn by the parent company. That made him suspect number one.

Smith leaned back in his chair. "Avoid him, Jim. Don't tell him anything."

Then, just like that, he let me out of his office with a slap on the back and a smile.

"Just keep me up to date, Jim. I'm always here if you need me."

When I updated Jim O'Neil, he was alarmed and arranged a high-level meeting at his house with Charles Striker, a Whitworth main board director, along with David Muir, the current HR manager, and John Kilbride, head of administration at Westhorn. John was an external consultant who had moved into the company with a permanent contract—ex-Rolls Royce.

After this meeting, I was given a clear brief: secure the evidence as soon as possible.

I had a hunch that the plant manager, David Ferrie, might be able to help. I genuinely considered him, along with several others, good people who had been caught up in this web of crime. Searching through Jack's cupboards, I discovered a 'black museum'—exhibits of the many devices used to steal whisky. Small hand drills, water bottles, thermos flasks—all adapted for siphoning off whisky for drinking or sale. The most ingenious was a padded jacket with a long length of plastic tubing sewn into the middle layer of fabric. One end was sealed, while the other had a small plastic valve.

The method was simple: a vacuum was created inside the tube using a small pump, and the valve was closed off. From any source on-site—cask, tank, or pipe—the nozzle could be inserted, the valve opened, and whisky would be sucked into the tube. Each time, about three bottles could be removed. If it was cask strength, it could be diluted to create six bottles for sale or consumption.

The investigation revealed that this man had been taking neat whisky every working day for three years—worth about £20,000 on the black market.

In one of Jack's locked drawers, I also found a pile of poison pen letters. It would be delusional to think company directors don't know what goes on in their factories, shops, and offices. Reading these letters convinced me that human beings are capable of astonishing mischief and destruction within organizations. Affairs, thefts, sexual abuse, cruelty, alcoholism, racial and sexual orientation hate, nepotism—you name it. Some individuals were extremely keen to ensure directors knew exactly who was doing what, when, and where. The directors had passed these letters on to Jack for investigation. When I enquired with Personnel about the outcomes, about half were substantiated. The rest were just malicious.

Taking a chance, I asked David Ferrie if there was an archive store on-site for old records. He was sure there was and directed me to a storeroom near the old cooperage. He pointed to two broad metal cabinets, held shut with nuts and bolts. David helped me open them and inside were all the diaries— at least ten years' worth. A quick look confirmed everything: the weekend movements of the Gang of Four, transport records, even vehicle registration numbers.

I asked David to keep this quiet, and to his credit, he did. He was like many of the innocent, compromised employees—just trying to do a good job without getting tangled in organised crime.

Taking no chances, I waited until no one was looking, loaded all the diaries into my car, and left the site, heading straight for Terreagles Avenue.

Jim O'Neil was delighted. We could now proceed.

But it wasn't going to be easy. Or without risk.

It was a Friday in the second week of November when I received a telephone call from Ian Dewar, the Chairperson of Long John International and Chairman of the Scottish Whisky Association. He informed me that the "Gang of Four" would be summoned to HQ in Bothwell Street to discuss operational issues and that I was to secure the site. They were sent a taxi, leaving their company cars at Westhorn. The only problem was that Ronnie Jackson was running late.

The taxi picked up Smith, James, and Mac, while Smith was frantically trying to find out what was happening. I locked all the offices and stationed a security guard at every door. About an hour after the others had left for head office, Ronnie Jackson arrived. As soon as he parked his car, I intercepted him.

"You need to go straight to Bothwell Street for a meeting with the Chairman. A taxi has been arranged."

He hesitated. "Can I just grab something from my boot?"

I reluctantly agreed, and when he opened it, it was full of whisky cases. He knew the game was up. But instead of reacting, he simply asked, "Do you know what's going on?"

"All I know is that you need to go to Bothwell Street." He glanced towards his office. "Can I get back in?" "The doors are locked," I replied.

He took in a deep slow breath. "This must be serious, then. Do I need a lawyer?" "I think you should just go to the meeting."

The taxi arrived, and he left. I never saw any of those men again.

Back in the offices, the atmosphere was buzzing. Everyone knew something serious was happening, and for the moment, I was in control of the site. An hour later, Ian Dewar called again.

"The four managers have been summarily dismissed. They won't be returning to Westhorn."

I was also invited to an afternoon meeting to help plan how the company would continue operations after losing four senior managers. It was agreed that Adam Johns, the Manager of Tormore Distillery, would act as temporary General Manager.

Over the following days, whisky operations continued as normal. I had to pack up the personal effects of the Gang of Four and send them to their home addresses. A list had been drawn up of all the key figures in the "Smith Empire," detailing who should be replaced and when. The problem was that the corruption ran so deep that if we cut out all of it at once, the company would collapse. So, over the next year, major staffing and management changes were planned.

Phil Judd left to return to a Whitworth transport job in England. Some older staff members were retired early, and new people took their places. The first big change was that I was replaced by Roy Standhope, the new Security and Safety Adviser—an ex-Military Police Major who had moved to Glasgow with his family. Next, I was promoted to Operations Manager, overseeing production, warehousing, vatting, and engineering.

A few weeks later, Jim O'Neil took me aside.

"You have a great future ahead," he said. "I'm heading back to Whitworth Retail in Bedford."

I was disappointed. I believed he was needed to help stabilize the new organization. On top of that, with the exposure of the crimes, we had serious investigations underway—from Customs & Excise to Special Branch, not to mention the gun and ammunition found in Smith's office. Smith had been charged with possession of an illegal firearm—one that had my fingerprints all over it.

Company lawyers and Smith's legal team were preparing for trial. Smith had hired Joe Benson, the famous Glasgow criminal lawyer, known for representing the underworld figures like Arthur Thompson. The trial was set for April 1983.

As Christmas approached, I was scheduled to conduct a final inspection of Strathclyde Distillery in the Gorbals, near the city centre. Walking past the tank farm, I suddenly heard two shots. The bullets ricocheted off steelwork. Instinctively, I threw myself behind a tank and stayed put.

I grabbed my radio. "Control, I need police here. Now."

An armed unit arrived within ten minutes. They searched the entire high-rise block overlooking the site, but no weapon or sniper was found. The officers told me it was meant to scare me. It worked. The bullets were 0.22 caliber. I had to file a full report.

When Jim O'Neil heard what had happened, he came to my house.

"Don't worry," he assured Elaine and me. "I'll make sure you're safe."

That night, I looked at my kids and thought about what life would be like for them without a father. I knew I had to change things—soon.

I took a few days off. When O'Neil called, he said it was safe to return.

Back at work, Christmas was approaching, along with the annual company dinner dance—an extravagant black-tie event where Long John spared no expense. That evening, O'Neil pulled Elaine and me aside into a private room.

"Arrangements have been made," he said. "You won't be in danger anymore."

Whatever Whitworth did remains buried in some corporate file, but there were no further incidents. That was good enough for me. Still, I had made up my mind—I needed a new plan.

I was then formally appointed as the new Production Operations Manager.

The New Production Operations Manager

1983

I got on with my new job and spent some time helping Roy Standhope familiarize himself with the company and find a house. Over time, Roy became a great friend, and we travelled extensively throughout the UK and Europe.

In April, we were summoned to court as witnesses for the prosecution. There were three of us in the witness room at Glasgow Sheriff Court—me, Jim O'Neil, and John McDade. We arrived at 10:00 am, none of us looking forward to facing Smith. By 2:00 pm, Jim O'Neil was getting agitated and asked why we hadn't been called in. Fifteen minutes later, we were informed that we wouldn't be needed Smith had pleaded guilty and wasn't offering a defense.

After that, there was no further mention of the UDA, although Long John had to pay a massive settlement to Customs & Excise for lost revenue on stolen whisky.

As Operations Manager, I threw myself into the job, usually being the first manager in and the last to leave. I had to decide how best to secure my family's future—whether to climb the greasy pole at Whitworth PLC or start my own business. After everything I had been through, I knew it had to be the latter, but first, I had something to complete.

The Chartered Graduate author

After finishing my DMS postgraduate course, I had enrolled at the University of Glasgow Business School to pursue an MBA. It had been my ambition since 1977, knowing that it was a prestigious qualification that would benefit me—whether in my own business or elsewhere.

Returning to Business School, I once again met David Boddy, who interviewed me. He remembered me from three years earlier and was impressed by my distinction in the DMS, as well as the strong academic references from Dick Weaver and Norrie Train at Glasgow College. He shook my hand and welcomed me in.

I phoned my friend, Jim Green#2, to share the news. The best part? Long John International was covering all my fees. An MBA at Harvard would have cost $100,000, so completing it while staying with Long John was well worth it.

CHAPTER 29:
THREATS AND RETRIBUTION

The children were growing up, and we indulged them as best we could. Jamie loved the outdoors, so when we went on picnics up north, he would wander off to explore. We tried to get away most weekends. Elaine took the girls to the Helen Young School of Dancing, while Jamie helped me with routine jobs around the house and garden. He was getting bigger, and up until now, he had been sleeping in the box room, which was becoming too small for him.

He was due to go on a school trip to France for two weeks, so Elaine and I decided to surprise him by converting the attic into a studio while he was away. We had a Velux window fitted and, over the two weeks, transformed the attic into a proper room for him—fully decorated, with a new bed and an access ladder. He was thrilled when he saw it, and Elaine and I were utterly exhausted after working into the small hours to get it finished.

At work, I had been tasked with improving efficiency and was invited to join Whitworth's Scientific Committee forum that explored new ways of enhancing business through technology, science, and process improvements. It was particularly useful for me in understanding innovations such as IT, gene manipulation of yeast strains to increase alcohol yields in brewing, and heat recovery for distilleries. I gained insights into the difference between efficiency and effectiveness and how corporate decisions were made. After a year, I was made Chair of the committee.

I applied these skills to develop plans for improving production by investing in new equipment. I also studied and became a member of the Institute of Packaging. People in industry began to network with me, and on more than one occasion, I was asked to produce business plans for other ventures.

I improved production by 40%, reducing unit costs and significantly boosting LJI's profits. I received letters of appreciation from Ian Dewar, along with bonuses and shares.

Having completed the first wave of improvements through equipment and systems, I now faced a difficult task—reducing the workforce by about 10%.

Half of the employees wanted redundancy, while the other half did not. Some women in their 30s, who had been with LJI since they were 15, were entitled to substantial lump sums. Many wanted to start a family or buy a new house. The challenge was that some of them were among our best employees, and I needed them. On the other hand, an older engineer—who I was keen to let go—fought to stay, fearing he would never find work again. In the end, I managed the process as best I could, but there were tears and gnashing of teeth.

One incident I remember well from this time involved an employee with a notorious reputation. He was a hard worker but known as a "razor king"— someone who would quite literally cut your ears off for no reason. Willie "Cut-the-Lugs" was about 28 but looked much older.

One day, I was on the observation deck overlooking the bottling operations when I saw Willie violently hurling his hand truck at a pallet. I shouted at him to stop and report to my office, which he did—reluctantly. We had a quiet conversation where I made it clear his behaviour was unacceptable, but he leered at me in a defiant and aggressive manner. I issued him a verbal warning in front of his supervisor and recorded it in his HR file.

An hour later, I was back on the observation deck when I noticed Page making a gesture to me—dragging his finger along his ear, implying that mine would soon be coming off. I immediately called security and had him removed from the site. Officially, he was suspended pending an inquiry. However, that night, he attended a stag party, got drunk, and picked a fight with the wrong man. He was taken outside and beaten within an inch of his life, landing him in hospital for six months.

When he eventually was allowed to returned to work, he was full of apologies—both to me and to others. He also underwent aggression counselling.

The strange thing about all of this was that it left me with an unexpected reputation—as a spy, a giant killer, and a gangster. This created a mix of fear and perfunctory respect. From that point on, my working life became considerably easier. While I still faced plenty of challenges, I felt stable and happy.

Whitworth PLC had already appointed the new general manager, Adam Johns, bringing him down from Tormore Distillery to stabilize operations. From day one, it was clear he didn't like me. He was listening to too many stories and saw me as a threat.

I needed to recruit a new Engineering Manager, so after running a recruitment campaign, I shortlisted ten candidates. I took the list to John Kilbride, now Head of Production.

"What interview technique did you use to prepare the list?" he asked.

"I used the Whitworth WASP technique, John."

"Great stuff—so how come we have a guy called Brendan O'Hara on the list?"

I had never been bigoted, so I replied, "W= Welcome, A = Ask questions, S= Supply information, P = Part on good terms."

"Naw, naw, naw, son. White Anglo-Saxon Protestant."

In the end, I appointed Douglas Smith, the Bottling Manager at W. Grant & Sons whisky operations in Paisley. I had known Douglas from school, and he had defended me from his pals at college during a fight, and we were both at Camphill together. He had a solid reputation as a good manager. Adam Johns immediately took a liking to him, and Douglas saw his future with Adam Johns. John Kilbride was also pleased, as Douglas was "a true-blue nose."(Rangers Supporter)

All the old directors had now left the company. Whitworth was more than displeased that Chic Smith had managed to get away with his crimes under their noses. They appointed a new Technical

Director, Ian Wilson, who asked me to draw up plans for a revitalized bottling operation.

I identified all the limiting factors and issued a proposal, and the board approved a significant budget—£2.5 million—to make the bottling operations more efficient.

CHAPTER 30:
EUROPE AMERICA AND
CANADA

During the last six months of 1983, I went on several trips to look at new packaging equipment for the bottling operation. The first trip was to various locations in the UK. John Kilbride, the production manager, wanted to accompany me, which was great as we got on very well. We booked into the Tollbooth Inn in Dedham Vale, where the guest chef at the time was the celebrated Robert Carrier.

John loved to travel first class, and before we set off, four bottles of whisky were packed in our cases—meant as gifts for our hosts at the various packaging equipment sites. However, I suspect John drank them over the course of the week.

Our next trip was to a large packaging exhibition called All-Pack Emballage in Paris located in the Nord 2 area, where all the major equipment companies—Stork Bepak, Krones, Bosch, and Stackpole Phin— were highlighting their latest innovations. These companies were keen to secure a share of the £2.5 million budget, so John and I were in high demand at their stands. Stork Bepak invited us to a reception at a luxury hotel in Paris. The young hosts, all dressed in Scottish kilts, ensured there was plenty of champagne.

John, feeling peckish, asked if there was any food, and the hosts directed him to a table piled high with canapés filled with red and black caviar. Unaware of its value, he ate what must have been about £1,000 worth of Royal Beluga caviar. Still hungry, we later found a French restaurant for dinner. The menu was entirely in French, so we ordered somewhat blindly. John grinned when his beef bourguignon arrived but nearly fell out of his chair laughing when he saw a waiter pushing a trolley laden with live seafood towards me on ice.

After dinner, I felt a bit queasy from the seafood, so John took me to the hotel bar and ordered a double cognac to 'kill off' whatever was still alive in my stomach. That night, we met up with John

Dougal, the LJI QA Manager, who had also been invited to the exhibition. Keen to do his own thing, he soon left us to it.

From Paris, John and I flew first-class on Air France to Chicago O'Hare, on route to another exhibition at the McCormick Place Convention Centre on East Lakeshore (Michigan). Jet-lagged and hungover, I suggested we check into our hotel, the Palmer House on East Monroe Street, for a couple of hours' sleep. After an hour, John was banging on my door—not wanting to waste any drinking time.

We went down to the Potter's Bar, which was filled with well-dressed, middle-class Black professionals, mostly from Chicago University and IBM. Though we were the only white faces in the room, we were warmly welcomed and had a fantastic evening, drinking large Jack Daniel's bourbons and chatting with the locals.

The next day, we attended the exhibition. I usually spent my time at the various stands talking to the technical teams, taking notes on my Dictaphone. That evening, I parted ways with John, as he had been summoned back to Westhorn, while I planned to travel up to Canada. Before I left, John informed me that John Dougal had been mugged in Paris, losing his wallet in the process.

With time to kill before my flight, I went to the Palmer House basement, where I got an excellent American-style haircut, complete with a head, neck, and shoulder massage.

In Canada, I met Neil James from Stackpole Phin Labelers, based in Scarborough, Toronto, and Gus McDonald, the sales director for Krone, also based in Mississauga, Toronto. I spent the first few days with Gus, inspecting Krone's filling equipment. A Scotsman originally from Broxburn, Gus had settled in Scarborough with his wife, Mary, and their young daughter in a three-storey townhouse. Knowing I had been away from home for weeks, he invited me over for dinner. In his basement, he had created a Scottish grotto dedicated to Glasgow Rangers and pipe bands. We ate mince and tatties, washed down with McEwan's Export beer.

I was staying at the Plaza II Hotel on Bloor Street, where I later met Neil James for dinner. He brought his wife and her friend to make up a foursome, and they gave me some great insights into Canadian culture.

The following day, Neil took me to see several locations where Stackpole had installed its machinery. First, we visited a contract packaging company in Scarborough that filled and labelled plastic lube oil containers. Then, we toured the Noxzema cosmetic factory in Toronto. After that, I arranged to travel from Toronto to Windsor, on the Canadian American border, to visit the Canadian Club distillery on Riverside Drive.

At the distillery, we were greeted by Len Morhalo, the general manager, who was the perfect host, giving us a tour of the historic property. The distillery had once belonged to Hiram Walker and had reportedly been a favourite haunt of Al Capone. There were rumors that the Canadian Club was run by the Mafia. While I knew of a Canadian Mafia cell in Brownsville, it would be unfair to speculate further.

However, I did see firsthand how much the Mafia valued alcohol. A few weeks after I returned from Canada, we received a visit from an Italian distributor requesting a supply of 3-centilitre miniature whisky bottles with export label strip stamps. When they arrived at Westhorn, they were mob-handed, and their leader introduced himself simply as 'Don.' John Dougal, not catching the significance, turned to me and whispered, "That's a funny name for an Italian."

Whoever these men were, the request was taken very seriously. We were tasked with finding a way to produce 3cl whisky miniatures with no budgetary restrictions. Their only additional requirement was that the bottles had to be plastic for the airline business.

This set in motion a series of related trips abroad—each one memorable in its own way.

The first trip was to Stork Bapak's factory in Utrecht, Holland, where I took Douglas Smith with me. We had to meet the sales director, Pym Van Duisburg, who was working on a technical solution with Stork. We stayed at the Sonesta Hotel in central Amsterdam, and Pym treated us to a night in the town. The next day, he drove us to Utrecht, where we met the rest of his team, including Renus Van Dongen and Bus Dunevik. We were pleased with the technical specifications and the price, so we placed a purchase order and vowed to return for testing later in the year.

Douglas and I checked into a local hotel (the Holiday Inn) in Utrecht that afternoon. Before dinner, we decided to go for a sauna and swim. I didn't have any swimming shorts, so I wore my Y-fronts back to front, which Douglas found hilarious. We swam, went to the sauna, and took a cold plunge. On our final visit to the sauna, we unexpectedly found ourselves in the company of two naked women, which made me smile and Douglas laugh. He kept laughing, and when I asked what was so funny, he pointed at my crotch. My cold-shocked manhood had popped out of a hole in my shorts like a fat prawn.

That evening, we met up with Pym and his team for a meal and a tour of Canal Strasse, where we got very drunk. In the morning, Renus picked us up and took us to the airport, where we had arranged to fly over the Alps to Bern, Switzerland. I was completely hungover as we boarded the 24-seater Cessna aircraft. I was sick during the flight and must have smelled awful, as I got many unpleasant looks from my fellow passengers. I looked like death and received a hard time from border control.

On our way to BCM in Hésingue, on the French border with Switzerland, I asked Douglas to take the meeting and pretend to be me. Douglas, being Douglas, agreed. I sat quietly taking notes and excused myself every 15 minutes to be sick. We ordered a BCM 1000 unscrambler for plastic bottles.

When we returned to Glasgow, I was summoned by Adam Johns, who told me that the director of BCM was pleased to receive the order but felt it would be best if Douglas didn't return to the factory until he had recovered from his sickness.

The next trip was to find a Monoblock machine that would fill and cap the miniatures. There was only one such machine in the world, produced by the TI Group, which owned Rolls-Royce. The contract for this machine would go to either Stork or Krones, who would manage it as a turnkey project. John Smyth, the senior sales engineer from Stork, arranged a visit to the only Monoblock producing miniatures, located at the Martell Brandy operations in Cognac, France.

A few days before our flight, John Smyth told us that a unique opportunity had arisen— the company's private jet was available to take us from Glasgow to France. There were 10 seats on the jet, and we were allowed to bring our wives. Adam Johns declined, but I invited Elaine, as she had never flown before.

At Glasgow Airport, we met the two pilots, who personally carried our baggage onto the aircraft. Security was much laxer in those days, and we passed through customs with ease.

The jet had the letters G-BIZZ on the fuselage. We climbed a short step into a beautifully appointed interior with dark blue velvet upholstery. The pilot pointed out pull-out drawers under the seats containing safety equipment and a compartment stocked with wine, beer, and snacks. Elaine looked a little apprehensive, but the pilots soon put us at ease, and we were on our way.

Taking off in a jump jet is unlike any other aircraft— the runway time is short, and the ascent is steep. Elaine's eyes twinkled with excitement. Also on board were Adam Johns and John Smyth.

When we reached Paris, the pilots invited Elaine into the cockpit for a circular tour of the city, including the Sacré-Cœur. It was a special moment for her— I imagine that if you've never flown before, it doesn't get much better than that.

We landed at a private airfield in Cergy, north of Paris, and were driven in a black Citroën limo to the Belin Biscuit Factory in Évry, south of Paris, to inspect palletizing machinery. We then returned to the airport and flew down to Bordeaux, where another limousine collected us.

Driving north over the Dordogne Bridge on the A10, we headed towards Cognac. As it was quite late, we went straight to our hotel, Hôtel Françoise, in the town centre. The hotel had a classic French style, with tall windows and doors. After settling in, we took a short taxi ride over the Pont Neuf to L'Atelier des Quais, a fine-dining restaurant on the banks of the Charente River. With Christmas approaching, the whole evening felt magical.

The next day, we visited the Martell Brandy factory, also on the Charente River. Outside, a large group of farmers were protesting for the right to produce champagne, which was restricted to just six regions in the Cognac area.

Inside the factory, we were given a tour of the bottling operations and saw the Monoblock machine producing Martell Brandy miniatures at high speed. I was thoroughly impressed and immediately decided to purchase one.

During the tour, I noticed a small man resembling Toulouse-Lautrec following us. I asked John Smyth who he was, and he explained that his name was Remy Touchard, a direct descendant of the Remy Martell Brandy founder. He didn't speak English but liked to be part of visiting parties.

I had brought bottles of Laphroaig and Tormore malt whisky as gifts for our hosts, as was customary, and they were well received. After the tour, we were taken to the low-level buildings housing the hospitality suite. Inside, an old room filled with brandy memorabilia, we were seated at a Louis XIV table and cabinet.

Our host produced a key, unlocked the cabinet, and revealed a set of six crystal-cut brandy glasses with the letter 'N' cut into the glass. He then brought out a bottle of brandy dating back to Napoleon's time. Announcing that the aged brandy was most fitting for the occasion— as the glasses had belonged to Napoleon himself— he poured us a taste. It was an incredible honour to sample such exquisite brandy in such historic glassware.

Elaine, however, asked for lemonade, much to everyone's amusement. Remy did not smile.

We spent an hour strolling through Cognac before rushing back to Glasgow for the University Ball that evening. I bought Elaine a French shawl wrap and a white silk scarf for myself as souvenirs. We then flew back to Glasgow in the jump jet.

That evening Francis Quinlan, our marketing lecturer, had organised a 1920s-themed evening with white tuxedos and ballgowns, the perfect opportunity to wear our Cognac purchases.

Doing the MBA at Glasgow was one of the best things that ever happened to me. My friend Jim Green #2 was my companion in the classes, and we were both popular among our peer group and with the lecturers. The course was set to last three years and was highly intensive. However, in late September, we had a weekend event at various locations, usually Hamilton Hall in St Andrews. Jim and I relished these weekends, having done the same when studying for our postgraduate diplomas between 1979 and 1982 at Glasgow College.

The MBA lecturers always invited outstanding speakers from industry, such as Jimmy Gulliver from Argyll Stores, the forerunner to ASDA, or the Managing Director of Rolls-Royce. On one occasion in 1983, we were graced with the presence of Mr Albert S. Humphrey from the Stanford Institute, the proponent of Team Action Management and the famous SWOT analysis. What was more intriguing about Albert was that he had recently married Myriam, having sacked his first wife and left his four children for this extremely attractive Belgian aristocrat.

Jim #2 was particularly fascinated, as he saw Albert as something of a role model. He was an engaging speaker, and we had dinner together, where Jim #2 took the opportunity to chat with Myriam. Albert was personable, with more depth than first met the eye, and we developed a good friendship with both him and Myriam, even visiting their flat in Osnaburgh Street, London, near Regent's Park.

Later that year, I was invited to the Institute Of Packaging dinner at the Grosvenor Hotel in Park Lane as a guest of Stork Bepak. Before heading to the function, I stopped by Humph and Myriam's for an hour. They were both in good spirits, and Myriam announced she was expecting a baby.

On another occasion, I was visiting Queen Anne's Gate with Roy Standhope at LJI HQ. We took Humph and Myriam out to a restaurant in Covent Garden, as Roy was keen to quiz Humph— he was convinced he was a CIA agent.

I thought the evening went well, but Roy was adamant. As an ex-Major in the British Army and former Second-in-Command of the Maze Prison in Northern Ireland, he had an eye for these things.

Taking his advice, I never saw Humph again. He passed away in 2005.

The next trip I took was with Roy. Since joining LJI, he had done a great job re-establishing the security function, particularly at Westhorn. I helped him build a new security facility at the site entrance, and he systematically replaced questionable security officers with ex-military personnel from the Military Police and Parachute Regiment.

Now responsible for safety, Roy needed to review packaging equipment I was set to purchase from SIG-Pack AG in Beringen, Switzerland. Negotiations were well advanced, so Jim Quinn, the LJI Purchasing Manager, accompanied us. We flew from Glasgow to Geneva, where a SIG-Pack car picked us up and took us straight to our hotel in Schaffhausen, which had a spectacular view overlooking the Rhine Falls.

After a long day of travelling, I entered my room, which had an outstanding view of the Rhine and the fields beyond, and collapsed onto a luxurious four- poster bed, instantly falling asleep.

An hour later, Roy was banging on my door—we had a dinner date with some of the sales engineers.

The food and company were excellent. I opted for a fish dish (pike/perch), as the restaurant manager assured me it was his specialty, caught fresh that morning. Roy rounded off the dinner with a fine black cigar. Jim Quinn was keen to visit a club, so we followed him into Schaffhausen, had a single beer, and returned to the hotel.

The next day, we were picked up by SIG-Pack and taken to their factory in Beringen. The equipment was in excellent condition, and we arranged for our technician engineers to travel out the following week to assist with installation and commissioning.

Once negotiations were finalized—where Jim Quinn secured an exceptionally good deal—we retired to a Tyrolean restaurant high in the Alps. The scenery was breathtaking, and I wandered to a viewpoint with a swing, sitting there for five minutes, wishing I had brought a camera.

Another Feg

Before heading home, we spent an hour in Schaffhausen shopping for gifts. I bought a Florentine print of the town for about £150, which, on my return to Glasgow, was confiscated as a Swiss national antiquity. After filling out the necessary customs forms, I forgot all about it—until it arrived six months later. Fortunately, the snow globes I bought for the kids made it through customs without issue.

CHAPTER 31:
BACK AT THE FARM

Back in Westhorn,* I was in my office when I got the call about a security problem involving one of my staff members in the Quality Control Lab.

*Originally a farm to the east of Glasgow near Parkhead, home of Celtic FC.

LJI, like all whisky companies, carried out extensive QC tests on all products. Part of this procedure was a blind tasting system. The lab was set up so that members of the tasting panel sat on one side of a wall with a rotating table and door. The Lab Assistant would present three small tasting glasses with whisky samples—one being the standard and the other two being samples. The tester's job was to assess whether each was a sample or the standard. The theory behind this was that the more accurate the assessment, the closer the batch samples were to the standard.

Next to the rotating table was a funnel where the tester would spit out the contents of the taste sample. However, on this occasion, the tester had decided to swallow all the samples and, in his haste to get another drink, reached into the rotating door system—getting his entire arm caught.

We got him out, sent him home in a taxi, and issued a three-day suspension along with alcohol counselling. Although technically a dismissible offence, the managers were in stitches when they heard about it.

Before the end of the year, we had purchased most of the necessary equipment and planned for its installation as soon as possible in 1984.

There were two events that all managers had to endure before the end of the year—and one pleasant one. The pleasant one was the LJI Christmas party for employees' children. Santa was played by John Kilbride, and Sutcliffe's handled all the catering for the kids, mums, and Dads. It was usually held on a Saturday, and, to LJI's credit, no expense was spared. The kids were well entertained, and

John, even he would admit, looked exactly like Santa— especially when sober. The children received expensive presents, and LJI provided games and entertainment, giving parents a well-earned rest.

The less enjoyable events were the company dance for management and the works do.

The company dance was usually held in the ballroom of the Central Hotel in Glasgow, hosted by the directors and the chairperson, Ian Dewar. It was an extravagant affair with cigarettes, wine, and whisky on every table. A black- tie event, all partners were invited, and they could dance to the Jack Patrick Quartet. Unless you were "not in the game" as a career-climbing socialite, it was a good night out, though as always, politicking and brown-nosing were rampant. Staying on the dance floor was the best strategy. I was usually seated at the director's table, which sparked some jealousy and comments back at work, but I never let it phase me.

The works Christmas party was usually held at the County Inn in Cambuslang. The General Manger allowed every manager to withdraw £400 from petty cash to ensure their workers had an enjoyable evening. It always started off civilized but, as the night progressed and the workers got drunk, things tended to unravel. The women were outrageous—I was pinned against the wall on more than one occasion, with or without mistletoe tongues were exploring my mouth. The men, on the other hand, often got aggressive, so I arranged for four security officers to keep things under control.

One year, I made the mistake of bringing Elaine, and she vowed never to come again. As I got older, I developed the habit of leaving around 9:30 pm—before things got too experimental.

Christmas at home with Elaine and the kids was always a whirlwind. Jamie was now in secondary school at Stanley Green, and the girls were both doing well at Brediland Primary, conveniently just across the road from our house. The children were beside themselves with excitement as we put up the tree, and Elaine went into full Christmas mode, making it a happy time for us all.

The only problem was that I suffered from SADS and would usually slip into a dark depression due to the lack of light. I also tended to run myself into the ground, inevitably spending at least three days in bed, feeling sorry for myself with a bad case of 'man flu.'

Trouble at Westhorn.

Back at Westhorn, a new problem was emerging. John Kilbride had begun drinking heavily during the day, revealing a darker side to his personality. He was regularly bullying staff, and it was clear that he was spiraling out of control. I liked John, but his behaviour was unacceptable. He was picking arguments with everyone.

One afternoon, I got a call from security—he was in the recreation building, drunk. Douglas Smith and I drove over, and when we arrived, we found him supposed to be hosting a pensioners' event. Instead, he was sitting at an upright piano, pretending to be one of the Marx Brothers, balancing a polystyrene cup on his nose and hammering at the keys manically.

As soon as he saw us, he declared he was being attacked by the "Paisley Mafia." We manhandled him out of the building and bundled him into the car, much to the relief of the pensioners and security guards. I drove while Douglas fended off blows and kicks in the back seat. We took him home to East Kilbride, where his wife, Jessie, thanked me for bringing him back.

Back at Westhorn, the General Manager, Adam Johns, and his deputy, John Dougal, hesitated to take action. The next day, John strolled into my office as if nothing had happened and asked about the production lines. I listed the products, and he stopped me when I mentioned that we were bottling Royal Choice 21-year-old deluxe whisky for Brazil.

"We need to check that out in the vat room," he declared.

I knew this was going to be a problem and tried to dissuade him, but he stormed out of the office and down into the bottling hall. He took the stairway up to the vat room, and I followed. He asked which vat the 21-year-old was in, and I told him—Vat 25. Grabbing a stainless-steel sample beaker on a chain, he climbed the ladder to the access platform, opened the top hatch, lowered the beaker in, and pulled out nearly a pint of one of the most expensive whiskies in the world.

Back in the QC room near the vat, he produced two nosing glasses. Then, with exaggerated ceremony, he assessed the whisky.

"Colour: good, T17. Nose: excellent, slightly buttery. Taste: fucking excellent."

He offered me a glass but then drank the entire contents himself.

John was robust—he could hold his drink without stumbling—but his mood swings unsettled everyone. Normally, he was great company, funny and engaging, but beneath it all lurked something far less pleasant.

A Brewing Confrontation.

Over the next few days, John and I clashed frequently. I tried reasoning with him, but he had already gone to a dark place. He accused me of not making "the big decision."

"What big decision?" I asked.

He brought up a recent issue with a broken filling machine. When the gearbox failed, we had two options: wait five weeks for a replacement from Italy, costing £10,000, or have it refurbished locally by a company owned by one of his friends—for £25,000, in just three days. I saw the clear conflict of interest and discussed it with John Dougal, who hesitated before eventually approving John's friend's overpriced repair. John was obviously taking a cut. He was right about one thing, though—I needed to start making big decisions myself.

The next day, John barged into my office while I was speaking with Heather from logistics. I told him to leave and calm down, but he was after my keys to the hospitality suite. His had been confiscated after recent events, and I wasn't about to hand mine over.

I ignored him and left for Head Office in Bothwell Street for a negotiation with Stork Bepak. During the meeting, I got a call from John Dougal—John Kilbride had accused me of assaulting him.

When I returned to Westhorn, the situation escalated quickly. My discussion with John Dougal and Adam Johns turned hostile, and

I realised they saw an opportunity. John Kilbride and I had been instrumental in removing the previous management team, and now the tables had turned.

I took a calculated gamble and accused them of dithering over the disciplining of John Kilbride, pointing out that there were plenty of witnesses willing to come forward. I also told them I was going home and contacting Whitworth to inform them of what was going on, giving them 24 hours to sort it out. It was a battle of tooth and claw, and I had learned early on to play the game hard.

When I got home—after about an hour—Elaine said that John Dougal had been calling for me. When I phoned him back, he told me not to contact Whitworth and assured me he would handle the situation.

The next day, John Kilbride was back at his desk as usual. I confronted him, and he said, "You know you hit me, and there are witnesses." The only person who had heard our argument was Heather. I went to her office and asked if she had seen me attack John. She said no—she had not seen me hit him.

The following two days were exceedingly difficult, but I did phone Jim O'Neil to let him know what was happening. Then I got a call from John, saying he was going to kill me, as he had been suspended pending an investigation. That never came to pass. Instead, John was seconded out to an industrial initiative in Ayrshire for two years.

Living a good life at work can be a sharp contrast to normal family life when you're on a tight budget and struggling to pay the bills. It was becoming clearer that my position at Westhorn was getting more difficult—the new managers were not fans of me or my corporate history. The situation was unlikely to change quickly, but the prevailing forces were clearly working to a plan.

Every other day, I was receiving job offers to join Whitworth, thanks to the good offices of David Muir, the Marketing Manager based in Chiswell Street near the Barbican in London. Amongst them was a personal invitation from Jim O'Neil before he left, asking me to join him in Whitworth's retail division. He invited Elaine and me to dinner at the Excelsior's Academy Restaurant, near HQ in Bothwell Street. Over good food and fine wines—Fleurie and Vouvray—he presented me with a new job as a director in a new venture called TGI Fridays. The position required relocating the whole family to Luton in Bedfordshire. He gave us a few days to decide, and in the end, we chose to stay in Scotland.

Roy Standhope said we were mad to refuse, given the fantastic package on offer—resettlement costs, an executive car, profit-sharing, shares, and bonuses. This was, for me, one of those sliding doors moments where our entire family's future could have taken a vastly different path.

I've always believed that if you roll up your sleeves and work hard, you can make it anywhere.

Jim O'Neil was disappointed with my decision and said he would try again with other opportunities in the future. He returned to Luton and set up a new home for himself and his daughters in Bedford. Elaine and I visited him once—he had a big old executive house next to the local golf course. During that visit, he took me aside and made one final offer.

At the time, AIDS was becoming a worldwide scare, and the Parent Company was concerned about their vast retail empire being at risk if chefs or bar staff were found to be HIV positive. My job would have been to go to America as a business auditor and identify where all the gay employees were working. This was more like corporate espionage. It was also deeply distasteful and highly dangerous if I had been exposed. I didn't need much time to decide— I declined and left. I never saw Jim O'Neil again.

I needed a breath of fresh air, so I took up running marathons. I had always been fit—playing squash and swimming—but I wanted to push myself further. I bought a cotton tracksuit, shorts, and good running shoes. After work, I would change and run around our local estate. Within a few weeks, I was running seven miles every evening. At weekends, I stretched to ten miles. I felt fantastic and even started running during my lunch breaks at Westhorn.

My week usually consisted of working as an Operations Manager for LJI, running twelve miles a day, studying for my MBA, and trying to be a husband and Dad. I was lucky to have Elaine at home—she was a wonderful mother and an understanding wife. Most weekends, we tried to get away with the kids—on a picnic down the coast, up to Loch Lomond, or down to the Borders.

That summer, we borrowed Jim Kennovan's our next-door neighbor's trailer and headed to the Highlands for a camping holiday.

Back at work, I received orders from our new LJI Technical Director, Ian Wilson, to prepare plans for moving gin bottling operations from Plymouth to Westhorn. I knew this would not make me popular with the local workforce. However, the main board considered the current process— transferring rectified spirit from Strathclyde Distillery in Glasgow to Plymouth by tanker, double rectifying it in the gin still at Plymouth, bottling it there, and then transporting it back up north for dispatch—inefficient.

I took two packaging engineers from Westhorn Operations to Plymouth to assess a decommissioning plan. It meant around twelve bottling workers at Plymouth would be made redundant.

Over the next few weeks, we prepared the new gin line, installing it over a weekend. With record production levels and unit costs tumbling, I was receiving praise from the LJI Board—but the local managers had other plans for me.

Line 3 in the bottling hall was the high-speed line and could produce 4,500 cases per shift. However, after I revamped it, we were producing 8,000 cases per day. I now know that my main opposition was Adam Johns, who saw an opportunity to suggest to the board that I should specialize in production systems and move out of my line functions into a technical advisory role, bringing me closer to Whitworth PLC. I had already made up my mind to leave as soon as possible, though that would take some time.

Towards the end of the year, I was made Production Systems Manager and reported to Mike Trotter, the Technical Manager. My last appraisal from Adam Johns read: "Channeled properly, Jim has a lot to offer the company." (Bastard.)

The truth was, if I had continued in the Operations Manager role much longer—given my results—I would have been the new General Manager. That meant Adam and Dougal would be moved back to remote distilleries. I didn't resist the change, as it gave me a low-stress job where I could plan my future elsewhere.

I made the most of my time by training in Synectics (Creative Problem Solving), as practiced by the Abraxas Group in Leighton Buzzard England. I started at the basic level and worked my way up to become a trainer. John Alexander, the senior trainer, offered me a job, but I declined. The process forced me, for the first time, to take a long, hard look at myself—how I behaved and what I really wanted out of life. Up until then, most of my ambition had been for me. Now, I wanted something good and different for my family too.

Mike Trotter arranged for me to have a new office, tucked away, and fitted out with fresh décor, furnishings, and an IBM PC XT.

I was now Chair of Whitworth's Scientific Committee. The committee consisted of scientists and engineers exploring new products and technologies for Whitworth—heat recovery projects in distilleries, DNA manipulation of yeast strains to improve sugar conversion and alcohol yield, the use of lasers, IT development, and business and management systems. I learned more in those six months than in six years of MBA and DMS postgraduate courses.

I still hadn't finished my MBA and had a lot of studying to do. Mike barely supervised me, leaving me to my own devices.

During the holidays, I took the IBM PC XT home and let Jamie play with it. It had a remarkable effect—he regularly got caught playing Pac-Man at three in the morning. It's no coincidence that Jamie's first job after university was with IBM.

Running...

In July, I ran my first full marathon in Inverclyde. The week before, I had done my 21-mile run and then rested. On the day, I lined up with John Waters, a seasoned marathon runner who had already completed the London, Boston, and New York marathons. He had inspired me to give it a go.

Marathon Man

We started at the esplanade in Gourock on the banks of the Clyde—the same spot where Bob Marshall and I once shared some Four Crown wine. It was exceptionally hot. John Waters pulled away early with some of his running friends. We ran up to the Cloch Lighthouse and then returned for the 17-mile stretch into Greenock. The heat was brutal. Running past Lithgow's shipyard, the heat reflecting off the south-facing wall was causing heat stroke problems. My brother-in-law, John, who ran with us, was just behind me and feeling the heat also, so I left him dunking his head in a bucket of cold water.

About a mile from the finish, I caught up with John Waters, who had slowed down—blood was spurting out of his trainers. I asked if he wanted company, but he said he wanted to finish in his own time. I carried on and finished in 3 hours, 50 minutes. John finished not long after. We collapsed on the promenade with our bronze medals, eating chocolate bars. If I'm being honest, I never hit the wall or felt exhausted—just relieved it was over. The next day, I tapered off with a seven-mile run and continued training until September, when I ran the Glasgow Marathon.

That was a different experience altogether. I stood among thousands of runners in black bin bags to keep out the rain, the air thick with the smell of embrocation. By then, I had learned how to avoid serious chafing— Elastoplast over the nipples and liberal amounts of Vaseline on my feet and inner thighs.

We set off through the city, heading out towards Maryhill before turning back towards the Jamaica Street Bridge. As I crossed the bridge, I felt a sharp pain in my knee. That was it—I was crocked. I should have stopped, but I pushed on in severe pain. Soon, everyone was overtaking me—then it was the grannies and grandpas overtaking me—and the crowd started heckling me for being at the back.

It took me six hours to finish. Elaine and the kids had been really worried. After that, I stuck to half-marathons and short runs until 1986, when I stopped running for good reason.

Towards the end of the year, Mike Trotter called me in for my appraisal. He was clear that he saw my future with Whitworth and that there were no immediate promotions available—odd, considering I had never asked for one. I was content focusing on my studies, churning out grade-A coursework in my remote office for the MBA. I had also finalized my thesis topic: Creative Problem-Solving, aligning with my Synectics training.

My plan was simple: finish the MBA and start my own business as soon as possible. When Mike asked what I really wanted to do, I told him. A few days later, he came back and said he might be able to get me a redundancy package, though it would take some time. That suited me—I knew it would give me the capital to start up.

Originally, I had planned to go into business with my namesake, Jim Green #2, but that proved difficult. As other investors doubted our chances and didn't want to take any risks. They argued that if they put up 50% of the capital, they should get a shareholding which was fair enough. I'd be working my socks off for just a 25% stake.

Jim#2 and I had also been arguing about the nature of the business and the company name, and eventually, we fell out. I had hoped we could resolve things by the time we graduated, even if it meant running separate businesses. It took ten years before we made it up again.

Just before Christmas, Mike Trotter told me he had arranged my redundancy package. It wouldn't go through until April 1985, and he wasn't sure how much I would get—but Whitworth planned to make it attractive. I was offered a package worth £20,000 plus allowed to keep my brand-new company car. (Result)

CHAPTER 32:
1ST ADDITION LTD. IS BORN

In 1985, I pushed my output in my remote office, getting well ahead with my thesis. I also began applying my business skills to conduct a gap analysis of the building industry in my hometown. Although Jim#2 and I initially thought an attic conversion company would be a good venture, the data did not support that. I had gone to the district council and examined the major and minor warrant books, taking detailed notes. It became clear that the best type of business would be a general building or shopfitting company. The largest domestic market was in home extensions.

When Jim and I brainstormed names for an attic business, we came up with Attack the Attic. It was a strong name and secured an early listing in Yellow Pages. However, over the next few days, a different idea took shape in my mind. I settled on the name 1st Addition Ltd, registered it, and booked advertising.

In January, LJI participated in the annual Whisky Curling Bonspiel in Aviemore, in the Scottish Highlands. It was a weekend event, with every whisky company fielding a curling team. Douglas Smith and I founded the first LJI curling team, with Douglas as skip. John Dougal attended to represent the company and play as part of the team. Elaine came along for company. The freezing temperatures outside were in sharp contrast to the indoor curling rink.

One of the opposing teams was J.W. Grants. Beyond the main event of the Friday evening was a heavy drinking session. The competition began on Saturday morning, and John Dougal was clearly worse for wear. His curling was erratic—at least twice, he sent his stones careering into an adjacent rink. Douglas and I tried to reason with him, but he was unbiddable.

In the end, we were soundly beaten and sought consolation in the handfuls of whisky miniatures handed out. Elaine and I retreated to our warm room in the afternoon, had a bath, and fell asleep.

That evening, we enjoyed a pleasant dinner with our teammates, though it was noticeable that John Dougal was missing.

By Sunday morning, he was still absent, so we contacted the police, who informed us he was in hospital—he had been mugged. I phoned Roy Standhope the LJ security manager to inform him. This was John's second mugging in a year, which immediately raised suspicions. Roy said he would launch an investigation on Monday.

We had planned to visit John in hospital after lunch, but he reappeared, battered, and bruised, sporting a black eye. Roy travelled to Aviemore to speak to the police and locals, trying to piece together what had happened.

Although I got on well with Roy, he came down hard on Douglas and me, suspecting that we had either orchestrated or carried out the attack. I was deeply disappointed by his lack of trust. I had befriended Roy, yet he believed I was withholding information. Theoretically, anyone on the team could have been involved, but I assured him I knew nothing. I was aware that John had a drinking problem and a troubled marriage, but that was all.

Elaine and I were relieved to return home to the children, where her parents had been babysitting. The kids adored their grandparents. Elaine's Dad took them swimming, while her mum, May, often took them on picnics along the Ayrshire coast.

Jamie had started secondary school at Stanley Green School at the foot of the Glennifer Braes, the same school attended by legendary Scottish footballer Archie Gemmell. I had once worked with Archie's father at Babcock's, where he was a general labourer. Willie Gemmell had invited me to his high-rise flat in Gallowhill, just five minutes from my mother's house in David Way. Archie had sent his trophies there for safekeeping, and the little flat was crammed with his cups, caps, plates, and medals.

Jamie was incredibly bright, with phenomenal general knowledge. He constantly amazed me with his grasp of nature, science, cars, and current affairs. His teachers were impressed, though his marks for written work were poor. On a parents' evening, my old science teacher, Colin Jackson, pulled us aside. He showed us Jamie's results for multiple-choice exams—he had scored 100% every time. However, his marks plummeted when required to write narratives. It took another year before Jamie was diagnosed with dyslexia.

The girls were also doing well in school. Watching Emma cross the road to Brediland Primary was heart-wrenching. Every few yards, she would turn and wave to Elaine, lingering at the last corner for a final farewell before the school bell rang. Jennifer, in contrast, strode off confidently, only occasionally glancing back for a wave. Elaine was always there for them, which was one of the great luxuries of our family life.

In April, I completed my final MBA exams, clearing my thesis in May. Out of 40 students, only seven of us graduated in the first round.

It was a proud moment—not just for me but for my entire family. I was the first university graduate in the Green family.

Elaine did a great job getting the kids fitted out with new, expensive clothes. The girls got outfits from Hopscotch in Glasgow, while Jamie got a new double-breasted suit from Frasers. We had family portraits taken after graduation.

The graduation ceremony on 6th June was quite an event in Bute Hall, with a sherry reception where all the bright young things mingled with their families and academic staff. The graduates were taken behind the main platform for a last-minute briefing on how to conduct themselves on stage when being capped and gowned. The University of Glasgow uses only natural colours for hood linings, such as red, green, blue, white, and gold. The MBA hood is gold. Gowns come in various lengths for PhDs, Masters, and Bachelors.

I remember that after I was capped and hooded, I turned and saw Elaine and the children in the audience. I immediately felt pleased with myself and with them—it was they who had been denied my presence and attention during the years I was studying.

As I returned from the rostrum, I saw a sea of bright, clean faces filled with hope and expectation for what life and careers might bring. It was a special moment indeed as I could feel an incredible energy from those bright young people.

After the ceremony, we went to the photographer and then to the Ubiquitous Chip restaurant in Ashton Lane for a celebratory meal.

Since the number of tickets for the ceremony was limited, I popped over to Mum and Dad's house in Gallowhill to show off my scroll. I don't think either of them fully understood how significant it was for me. Dad had a wee drink and commented that it was all very good—but how much money did I have in the bank?

The comment stung at the time, but he was right. There I was, studying, running marathons, playing squash, and exhausting myself as the Production Systems Manager for LJI. Though I had a good salary and a company car, Elaine and the kids were living in relative poverty—we struggled to pay the utility bills after covering the mortgage. Something had to change. I had a plan, but now I became even more focused on making it happen.

After a few months, things settled again, and we completed the new engineering in production operations. All was well at Westhorn—until 23rd September, when the River Clyde burst its banks, flooding the oxbow land around the site and forming an oxbow lake. The warehouses ended up under several feet of stormwater. Some warehouse barrels floated away, while hundreds of empty barrels drifted down the Clyde, eventually reaching the open sea. A salvage team was sent out at huge cost to LJI.

In November, my new boss, Mike Trotter, was called away when his son was hospitalized. The next day, he returned to work, only to receive a call that his son's condition had worsened. That same day, his son—just 21 years old and newly graduated—died. Mike returned to work the day after the funeral. I found this odd at the time, but as an older man writing this, I now understand—he needed to focus on something other than his grief.

To Mike's credit, he was incredibly supportive during my annual appraisal. When I told him I wanted to leave and start my own business, he acknowledged my potential within Whitworth but said he would see if the directors would approve a redundancy package.

By December, Mike informed me that a package had been agreed upon, and I would leave in April 1986.

I registered my company, 1st Addition Ltd, and took out an advert in the West of Scotland Yellow Pages, set to launch in April 1986.

1986

The first three months were all about planning my departure and preparing to start my building company. In March, Mike came back to me with the severance proposal from the directors. I was to receive the financial package worth £20,000, with the option to keep my existing company car—an Austin Princess hatchback— or select a new car from the Whitworth fleet, provided I paid one-third of its value. I opted for a new car—an Austin Montego in white.

On the first Friday in April, the managers held a farewell lunch in my honour. Sutcliffe catered a full four-course meal. Earlier that day, a contingent from the shop floor and staff had presented me with a good luck card, covered in hundreds of signatures and well-wishes. The managers gave me a leather briefcase with gold fittings and a bottle of Royal Choice in a blue velvet presentation box.

I thanked them all for putting up with me and made my final goodbye brief.

On the way home, a wave of regret hit me. Had I just made the biggest mistake of my life?

CHAPTER 33:
TIME TO GET MY HANDS DIRTY

In March, I visited my brother-in-law, Bob, to get some advice on running a building company. I had helped Bob and my sister, Ellen, just after they got married when Bob was made redundant from a local joinery company by guaranteeing a loan against some purchases they made. Bob had started with a beat-up van and now had his own premises on Underwood Road in Paisley. From what I could see, he was doing quite well. The only piece of advice I remember him giving me was never to do cash jobs. It turned out to be particularly good advice, keeping me on the right side of the taxman.

Before the new Yellow Pages came out, I was already getting contracts from friends who had kindly trusted me to do a good job. My first job was for Elaine's old school friend, Moira, who had recently married David after a short engagement. I was hired to construct a wall and patio area.

The week before I was due to start, I asked my Dad if he could help with the work and bring in old Martin Kiernan, the bricklayer. Dad agreed, as he was idle at the time.

On the first day, it was raining, but I turned up to pick them both up. Dad advised that it was too wet to work, so I went home defeated after so much anticipation. By lunchtime, it had cleared up, so I decided to try for a late start. Mum told me Dad and Martin were at the British Legion playing snooker. (*Indulge me in this little story*)

Martin the Brickie:
The Builder's Boys (A true story)

The word "boys" isn't exactly accurate because they range in age from thirteen to eighty-five. I'm Jimmy, the owner of a building company. The story I'm about to tell is all true. I could write a book about any one of my boys, and one day I might. But for now, I'll focus on one man—Martin the Brickie.

This is a unique insight.

Sit tight because... Builders don't normally write.

It all started with Maggie Thatcher's ethos of selfishness—"no such thing as society." I had spent three years studying at business school and six years teaching undergraduates.

I figured out that having a business degree without a business was like being a dentist with no teeth to practice on. So, I engineered my departure from my employer, Long John International Ltd whisky producer in the East End of Glasgow, where I worked as Operations and Production Manager. With what investment money I had, I started my building business with an advert in Yellow Pages.

My first port of call was my father's house. I explained my grand plan.

"Whit? Ye must be mental to leave a job like that. I've nearly killed masel twice! You should know better—it wis you that hid tae lift me back and forward tae the toilet for two years."

Dad was right. I knew it was a hard game, but it was locked in my psyche. I wanted to be out in the fresh air. I wanted to be a man. And I wanted money. More than anything, I wanted to escape the petty office politics and betrayals that made working life miserable for most decent people.

I let Dad rant until he calmed down. "So, have ye got any contracts yet?"

I had one. A good friend knew I was starting up and had asked me to build a wall at the back of their garden.

"We start a week on Monday. How good is your brickwork?"
"Me? Ah don't lay bricks."

I had known my father all my life, and I swear to God, I always thought he was a bricklayer. I had been relying on him to be my brickie.

"I'll phone Martin. He's available, and I'll dae the laboring."

I decided to see Martin. I knew he was getting on a bit, in his late sixties. A veteran of Dunkirk, he had a huge family, loved dancing, had been a supervisor for Wimpy Contractors in London for fifteen years, and had a reputation for solving problems with his fists. He also never drank until he was sixty—and rumor had it he was trying to catch up on lost time.

I knocked on the door of his council house. It took some time, but eventually, Martin answered. You couldn't help but like this old man—he looked like Uncle Albert from Only Fools and Horses and even sounded like him, with his hoarse voice.

I stepped inside, passing through the hall into the living room, where his wife, Mary, was making his tea. She was beginning to show signs of dementia and kept reminding me that she knew my mother. The house itself was showing signs of neglecting, a n d all the middle-age energy had faded.

Martin agreed to be my brickie for £40 a day.

On the day the contract was due to start, I arrived in my new car to pick up Dad. It was raining, but I was excited and eager to get going.

"You'll no be daein any work the day, son. It looks as though the rain is oan fur the day."

I was gutted. Dad was so final about it. I had a cup of tea and returned home.

I paced up and down the front room, tearing at the avocado coloured Venetian blinds, when I noticed a large patch of blue sky breaking through.

It was just afternoon. I jumped in the car and headed to Dad's house. My mother came to the door.

"Hello, son. Yer faither's away ower tae the Legion wi' Martin."

I got back in the car and sped the half mile to the British Legion Halls at the bottom of Renfrew Road in Paisley.

Dad and Martin were deep into a game of snooker and had already had a couple of specials—a half pint of beer with a whisky chaser.

"Sorry, son, but we're settled for the day. We'll have a go the morra."

I was gutted. As a senior manager, I would have sacked anyone who so much as smelled of drink. That day, I realised the building trade was more complicated than I'd anticipated. I was now in a very different world.

Two days later, we finally got started. A lorry load of cement had arrived outside the site. I had swapped my dark blue pinstripe and black Oxfords for a pair of ex-army combat trousers, a white T-shirt, and heavy, tan-colored construction safety boots. Keen to prove myself, I was first to grab a bag of cement. It bent, and I didn't have the strength to lift it. Fifteen years of pen-pushing had rendered me a weakling.

Martin, with a knowing smile, gently moved me aside.

"I'll get this wan—you get us mair work. That's whit you should be daein'."

He was right. My romance with being a builder was only going to work if I could bring in plenty of contracts.

It took a few months, but eventually, the work was flowing in, and slowly, I was getting fitter. The fresh air and summer sunshine were good for me—I was tanned and healthy.

"Martin, do you always wear that bunnet and jacket?"

"Aye, son. When ye get aulder, yer blood gets thinner, and ye learn that the sun can be dangerous. Summer or winter, ye always cover up."

We'd made enough that year to cover our costs, but as winter set in, the work started drying up.

We were back on our feet by the summer, and I had been awarded a contract to build an office extension for a foundry in Craigton, Glasgow. The first week had been problematic because I'd started my younger brother, Steven, as a labourer, and he'd overslept the day he was supposed to receive nine cubes of concrete on-site. I was attending to another contract elsewhere when I got the message that the concrete had been turned away, and we were liable for the cost of the load. I told Martin the story and that I'd fired Steven for letting me down. He suggested his son, George, who was not only a good labourer but could also lay infill brickwork to Martin's brick lines and corners. I hired George.

George was nowhere near as sharp as his father. He also looked unwell, with dark circles under his eyes. I'd heard he was living in one of the poorer areas of Paisley, and his track record was a bit dodgy.

At 10:00 a.m. on his first day, George approached me.

"Excuse me, James. Sorry tae disturb ye, but I wis wunnerin' if ye could dae me a wee obligement?"

"Whit wid that be, George?"

"Could ye gee me a wee sub tae get a message fur ma burd?' (girlfriend)

I'd been in the building game long enough to know that one thing you never do is give a man a sub on his first day—never on a Monday and certainly not before 10:00 a.m. But I didn't know that then.

"Twinty quid wid be guid, James. Jist take it aff whit am due on Friday."

I felt sorry for George. Some boys just need a break, so I handed him twenty quid. (£20)

At lunchtime, I was inside a portacabin in the foundry, talking to the manager about the ongoing works. Looking out the window, I saw my father helping what looked like a semi-conscious George towards the toilet area. Dad quickly laid George against the wall and hosed him down using the mixer's water supply. Without alarming my client, I excused myself.

"Whit the fuck happened here?"

"Ask Martin. C'mon, George, we don't want the foundry boss seeing you like this or we'll be bumped aff the site."

We tidied George up and gave him a cup of sweet tea.

I assumed drugs—there was no smell of drink. But I was wrong.

Apparently, Martin and George had a history. George had been borrowing money from Martin for years without paying it back.

He was borrowing all over the place and never settling his debts. Before he started working for me, Martin had warned him not to ask me for money or he'd be in trouble.

At lunch, Martin had caught George trying to sneak away. When he pulled him up and heard the truth, he decked him—nearly knocking him out. That was how Martin, like Dad, solved problems: with his fists.

Despite the setbacks, the business continued to grow. Most weekends were free, which meant family time for me and the British Legion for Martin, Dad, and Big Charlie dad's cousin and resident plasterer. They all loved snooker, but Martin's real passion was dancing and the ladies. On Saturday nights, the Legion hosted a dance, and Martin would spend most of the night drinking and twirling the women around the floor.

This was a different Martin from the poor refugee who'd shivered on the roof of the Excelsior. He was charming, always dapper in a smart suit, crisp collar, and silk tie. He was also minus poor Mary, who was at home, convinced he was at evening Mass at St Mirren's Cathedral.

One night, he was well-oiled, and a steward approached him, sensing trouble.

"C'mon, Martin, mibby ye've had enough."

Davy Newton, British Legion steward, never saw it coming. Martin shot a full-weighted uppercut at his chin, flooring him on the spot.

The Legion had him escorted home and called him to a hearing, where they suspended his membership for three years. He was sixty-nine years old.

Meanwhile, work was steady. An old friend from my management days rang me for a quote to rebuild her front garden wall in Clarkston.

I carried out a site visit, agreed on a price, and we got started. The job involved cutting back hawthorn hedges that had burst through the random stone wall and onto the pavement. Martin loved this kind of work, and we agreed the entire wall should be knocked down, with the hedges rooted up and removed.

I'd hired young Alistair to labour for Martin and Dad. Martin was taking down the wall, Dad was stacking the stone for rebuilding, and Alistair was wrestling the hawthorn bushes into a roadside skip.

Suddenly, an old woman appeared from next door.

"Are you in charge?"

"Yes."

"Do you realise that those bushes are part of the original Clarkston wall boundary and that there's a preservation order on them?"

I explained to the woman that the property owner had contracted me to remove them and rebuild the wall, as it was a matter of public safety. She marched off, muttering that she was calling the police and that her son was a senior officer.

An hour later, the police arrived, and a big ginger police sergeant approached me.

"Is that your skip?" "Yes."

He took me to one side so nobody else could hear. "Then get it tae fuck out of here or I'll book you for obstruction. Have you got a license for it?" "Yes, it's in the post," I lied.

He never mentioned the protected hawthorn hedge and was off with a promise to return to check that the skip had been moved. The problem was, there was so much hedge that I'd need at least another skip as soon as possible. Alistair packed the existing one so tightly I reckoned they'd have to burn the bushes out.

A new skip arrived at 3:00 pm, and just as we were filling it, the police turned up again.

Ginger approached. "What the fuck is that?" "A skip."

"I told you to get rid of it."

"I did. That's a different skip."

"Listen carefully, smart arse—if that's not gone by the time the traffic builds up, you'll be reported to the Procurator Fiscal."

We moved the skip.

The job was done, and Martin was finishing the pointing on the stonework.

My client called me in and paid me. She also had two big black bin bags at her back door.

"Jim, I wonder if you'd be so kind as to drop these off at the local charity shop for me?"

I got Alistair to put the bags in the back of the van, and as I got into my car, I spotted Martin and Alistair rummaging through them. I was shaking my head when Martin pulled out a pair of fancy brown leather cowboy boots. He was trying them on. I got back out of the car.

"Jim, look at these. They're crackers—jist whit ah need fur the dancing."

He strutted up and down Clarkston Road, muttering, "Perfect fit."

A few weekends later, I was driving through Paisley town centre on a Saturday afternoon when I saw Martin standing at a bus stop.

"Get in, Martin." He was well dressed for action. "Naw, ah'm ok, you carry on."

"Where are you going?"

"Tae the United Services Club in Johnstone." "Aye, you'll be missing the Legion."

"Aye."

"Look, Martin, get in. I'll take you there, no problem."

He hesitated, awkward and coy. "It's jist that…" "What?"

"A've got somebody wi me." "He can come as well."

Martin waved his friend over, and I saw that 'he' was very much a 'she'— an attractive blonde in her fifties. They both got in the back of the car. I caught Martin's eye in the rear-view mirror, and he was smiling in silence.

I repeated myself. "So, are ye really missing the Legion, Martin?" "No, not really."

He grinned.

"By the way, these boots are fuckin' marvellous!"

End of Story

We worked like dogs on that first contract to get that patio and wall out of the ground, and after a couple of weeks, it was done. After paying wages and materials, I only made about £200, but I did have a good customer references. Next was another wall—an insurance job from my old friend Brian.

Before the contract started, I realised that while the Montego was great for sales calls, it wasn't practical for transporting men, materials, and equipment. So, I headed to Newmains Auction Market near Wishaw, accompanied by my father-in-law, James. After missing a couple of bids, we finally agreed on a used white van for £400. I handed over the money, got the keys, phoned for a cover note, and signed for the logbook transfer.

Elaine's Dad took my car and followed me out of the auction yard. We turned right and headed for the roundabout, about 100 yards away. As I turned, the main driveshaft fell off at one end and scraped along the road. I suddenly came to a stop on the other side of the roundabout, with Jimmy pulling in behind me. Crawling under the van, I saw that the flange bolts for the driveshaft had sheared. Fortunately, we had broken down just 50 meters from a Kwik-Fit depot. I grabbed my tools from the car, sent James home, then bought some set pins, bolts, and washers from Kwik-Fit and did the repair myself.

When I finally drove away, the van ran fine. It lasted us a whole year before eventually giving up.

In May, I got my first truly profitable job—building a carport for a family in Crosslee near Houston, Renfrewshire. On the job were me, Martin Kiernan, and Dad. Dad and Martin handled the slabbing work, while I did the steelwork, which I designed and had fabricated by John McLean Metal Workers. John had started his own company, Abbey Metal Ltd., around the same time as me. We struck up a friendship and, in the years ahead, did plenty of business together.

During the carport construction, three key events changed the way I approached things. As a trained manager in a large corporate organization, I was used to systematic ways of handling issues, with ample resources and sophisticated processes. But as a new, small-scale building contractor, I had to become streetwise—fast.

The first lesson came when I had to collect the plastic roofing sheets from JW Grants Builders Merchants in Love Street Paisley. I loaded up the old white van and decided to drive through my old scheme in Ferguslie Park Avenue. As I was leaving via Candren, I noticed the van doors weren't shut properly. When I checked, I realised all the plastic sheets had slipped out of the back door— somewhere in Feegie. Retracing my journey was pointless; the sheets had magically disappeared.(Feegie magic)

Back on-site, I told the boys what had happened—they found it hilarious. Lesson learned: always secure your load and avoid Feegie. In the years ahead I never took on work there.(experientia docet)

The second lesson came while fitting the sheeting onto the steelwork. My drill slipped, and I twisted my back. It wasn't a serious injury, but it led to a conversation with Martin and Dad. They told me to hire a labourer so I could focus on winning contracts rather than doing manual labour. They were right. My dream of escaping air-conditioned offices for outdoor work and hard graft was short-lived.

When we finished the carport after two weeks, I drove home from Crosslee with a tidy profit of £1,800. I realised I could earn more than a monthly salary—but only if I got back into a suit as soon as possible. I also needed to find a labourer.

Contracts were still slow, so I had to keep my boots on and help out. I secured a job building a dining room extension and patio on Paisley Road for an old Camphill FP, Andy Heron. Andy was great to work for and let us get on with it. Part of the job involved tearing down an old washhouse ceiling to replace it with a new one.

The old boys weren't keen on working late, but I wanted the new ceiling up over the weekend. I told Andy I'd be back to handle it myself. That Friday evening, just as I sat down for dinner, a young man in his late teens rang my doorbell. He apologized for disturbing me and asked if I needed any workers.

I asked about his skills—he was the perfect labourer: strong, fit, multi-skilled, and able to drive. I asked if he was free that evening. He said yes, though he wasn't dressed for work. I handed him some work clothes, made a cup of tea, and we set off in the van to Glasgow Road.

Tearing down the ceiling didn't take long—until a large piece hit me on the head, knocking me out for a few seconds. Alistair splashed me with cold water, helped me up, and kept clearing debris into the skip.

On the way home, we stopped for fish suppers. Alistair asked if I could drop him at his girlfriend's house in Foxbar—I agreed, only to learn he'd stood her up to come and work for me. He ended up working for me for the next ten years.

That summer, Jamie joined us. At only 12, he held his own, picking up new skills from the older boys. There's a myth that building is easy—especially among DIY enthusiasts—but in reality, it's incredibly tough and requires real skill to achieve quality work. Most days, you go home exhausted. In the West of Scotland, you're either soaked through or frozen solid in winter.

As a trained manager and HSE specialist, I tried to maintain good safety standards. But it would be disingenuous to say we weren't taking risks— costs and deadlines were often dictated otherwise.

As summer rolled in, I got a call from Bob Jack at Lambert Contracts. He wanted me to do subcontract work for Hamilton District Council on water ingress repairs at £5.00 an hour. It was hard, low-paid work. Worse still, he insisted that if I took the contract, I had to paint over my company logo on the van.

There wasn't much else on, so, with a heavy heart, I painted out the livery and became just another "white van man."

At this end of the construction world, it's hard going, and the weather in the West of Scotland is a constant tormentor. However, Bob wasn't too bad at paying, so it kept me going for a little while.

Just like with my Dad in earlier years, work tapered off in the winter, and I only had one contract come in from my brother-in-law, Bob Gibb. It was guttering work in Barrhead, valued at £2,000. We did the work in November, and my reserves were getting exceptionally low, so I approached Bob for payment. That was another lesson—Bob advised that I get would not get paid until he got paid. From then on, I always made sure to get a substantial deposit or clear payment terms. Thanks, Bob.

This left me in a bind, with Christmas approaching and money running out fast. After receiving my lump sum from LJI, I had invested £1,000 in penny shares in a company called Common Brothers, which owned a shipping line in the States. I had 22,000 shares, now worth £3,000, so I had to sell them to get through Christmas and the winter season.

As a side note, on 26th April 1986, the nuclear reactor at Chernobyl melted down, releasing a huge radioactive plume across Europe. Hardly anyone from America travelled to Europe that year. That same year, the Norex Corporation bought out Common Brothers, which specialized in Caribbean cruises. By late summer 1986, those shares would have been worth £83,000. Thanks again, Bob.

By now, I was fully in combat mode for business, so the suit was back on. I started targeting bigger companies, and my first break came with a call from Graham Gold, the facilities manager at the Royal Alexandra Hospital (RAH) in Paisley. It was a routine call-out to board up a door, as we had advertised 24-hour emergency repairs in the Yellow Pages. We never got much more work from RAH, but Graham was pleased with our job. Later, when he became Facilities Manager for the Allied Building Society(ABS), the work started pouring in.

I began building up my team. Rab Scott became our new joiner, and my Dad's cousin Charlie Green became our resident plasterer.

Contracts started flowing nicely, and my bank balance was looking extremely healthy. After just one year of trading as a limited company, we got a visit from the tax man. Elaine and I had been running the business from our house in Tantallon Drive, Paisley, doing our best to keep good books. That paid off—despite having no previous accounts, the taxman's estimates of our first-year turnover were within a few pounds of the actual figure. Also, thanks to Bob Gibb's lesson, the only cash job we ever did was fully receipted and banked.

One of our jobs was a structural alteration in Walker Street, Paisley, and we needed a good brickie. I had been in touch with Reid Kerr Technical College, and they had given me the name of their Bricklaying Apprentice of the Year—Peter McGlade. He was from Linthouse, near Govan, had recently got married, and was indeed a good bricklayer. However, they hadn't taught him how to cut a reinforced lintel properly. Alistair came to see me, explaining that Peter was trying to cut the lintel with a bolster, not realizing it had two reinforced steel rods inside. Alistair showed him how to do it with a Stihl saw. Peter moved on, but a few years later, we hired him again—this time, he was a well-seasoned and capable trowel. (Bricklayer)

That year, I didn't take a holiday, as I was focused on bringing in more business for the winter. Elaine took the kids to Estartit in northern Spain by coach, along with her family. My mum took my place on the trip. According to reports, it rained the whole holiday, and it took a long time before the smiles returned to their faces when they got back home.

Contracts kept coming in, and we got a new van from Melville Motors in Glasgow. Not only that, but we also landed a contract to build an extension for the sales manager's house in Burnside, Glasgow. The new van looked great in its fresh livery, and Alistair got to drive it.

Graham Gold from ABS started giving us work all over Scotland, so we had to expand the team again. I hired Jim Usher, an excellent joiner. Later that year, as work from the building society grew, we took on more joiners. At that time, I subcontracted most plumbing and electrical work—plumbing went to John McDonald Plumbers, Paisley, and electrical work to Ace Electrical, owned by my cousin Fiona's husband, Malky Adams.

Running the business from home was no longer sustainable. To maintain proper administration, we needed office and storage space.

1987

We kept pushing forward, working non-stop with our private and commercial customers. Bob Jack introduced me to contract manager Jim Harvey at British Airways (BA) at Glasgow Airport. Bob only wanted me to get a small share of the contracts, but within a year, we were getting a lot of work from BA and had stopped working with Lamberts, apart from the occasional domestic job from Bob's co-director, Joe Moreland.

One of those jobs was building a conservatory for Joe at his home in Kilmarnock. It was an expensive contract, but Joe seemed to think he was getting it for free since we had been doing work for Lamberts. I had already asked for payment twice, but things escalated when, during construction, he was unpleasant to my son Jamie, who was working with us over the summer.

I was in no mood for niceties. Joe got a verbal blasting, and I told him I wasn't leaving his office until he paid me. Bob Jack tried to smooth things over, but I eventually walked out with my money— and no more contracts from Lamberts.

What Bob hadn't factored in was that Jim Harvey's boss, Bob Provan, and I had been at college together during my DMS days. And Bob Provan wanted Lamberts out.

Over the next few months, I travelled to London, Edinburgh, and Aberdeen with Jim Harvey. It was always satisfying to receive those colorful BA cheques each month.

During the summer, Elaine and I took the family to an apartment in Alcúdia, in the north of Majorca, in the Spanish Balearics. The beach there is particularly good for children, as it remains shallow for a long way out to sea, with soft sand and great nearby amenities and restaurants.

On our first Sunday, the kids were playing in the pool within the apartment complex. Emma had her favourite soft toy with her, which fell into the water. When she came back, we placed the toy—called a "Puffalump"—on the veranda to dry in the sun. That morning, we had planned a visit to the Roman ruins at Pollentia, near Alcúdia, which we did. When we returned in the afternoon, Emma rushed inside to check if her Puffalump had dried out.

Earlier that day, I had put orange stickers on the patio door leading to the veranda. The glass was only 3mm thick and so clear that we had already accidentally walked into it. However, while we were out, the local housekeepers had peeled the stickers off.

In her excitement, Emma ran straight through the glass, with horrific consequences. She suffered numerous cuts to her arms, legs, and body, and glass had entered her eyes. Blood was spurting everywhere. I lifted her up and carried her to our hired Fiat Panda, driving straight to the complex's first aid station. Elaine held her in the car while my hands stuck to the steering wheel with blood.

At the first aid post, a military paramedic quickly realised he could only do so much and called for medical backup from the army. Emma had a deep cut under her armpit, which had bled heavily onto Elaine, making it look as though she had also been injured. Emma turned to me and asked, "Am I going to die Daddy?"

A military ambulance took Elaine and Emma to A&E in Palma, about an hour's drive south. I followed with the other kids in the Panda. It took a couple of hours to patch her up and remove the glass from her eyes, but she was safe.

Back at the apartments, I was furious about the glass. Since our room was now unserviceable, I insisted on a new one. On the new veranda door, I wrote "DANGER" in Elaine's lipstick. Later, due to issues with her medication, Emma needed a fitness-to-fly certificate, which meant more medical examinations. We were relieved to leave Majorca behind and have never returned.

When we finally arrived back in Manchester, where I had left the car, it was 2:00 am. We were exhausted but grateful to be heading home. As we drove through Scotland, somewhere on the A74 south of Abington, a woman two cars ahead of me fell asleep at the wheel and crashed into the barriers causing an immediate pile-up. The car in front of me and I managed to swerve past the crashed vehicle, but we collided in the emergency lane. Our car the Montego was written off.

Luckily, we were all okay. I had sore wrists from bracing against the steering wheel, which had bent on impact, and Elaine had a bruised leg. The kids, safely strapped in, were unharmed.

The police and ambulance arrived, and I was breathalyzed, which came back negative. A local recovery company from Abington towed the car, and the owner kindly let me use his personal vehicle to get the family home. When we arrived, Elaine went straight to bed and didn't get up for two days.

The following day, a low-loader arrived with our wrecked car. The driver, an elderly man, was lowering the ramp when it suddenly fell, narrowly missing his head by mere inches. People say bad luck comes in three—I was relieved we could move on without further incidents.

In September, Alistair approached me for a loan. He wanted to marry his girlfriend, Shona, and I was happy to help. I also assisted him in getting a council flat in Glenburn's high-rises. One Saturday morning, he rang me, panicked. Our new van had been vandalized in the car park, and he was too afraid to leave his flat.

I grabbed an iron bar and drove over. When I arrived, I saw the damaged van, its window was smashed, but there was no sign of any troublemakers. I found Alistair safe inside his flat.

With a better salary, he started a family. When his daughter, Lisa, was born, he moved to a flat in Paisley town centre.

CHAPTER 34:
1ST BUSINESS STRATEGY

In 1987, we took a lease on an office in Mirren House, located on Back Sneddon Street in Paisley, owned by the Dinardo Company. It was just one room, but it helped carry us through the most profitable period the company had ever seen. Clients need a sense of security before engaging with a builder, so advertising had to be well-phrased, and certain elements needed to be in place. Genuine, high-quality clients won't hire a cowboy builder. Using my training, I developed a business strategy:

- Advertise as quality builders.
- Gain membership with the Federation of Master Builders.
- Secure a prime listing in Yellow Pages.
- Hire skilled tradespeople.
- Diversify into shopfitting.
- Register for VAT.
- Pay all taxes.
- Establish reference sites.
- Provide proper PPE with company logos for all workers.
- Move administration to Mirren House.
- Find additional storage space.

We implemented all of this; however, storage became an issue, taking over both my garage and my father-in-law's garage in Foxbar. Despite this, we successfully operated from Mirren House until 1989.

By this time, we had several workstreams:

- Domestic Contracts – Extensions, repairs, attic conversions, new kitchens and bathrooms, landscaping.
- Commercial Contracts – Shop and office fitting for clients such as ABS, William Hill, Ladbrokes, The Body Shop, Duncan Rogers, British Airways, and Lambert Contracts.

Our turnover grew from £100,000 to £500,000 over two years. During this period, Elaine hired one of her cousins who proved to be an excellent worker.

At home, we faced a major decision regarding Jenni. She had won a scholarship to the Dance School of Scotland in Knightswood, Glasgow. We didn't want her to board, so we arranged for her Papa, James Keenan, to drive her to and from school daily, often using my company car. Sometimes, I made the trip myself. Jenni would always be exhausted and starving after classes, so I'd stop at a local chip shop at Anniesland for a burger and a Coke before heading home. This routine continued until 1990.

One of our key contracts was with the Margaret Blackwood Housing Association, which managed various properties around Glasgow. Their Glasgow location was on Argyle Street, at the corner of Perth Street. We secured regular work from them, and their favourite joiner was Rab Scott.

Rab was a fantastic worker but also a bit of a devil. One day, he arrived at reception in high spirits, only to find everyone looking somber. In his usual bouncy way, he quipped, "What's the matter, folks? Has somebody died?"

He turned the corner and came face-to-face with two coffins resting on trolleys, waiting for the undertaker.

Rab was always up to mischief. I once saw him walking behind a man with macrocephaly, a condition that caused his head to be three times the normal size. Rab had joked before that he feared the man's head might explode. As the man got closer, Rab reached into his tool bag, pulled out a 4-inch nail, and held it over the man's head b e h i n d h i s b a c k with a devilish grin. Naughty Rab.

On 6th July, the tragic Piper Alpha disaster struck in the North Sea. An explosion claimed the lives of 167 men. The news had a profound impact on me and has stayed with me ever since.

1989

Early in the year, we received news that Jamie's school, Stanley Green, was set to close. All local secondary school pupils would now have to attend Paisley Grammar School. Elaine led a campaign to keep Stanley Green open, as they had recognized Jamie's dyslexia and were providing excellent support.

Unfortunately, the campaign was unsuccessful, and Jamie was sent to Paisley Grammar to complete his schooling in preparation for university. This wasn't necessarily a bad thing—Paisley Grammar had a strong reputation, having once been a fee-paying school. My sister Anne had her education there and as she went on to become a Cambridge PhD. being and old Grammarians had a certain cache.

When the local council attempted to close it, the proposal attracted the attention of Mrs Thatcher, Andrew Neil, and the then-Secretary of State for Scotland, Michael Lang, ultimately saving the school. That said, Jamie hated it, however his Higher exam results were enough to secure his place at university in 1990.

The business continued to grow, prompting a move to new offices at 4 St Mirren Street, Paisley. We also hired Vera Gordon—Elaine's brother John's mother-in-law—as office manager, followed later that year by Lee McCrimmon as an admin secretary. I bought Elaine a new car: a white Nissan Micra.

At the time, I was receiving many requests for electrical and plumbing work, so I registered a sister company, Fastex Ltd. I organised electricians and plumbers, each with their own contracts and marked-up vans. However, after about a year, it became clear that a significant amount of materials were going towards "homers" (side jobs), turning the venture into a loss-maker. I shut it down and got rid of the thieves.

That summer, we visited Cambridge to spend time with Anne and Gordon. Anne was pursuing her PhD at St. John's college,(Johns) and they had invited us to the Summer May Ball. Elaine bought a designer dress from Roberta Buchan's in Glasgow, while I wore my kilt. We attracted a lot of attention from photographers, and the highlight came when they asked the Master, Robert Hinde—

Anne's professor—to step aside so they could take a photo of just Elaine and me.

Elaine Cambridge Ball at John's July 1989

1990

Business was booming. I had just finished renovating our house in Tantallon Drive and treated myself to a new Honda Prelude EX. Around this time, I got a call from Brian Kell, an old university friend from my MBA course.

Brian's family-owned large parts of Glasgow's East End, including the arches at Paddy's Market and various properties near the Barrowlands. One of his trading units in the arches had burned down, and he needed repair quotes. I agreed to meet him there the next day.

The moment we arrived, the stench hit me. Both ends of the arch tunnel had been boarded up, and inside, there was no power, as all services had been cut off. Armed with a large flashlight, I shone a beam over the charred debris— only to see dozens of rats scurrying away. This wasn't going to be an easy contract. Brian and I had a serious business discussion, and I ensured that I'd be paid properly.

We struck a deal: he would pay me in cash, in stages. On the first day, when I took the boys to see the site, they were gagging at the sight (and smell) of the place. Understandably reluctant, they only agreed to get started after I offered £5 per day in "dirty money" plus a £100 completion bonus. Big Charlie, our plasterer and my Dad's cousin, taped up his trouser bottoms, as did the rest of the crew. Two days later, the debris was cleared, packed into a 12-yard roll-on/off skip.

We waterproofed the arch, re-sheeted it, and built new end walls with doors. Brian handed me my first cash payment in a plastic bag full of bundled fivers. He passed it to me in the Blue-Chip pub next to Paddy's Market. I took it home and stuffed it in the bottom drawer of my bedroom until I could deposit it.

A few days later, on a Friday night, Elaine asked for some spending money for a meal and drinks with her friends. I told her to check the bottom drawer. Her scream still echoes in my mind— she thought I'd pulled off a bank robbery!

Three weeks into the job, Brian asked when we'd be finished. I estimated another month. Then he hit me with three new requests:

Work faster.

Increase the number of hawker bins from 80 to 100.

Build a new restaurant at the back of the unit on Merchant Lane.

I recalculated the costs, and he agreed. However, I questioned how I was supposed to fit 100 hawker counters into a space meant for 80. Brian, who had a congenital speech defect, replied, "Make them wee-er" (smaller).

Doing the sums, I realised Brian was raking in at least £500 a day from the hawker stalls alone, not to mention profits from his greasy spoon café catering to the Paddy's Market crowd. I crash-programmed the work, brought in extra agency trades, and finished three weeks later. I walked away with a decent profit for six weeks' work.

Despite its rough reputation, Paddy's Market was a fascinating place, full of resilient people making a living on the margins. Sadly, the District Council shut it down in 1996, ending a 200-year-old way of life.

We did more work for Brian, including jobs at his industrial units near Bell Street in the Barrowlands. Two incidents from that time still make me smile.

The first: one lunchtime, our aluminum scaffolding disappeared. When I rang Brian to report the delay, he said, "Hold on, I'll call you back." Ten minutes later, he confirmed that our scaffolding had been cashed in at his scrap yard—run by his own brother!

The second: when we arrived, there were old Rexene benches from a closed shop. Old Martin, one of the crew, said he'd love to keep one for his garden in Gallowhill, Paisley. Sure enough, he took one home. Every time I passed his house; I saw that bench sitting proudly in his front garden—it even outlasted Martin.

Running a business with your wife brings unique pressures. I was fully immersed in the company, while Elaine was balancing her support for me with managing the household and raising the kids. Naturally, this led to arguments, and there were nights I ended up sleeping on the couch. I don't blame Elaine—back then, I was ruthlessly focused, spending sleepless nights planning the next day, week, or month.

One night, around 1 a.m., I heard noises outside. A group of teenagers were taking drugs on the stairs near our house. That was the final straw. After some discussion, Elaine and I decided it was time to leave Tantallon Drive.

CHAPTER 35:
THE HALL OF CALDWELL

In early summer, we moved from Foxbar to Caldwell, taking up residence at the Hall of Caldwell—an attached property dating back to the 1600s. It was a country house with four bedrooms, a bathroom, a shower room, a kitchen, a toilet, a large lounge, an outhouse, and a tennis court. Emma was still at school, Jamie had started at the University of Paisley, and Jenni was being driven back and forth to the Dance School of Scotland in Knightswood on the north side of Glasgow.

Our neighbours, Peter, and Diana were distinctly middle class and made early moves to welcome us to Caldwell—this, apparently, was how things were done. Their family had grown up in Caldwell, but by then, it was an empty nest. Diana was a senior physiotherapist, and Peter was a board member of the Irvine Development Trust; they were also both Lloyd's names.

I arrived in a tracksuit, which was somewhat at odds with the conservative attire of the other neighbours at Waverly Cottage on the north side of the house. Jim Dempsey was a local architect and had been acquainted with all the other neighbors for years. His wife, Valerie, was a genuinely lovely woman—unlike some of the others, who had difficulty even saying good morning once they'd laid down the unspoken rules of Caldwell.

Caldwell itself is a small hamlet about half a mile uphill from Uplawmoor, passing the local golf club and Caldwell Tower. Our local farmer, Alec Mitchell, would visit us occasionally. A typical farmer, Alec, made his money breeding Shire horses and sheepdogs. His farmhands, Leslie, and Sandy were the kind of characters Roald Dahl would have loved.

The Hall of Caldwell

Leslie, of Irish stock, was rumored to have been jilted by his fiancée. He'd run away to Scotland, leaving behind a family farm now managed by his four brothers. When he wasn't working for Alec, he took on jobs for other farmers in the area, like the King family. He lived in a dilapidated farmhouse and frequently clashed with Alec—especially when drink was involved.

A typical Friday night at the farm saw other heavy horse farmers arriving to have their mares sired by Alec's breeding colts. This inevitably turned into a drinking session, culminating in a gathering at Sandy's caravan, where they'd polish off bottles of John Barleycorn whisky, accompanied by Sandy's accordion playing.

A few days after we arrived, Jenny and Emma darted behind the furniture when they spotted a disheveled man approaching our garden. It turned out to be Alec, who, to put it mildly, had seen better days. His clothes hadn't been washed since his mother died in the 1950s. When he asked if I had anything for his arthritis, I poured him a stiff whisky. He took a sip, surveyed the room, and declared that my wife was "a real wumman."

I could write a book about those early days in Caldwell—it remains a blessing to have become part of country life.

Eventually, Leslie fell out with Alec and moved in with young Davy King, who owned the land around the old castle. One morning, as he was having breakfast, he simply slumped in his chair and died. A few days later, his four brothers came to take his body back to Ireland. I had met him not long before at the ABS in Paisley, at St Mirren Brae. Immaculately dressed, he was unrecognizable at first, attending business and the monthly farmers' market in Paisley.

Within a few years, Alec had also succumbed to "arthritis," not long after I last saw him at our neighbour's house, "Crossburn," where Anne and Colin Sparrow lived next to the Mitchell farm. Propped up in a chair at the centre of a room filled with guests, he was unusually well-dressed. Newspapers were spread around his seat—Alec had become incontinent. The previous year, he had been burgled and beaten; rumor had it he had £180,000 in cash hidden under his bed. He died not long after.

Sandy, meanwhile, carried on in his caravan at the back of the farm. On weekends, we'd hear his accordion playing late into the night, and on occasion, he'd head into the fields, lamping foxes before dropping them with his shotgun.

When Alec was still alive, he had let Sandy move into a new bungalow on another Mitchell farm, about a quarter of a mile from Caldwell. In Sandy's absence, he rented out the caravan to transient road tarmac workers— "boys from the black stuff." They got drunk one night and set the caravan on fire. When Sandy found out, he went on the hunt with his shotgun—there are some black toppers out there still nursing buckshot wounds.

He found out he had Parkinsons disease and died not long after, bringing his story to an abrupt end. The local farmers gathered at the hillock where he used to train sheepdogs and scattered his ashes to the sound of an accordion playing "Dark Lochnagar." A lot of malt was consumed that day—it was the end of Sandy.

The next morning, passing by the farm, I noticed the sheep gathered on the hillock, grazing. I think Sandy would have liked that.

That summer, we took the kids on holiday to Florida. We visited Disney World and Universal Studios, with a stop at Chicago O'Hare before transferring to our Miami flight. Preoccupied with the airport shops, we barely noticed the Tannoy announcement:

"Would the Green family please proceed to the gate? Your flight is closing." We ran like the wind—a long, arduous sprint for Maw, Paw, and the weans—boarding to a chorus of disapproving tuts.

Arriving in Miami at 2 a.m., we were met with the news that the airline had lost our luggage. After hiring a Lincoln Town Car, we set off for a one-night stay at a Holiday Inn. Getting lost in the Miami suburbs was not part of the plan, and with no satnav in those days, I pulled into a petrol station to ask for directions. Leaving Elaine and the kids outside, I approached the pay cabin, where the attendant—apparently alone—was doing press-ups on the floor. As he sprang up, I caught sight of a handgun on the counter.

The moment was awkward, to say the least. After delivering a lecture on the dangers of the neighborhood, he pointed me back towards the interstate. We still had to locate one of five Holiday Inns. Eventually, we found it, and the next morning, after a hearty American breakfast, we continued to our hotel in Kissimmee.

It was the Fourth of July.

We were all excited, and the heat was intense. I slipped away to a local shop while the family enjoyed the hotel pool. When I returned sometime later, I was dressed in a Florida summer beach outfit—a luminous green creation courtesy of Panama Jack. I can still hear the kids laughing at their naff Dad.

Over the next two weeks, we toured the entire area. Our first stop was Disney World, where we visited the Epcot Centre. I have to say, we had a fantastic time. The kids loved the razzmatazz, and Elaine and I soaked it all up like big kids. At one point, Elaine went missing. I eventually found her sitting on the steps of Minnie Mouse's little house, wearing an Alice band with ears.

We didn't miss a trick, staying for the evening concert and light show. Disney is for all kids, no matter their age.

After a couple of days at Disney World, we headed to Universal Studios. It was just as brilliant walking through movie sets, watching the Indiana Jones stunt show and feeling the heat from the special effects. The Bond movie stunts, and cowboy gunfights were pure magic.

Jamie Jennifer and Emma were all thriving and Elaine and I were so proud of them as the were starting out in life and getting ready to become married and becoming mums and dads.

Jennifer Jamie and Emma

1991

Back home, we faced the decision to finally let Jennifer go to London. Jennie and her mum had already travelled there to scout out Theatre and Dance colleges, eventually settling on Arts Educational School in Chiswick. We booked her a room at the Brookes Hotel for the first few weeks before finding her a flat above an old fruit shop next to Chiswick station. The place was owned by an elderly Italian lady, Mrs Biscetsca.

My Daughter the actress Jenni Keenan Green

Those were tough days, worrying about our 16-year-old daughter living alone in London. Eventually, she moved in with her classmate Alexa, which eased our worries slightly.

For the next few years, we made regular trips to Chiswick to visit Jennie. We often had a drink at the Tabard Pub and dined at local spots like Chimichanga and The Piano.

Business was booming, so we took premises at No. 4 St Mirren Street, overlooking Dunn Square Gardens in the centre of Paisley. Elaine had hired Vera to help manage the office and later brought in Lee McCrimmon as an office assistant.

One of the perks of running your own business is the flexibility to fit work around life. Elaine would bring our two Bichon Frisés dogs, Daisy, and Blanche, to the office, and on the way home, she'd stop by M&S for something tasty for dinner. Our office had its own balcony, with views of Paisley Town Hall where we had our wedding reception with its impressive clock, and Paisley Abbey—where we got married.

Towards the end of the year, the surveyor for ABS asked me to inspect an apartment on the top floor of No. 4 St Mirren Street. The property belonged to ABS, but the tenant, Mr Kelly, had a lifelong right to live there due to a clause dating back to when his father, a banker, had lived in the building.

The surveyor collected the keys from Mr Kelly, and we headed upstairs. The first thing I noticed was the complete darkness—old wartime blackout blinds still covered the windows. The flat hadn't been decorated since the war. Each room was a time capsule, unchanged since Mr Kelly's parents had passed away just after the war.

In one room, an old gramophone sat with a Bakelite record of Al Bowlly's "Goodnight, Sweetheart" still on it. I lifted a clock from the mantelpiece, revealing a shiny black square where it had once stood, surrounded by decades of dust.

I believe ABS made Mr Kelly an offer he couldn't refuse, and the flat was eventually sold.

CHAPTER 36:
BUSINESS EXPANSION

By the summer of 1992, we had about 20 men working for us, so we expanded further, taking up an industrial unit at Abbeymill Business Centre. We refitted the unit with an office and workshop, and every morning, the boys would meet with me so I could assign their jobs for the day or week.

I had hired Kenny, whom I'd known since school and had even been best man at his wedding. Kenny was a great joiner, and on his 40th birthday, I promoted him to Contracts Manager and issued him with a company car. He was a real character, always in good humor, with an eye for the ladies, and he built a solid team of joiners and shopfitters around him. The orders kept coming in, particularly from the ABS, which had us working all over Scotland and Northern Ireland. Most of the work involved general repairs, so I split the boys into various teams.

Alistair headed up the building team, which focused on brickwork, concrete work, plastering, structural alterations, and foundations. Alistair was always my second in command, though this didn't sit well with either him or Kenny. So, with Kenny as Contracts Manager, Alistair could get on with the work without any disputes.

Jim Ford was hired to head up the electrical team, which included two others: Maxi Nelson and an apprentice, Alan. Alan had been recommended by Kenny, but it quickly became clear he was struggling with his exams, even after I arranged for Jim Ford to give him one-on-one tuition during overtime. Elaine was looking out from our office at No. 4 St Mirren St. and spotted Alan wandering through Dunn Square Gardens without a care in the world when he was supposed to be at college. When we checked his attendance, we discovered he was a regular absentee, so I let him go. Alan then took the company to an industrial tribunal, which he lost—much to his embarrassment.

We hired Larry and Eddie to form our decorating team, which was a little awkward at first, as Larry had been hired first and was made lead decorator, while Eddie, who had originally been Larry's journeyman, was now working under him. To their credit, they handled it professionally, and their work was immaculate.

Later that year, Larry and Eddie were on a night shift in an ABS branch on Oxford Street in Glasgow when they found a black bin bag full of money on a chair. Larry phoned me straight away, and we followed protocol by calling the police, the branch key-holder, and the local surveyor responsible for the works. It turned out there was approximately £90,000 in the bag. Larry and Eddie were rewarded with a good bonus from ABS. This, of course, caused quite a stir among the rest of the team—some of whom didn't entirely agree with their honesty. To avoid any potential issues with my clients, I recalibrated the team after a few days to ensure we remained professional and trustworthy.

Mark Grey was brought in to head up our plumbing and heating team, later joined by Paul McManus and, occasionally, Paul's Dad, Charlie, who was highly skilled in plumbing and tiling.

Our plastering and roughcasting team consisted of Duncan McClelland, Alec Sellars, and Big Charlie Green, my father's younger cousin. Duncan was the nicest man ever to wield a hawk and trowel—bright but overly sensitive. Unfortunately, that wasn't the best trait to have in the construction world, where banter could be brutally rough. It was very much an acquired taste for bastards. More than once, we arrived at the office in the Mill to find a resignation letter from Duncan. Each time, I sent Kenny to fetch him back and reassure him how much we valued him.

With such a big team, we were regularly out for birthdays, stag nights, and boxing events we sponsored. These nights out were usually riotous, and some often drank so much they could only crawl on all fours like a dog— barking, since they couldn't form words.

One particularly memorable night out was our Christmas do in 1992. One of our new young labourers, James—who had been hired by Alistair and was "a halfpenny short of a shilling," as they say—stood up in the middle of the group and burst into song. He started with Jingle Bells, then, by popular demand, kept going as the drinks flowed. Because of James's mental impediment, it was outrageously funny—some of the boys were rolling on the floor laughing, and even the older lads were wiping away tears.

Normally, they were a bit better behaved when I was around, so I had a policy of leaving at 9:00 pm to avoid any trouble. One night, Alistair, his brother Tommy, and some of the lads headed to La Verty's Bar, opposite the Russell Institute at the bottom of New Street in Paisley...

Just to give you a bit of background on this night out—Alistair and Tommy were drowning their sorrows, as their Dad had been killed the week before when a bus ran over his head about a hundred yards from La Verty's. Tommy had been hired by Alistair with my blessing to support the building team and, like Alistair, was a good worker. However, Alistair confided in me that both he and Tommy had been taken out of the family home and placed in care in Dumfries. We later found out the home had been abusing several of the children, including Alistair and Tommy, who had tried to escape as young boys, only to be returned and further abused. I also discovered after this event that Tommy had clearly been traumatized by it all and had a resulting violent temper.

Somebody made a comment about their father, and a melee ensued, leading to the police being called. Several of the boys were arrested, and it was reported that Tommy was handcuffed behind his back, thrown face first into the police van, and charged with causing a breach of the peace. I really liked Alistair and Tommy, so we just drew a veil over the incident.

The boys were always challenging, usually because of their personal lives. I had a policy of only hiring apprentices from single-parent families, typically from Linwood, which had been devastated by the loss of the car factory. This had forced many fathers to seek work elsewhere, leaving behind broken marriages or, in some cases, dying too soon—such was the case with Michael and Gary. Other apprentices included Billy, Graham and, as mentioned before, Alan.

Alec Sellers, in his early twenties, was living alone in a council house in Glenburn, Paisley, and was in deep trouble with a local gang that had threatened to murder him. He had asked Alistair for help, so I gave him a start as a labourer for the plastering team. In fairness to Alec, he learned fast and became a good plasterer under the tuition of Duncan and Big Charlie. He only let me down once in his career with us—when we were carrying out alterations to a tenement flat in Hampden, Glasgow. According to reports, Alec, in a high-spirited moment of comedy, took a pair of knickers from a drawer in the householder's bedroom, put them over his head to entertain the boys, and walked straight into the woman owner as she returned home early. I had to redecorate the entire bedroom to her taste to keep the story out of the papers. Alec never got a raise after that event.

During the summer, ABS asked us to alter their branch in Blairgowrie, and Kenny put a team together, including a new joiner, Gerry.

Gerry, in his late thirties, was a particularly skilled joiner. He had seemed a bit subdued for a couple of weeks, so I asked if he was all right. He replied, "I'm not getting on with my wife—it's a long time since I had any nookie, Jim." I told Kenny to see if he could help Gerry after work.

The story goes like this: after work, Kenny takes them into a bar in Blairgowrie where there's a decent crowd. Kenny scans the room, sniffing the air like an animal before zoning in on a group of women out for the night. "Follow me, boys." They have a good night, pairing off with some of the women. Later, Gerry and Kenny treat the girls to a fish supper and invite them into the large shop-fitting van. Kenny sits in the front while Gerry is in the back with a suitably fed local woman. Kenny hears Gerry ask, "Did ye like that fish supper, hen?" "Aye, I did, Gerry." "So, am I getting it or whit?" Details are a bit hazy according to reports, but Gerry was in a much better mood after that.

The building team was in high demand, so I asked Alistair to find another labourer. Without asking too many questions, a big, strong young man joined the team and gave a good account of himself for a few days—until I noticed he had started limping. I stopped him and asked why, and he said he had a sore foot from a burn he had received a few days earlier while working with a road gang. A hot chipping had got inside his boot and burned the side of his foot. As a trained first aider, I asked to see the wound. He removed his boot gingerly, peeled off his sock, and revealed a suppurating mess about the size of a lemon. I asked why he hadn't got it treated already, and he said he hadn't realised it was that bad—he hadn't taken his boot off to look until now. "But you must have been in agony," I said. He then admitted he was homeless, living in a lodging house where, if you left anything out at night, it would be stolen—so he slept with his boots on. Poor bugger. We took him to the hospital where they patched him up and he made a full recovery. I bought him a pair of safety boots and a bundle of work socks.

I often left recruitment to Alistair, Kenny, or Dad, as they had numerous contacts. Sometimes, I advertised in the Evening Times or Daily Record newspapers, but when it came to interviews, it was usually a case of not too many questions and a firm handshake sealing the deal. With tradesmen, I always checked their tool bags—it was a great guide to their skill.

Alistair once brought a labourer onto the site to help lift a heavy concrete lintel into place. He did well, but when I asked about his background, Alistair was unusually evasive. Digging further, I discovered the man was his mother's ex-boyfriend—who had just done eight years in Barlinnie for murder. After that, I started using my HR training techniques.

Each morning, I organised a breakfast for all the boys before they started their shift. This served several purposes. Firstly, an army marches on its stomach, and a building company needs its team fueled up. Some of the boys came from poor backgrounds and wouldn't have eaten before work. Secondly, stopping on route for a greasy spoon shop or burger van meant less time on site. Thirdly, it gave us a chance to bond as a team and learn from each other.

One morning, as we all sat around the mess room table, Craig— one of Kenny's joiners—pulled out a used condom with some contents still inside. He held it up and accused Kenny of being "a durty bastard," saying he'd found it stuck to the side of the works van. Kenny asked to see it, and Craig handed it over. Without hesitation, Kenny dipped his finger into the contents, slowly tasted it, and declared, "Not mine—I don't recognize the taste." The table erupted half in disgust, half in laughter. Nothing beats a fun start to the day. Thankfully, it was all a planned stunt between Craig and Kenny—the contents were condensed milk.

In construction, people let you down all the time, and you need a strong resolve not to let it get to you. My next disappointment came when I hired a relative. He was out of work, and his mother had appealed to me to give him a job.

He was supposed to be at the Graigton site early to receive a concrete mix for some foundations. Instead, I got a call from the concrete company saying no one was on site to direct them, so the load was redirected to another contract before it started to cure in the drum. I rang his Mum, and she told me he was still in bed. So, I sacked him.

Employing friends and relatives can go well, or it can go badly—just like hiring anyone else. My policy was to keep the good ones and let the bad ones go.

A similar situation happened when Alistair asked me to give his wife Shona's young brother a job of laboring. We were doing some landscaping work for Elaine's uncle, Peter, in Glenashdale Way, Hunterhill, Paisley. A load of sand and gravel had been delivered in 40kg bags, which had to be hand- balled onto the site.

I watched the young boy struggle to lift a gravel bag, only for it to slowly slip back to the ground. He tried resolutely before finally giving up. He only lasted one day; however, he went on to become a top chef.

In April, we got a contract to refit the ABS branch in Dumfries. It meant mobilizing the whole team, travelling on Friday afternoon with a fleet of vehicles loaded up for a weekend campaign. Elaine had arranged a B&B for the men, while I was booked into the same hotel as the ABS surveyor—a mistake for two reasons, which I'll explain.

On the Friday night, after the boys checked in, they went out on the town. I had recruited a new brickie—let's call him Barry—to assist with underbuilding work where emergency bandit screens were to be fitted in the basement. Barry, however, decided to share various drugs with the lads, with catastrophic effects.

They went crazy, decorating the entire B&B with different-coloured string foam. The B&B owner called Elaine with a serious complaint. Since I didn't have a mobile phone in those days, Elaine drove from Paisley to Dumfries on Saturday to see what was going on. By then, the latest update from the B&B was that the neighbours had complained about men taking women into the shop-fitting vans in the early hours, with very noisy "goings-on."

On Saturday morning, the boys were late for work. I was raging. When I found out what had happened, I dismissed four of them immediately despite their protests. I then made some calls to get replacements as soon as possible.

The atmosphere was subdued, but they got their heads down. Elaine arrived that afternoon and went straight to the B&B to assess the damage, arrange cleaning, and pay compensation. She wasn't happy that I was staying in a different hotel, but hindsight is a perfect science—I hadn't foreseen the drugs issue.

With the new workers in place, progress had picked up. I think the remaining lads, earning three times their usual wages, saw the risk of losing their jobs too, so a bit of competition emerged, and we caught up with the schedule.

Before the end of the shift, I warned them to behave and not be late on Sunday morning.

Now, my next challenge was convincing Elaine that things were back under control. We went for a nice dinner and, afterwards, sat on a bench in the town square, enjoying a lovely evening and watching people go by.

The boys had been off shift for about an hour when I spotted a crowd of them leaving a pub and heading for a kebab place. As they emerged, Duncan was leading the pack, looking in good spirits—already drunk. He spotted me and Elaine sitting on the bench, got about ten feet away, and shouted, "Jimmy!"

Then, as if it were a Glengarry cap, he slapped his kebab onto his head and saluted me, sauce and lettuce dripping down his face.

It was hilarious. Even Elaine struggled to hold back a smile.

"Fit for work?" I asked. "Guaranteed, boss!" Duncan grinned.

Kenny reassured me he'd keep an eye on them. Elaine had to head home, so we said our goodbyes, and I returned to the Station Hotel.

The ABS surveyor was already drunk, having joined a golfing team in the lounge bar. I had a couple of beers, glad to unwind after the madness of the past 24 hours.

The golfers were playing drunken party games, one of which involved pretending to be engines on a Lancaster bomber. As part of the game, someone declared my engine was on fire, at which point I was doused with several pints of beer and lager.

I fucking hate golfers.

That winter, work began to thin out for the building squad. Then, an order came in to supply bricklaying teams for the new International Arrivals Hall at Glasgow Airport. I provided two squads—each with two brickies and a labourer—and left the organization to my Dad. My number one squad was Martin and Jakey Laird, with my Dad as the labourer.

The job was progressing well, so I thought it'd be a good idea to take some photos for a new sales brochure.

When I arrived on-site and pulled out my camera, the reaction was as if I'd drawn a gun.

The construction industry is rife with casual workers, many of whom claim benefits while working "on the grip." The last thing they wanted was photographic evidence of them on the job. That's why, in most construction photos, men are either hiding their faces or turning their backs.

We were receiving many requests for extensions and attic conversions. Clients often wanted to avoid paying VAT, which made things tricky, as we were under the scrutiny of the taxman— and make no mistake, they are not stupid. Some clients offered cash, but we still had to account for wages and materials bought on account.

After one tax inspection, we had to drive at great speed to the Tax Collection office in Greenock to update our payments and avoid heavy penalties. It's also worth remembering that if you collect VAT, it is not yours—it belongs to Customs and Revenue.

One of the extensions we built was in Govan, a bedroom extension with an ensuite bathroom. I subcontracted John Timlin to fit the new Jacuzzi pool. We were just finishing the contract when John and his apprentice carried in the exceptionally large and expensive Jacuzzi. The pool was fitted, and all that remained was installing the extremely costly mixer tap. John asked his apprentice to hand it over, but it slipped from the boy's hands and put a hole in the pool. I have never heard anyone get such a tongue lashing. Take it from me—never fall out with John Timlin.

Working at Abbeymill Business Centre presented new opportunities with the local facilities, managed by Malcolm McMin. The entire Mill site was owned by the Watlings Group, and we were regularly awarded contracts for repairs and office alterations. I got on well with Malcolm, who knew the buildings inside out, having previously been the fire master when Muir was in operation. We often walked the site together, as he explained the history and uses of the different buildings. Many of them were due to be demolished to make way for a new Morrisons supermarket and car park.

Security at the Mill was poor. Thieves frequently broke in at night, stripping the old buildings of slates, aluminum, and lead. Malcolm invited me to tender for the removal of all old slates and scrap metal after one thief fell from the roof, leaving a trail of blood behind. The deal was that we would remove the materials at no cost but retain the salvage value.

These were high-quality Ballachulish slates, around 100,000 in total. I struck a deal with a slate recovery company in Glasgow and made a good profit— some of which I gave to Malcolm so he could take his wife on holiday.

On one of the higher roofs, I sent Alec Sellers to help with repairs. However, Alec suffered from vertigo but was too scared to tell me. Determined to overcome his fear, he crawled out of the skylight onto the apex and made it about five feet along the ridge before freezing. He was unable to go forward or back. I had to call in Big Charlie Green, my Dad's cousin, to get Alec off the roof. It took some effort, but we eventually managed to pull him back into the attic space, where he was suitably sick.

After that, we needed to inspect the roof with a cherry picker. I went up in the basket with Malcolm, and after finishing the inspection, we lowered the basket to the ground. As I swung off, I reached for the handrail to lower myself—but it wasn't secure. I fell with my full weight onto the basket's kickplate, hitting my back so hard that I couldn't breathe. Malcolm thought I was dying. An ambulance took me to the hospital for an X-ray, where the consultant told me I was incredibly lucky to have avoided spinal damage— because I was fat.

On 14th November, I got a call from the ABS surveyor, who informed me that a bomb blast in Coleraine, Northern Ireland, had caused serious damage to their branch there. The surveyor, Graham, arranged for us to fly to Belfast, where we would hire a car and drive to Coleraine.

We flew into Belfast Airport, hired a car from Hertz, and parked in Patrick Streetcar park before heading to the ABS branch on Royal Avenue, near the Europa Hotel. Any risks associated with this visit were at the back of my mind, although being near the Europa was always a concern as it was the most bombed hotel in Ireland. Graham wanted to check in at headquarters before we travelled to Coleraine.

Driving north through Ballymena, I was struck by how much the landscape resembled the West of Scotland. The houses in North Belfast were covered in Union flags, with kerb stones painted red, white, and blue.

Arriving in Coleraine, the devastation was plain to see. Shrapnel had left claw-like marks on the town hall opposite the ABS branch, which had already been boarded up by another construction company. As soon as I stepped inside to assess the damage, I got a call on the internal line from Eamon from an Irish building company. He was very polite but wanted to meet me for a chat. I was beginning to think that before the day was out, I'd have a bullet in the head—or my kneecaps.

I asked Graham how this guy knew I was here. He just shrugged. I had heard stories about Irish contractors not taking kindly to firms from the mainland "cutting their grass." I was on dangerous ground.

Eamon explained that he was my sponsor. When the work was complete, I had to send my invoices to his company. This made me even more uncomfortable. Graham assured me it was fine—the sponsor company would take a percentage of the contract value. To my mind, this was just extortion, but if it kept me and my people safe, so be it.

Back in Paisley, I asked for volunteers and agreed they would get treble time, with all transport and accommodation costs covered. We hired a white van, and the team travelled via Cairnryan to Larne within a few days.

Towards the end of the contract, Larry and Eddie called, desperate to come home. They had been questioned in their Coleraine hotel and were feeling threatened. I brought all the men home.

We completed the work, and I sent my invoice to ABS, with a copy to Eamon. Graham and I had one last trip to Belfast to sign off on the work.

Again, we hired a car, and parked it in Patrick Street car park, and attended a short meeting at the ABS branch.

On our return, we found the street to the car park blocked by two Ulster Constabulary officers with machine guns. We explained that we needed our car. The officer asked what colour it was. "White Ford Sierra, hired from Hertz," I replied.

His face darkened.

"We're investigating a bomb in a white Sierra in the car park," he said.

After that, I asked Graham for my return ticket and left him behind. If I was being scared off, it was working. I took a taxi straight to the airport and said nothing.

On the flight back to Glasgow, I found some comfort sitting next to Willie Henderson, the famous footballer and manager. But it was a long time before I set foot in Northern Ireland again.

CHAPTER 37:
BANK ROBBERS AND
CAMBRIDGE

In early 1993, we got a major break in contracts from ABS. The company was introducing a new counter-based IT system called NIXDORF, requiring every branch's counters in Scotland to be altered to accommodate the new hardware. The challenge was that they wanted it done quickly so the IT installers could meet a rolling programme. I split the joiners into three teams. They had to work outside normal hours, staying in B&Bs during the day for sleep and working after hours until the job was done.

One team covered the West of Scotland, from Dumfries to Oban; another covered central Scotland; and the third, covering the east, consisted of Timmy Sillars and Jim Usher. They were working over the weekend, so I visited them on Saturday afternoon. The branch had closed early at 12:00, and Timmy was hyper, convinced he'd found the key to the safe.

"So, what's the next move, Timmy?" I asked.

"I'm going to rob this place and fuck off somewhere nobody can find me," he replied. I knew he was serious—when Timmy got mad, he became very polite. When I told him it was just the skeleton key and the active insert was in the head teller's purse, he was devastated.

I should have got rid of Timmy right then, but I didn't—and that was a mistake.

When all the NIXDORF work was completed, I had delivered the programme, made a tidy profit, and the joinery teams were all incredibly happy. At the time, I was building a dormer extension for an old family friend, Jannette Kennovin, in the Meikleriggs estate. I had known Jannette since she was a little girl living next door in Tantallon Drive. Now she was married and had given me the contract, as I had done work for her father, Jimmy, in the early days of my business.

Timmy was transferred to this job to work alongside his brother onsite at the dormer site. We were working on the roof and had brought a tar boiler onto the site. It was Timmy's job to keep it topped up and prevent it from catching fire. The week before, he had been earning about £800 a week, plus expenses. Now, he was working for his little brother, boiling tar, on a basic wage of £200.

The boiler caught fire, leading to an argument between the foreman and Timmy. I was on the roof when I saw Timmy throw a spade at the foreman, just missing his head. Kenny and I shouted at Timmy to behave, but he had completely lost it and started climbing up the scaffolding towards us. We knew we couldn't let him onto the roof, so we moved to the edge to meet him. Seeing us waiting with claw hammers, he jumped back down and disappeared.

I gave him ten minutes before going after him, knowing he was in a dangerous state. I found him at a local bus stop, where he had been violently sick. He was as white as a ghost.

"I'm sorry, Jimmy. I just lost it."

"You need some anger management, son." "So, I'm sacked then?"

"It certainly is, Timmy."

I took him home, and that was the last I ever saw of him.

On the family side, it was my brother Charlie's 40th birthday, and his family had asked me to prepare a big red book on his life so far. It was fun to put together, collecting stories from the rest of the family. Charlie had recently graduated in his church, so I got a photograph and did an oil painting as a present.

Down in Cambridge, my sister Anne was about to graduate with a PhD from St John's College—known simply as 'John's.' Most of the family went down for her special day. Ron, her next-door neighbour and a master tailor in Cambridge, had fitted thousands of graduates for their ceremonies and made sure she was perfectly dressed in her black doctorate cape and purple hood. It was warm and sunny, and the procession from John's to the Senate House was a remarkable sight, with Anne at the front among the graduates—not bad for this "Dr Feg."

My sister Anne on her way to the Cambridge

Senate House for her PhD with our proud Dad looking on.

Over the years, we visited Cambridge regularly, and it was always a great delight. Anne and Gordon were the perfect hosts. We often attended the Cambridge Balls—an experience in itself—partying through the night until breakfast, only to find myself sleeping in Jesus Green overnight and being woken by the park attendant. Many lovely mornings were spent sitting on a bench in Jesus Green, looking over the Cam, enjoying the vista and the sound of the little burn that bordered the Green.

In summer, we would take the children down for a holiday, punting on the Cam—a perfect way to spend a summer's day. Often, we would take the split trip up to Grantchester, disembark, and have tea in the orchard next to Jeffrey Archer's house.

CHAPTER 38:
FLYING HATS AND FAECES

It was the start of 1994, bitterly cold, when we secured a contract to carry out work at the Excelsior Hotel at Glasgow Airport. The job involved roof works, including repointing all the brickwork on the services building, acid-cleaning the chimney stack, and fitting structural bands around it to prevent further deterioration. We also had to carry out lead-burning work on the flashings and, most importantly, drill and fix several large metal covers that had occasionally been blown off—sometimes landing on the airport runway.

I hired a scaffolding company to bridge out the intersections, as the Excelsior was built in the shape of a cross.

It took us a couple of days to haul all our equipment up to the top of the building using the service lift. Inside the service room, where the boiler was, it was warm and dry—just as well, because outside, the wind chill was well below freezing. Martin, Dad, and Big Charlie started the pointing work, with the freezing updraft blowing the loose mortar upwards before it fell back down. We kept the boys going with plenty of hot, sweet tea and frequent visits to the boiler room to thaw out. The hotel kitchen kept us all going on bacon rolls.

Martin and Dad were both well into their sixties but worked together seamlessly, often without saying a word. It was Big Charlie who kept everyone in good spirits. Jamie, now 13, wanted to be part of things, so he worked with the squads at weekends and during school holidays. Our main task was to design and fit the steel rings to the chimney stack, but first, we had to complete the acid cleaning—a dangerous and difficult job due to the high winds and the fact that the stack itself was even taller than the service building.

We managed to get it done, though I suspect some cars in the airport car park received an unexpected new paint effect.

Dad and Martin were working together at one of the intersections when Martin nearly vanished—one of the scaffolding infill pieces had come loose. Dad moved like lightning, grabbing him before he could fall to his certain death 14 floors below. Unfortunately, Martin's bunnet was swept away, soaring high into the air and out of sight.

We took him inside, gave him a cup of tea while the boys secured the loose board, and then he got straight back to work. He was a tough old man, having served in the Army during the Second World War and seen plenty of combat. On this day, however, he was more upset about losing his beloved bunnet than nearly losing his life.

Two days later, Alistair was driving the works van back into Paisley to drop the boys off after work when Martin suddenly became animated. He was convinced he had seen his bunnet stuck in a tree at a roundabout near the airport. Alistair pulled over, and sure enough, there it was. Martin was reunited with his bunnet—still dry—and sat in the front of the van, grinning from ear to ear, delighted at the reunification of man and hat.

By this point, we were getting a lot of work from Jim Hartley, the facilities manager at British Airways in Glasgow. I had gone to college with his boss, Bob Provan, who must have put in a good word for me. We soon found ourselves handling runway repairs and general building maintenance. Eventually, Jim started taking me to BA operations in London, Edinburgh, and Aberdeen.

That summer, Elaine and I took the kids to a villa in Spain, near Puerto Pollensa in northern Majorca. It had a pool, and we stocked up on good food and wine. We hired a car to explore the island. The weather was fantastic, and we took the kids to some great restaurants. Some evenings, I would fill a water gun with pool water and squirt it into the air so the local bats could drink. I have always hated mosquitoes, so in the early evening, I would go on a hunt with my spray. If they got inside the house, I would track them down and splatter them against the walls. On one occasion, I hit the wall so hard I blew the fuse, plunging us into darkness.

Back home, work was picking up again. We secured a contract for plumbing work at a house in Fairlie on the Ayrshire coast. The house was owned by two retired women—one suffering from cancer, the other feisty and well- spoken.

We installed a Sani Plus unit behind their downstairs toilet to save her friend from having to climb the stairs. The unit macerates waste so it can be pumped through a 22mm copper pipe.

The plumber on the job was Garry Lomas, who had started with us as an apprentice and had since become a skilled tradesman. At one point, the feisty lady called Garry over and said, "This Sani Plus unit isn't working properly."

"How do you know?" Garry asked. "Because there are faeces in the pan."

Garry grinned. "I know we're near the seaside, but there's no way there are fishes in the bowl."

"Shite, Garry! Shite!" she snapped.

That story kept us all laughing for quite some time. We fixed the Sani Plus, said our goodbyes, and left.

CHAPTER 39:
BLOOD, SEWAGE MUD AND BULLSHIT

I got a call in 1995 to quote for brickwork on a labour-only basis from Norwest Holst, who were building a new pumphouse for Scottish Water at Barassie. The purpose of this pumphouse was to pump sewage from the local community out to sea. It also had to resemble the local bungalows, with two-thirds of the structure built below ground level. We won the contract, and I built up the team with Martin and Jimmy Laird, Frank McColgan, my Dad doing the laboring, and Elaine's Dad driving them to and from the site.

I had just bought Elaine her first new car—a Nissan Micra—and because of the logistics, we had to borrow it to get the men to the site every morning. Elaine's Dad, who was recovering from face cancer, took on the driving, which he loved. He could take the men down the coast and then have the day to himself in the Micra—unless Elaine needed it. He loved his music tapes and a smoke, often saying, "I can't believe you're paying me for this."

I could always rely on Martin and my Dad, but Jimmy Laird and Frank McColgan were only interested in one thing—drink. It was a pity because Jimmy was one of the best bricklayers I'd ever seen. He was the only man capable of forming the intricate corbels and bullseyes required for the job. He was fine right up until the last week when he failed to turn up. Elaine's Dad was with me when I realised Jimmy hadn't arrived for his shift. I phoned him and gave him a flea in his ear. His response?

"I don't give a fuck, Jimmy. There aren't enough hours in the day for me to drink, so goodbye."

I had to find replacements quickly. I contacted some local 2+1 squads who had the Ayrshire brickie supply market sewn up. Alfie came to see me on- site. I explained I needed him to build the boundary walls, and we agreed on a rate. He was confident he could meet the deadline but laid out his terms:

328

"I won't work Mondays, I'll leave on Fridays at 12:00, and you'll pay me before I go."

I replied, "Here are my terms—provided you build the walls to good quality and complete them in two weeks, I'll pay the rate agreed."

To be fair to Alfie, his team was fantastic. They even finished a day early.

I replaced Jimmy Laird with a much-improved Peter McGlave, but imagine my disappointment when, a few days later, I arrived on-site to find they had all gone to the local pub/hotel to "keep warm." Aye, right.

So, what would you have done? Sacked your Dad, his best pal, and the apprentice of the year? Like it or not, in those days, you had to deal with men who drank—and some who did drugs.

We worked for a lot of big construction companies—Norwest Holst, Balfour Beatty, Kier Contracts, Wiggins Group, and Babcock Energy—but they all made you wait for your money. Over a couple of years, I lost £70,000 to Balfour Beatty and Norwest Holst alone. My accountant, George Walker, pursued the debts and eventually advised me to accept percentage offers or tie myself up in court for years : I lost £35,000 on that deal. At the time, if you had a £6,000 debt, it was often better to write it off because taking it to court would cost the same in legal fees.

During the bricklaying works at Barassie, we passed a construction site in Irvine near Girdle Toll every day. The squad would always comment, "Thank God we're not working on that site," because it looked like a muddy battlefield. Naturally, when the next contract turned out to be Girdle Toll, they weren't pleased—but work is better than no work.

On our first day, the men had to sign the site induction register and left their tools outside the portacabin. The forklift truck driver ran over their tool bags. Martin was raging, and straight away, I smelled a rat. I drove into Irvine and bought new tools. When I got back, the men had been directed to the worst, muddiest part of the site. It soon became clear that the other local squads had paid off the FLT driver to sabotage our operation—getting rid of the competition. The site agent was useless, so I decided to cut our losses and withdraw the squad. Workers aren't always comrades, and when it comes to money, beware of cartels and the men who benefit from the contracts.

I found other work for the squad, building extensions all over the West of Scotland.

One dormer extension for joiners in Burnside, south of Glasgow, was memorable. When we arrived, the owner asked us to clear his attic, agreeing to pay extra. We cleared most of it into a skip, but some of the items were decent art. Normally, any salvage was shared among the men on the job. This time, I got the artworks valued—they were worth about £800—so I kept the art and gave the men a bonus.

That contract also nearly killed me. I was on the outside of the dormer frame Kenny had built when I slipped. I rolled backwards down the roof, heading straight for certain death. Luckily, Kenny grabbed my ankle just before I went over the edge.

Later, I built an extension for friends in Paisley. They asked if I could send joiners up to Aberdeen to repair a flat they had bought for their daughter at university. I sent Kenny and two others, expecting a two-day job. Kenny called on Friday to say they had found rot in some timbers, and the client agreed to pay for the extra work. I told them to get on with it after checking with the client.

On Monday, Kenny was moaning about going back, and I knew something was up. Turns out, the flat was full of young female students. That explained the sudden enthusiasm to work weekends. I never let them go back—and I didn't pay them for the extra days.

CHAPTER 40:
THE WORST STORM AND THE BIGGEST BETTING SHOP

In early 1996, we won a contract from Ladbrokes to fit out their new betting shop in Ayr, on the west coast of Scotland. This was set to be the biggest betting shop in Europe, with state-of-the-art shopfitting. The contract went very well, though I later heard that all the shopfitters were placing bets. As long as the job was running smoothly, that was none of my business.

Eventually, we completed the project, and there was a grand opening ceremony where Johnny Francome, the racing jockey and broadcaster, cut the ribbon in front of the media. Elaine was there and asked him for a tip, which he gave her for a horse running the next day. We placed a bet for fun, and sure enough, it won—happy days. The surveyor on this job was Gordon Reece, and based on our work, we secured a second betting shop refurbishment near the main railway station. When the job was done, we submitted our invoices, only to be told that we'd need to deduct the VAT. Gordon had made a mistake, and since we were old friends, I took the hit. Sometimes, in business, you have to make compromises and work with people you wouldn't normally. That's just how it is.

Around that time, we also got a refurbishment contract from A.T. Mays (Travel Agents) in Ayr city centre. Our task was to upgrade the front façade stonework, which needed shot blasting and repairs. I built a team around Alistair, with my Dad, Paul McManus, and his Dad, Charlie. The first job was to erect scaffolding. A few days in, Alistair came to see me, concerned about my Dad. Alistair and the team loved him, so he was reluctant to say that Dad had hurt his hand while loading the scaffolding poles. He kept mistiming the handover to the men on the scaffold.

I checked Dad's hand—it was more than a superficial cut. Over the next few days, we kept an eye on him. It's hard to admit when a loved one starts showing signs of ageing. Lately, Dad had been misplacing his glasses and stumbling, but I never thought it was serious. Then, a few days later, Alistair called from Cupar in Fife, where they were doing building repairs for the ABS.

"Hi Jimmy, we've lost your Dad," he said. "He went to the toilet and never came back."

I told Alistair to spread the team out and check all the pubs and bookies. Eventually, they found Dad—completely lost.

The next day, we kept him in the workshop to observe him. That Friday, we had a team night out at the Tudor Bar in Paisley. The place was packed, and Dad looked uncomfortable. I asked if he was all right. He nodded but then quietly asked me to take him home. On the way to his house in Gallowhill, he said, "I'm not viable anymore, son."

I was stunned into silence. I tried to reassure him. "Let's get you to a doctor, Dad."

A few days later, my sister Ellen took him to the GP, where he was diagnosed with possible dementia. Ellen adored Dad, so I agreed to take him to a specialist at Dykebar Mental Hospital, on the outskirts of Paisley.

When I was a boy, I hero-worshipped Dad. As I got older, we fell out—like many fathers and sons do when one turns eighteen. Seeing this once-strong man diminished like this was hard to take.

At Dykebar, the consultant asked Dad some basic questions. "Who is the Prime Minister?" No answer. "What's your date of birth?" Nothing. Then he asked Dad to draw a square, but all he could manage was a squiggle.

I don't know how Dad felt, but I hoped his cognitive decline spared him from fully grasping what was happening.

Years later, while working in Derby, I experienced a brief but total loss of memory. It lasted only a few minutes, but it was terrifying. I can only hope that, in the fifteen years before Dad passed, he never felt that same fear as his regimental motto was "Sans Peur"

I spoke to Mum. She was perplexed but knew her husband was gone in all but body. I tried keeping Dad busy at work, just tidying the workshop and office, but he didn't know where he was and started arguing with other tenants at Abbey Mill Business Centre. One day, he was sweeping debris onto the neighboring work unit's doorstep. When the owner confronted him, the old fire still burned in his eyes.

Then came the breaking point—Dad was cleaning a table saw when we realised how dangerous this was. I went to see Mum, who was with my sister Caroline and brother Steven. I suggested Dad just needed some TLC. I had no choice but to take him with me for a while, however it was time for the whole family to step up and help Mum.

I spent weeks filling out forms to get them the proper benefits. Eventually, with disability and care allowances, Mum eventually had more income than I had been paying Dad.

As winter set in, we secured a contract to refurbish a property in Fox Street, Greenock. This involved building a new apex roof over the existing flat roof and re-roughcasting the entire building. We got on well with the tenants, especially the family in the top flat, Jimmy and Rita.

One Friday night in November, Jimmy called me—water was pouring into his house. I got in my car and drove the 30 miles back to Greenock. It was 11 pm, with driving wind and rain. Alone, I climbed the scaffolding to find that the plumbers hadn't connected a temporary downpipe—bastards. I had tea with Jimmy and Rita, inspected the damage to their bedroom ceiling, and promised to redecorate. They took it well after that.

Whenever we refitted an ABS branch, we kept or disposed of the old furniture and fittings. I asked Marcus Dean, whose company had taken over Abbey Mill, if I could use an unoccupied flat to store surplus equipment. He agreed, in exchange for some minor repairs. Eventually, the flat was full of office furniture, including a computer I thought we could use in the workshop.

I asked Jim Ford, our electrician, to check it out. A few days later, the computer disappeared. I suspected Big Kenny—Malcolm Morrison's son, who had access to spare keys through his Dad.

We'd already noticed someone making calls to sex lines from the workshop's phone, and all fingers pointed to Big Kenny.

We had previously accused him of stealing a ladder, which caused an uproar with his father, so we decided not to pursue the phone calls. Instead, we tightened security.

But the missing computer had been on the electrician's bench. Big Kenny hadn't been at work that day, so it had to be someone on our team.

I gathered the crew. "Return the computer, and nothing more will be said."

The next day, the computer was returned; however, that was not the end of it. Jim Ford had booted it up and found that all the telephone contacts. It turned out that my contracts manage had taken the computer for his son.

I had already reached the end of the road with him for several reasons, so I suspended him for three days.

Funny how actions like that encourage more information to surface. Some of the lads, who hadn't been keen on the contracts manager but had kept quiet out of loyalty to me, started coming forward. With this new information, I decided it was time for him and me to part ways.

We arranged to meet at the Lord Lounsdale pub in Paisley, next to Ferguslie Cricket Club. I had a cheque for him—£2,000 to settle things. When I arrived, he was immaculate, dressed in a brand-new dark suit and a white polo neck. I handed him the cheque and told him it was over.

The lads accepted the decision and got on with things, but we all missed him—he was such a big character.

With Dad gone, I felt as if I had lost my lucky mascot, and it started to affect the business. Since Black Wednesday, things had been slipping, and our overheads were high.

The bills kept coming in fast, and the work was barely covering our position. I was constantly scraping together what I could to pay creditors, but this went on for months. The final straw came when one of the scaffolding contractors, whom I owed £2,000, sent some

guys with baseball bats to my house. Jenni answered the door—
I was in Paisley at the time."

I had to sell the cars to raise the cash to pay them off. It was brutal,
watching my empire collapse around me.

Then came one last roll of the dice. Blick Services offered me a
contract to completely refurbish their offices over the Christmas
period for £65,000. I pulled a team together, and we worked
through Christmas and New Year. They paid quickly, and I
banked the cheque.

Then, the Clydesdale Bank froze my account the moment the
money landed. They informed me they wouldn't be paying wages.
This was preferential alienation—we also had to settle with the
taxman and pay the VAT. I was sunk.

I had no choice but to put the company into the hands of a Receiver.
As soon as that happened, it was all over.

Some of my creditors were understanding; others were not.
There's a terrible stigma attached to failing to pay your bills and
liquidating a business. The lads were all laid off, though they
received redundancy from the government. Still, I felt I had
failed—myself, my family, the lads, and my suppliers, who had
lost out.

What made things worse was that my son Jamie and his fiancée had
planned their wedding for the summer, and I had no money to
contribute. We agreed to buy them a designer settee and helped
with some champagne, but it wasn't nearly enough.

CHAPTER 41:
TRIALS AND BANKRUPTCY

The whole process of losing the business and facing diminished financial circumstances consumed my every thought. I knew we might lose the house, and all our business premises would be closed. Fortunately, my neighbour, Drew McDonald, let me use his outbuildings at Caldwell to store my tools and supplies. All the surplus equipment I had at the Mill was auctioned off by Shirlaw and Allan. I estimated it was worth about £20,000, but after costs, I received a cheque for just £1,300, which went straight to the receiver.

The hardest part of the process was watching my assets being stripped away while depression set in. It affected the whole family. We had everything, then suddenly, we had nothing. Just when I thought we'd hit rock bottom, the Clydesdale Bank began proceedings for a division and sale of the house. Over the next year, I made several court appearances to defend the action.

When I turned to my long-time lawyers, Cochrane Dickie and McKenzie, Mr Black informed me they couldn't take the case due to a conflict of interest— they handled conveyancing work for the Clydesdale. I then went to Scolarius Lawyers in Moss Street, Paisley, who agreed to take the case and applied for legal aid. However, I soon realised I was on a slow slide to the bottom.

At a family gathering, I had the chance to speak with my nephew, Steven, who had worked at the Clydesdale Bank and knew my bank manager. Steven told me that the manager had said my business was finished a year earlier—this was shocking, as at that time, the business had been doing fine. I asked Steven if he would provide a statement for me, and he agreed. I took this new information to Scolarius, hoping to present it in my defense regarding preferential alienation. However, soon after, I got a call from Steven—he had been summarily dismissed by the Clydesdale Bank.

I was gutted. Steven was a good man, and now he had lost his job because of me. I no longer had faith in the lawyers, who were clearly in collusion with the bank. In desperation, I tried to find new representation but had no success. Instead, I bought a book on Scots law and decided to defend myself. The bank did not like that. I was accused of being unprepared and unlearned, but the judge granted me time to prepare. By my next court appearance, I had improved.

The case dragged on until my old neighbours from Tantallon Drive, Jimmy, and Betty—both devout Christians—recommended a lawyer from McClure Naismith in Glasgow. I met Mr Smith on the steps of Paisley Court. He told me that if the hearing went against me, he would need to be paid before entering the courtroom. I emptied my pockets, handing him every penny I had. It wasn't enough, but he agreed to represent me.

When we were fighting to keep the house, we sought advice from our local MP, Jim Murphy, who had recently been elected as the Member for Eastwood in 1997. At the time of my court battles, I had nowhere else to turn, so I went to his Friday night surgery in Barrhead. Jim, along with his secretary Marion Anderson, listened carefully and took notes.

He sent a letter to the court when I was unprepared, written on House of Commons paper:

"I have examined the subject matter of Mr. and Mrs. Green and find it to be good. Please consider dealing with this case sensitively."

That letter bought me precious time—just enough to try and get back on my feet. I was incredibly grateful for his help, so I joined the Labour Party. It turned out to be one of the best decisions I ever made.

The bank's action against me was "summary diligence," their argument being that since I was unemployed and on legal aid, the asset in question (the house) was at risk of falling into disrepair and losing value.

The judge addressed me:

"Mr Green, do you accept or deny the debt?"

"I accept the debt, but there are strong mitigating circumstances you need to hear, Your Honour."

"I'm sorry, Mr Green, you have accepted the debt, and I therefore declare you bankrupt."

I heard his gavel hit the bench. Several bank lawyers shook hands and smiled at me. My lawyer never spoke to me again. I never saw him after that.

Stepping outside into the fresh air, I was gutted. I had lost everything and was now completely penniless. I walked to Ian McNeil's garage in Moss Street. Ian was a good friend—I had given him all our fleet's garage work over the years. I told him what had happened and apologized, as I owed him about £1,800. Ian was gracious. He told me he would write off the debt and offered me a cup of tea.

I still had my work van, so I drove home, composed myself, and walked inside. Elaine met me at the door, Emma by her side. I told them what had happened, and we just hugged each other. I had lost so much, but with Elaine and the kids by my side, I was still a lucky man.

I had barely sat down when the phone rang.

"Good afternoon, Mr Green. I'm Brian G. LeMay, your Trustee in Bankruptcy. I'd like to meet as soon as possible."

I suggested the following morning.

"I'm outside your house," he replied.

I had been preparing for this moment. I had gathered all our bank statements, passbooks, and a list of our assets in one box. In another, I had a pile of all the outstanding bills.

Mr LeMay took the box of bills.

"These are now mine. If you have any contact with these organizations or their lawyers, direct them to me. I'll write to them today and advise them of your bankruptcy."

He then produced a thick A4 booklet and began discussing the house, its contents, artwork, antiques, and any inheritances I might be due. He toured the entire house, taking notes as we filled out the booklet. Before leaving, he told me he would return the next morning with a proposal regarding my future as a bankrupt.

The next day, he outlined the conditions:

He would make no claim on our assets except for business-related equipment and stock.

I would be allowed to keep my work van and tools. All domestic assets would remain untouched.

My pension funds were not vested in the trustee and would be protected.

I could earn up to £12,000 per year, but 50% of every pound earned beyond that would go to the trustee (e.g., if I earned £20,000, I would owe £4,000).

I would report to Mr LeMay every six months to review payment progress.

At the time, it felt devastating, but with the mountain of bills now gone, I felt an enormous sense of relief.

The bank immediately began proceedings to sequester the house. In Scots law, this is exceedingly difficult to do when the marital home houses children under 18 (Matrimonial Homes Act), and at that time, it had never been done. However, banks wield incredible power and can afford the best legal teams, so the pressure was on. They sent out valuers to survey the property, but this did not go as expected. The valuation came in lower than anticipated, meaning a sale would leave them with nothing but more legal costs.

Elaine was fantastic in fighting to keep the house, bombarding Lord Nixon, CEO of Clydesdale Bank, with letters of appeal. Working with her lawyer, Brigit McLaren, she eventually offered

£2,000 to remove the second charge—despite the bank seeking £40,000. Faced with legal costs and no better alternative, they had to accept.

A few weeks later, we received the discharge papers from the bank. Well done, Elaine.

A few years earlier, I had helped two friends, Douglas Booth and Robert Graham, both managers at Turner Aviation Ltd. in Thornliebank, start their own company, Avotec Ltd., specializing in aircraft part repairs. Now turning over enough to secure new premises in Bellshill, their sponsoring business partners advised them to bring in more experienced people. They invited me to join as Associate Director and temporary CEO. We secured premises at Wren Court, Bellshill Industrial Estate, outfitting them to satisfy the CAA and FAA in America and obtaining licenses to repair aircraft starter motors and simulators for Avial in Prestwick.

Ian Lang, Secretary of State for Scotland, attended the factory's official opening.

After a few months, my fees began draining the company's cash reserves, so we parted on good terms.

I now had to rebuild a business to keep paying the mortgage, so I started trading as Allied Contracts as a sole trader. Jamie was supporting me in various ways while considering marriage to Ruth, who was finishing university to become a doctor.

We set up Allied Contracts, using an old white Astra estate van, and became jobbing builders.

Jamie and I endured incredible hardships just to keep a roof over our heads, often taking safety risks. I remember one occasion in Uplawmoor, working on a roof. I asked Jamie to edge down and fix some slates while I remained at the apex to anchor the rope. We debated the risks and eventually Jamie took the rope down the roof.

I know for certain how much Jamie cared for me, especially when I got a call to unblock the toilets at Williams Rover on New Sneddon Street, Paisley— just yards from where my mother grew up. The main sewer was completely blocked with all manner of filth.

"I'll get it, Dad," Jamie said. "No, I'll do it, son."

Neither of us wanted the other to endure what was undoubtedly a low moment for two graduates.

In the winter of 1999, we secured a contract to install a flagpole at a new housing development in Bellshill. We marked out the hole for the foundation, but when Jamie struck the ground with a spade, it bounced off the frozen earth. Even using a pick and mattock, the ground remained stubbornly hard. Eventually, we dug it out and drove to a builders' yard for concrete mix. The cold was so bitter we stood in an old site bothy, warming our hands by a coal fire.

Next, we took a job repairing a roof beam in Carmyle, near Glasgow's east end. Fully loaded, we were driving along London Road, near my old Westhorn offices, when there was a loud bang and a violent shudder. The Astra's rear offside gas strut had fractured under the load, puncturing the tyre. We emptied the boot to reach the spare wheel and jack, but the wheel nuts were jammed solid. Having served my time as an engineer, I knew I needed a metal tube to extend the leverage. I walked to a nearby industrial estate factory and convinced an engineer to let me have a scrap piece. Back at the car, the nut cracked open with a loud snap, and we fitted the spare before tying up the broken strut to prevent further damage. We carried on and completed the job.

If I'd had spare cash, I would have taken the car to a garage. But with no reserves, we pushed on, securing a block paving contract in Port Glasgow. Loading up the Astra, we headed along Greenock High Street towards Larkfield Hill. We didn't get far before we saw blue flashing lights—the local traffic police.

"We've stopped you because this vehicle doesn't look fit for the road, sir," the officer said.

He didn't need to convince me—I knew it was in a poor state. He issued a ticket, giving me a week to either repair or scrap the car and notify the chief of police.

Still, we continued to the site with our seven-day license. Approaching Larkfield Hill, the Astra simply gave out. I got out, and Jamie took the wheel as I pushed. Eventually, we completed the job on Friday and got paid.

We drove into Paisley, and to celebrate, we went to my father's old pub, The George, at the bottom of George Street. We had a couple of beers, and I can tell you—after working hard and being under stress—those beers were a most welcome treat.

On the gantry behind the bar, we noticed a bottle of Antiquary Deluxe Whisky and got chatting with the bartender. He told us that my Dad had been the one drinking from that bottle but, due to his dementia, hadn't been in for some time. I explained Dad's situation to him, and before leaving, we both had a Deluxe in his honour.

To my shame, I started to drive home in the old Astra. As I reached the hill before Brodie Park, the front steering column collapsed, and the car ended up straddling both sides of the road. I phoned Jamie and Elaine, but it was Jenni who got there first. She hauled the Astra to one side, pointing it back downhill on a bad bend. I called for a recovery vehicle, and within 15 minutes, the Astra was towed onboard.

Elaine smelled the drink on me and quickly got me into Jenni's car—just as the police arrived. They cruised slowly but didn't stop. There's no doubt that if my family hadn't come to my rescue, I'd now possibly have a criminal record.

Those days were tough. Just keeping going was a struggle. Jamie was incredibly supportive and knew I was drowning under the burden. He worked for me for several weeks without pay. Eventually, he had to find work, so he got a job with Manpower at IBM in Greenock. Before long, he was appointed directly by IBM and spent the next few years managing their call centre.

My old pal Ronnie Syme was a great help, keeping me going with maintenance contracts at the Babcock Research Station in Renfrew. On one occasion, Jamie and I had to do some roof repairs and hired a three-layer pulley ladder to reach the height we needed. It was so heavy that just getting it from horizontal to the correct angle was a challenge. As we tried to maneuver it into position, I felt a hot, searing pain as my groin muscles tore. Over the next few days, an unwelcome bulge developed—an egg-shaped lump in my groin where my stomach was trying to exit my body.

The doctor diagnosed a double hernia, and within weeks, I underwent surgery. Foolishly, I tried to get back to work too soon and ended up in a heap of pain in a garden in Elderslie.

At this point, I was on my own and took up premises at 33 Moss Street in Paisley under a lease from the Holehouse Properties Company. It was a two- floor workshop behind a kebab shop and the Job Centre on Hunter Street. Various men helped me on a casual basis. Jennifer had got engaged to Paul Cassidy, who came to work for me, along with Garry Lomas (a plumber) and Davie Hegarty (a joiner).

Davie was fascinating. Once in the topflight of Scottish boxing, he was a lovely man with great manners and a skilled joiner— though a bit "punchy."

We fitted a new suspended ceiling and installed new windows, but the place was so run-down that it would take a fortune to fix properly.

I was earning just enough to cover the mortgage (interest-only) and had used a small reserve to buy a Volvo estate, which kept us going for the next two years.

I had constant arguments with the kebab shop owner about leaving large cans of solid fat in the link corridor to the workshops. The lighting was faulty, so I had to use a torch to find the switch. One morning, I slipped on the shop's rubbish, hurt my knee badly, and limped for weeks.

The final straw came when, while trying to find the light switch, I shone my torch up the corridor and saw hundreds of big black rats swarming over the grease cans and rubbish. They scattered frantically, but now I could smell them everywhere. I reported the owner to the Environmental Department, who advised me to get pest control in. Instead, I bought rat poison, put it down, and locked the doors for three days as instructed.

I'll never forget what I saw when I reopened the workshop— hundreds of dead rats, with about twenty piled up around the toilet bowl, desperate for water. Emma and her boyfriend, Gordon, helped me clear them out and disinfect the place.

Those were dark days. I was exhausted, barely holding things together, and having to do all the work myself.

I got an appointment with the doctor as I was clearly depressed, and he referred me to a psychologist for talking therapy. This was very helpful as over the first three of ten planned session I realized that I had lost my center and had to refocus on me rather than all the distractions that were no up close ands present in my life. I was now back on track and back to identifying as Jim, not Jimmy or James my other selves.

CHAPTER 42:
COMRADES AND CONTRACTS

Getting involved in politics was a whole new world for me, offering both a distraction and a complement to my business. If truth be told, my politics were left of centre, but in my twenties and thirties, I had great sympathy for the nationalists—mainly after watching Braveheart. However, having lived through the Winter of Discontent, I believed Maggie Thatcher would sort out the country—and she certainly did, much to the disdain of the left. The Poll Tax in Scotland marked the beginning of her downfall and planted the seed for a Scottish Parliament.

Jim Murphy was keen for me to join the Labour Party, so I did. In my mind, I pictured the cloth-cap working class with Bolshevik attitudes. I was surprised when my first meeting at McGuire Hall in the centre of Barrhead turned out to be sensible and procedural. However, after three meetings, I had met most of the activists and officers and was beginning to get bored.

Colin Roberts, the CLP Chairperson and a local Justice of the Peace, tugged on my sleeve as I left a meeting. He invited me to his house that weekend to discuss an upcoming selection process for candidates for the first Scottish Parliament, which would be established in May 1999.

Colin and his wife, Isobel, lived in Neilston and had created a political hub for elected members and activists. The discussions were stimulating and intellectual, and Isobel was the perfect host, keeping food and refreshments flowing in her warm, cosy home.

Labour Party members are generally very comradely, and I began to enjoy the debates and helping out. I say generally because when it comes to elections, selections, and career ambitions, the tooth and claw are never far from the surface—on occasion, it's even been known for fists to fly.

I tried to bring my managerial experience into the processes, but Labour has its big red book, and although they paid lip service to my ideas, it soon became clear that I had a lot to learn. In the early days, my friendship with Colin Roberts grew stronger, and we would go fishing together on his stretch of the River Doon near Dalmellington, where the salmon fishing was good.

I got to know all the councilors, especially Owen Armstrong, the Leader of the Council.

After my first year, I was elected Political Education Officer and Deputy Chair of the local Barrhead and Neilston branch. I also joined the Fabian Society, which held meetings at Strathclyde University. By now, I was taking a serious interest in politics and developing my own opinions—sometimes at odds with my comrades.

(The term "Comrade" is used in the Labour Party as a tradition from the early Labour Movement, emphasising that the struggle for power is ongoing, with a clear enemy in the Tory Party. Tony Blair had not long been elected, and with New Labour came changes. "Friends" or "Colleagues" were the preferred terms, but they never really caught on. During the the time of writing, "Comrade" made a comeback as the Momentum group took over Jeremy Corbyn's Labour Party which eventually was supplanted by Sir Keir Stammer's new vision.

Jim Murphy was now a member of the Blair Government. He had started his career as President of the National Union of Students (1994–96) before being selected to contest the East Renfrewshire parliamentary seat in 1997. It had been Tory since 1922, and he was expected to lose—but he won, taking the seat from Alan Stewart (Conservatives) with a majority of over 3,000.

Getting involved in politics was refreshing, and I played my part well. The comrades came through for me, rewarding me with many contracts to repair their homes and fit new kitchens and bathrooms. This helped me start recovering my business, and I will always be grateful for that support.

With some spare cash, I was able to book a holiday villa in Portugal, giving the family a break from the stress of bankruptcy. The villa, Casa Quilombo, was in the hills above Albufeira and owned by a British ex-pat writer. It was a beautiful spot, overlooking the Atlantic, with the scent of fruit trees filling the air as we swam in the pool. In the evenings, we watched fireflies dance around the streetlights. The setting was perfect for reflection, and I began writing this story—since the environment and circumstances were so conducive to it.

When we got back home, it was straight into business and politics. It was winter, and Allied Contracts wasn't getting much work, so I had some leaflets printed and decided to distribute them door-to-door in the area.

Before Jamie left for IBM we ventured as far as East Kilbride. As we neared the end of our leaflet supply, our last round took us to Elderslie, near Paisley. We were both freezing, and with all the leaflets used up, we headed home.

When I got back, I found a message on my answering machine from a homeowner in Elderslie who needed some work done. I arranged an appointment for the next day. His house was a new build, but the tiles were falling off the walls in his shower. We agreed on a price and returned a few days later to complete the repair. He was a nice man, and his house was a shrine to Elvis, filled with pictures and ornaments of the King. We were paid fairly, and before we left, he asked if I was interested in commercial work— which I was.

The job was in central Glasgow, where the man managed a large furniture shop in need of about £3,000 worth of structural and floor repairs. The only problem was that the worksite was on the first floor, and Miller Street below had strict parking restrictions. We managed most of the job with sheer physical effort and some creative parking. However, on the final day, we had a lot of concrete work to do, and it was just me and Jamie. I started feeling lightheaded and dizzy. Jamie pointed out that I was dehydrated— we had been working all day without a drink of tea or water.

Once the job was done, we were paid about a month later—but there was an issue. They sent us a cheque for £13,000 instead of £3,000. I called the manager, who advised me to bank the cheque and send a credit note. It turned out the cheque had been issued to my company in error because our name was similar to a carpet company.

I had a reasonable surplus in the accounts and waited for the formal letter requesting the credit cheque. A few months later, I received a note from a Receiver stating that the furniture company had gone into liquidation and that I would be contacted in due course.

A year went by before I was finally contacted by an accountant acting on behalf of the Receiver. He requested a face-to-face meeting. My biggest problem was that I had already used the money as working capital over the past year, and while I had funds incoming, it would take a few weeks. I explained my situation to the accountant, who was sympathetic and keen to resolve the matter quickly. Given the long delay, he said they would accept a settlement offer. He asked how much I could arrange that day. I told him about £2,000, which he asked me to bring. I did, and the matter was formally closed.

Outside of work, we were in the process of selecting a candidate for the new Scottish Parliament. After a series of hustings, Ken MacIntosh was chosen, and he asked me to be his agent, which I agreed to. I was also appointed his election coordinator. Ken had previously been a television producer with the BBC, working on news broadcasts and election coverage. We were delighted to have such a strong candidate. Jim Murphy was equally pleased and threw his full influence behind Ken's campaign.

Being an election agent is governed by the Representation of the People Act 1918, meaning strict rules had to be followed. This was sometimes challenging, as candidates would often prioritise family events over last-minute deadlines for legal forms.

The Labour Party's election machinery in East Renfrewshire was formidable, with funding coming from the unions, local fundraising events such as dinners and "cash and curry" nights, and personal donations. Colin Roberts and I put up posters on every lamppost in the constituency—some of which were promptly torn down by the local Tory Party activists.

In the end, Ken won comfortably and was elected to Parliament. Elaine and I were invited to the State Opening in Edinburgh, where we watched Ken being sworn in, both in English and Gaelic. It was a day of great celebration. A bus load of activists travelled to Edinburgh, singing "The Red Flag" and other songs. We watched the procession from the church on the Royal Mile, where the new members mingled with celebrities, including Sean Connery in a kilt, prompting plenty of jokes about James Bond's hairy legs.

Security was heavy, as a large mob of anarchists protested with placards, shouting, "No privilege for Scotland!" Unfortunately, we got caught up in the chaos and had to make a quick exit behind the barriers to avoid any risk of arrest or being mistaken for part of the protest.

The celebrations continued with a picnic in Princes Street Gardens, followed by a group dinner just off the Royal Mile. Later, as we walked towards the Assembly Halls in George Street, we met Donald Dewar, who would become Scotland's First Minister. Elaine asked him to sign her Saltire flag, and as we explained we were from the East Renfrewshire Labour Party, he joked, "I believe you, but thousands wouldn't." he signed the flag. Sadly, Donald, a driving force behind securing the Parliament, passed away in October 2000.

Back at work in Paisley, my old friend John Timlin asked me to look at some repairs needed in his tenement flat, where he was the "spokesperson for the close." In Scotland, the Law of the Tenement applies, meaning all repairs in a building are the shared responsibility of the residents. John had been elected to organize the work, which involved roof repairs and stone preservation on the building's exterior.

We had to erect scaffolding, and I was assisted on-site by Paul McManus, Jamie, and Garry Lomas. We used a shot-blasting pot powered by a compressor, directing the blast onto the stone. After a few adjustments, I put on the protective hood, while Garry managed the hoses. We were making good progress when Garry asked if he could have a go at blasting. I agreed.

We were on the scaffolding, and visibility inside the hood was poor— especially if you sweated, as it made the visor fog up. I was standing near Garry when he turned and accidentally ran the shot blast across my stomach. I was wearing multiple layers, including a boiler suit, but it felt like I'd been machine-gunned.

Thankfully, I only suffered heavy grazing and bruising, but had I been wearing less protection, the shot could have gutted me.

After the cleaning was completed, we applied several coats of sealers to the whole building to prevent green moss or carbon coating from the atmosphere taking hold. If you are ever in South Park Drive in Paisley, you will see one building with clean stone, demonstrating the effectiveness of those coatings.

However, we encountered another problem—we had not been very diligent when cleaning the stone. Despite plywood covers for the windows, we had hit much of the glasswork, leaving blast marks. It cost a small fortune to have all the glass repaired.

I was now working out of the house with only the basic tools I was allowed to keep by the Trustee. I had also purchased another good second-hand Volvo Estate, which was perfect for carrying tools, ladders, and materials on the roof racks.

I secured a contract to carry out a structural alteration in Johnstone Drive, Rutherglen, involving the removal of an internal wall in an old, substantial sandstone building, about a hundred years old. This required installing Acro-Props along the entire wall to support the structure above and cutting a pocket for a new structural steel beam, which was about five meters long and of heavy section.

I organised the beam from a fabricator in Clarkston, picked it up with the boys in the morning, and returned to the site. At 10:00, we agreed to have tea and rolls from the local greasy spoon takeaway on Stoneylaw Road, near the town centre. I took the order for the boys and jumped into the Volvo, which still had the beam on the roof. Unbeknown to me, one of the boys had loosened all the ropes, and the beam was just sitting on the roof racks.

I drove to the takeaway and only realised the beam had shifted and was untied as I got out. Just as I started to secure it, a police car passed by and barely glanced at it. It was a miracle that the beam never came off—it could have been catastrophic. I often drive with the driver's window down, resting my arm outside, and it could easily have struck another car or person or chopped my arm off.

Harry, our slater-plasterer, was doing a good job but was clearly struggling with life. He had been named Harry but, while drunk, got a tattoo that read "Hardy." It was a source of much amusement to the other boys but an embarrassment to him.

One day, I got a call from Harry saying he was going to kill himself. I spent hours on the phone talking him down before driving to Linwood to make sure he was okay. When I arrived, he was still in one piece, and we talked for hours about his past and current troubles, which now included drugs.

Harry told me he had grown up in a difficult home with an alcoholic mother and an absent father. His older sister had taken the kids, including Harry and his brother, for a walk along a railway line near Johnstone, where his older brother was killed by a train.

Harry worked for us on and off for a few years but eventually got into trouble with the police after a football match. His picture appeared on the front page of the Daily Record, brandishing a slater's axe during a melee after an Old Firm match in Glasgow.

On one occasion, it was just me and Harry in the Volvo on a very wet day when we had been rained off. Harry explained that he had been brought back to life twice—once after a motorbike accident and once after falling off a cliff near Stranraer in the Scottish Borders.

He wanted to place a bet, which I tried to discourage, but he was determined. So, I suggested we do a joint bet. We decided on a "mug's bet" since neither of us was any good at horse racing analysis. I suggested we pick horses based on the weather, given the rain. We selected seven horses with names like Stormy Weather or Go Like the Wind and placed a Union Jack Bet. Then, we had some hot tea and bacon rolls.

The weather improved, and we managed to get some work done in the afternoon. On the way home, we stopped at the bookies to check the races. Harry came out beaming—five of the horses had won, and we were waiting on the last two. I had worked out that, since we had placed a £20 bet, if the final two won, we stood to make £80,000.

We decided to wait and see. Harry went into the bookies while I made some calls. When he came out, his stammer made him incoherent. The last two horses had won. Then he said, "Don't kill me, Jimmy." He hadn't placed the Union Jack Bet correctly—his line had excluded the accumulator.

I rushed inside with the copy slip. The cashier showed me the bet. Instead of £80,000, we got about £60 back.

You can imagine the disappointment—the air was blue. But Harry had simply made a stupid mistake, and I should have supervised him.

At home, Elaine and Emma had just completed a self-development programme in Glasgow with the Mindstore Organization, run by Jack Black. Part of the technique involved making your dreams and wishes come true. Elaine had wished for a white Jaguar with leather seats, while Emma, fresh out of university, wished for a job.

At the conference, Emma asked Jack directly for a job—taking the forthright approach he advocated, where problems were no longer problems but "challenges." Jack advised her to phone him in a few weeks' time.

In the meantime, I thought I'd help Elaine with her dream. Without consulting her, I sold her new Fiat Punto in a straight swap for a second-hand white Jag with leather seats. It wasn't easy to find one, so the exchange took place as a private sale in the Tesco car park in Anniesland, north Glasgow.

I admit it had seen better days, but I thought she'd be delighted. Big mistake. After a few weeks and several breakdowns, I was told the Jag needed an MOT and £4,000 worth of repairs.

I traded the heap in for a second-hand Honda, which was even worse—it reeked of urine. It sat on our driveway for months before I finally had it towed away for scrap. Sorry, E.

Emma phoned Jack Black a few weeks later as advised, reminding him of her job request and the need to "take up the challenge." Jack replied that he didn't have a job to offer and that he had so many challenges, they were now a problem. So much for Mindstore, Jack.

I'd been working in the garden at weekends and needed help cutting back the huge hawthorn bushes on the north boundary of our property. I phoned Jamie to see if he could lend a hand. He sounded down and asked if he could come over to talk.

Jamie looked pale when he arrived and told me that he and his wife had fallen out badly—the marriage was over. Eventually, the house was sold, and Jamie moved in with us for a few months, but I could see the break-up had hit him hard.

Not long after, I got a call from Stephen Kerr, a good friend, as was his wife, Anna, who was close to Elaine. Stephen had to deal with his parents' house in Greenock—his father had passed away, and his mother had been taken into care. To make things worse, Stephen's brother, who had been living in the house, had set the bedroom on fire while in a heroin-fueled haze.

Stephen was still in shock from his father's passing and couldn't face going back, so it was Anna who showed me the damage. The bedroom where his brother had been sleeping was completely burnt out. On top of a wardrobe, I found drug paraphernalia—used needles, a spoon, and tie-off rubber tubing.

Anna wanted the entire house gutted and made ready for sale, including a new kitchen. I agreed a price and got started as soon as possible. Most of the furniture went to charity or the local skip. I briefed the boys, Gary Lomas, and Mick McGann, about the needles and drugs, so we proceeded carefully to avoid needle-stick injuries.

After a few weeks, the place was ready for sale.

I found two suitcases full of personal family letters and memorabilia, which I delivered to Anna's home in Johnstone. I couldn't bring myself to throw them in the skip, despite Stephen's request to do so.

The house, a three-bedroom villa on York Street opposite the local cemetery, was on the market for months without a buyer. Stephen eventually phoned me, saying the problem was that the structure was steel-framed, and building societies weren't lending on it. He asked if I wanted to buy it at a bargain price, but it occurred to me that, since the house was within walking distance of the IBM factory where Jamie now worked, he might be interested.

Jamie didn't waste time, he raised the funds, bought the property, and turned it into rental accommodation for IBM employees working on the international desks. He was able to charge a good rent.

It didn't take Jamie long to bounce back. With his own place, extra money coming in, and a few genuinely nice international ladies as housemates, he soon found himself in a much better place.

CHAPTER 43:
DISCHARGE AND DEMANDS

In 2001, I was fully discharged from bankruptcy. Although this marked a new chapter for me, I was still just getting by. The Labour Party provided a welcome distraction and friendship, and my comrades continued to give me work, allowing me to start paying the mortgage again in full. The Nationwide had previously let me pay interest only, which had been a lifeline. I had several pension plans, but I had to cash them in just to make ends meet.

No matter what I did, I had to start over and make new provisions for the future. Over the next two years, I took on numerous contracts and gradually rebuilt my reserves. Unfortunately, whenever money got tight, I had to dip into my pension funds, meaning my long-term plans for retirement had to be re-established.

We managed the occasional break, mostly to Cambridge or wherever my sister Anne was living with her husband, Gordon, as she built her career as a psychologist. One particularly memorable trip was a winter skiing break to the Alps in 2002. We hired a minibus, packed it with family, including Anne, Gordon, and Jennifer's friend Emily, and set off just after Christmas.

We travelled to Swavesey in Cambridgeshire to pick up Anne and Gordon, staying overnight before heading to Dover the next morning. I had set up a portable TV with videos in the back seat to keep the kids entertained— solving a major boredom problem. When they weren't watching, they were sleeping.

On the ferry, I was in the restaurant when I noticed someone staring at me. Looking up, I found myself face-to-face with my doppelgänger. The man was grinning at me, so I smiled back. I pointed him out to Elaine, and we were all bemused. I should have taken a photo, but instead, we let it go. To this day, I've never seen anyone else who resembled me so closely.

Once across the Channel, Gordon and I took turns driving towards Les Gets in the French Alps. We had rented a ski chalet from my old friend PJ Smith, who ran a chalet rental business. We arrived in Taninges late at night before making the final leg to Les Gets, where we found the chalet covered in a foot of snow, with huge icicles hanging from the gutters. The chalet maid had prepared supper for us, and the warm welcome was much appreciated.

The next day, we suited up in our ski gear and headed for the slopes. Elaine and I had skied before with PJ and his wife, Jackie. We were absolute beginners but willing to give it another go. On a previous trip to Morzine, PJ had taken us down a red run, but Elaine got fed up with him pushing too hard, so she and Jackie left us for some chocolat chaud.

I had my Canon camera slung around my back, as the views from the upper slopes were stunning, with Mont Blanc in sight. PJ warned me to move it to the front, saying it could snap my spine if I fell.

As the weather closed in, we tackled the red run. I was doing well until I fell hard—the camera slammed into my face, splitting my lip. Blood poured everywhere. PJ, ever the joker, quipped, "That's why they call it a red run." Very funny, PJ.

Once we had our ski passes, it was agreed that the less experienced skiers would take lessons on the lower slopes while the rest of us headed up the mountain. The scenery was breathtaking, and we had a fantastic time. Jamie, who had taken up snowboarding, proved to be very competent—good to see, given that he had previously ended up in the neurology unit in Glasgow after tearing the membrane at the base of his brain. Brain fluid had been leaking from his nose after a fall on hard snow. Thankfully, his then-wife, Ruth, recognized the symptoms and got him to the hospital in time.

Skiing was great fun, but the real highlight for Elaine, Emma, and Anne was their lessons with Fabrice, a handsome French instructor. They diligently attended each session but never actually ventured up the slopes.

Evenings were spent at the Alpine Tavern in town. Fondue was the favourite, followed by rich cream desserts. One night, Anne flicked a small bit of cream at Emma. What followed was chaos—Jamie, Jennifer, and Emma launched into an all-out cream fight, and soon, we were all involved. The restaurant was covered in cream, and only when the manager stepped in did we realise we'd taken it too far. We apologized and cleaned up, but the other diners found it hilarious.

On 30th December, after a day of skiing, we returned to the chalet for hot baths, tea, and cakes, all laid on by the chalet maid. Later, after a few beers in town, I was exhausted and just wanted to jump into bed. Unfortunately, when I leapt onto the big pine bed, it collapsed under me. The crash brought the whole family running. I wasn't hurt, but they were all in hysterics when I asked, "Has anyone got a hammer?"

PJ and I later had a disagreement about it—he wanted me to pay for the damages, but I argued that a man should be able to jump on a bed without it collapsing.

It was New Year's Eve, and we went into town to join the locals in welcoming the new year with fireworks and fun. The winter scenery was stunning, and the atmosphere was lively. We wished countless people a happy New Year, and before heading home, we stopped at the lower slope for a snowball fight and some sliding. We climbed about 100 meters, formed a human train, and slid down six at a time. Halfway up, a black object whizzed past me at around 70 mph. I followed it to the bottom, where Jamie emerged—wrapped in a black plastic bin bag.

On New Year's Day, we decided to travel to Geneva for a shopping trip. When we reached the border at Gaillard, we discovered we needed passports, so I had to drive back to Les Gets to fetch them, leaving the family in a local restaurant. When I returned, I got stuck in the snow at the chalet and had to fit the snow chains. Eventually, I made it back to the family, and we continued to Geneva. It never occurred to me that, being New Year's Day, the shops would be shut. Still, we had great fun and ended the day in McDonald's, feasting on cheeseburgers, coffee, and hot chocolate.

At the time, when friends and family heard we'd been to Geneva, they joked about me having a secret Swiss bank account. Since we had a business and a nice address, people assumed I had money stashed away for a rainy day. In reality, we were often just making the best of things with limited funds. AS mentioned earlier the Clydesdale Bank did pursued me through the courts, convinced I would produce the money at the last minute—much to their cost.

The Labour Party in East Renfrewshire was structured with a Constituency Labour Party (CLP) and two branches: Barrhead & Neilston and Eastwood. I was Vice Chair of the Barrhead & Neilston branch from 2001 to 2004,

Chairman from 2004 to 2007, Vice Chair of the CLP from 2007 to 2010, and Chair of the CLP in 2012. In 2004, I was also a candidate for the Scottish Parliament, standing on the West of Scotland list.

By 2002, preparations for the Local Council Elections were underway. We had set up a campaign shop in Barrhead shopping centre, and as election coordinator, I organised a group of activists to manage the shop and run the campaign. Key activists included:

- Eddie Pearson (Councilor) – Logistics
- Edwina Pearson – Chair of Barrhead & Neilston Branch, responsible for funds
- Charlie McLaughlin – Shop Manager
- Marion Andrews – Diary Secretary
- Danny Scott – Street campaigns

We also had support from local members, students, and union helpers. The shop was decorated with Labour Party posters and set up as a walk-in centre. On Saturdays, Eddie would organize long car cavalcades, with loudspeakers, posters, and balloons on the vehicles.

Children loved the helium balloons, and when we campaigned in marginal areas, we would stop the cavalcade and flood the local letterboxes with leaflets. Jim Murphy and Ken MacIntosh followed a timetable, ensuring each council candidate had doorstep engagement as part of the team effort.

Canvassing was a great way to stay fit, and those who weren't able to go door-to-door worked in the campaign shop, folding and preparing leaflets for the street teams. Depending on strategy, we sent targeted letters to marginal voters.

Councillors had their own ideas about campaigning, often refusing help beyond funding. Betty Stewart, well-known in her ward, ensured her constituents voted for her—either by taking care of their problems or, in a light-hearted but firm manner, threatening them with the local gangsters.

In the end, we won the election and formed a Labour-led council, with Owen Armstrong as Leader and Betty Stewart as Provost. I was appointed as an observer at Labour Group meetings with the council, where I began learning the realities of political life.

Owen was particularly supportive, wanting me to stand for council in the next election. He was a great mentor, guiding me in political strategy. I received press bulletins and regularly helped him prepare rebuttals to Tory narratives in the local press.

One of the most dedicated activists at the time was Danny Scott. Well-known in Barrhead, particularly in the Arthurlie Inns Bar, he had political ambitions. However, he had only just become a party member and needed at least one term to establish himself within the branches and CLP.

Danny had already clashed with Owen Armstrong over the proposed Lidl roundabout in Barrhead, creating tension between them. As the council elections approached, Danny recruited ten of his local supporters to push his candidacy. However, party rules required members to be active for at least six months before they could vote.

Seizing an opportunity, Danny waited until Owen was on holiday in Ireland before going to the press with a scathing article, attacking Owen over the Lidl roundabout. A few days earlier, at the candidates' elections in John Smith House, I had seen Danny try to shake Owen's hand—only for Owen to turn away. At that same meeting, Danny had pledged not to bring the party into disrepute.

His behaviour was noted. I immediately moved to have him removed from the party for his actions. I didn't stop there—I went to the Arthurlie Inns and gave him a piece of my mind. Danny was ambitious, ruthless even, but his timing was poor.

At that time, Eddie and Edwina Pearson were the backbone of the Labour Party in Barrhead. They built up the membership, started a bonus ball scheme for fundraising, and helped establish the local Credit Union.

Elaine and I were often invited to Eddie and Edwina's home for informal meetings and parties. I really liked them both. They weren't perfect—but neither was I.

They lived in a council house on Balray Crescent, Barrhead. Sadly, Edwina's mother passed away from cancer, and shortly after, her father died as well. Eddie and Edwina decided to buy her parents' house and asked me to carry out some major alterations before they moved in. It was a good contract for me and would keep me busy for a few weeks.

CHAPTER 44:
ME AND THE LABOUR PARTY

Rather than scattering my time in the Labour Party throughout the rest of the story, I will narrate it as best I can in this chapter.

As mentioned earlier, I joined and served in the Labour Party from 1998 to date. It was a natural fit for me after the bankruptcy left me isolated. Jim Murphy had helped me, and I was determined to help him in return. The Labour Party gave me friendship, and I enjoyed giving back by supporting them. Some councillors felt I was too loyal to Jim, which was fair enough, but I saw it as the best way forward. I was developing my own political ambitions, and Jim was the key to that door. The party is like a church—the more devout you are in your Labour politics, the more you are valued and given opportunities, at least until you come up against competition or the rules.

The first major challenge was the Iraq War. The councillors were firmly against it, as was most of the Labour Party. In East Renfrewshire, we held a summit meeting with all members and elected representatives. Most members of Parliament supported the war, citing the dozens of UN resolutions Saddam Hussein had violated and, eventually, the infamous "weapons of mass destruction" claim, which had been sexed up by Alastair Campbell.

As election coordinator and vice-chair of the CLP, I wrote to John Smith House and the Cabinet Office for guidance. It was suggested that I should remain neutral, as they were aware that the parliamentary vote on the war was imminent. Since Jim was a whip at the time, taking a position could have been politically embarrassing and a prime story for the Daily Mail. Owen Armstrong and the councillors made powerful speeches against the war, but nothing could stop the vote. As we know, the war went ahead, and the rest is a tragic chapter in history.

In 2004, Owen Armstrong, the longest-serving councilor in local government, made a fatal mistake. After a Celtic football match, he got drunk, went home, and allegedly assaulted his wife, Millie, ending up in the cells.

Behind the scenes most of the councillors decided not to support him, despite Millie's protests. When I attended the Labour Group meeting to discuss the emergency, the decision had already been made—he was to be suspended from the Labour Party. As chair of the "Zero Tolerance Group" against domestic violence, he had effectively hung himself out to dry. He lost his seat on the council, was expelled from the party, and returned to his job as a fire fighter.

The remaining councillors moved up a position, and Jim Fletcher became leader of the council. In fairness, they were right—Owen was now a "busted flush." Fortunately, the Labour Party still had a majority.

Jim's career in the Blair Cabinet continued to rise, and in 2005, he was appointed Minister in the Cabinet Office.

Danny Scott stood as an independent in the next election, won, and has been the local councilor ever since.

By 2004, my credibility in the Labour Party had risen as I had coordinated another victory for Jim Murphy, increasing his majority to over 10,000. John Smith House placed me second on the regional list for the Scottish Parliament. Labour performed exceptionally well, so the regional list was not called, and Jack McConnell formed the new Scottish Government.

Jim Murphy's appointment to the Cabinet Office in 2005 brought a noticeable change—he honed his whip skills and remained accessible to the local party.

Behind the scenes, I worked with Ian Fulton, Colin Roberts, and Nasim Khan to keep the local branches and CLP together. We were highly successful in fundraising and campaigning. We campaigned continuously in local council elections, Westminster, Holyrood, and the European Parliament. These were the halcyon days for Labour, particularly in East Renfrewshire, with the Blair government boasting a significant number of Scottish MPs.

The Westminster election campaign was gathering momentum, and I was Jim Murphy's election coordinator. We leased a shop in Barrhead shopping centre, which Colin Roberts and I fitted out for the campaign.

We received word that a VIP would be visiting Barrhead and our campaign. A few days before the visit, two burly men walked into the shop unannounced. I confronted them, as not all members of the public are Labour supporters, and the SNP can be quite aggressive. The first man flashed a badge and introduced them as Protection Officers—they were there to assess the shop. I immediately knew the VIP would be Tony Blair.

During most elections, the government is disbanded, but the Prime Minister remains in office to run the country.

When Tony arrived in Barrhead, he was early, meaning many of our activists missed seeing him. This is a typical security tactic, as it is always difficult to contain VIP movements. He addressed the local people from a street bench outside our campaign shop while his security detail remained vigilant. It would have been easy for the SNP's "angry squad" to give him a hard time—just as they did to Jim Murphy during the Scottish independence referendum.

He then entered the campaign room to address the activists, standing on a pile of wooden garden blocks donated by Colin Roberts. We presented him with a hand-painted picture of Donald Dewar, created by a member of the local art club in Barrhead. As he spoke to the activists, I noticed some graffiti high on the wall above his head: "Scotland Forever – Fuck off the English." Like so many things in politics, nobody acknowledged it, but it would have been a gift to the media if caught on camera.

Jenni interviewing the Prime Minister Tony Blair

The activists were thrilled, and we all put in extra effort to get the shop ready and push forward with the campaign. A Labour government was returned on 5th May.

In 2008, Jim Murphy was appointed Secretary of State for Scotland. Although I continued working hard behind the scenes for all elected members, my hopes of a political career were dashed for several reasons— primarily because I was bankrupt and, frankly, of more use as an election coordinator than a candidate. I have no doubt I was well liked in the party, but I had to face the facts: you need to be squeaky clean in Politics, or the media will tear you apart.

Our best bet for a political position was Elaine, whom Jim Murphy backed as a local councilor. She was elected in 2007 and served for ten years—first as Vice Convenor for Education until 2012, then as Convenor for Education until 2017. She also held various other positions, including Chair of Licensing.

In 2001, I was working on Colin Roberts' house in Neilston, which was great because his wife, Isobel, was the best hostess—keeping us going with breakfasts and lunches. In between work, we continued discussing politics and local party issues.

One day, while I was working on the roof, Colin told me he had to go to the doctor for the results of some recent tests. When he returned, he was subdued—the doctor had told him he had esophageal cancer. Colin decided not only to fight it but also to fight for other cancer sufferers. We formed the East Renfrewshire Cancer Care Group and enlisted the help of Jim Murphy and Ken MacIntosh. Jim raised questions in Parliament about Scotland's poor cancer care record, and Ken became Chair of the Cross-Party Cancer Group at Holyrood. We took our campaign right to the heart of the Labour Party, and in 2002, we attended the Party Conference in Perth, holding our own fringe event to discuss the way forward.

Colin's condition deteriorated. He lost all his hair, but he kept going. When he was receiving chemotherapy at the Western Infirmary, it became clear just how appalling cancer care was in the West of Scotland.

We visited various cancer hospitals, including the Beatson in Glasgow, and spoke to top consultants. Ken and I visited the Molecular Biology Unit, only to be told that thousands of tests for women with a family history of breast cancer had not been completed due to lack of funding. The more we uncovered, the uglier the truth became. It was no wonder Glasgow was the cancer capital of Europe.

Colin's treatment was horrific. He had to have a stent fitted in his throat just to swallow pulped food, and he was bleeding from all over his body— including from his nails. I visited him a few days before he died, and he indicated he'd had enough. He was one of the best friends I ever had and a stalwart of the Labour Party.

Despite his passing, we carried on the campaign, gaining the support of many MSPs for improvements to cancer care. Andy Kerr MSP was instrumental in securing funding for the new Beatson Centre and prioritizing improvements in palliative care, something Isobel had insisted on after witnessing Colin's painful final days.

In May 2007, the new Beatson West of Scotland Cancer Centre opened— Colin Roberts' and Scottish Labour's greatest legacy.

One of our activists, Jimmy Hay from Barrhead, was admitted to the Beatson in 2009. When I visited him, he was dying, but he told me: "Jim, they're so nice to me here, and the place is great. It's a good place to die." Compared to the old cancer ward at the Western Infirmary, it was indeed a better place to die.

In 2007, Jim Murphy was appointed Minister of State for Europe and immediately had to deal with the assassination of Alexander Litvinenko by the Russian FSB using Polonium. Litvinenko died on 23rd November.

New troubles emerged within the branch and CLP when Vince Watt infiltrated the party—not as a sleeper from another party, but as an ambitious opportunist who would do anything to advance himself. He ingratiated himself with elected members and used his cleaning business to gain access to parliamentary offices and their homes.

He was not popular with activists and struggled to get onto the CLP, attempting entry through the Fabians and then the GMB Union. He even told Jean Hunter, our oldest member, that it was "time to move over" as she was "too old."

Ian Fulton and I tried to warn elected members about the dangers he posed, but to little effect. Eventually, during the council selection process, Watt misrepresented himself and was caught lying—exposed at an appeals meeting at John Smith House. He claimed his case was prejudiced because his record as a member of various school boards and parent councils should not have been shared with the selection team. However, the record was damning—he had made life exceedingly difficult for teachers and board members.

At the appeals hearing, Watt burst into tears, claiming he was being treated unfairly and threatening legal action against the party. That did it—the decision went in his favour. Ian and I resigned as Chair and Vice-Chair of the CLP in protest.

Surprisingly, Watt withdrew from the council list and left Labour to join the SNP, where he immediately caused trouble for the local SNP councillors. His revenge came when he "masterminded" the SNP's election campaign against Jim Murphy in 2014, which resulted in Labour losing the seat. Unfortunately, I was working in Denmark at the time and missed the campaign and defeat.

Jim became Leader of Scottish Labour at the end of 2014 and led the "No Campaign" in the independence referendum. The No vote won, keeping the Union intact—but at the cost of Jim's political career. He spent so much time fighting for the Union that he sacrificed his own standing in the constituency.

Watt was eventually elected as an SNP councilor but lasted only one term—he was so disruptive that even his own party refused to work with him.

When Jeremy Corbyn took control of the Labour Party, Ian Fulton resigned completely, and Nasim Khan stopped attending meetings. With new constituency boundaries, Elaine and I found ourselves aligned with Paisley South and Barrhead. Elaine continued as a counselor, but for me, I had to take a backset now from politics.

I bumped into Jim occasionally at the airport—he was now working with in London and building up his own Consultancy—but my focus had shifted.

Ken MacIntosh MSP eventually rose to the top, becoming Presiding Officer of the Scottish Parliament. One of the nicest men in politics, he now holds no party affiliation.

Being involved in politics was an incredible experience. I met great people who became lifelong friends, visited Downing Street, attended the Queen's Garden Party, and shared countless events with Labour leaders. But it's the cancer care work that I am most proud.

Jim Green MBA

The author at No 10 Downing St

I am no longer as active in politics but remain a Labour Party member. My comrade, Ian Fulton, left the party after Corbyn's election to focus on his role as a board member of the Refugee Council in Scotland. Ian has since re-engaged with the Labour Party and remains a sage council for all.

Labour Party Comrades (with Ian Fulton)

10 Trades

I decided it was time to rebuild the business, so I created a new company, 10 Trades, and liquidated the Allied Contracts sole trader business. I got Jamie and my brother-in-law Gordon involved, and we each had white vans with the 10 Trades logo on the livery.

Gordon had been working offshore in the oil industry for about 25 years and had had enough. He asked if he could work with me on a casual basis to learn new skills. The plan was for him to develop the business north of the River Clyde while I focused on the south side. Jamie, meanwhile, would start his own company, Greenman Builders.

We set up a workshop and offices at Blackhall Street, Paisley, got everything fitted out, and waited for the work to come in. Jamie left IBM in 2002 and joined the company, but the work was patchy. My Labour Party comrades kept me going Isobel Roberts, along with Eddie and Edwina Pearson, gave me jobs fitting out bathrooms and kitchens. By November, however, we were struggling again. I was paying wages when I couldn't even take anything for myself.

We picked up a few extension projects, and customers were complimentary, leading to some referrals. However, extensions don't bring in much profit— bad weather slows things down, and workers are unreliable.

Then, I landed a big contract in Clarkston to build a two-level extension on a bungalow. It was worth around £60,000, but by the time I secured it, it was already November, and the customer wanted it finished by Christmas. I got to work immediately, but we ran into problems straight away. I had budgeted for four skips, but we ended up needing twelve. Then the rain came.

We managed to get the structure built and the roof on, but it was clear we'd have to return in the new year to finish. Some of the lads weren't pulling their weight, and the schedule slipped further. Three weeks into January, the money had run out. The customer had requested a lot of extras, and although the work was complete, I asked for the additional costs so we could finish properly. The problem was that the customer had also run out of money.

If I'd had enough funds, I could have completed the job, but as it was, I had to walk away, exhausted. A few days later, when I went back to collect my tools, I found three of my men working for cash to finish the job. I was gutted—by them and by the client—and it took me a long time to get over it.

Back at work, I took on a large extension project in Nethergreen Wynd, Renfrew, determined to make it a showpiece. I brought in Eddie the brickie to ensure the extension matched the house perfectly. He did an outstanding job, and we were nominated for the Federation of Master Builders award.

Interestingly, the site had been built on reclaimed land from my old employer, Babcock's. It brought back memories of working there 30 years earlier with Freddy Allen and the Pipe shop boys, killing time by shooting pigeons.

Just as we were finishing the project, I received a letter from our landlord at Blackhall Street, taking me to court for unpaid rent. Having recently been through bankruptcy, I didn't waste any time—I went straight to the landlord's solicitors in Glasgow and paid every spare penny I had to avoid legal action.

That wasn't the end of it. I had to clear out the premises immediately, but worse, I had to break up the partnership with Gordon and Jamie. I worked over the weekend to clear the workshop, with my old pal Fred Thorley helping me.

For a while, I licked my wounds and tried to manage work on my own or with one or two of the lads when they were available. Years of physical labour had taken its toll—some mornings, I needed two Solpadine pain killers just to get my boots on.

Jamie had started his own company, and we helped each other out when possible, working for each other on a daily rate when needed. We jogged along like that for a few months.

James And Ellen Together at Last

Towards the end of February 2005, I got a call from my sister Anne to say that Mum had been admitted to hospital as she wasn't well. At the end of 2004, she had already needed paramedics when she slipped into a coma. Mum was 75 years old, but she had walked into the hospital and onto the ward herself.

Anne later called to say that the consultant wanted to speak with the family, so we both agreed to meet with him. It was Thursday, 20th February, when the consultant told us that Mum only had a few days to live—her body was riddled with cancer, and her kidneys had collapsed. It was difficult to process, especially as she had walked into the hospital just two days earlier.

I let everyone in the family know so they can come and say their final goodbyes. This included the grandchildren who visited on the

Friday. After the evening visit, I agreed to sit with Mum through the night, and Anne stayed with me while the others went home.

By about 9:00 pm, Mum was clearly drowning in her own fluids. I asked the doctor to make her more comfortable. One shot of morphine, and she was gone within two minutes. Her feet stayed warm for a little while, but then I had to go and tell the rest of the family. The nurses prepared her for the mortuary, and the doctor handed me the death certificate.

Life is cruel—to have to ask for the person who gave me life to be "made more comfortable."

2006 was a horrible year, starting in the worst possible way.

Maggie Jamie's wife was due to give birth and had been taken into Ayrshire Maternity Hospital Complications arose, and their baby—a little boy—died in the womb.

Elaine and I drove to the hospital immediately and found Jamie and Maggie in a darkened room, with Jamie holding his dead son while the nurses attended to Maggie after the delivery. I can still picture that beautiful little boy in Jamie's arms, his lips tinged blue—the same as when my mother lost my sister Angela to stillbirth so many years ago. I never thought we would have to go through that tragedy twice.

Jamie and Maggie named their son Cailin.

The funeral was held in Dunlop. Jamie carried the small white coffin from their home on Dunlop High Street to the grave in the churchyard cemetery. Their eldest son, Robin, and others scattered paper butterflies into the grave. It was heartbreaking, and it took a long time for us all to recover. As if that pain wasn't enough, the hospital carried out an autopsy, and by some awful mistake, they sent the post-mortem photographs to Jamie's home. Our troubles weren't over.

Dad continued to deteriorate, and I visited him every week, feeding him ice cream and yoghurt. In the final days before he passed, he refused all food, pressing his lips firmly shut. Because of his condition, we had no way of knowing how much he understood, but one thing was certain—when I held his hand and asked if he'd had enough, he squeezed it.

Dad passed away on 20th July 2006.

Neither he nor Mum had to suffer the pain of losing each other.

Family Grave Hawkhead Cemetery Paisley

The last days of being a builder.

I jogged along for the next two years, sometimes working with Jamie and sometimes with the boys. Jimmy Boyle was amazing—he would handle all the brickwork, and working with him and Jamie on extensions was always a pleasure. Jimmy once told us that he had worked with my grandfather, father, son, and grandson as a builder.

The physical work was grinding me down, and on one occasion while working with Jamie, it nearly became fatal.

Jamie had a contract for structural alterations in a top-floor tenement on Alexandra Parade, on the north side of the River Clyde. I was helping move materials up and down four flights of stairs, but I became weaker and weaker. Eventually, the boys working with Jamie said I didn't look well. I could hardly walk, so I asked Jamie to take me home.

Once home, I just sat on the couch, unaware that the black stools I was passing were a sign of internal bleeding. Elaine was going out that evening, and I didn't want to worry her—I planned to see the doctor in the morning. I was beginning to drift off when the phone rang. It was my old pal Freddie Thorley, who asked what was up, as I usually went to the midweek cinema with Ian Johnston. When I told him about my day and the black stools, Fred told me to get to the hospital immediately. As a retired police inspector, he had seen too many people bleed to death overnight.

I called Jamie, who took me to A&E. Within minutes, I was admitted and handed over to the surgeons, who plugged the bleeding from two duodenal ulcers. The consultant said I was a lucky man.

The next day, while in the ward, they fitted a drip, but it fell out, and I bled from the vein—out of sight from me and the nurses. A huge pool of blood had gathered on the floor before anyone noticed. Once again, I survived to tell the tale.

It took a few weeks to recover, but between the ulcers and the hernias, I wasn't enjoying the challenges anymore. My only real pleasure was when Jamie and I went to the Arthurlie Inns in Barrhead after work on a Friday for a few beers. If you've worked hard all day and are covered in dust, there's no better pleasure than a pint of draught beer.

In the summer of 2007, I got a contract from a customer in Erskine to build a two-storey extension to a new house. I managed to pull together a good team, including Jimmy Boyle, and the job was going well—we were set to make a reasonable profit.

Every Friday, I would go to the bank to get the wages for the boys. On this particular Friday, I was on my way back to the site when, at the St James Interchange near Glasgow Airport, a young boy racer slammed into the back of my Volvo estate. I immediately felt pain in my lower back and neck. I returned to the site, paid the boys, and took the weekend off. The pain got worse before it eased, but my back still gave me trouble in the mornings when I got out of bed.

I recovered a bit, but my final contract was in my local village, where Jimmy and I did some stone repairs on a house in Tannoch Road.

On the last day, Jimmy gave me a book about the design and construction of the Guggenheim Museum in New York. He had often talked about working on it as a young man, but it wasn't until I flicked through the pages at home that I saw a picture of Jimmy and the other stonemasons with Frank Lloyd Wright himself. Jimmy Boyle passed away a few years later, leaving behind some of my best memories—working with him was always a pleasure.

My Last Day as a Builder with Jimmy Boyle

It had been my boyhood dream to become a builder, and I did. I learned to carry out most trades myself, hired and fired hundreds of men, and grew the business from nothing to trading over £1 million per year. We worked all over Scotland and Northern Ireland, meeting some of the best—and worst— people imaginable. In the end, I have no regrets about being a builder, because the skills I learned on construction sites would form the foundation for my next career.

CHAPTER 48:
A CONSULTANT IS BORN.

Elaine was elected as a Councillor in May 2007 and was now earning a salary every month, which meant I could start considering an alternative to being a builder. Aside from my solid understanding of construction, I also had a strong CV in health and safety management.

In 2005, the government introduced the CDM Regulations, which placed specific duties on those responsible for construction projects. This legislation created a role for CDM Coordinators, and I had a few friends working in the field. I thought this might be a good option for me, so I started applying for dozens of jobs—but with no success. It was incredibly disheartening. I believed my CV was strong, but there was certain information I had to hold back.

At 57 years old, I had a medical history that included ulcers, back problems, double hernias, and depression. On top of that, I was an ex-bankrupt with two failed businesses. If I were in an employer's shoes, I wouldn't have hired me either.

I had one last throw of the dice. A company called GHP, based near Ascot, was looking for a CDM Coordinator for a client in Scotland. I applied and secured an interview with one of the directors, Clair Thomas. The interview was scheduled to take place at the Excelsior Hotel at Glasgow Airport. By this point, I was so frustrated with all my previous failures that I was ready to pass on the opportunity. It was Elaine who persuaded me to go.

It was a Friday afternoon in late August 2007 when I met Clair and her HR manager, Kelly Dawes. Clair was a sharp, no-nonsense woman who had joined the company just a few years earlier and had already become a director. The interview was informal—Clair asked me what I knew about CDM, and I told her to ask me anything. I suggested we discuss F10s (formal CDM notification forms for the Health and Safety Executive), but she waved it off, satisfied. She then asked if I could wait an hour to meet her boss, Paul Davies, who was returning from holiday.

Paul arrived at the hotel reception in sandals, shorts, and a beach shirt— tanned and in good spirits. After he and Clair discussed her part of the interview, he came back to me and said, "When can you start?"

"Right away," I replied.

He then asked what salary I wanted. I said £40,000, to which he immediately agreed—and even offered me a company car. I was to report to Taylor Wimpey Developments' MD, Willie McDermott, the following Monday at their Livingston site in Central Scotland. I couldn't believe my luck.

Wimpey Developments had about 20 sites across the central belt, mostly new housing projects. It didn't take long to settle in, and I quickly built a good working relationship with the project managers and land purchasers. When Christmas arrived, there was a big workforce gathering in the boardroom.

As an external contractor, I wasn't planning to attend, but Willie McDermott insisted. He reaffirmed that I was part of the team. The boardroom table was stacked with Christmas gifts, each marked with a raffle ticket—contractors' tokens of appreciation for doing business with TWD. After the speeches, I returned to my desk to find two bottles of the finest malt whisky waiting for me.

The next day, I got a call from David Williams, the previous CDM Coordinator at TWD. He had since joined Mott MacDonald and had been checking in with his contacts about my performance. He asked if I'd be interested in a role with them. Within days, I had an interview at Canning Tower in Edinburgh with lead CDM Consultant Duncan Chisholm. I was offered a consultancy position with a salary of £50,000 per year.

I hate letting people down, but this was a fantastic opportunity with a top consultancy. Motts was unique consultants owned the business and shared in the profits.

Just before Christmas, Clair flew into Glasgow. When I told her, she was furious and called Paul immediately. I handed her my resignation letter, but she didn't even open it. When I tried to return the company car, she refused, saying she'd been drinking, so I ended up driving her to her mother's house in Saltcoats, Ayrshire.

That weekend, Paul bombarded me with calls and emails, offering "jam tomorrow" promises, including a director's job, but my mind was made up. I was heading to Motts.

I spent a month training in the Edinburgh office, meeting my fellow CDM Coordinators. Soon, I was appointed to several projects, including the New Museum of Liverpool. This was a major project that involved flying to Manchester, catching a train to Lime Street Station, and taking a taxi to the site at Liverpool Docks, right next to the Liver Building. The museum's modern design presented various safety challenges, especially the spiral staircase construction, which was a key feature. We managed these challenges well. I got on with most of the managers, though I clashed with the Director of Museums—a particularly feisty woman.

New Museum of Liverpool

I've worked for female bosses before, and I'm not sexist, but I've generally found them more stressful to work for than male bosses. After a year of tension, I was relieved to move on to another project, though I remained proud of the work we did on the spiral staircase—it was incredibly challenging.

Duncan Chisholm later asked if I'd be interested in offshore renewables work. The project was the Pelamis Wave Energy Converter (WEC), being built by BiFab in Leith, near Edinburgh. I was appointed as the CDM Coordinator, but offshore work required certification.

I was sent to the Petrofac Training Centre in Aberdeen for BOSIET and HUET training—courses that covered sea survival and helicopter escape.

Anyone who has undergone sea survival and helicopter escape training will tell you—it's not for the faint-hearted. During the helicopter escape drill, they simulate a crash, submerge the chamber upside down, and strap you in. You have to escape underwater.

On my way to Aberdeen, I met a young scaffolder from Ayrshire. He had saved up to take the course, hoping for offshore work with better pay. The training, including travel and accommodation, cost him about £1,500— money he couldn't afford to waste. During the helicopter escape simulation, he panicked, trying to get out before the water had equalized inside the chamber. The divers had to rescue him. Eventually, he completed the training and got his certificate.

A few years later, he was killed in a real helicopter crash in the North Sea.

CHAPTER 49:
THE GOLDEN SHILLING DIES

At home, I had been looking forward to the weekend. Slumped hard into the couch after dinner, I was dozing off when my mobile phone rang. It was Friday, 2nd March 2007. My sister, Anne, was on the line, incoherent. All I could make out was, "He didn't make it." Her husband—my best friend, Gordon—had suffered a massive heart attack and died.

I drove immediately to the Vale of Leven A&E unit, where I found Anne sitting behind some screens, devastated. Gordon lay on a bed, lifeless. There were burn marks on his chest from the defibrillator shock paddles, but other than that, he was still warm. He had just showered, his hair fresh and neatly combed and he smelled of aftershave. Anne had not only lost her husband and the love of her life, but also her chance to adopt children.

Anne and Gordon had applied to adopt three girls—triplets—who had an exceedingly difficult start in life. Their parents were drug addicts; their father was in prison, and their mother was completely troubled and unwell. For their safety, the State had removed them. Anne and Gordon had tried everything to conceive, even undergoing IVF in Cambridge, but without success. It was only a matter of days before the girls would have been placed with them.

Gordon had been terribly unlucky. The weekend before he died, he and Anne had gone to the cinema after a burger meal. Not feeling well, he called NHS 24, who advised him to take indigestion tablets, assuming the burger was the culprit. During the call, Gordon told them he had a family history of heart disease and was in his 50s. It was outrageous that he was not sent to hospital immediately.

The next day, still unwell, Gordon and Anne went to the RAH A&E in Paisley. It was a Sunday, and the department was understaffed. A young female doctor—who had only been in the UK for six weeks and at the RAH for two—failed to carry out a proper ECG. She applied only some of the required electrical leads and misinterpreted the data, not realizing Gordon was having a heart attack. She sent him home with antacid tablets and an antibiotic.

Though still feeling ill, Gordon assumed it was the flu and went to work in Dumfries on Monday. By Friday, his condition had not improved. He left his shift early, drove home, took a shower, and settled on the couch to watch TV where A Question of Sport was on. Anne asked if he wanted a cup of tea and went into the kitchen. Moments later, she heard a noise from the lounge. When she returned, Gordon was unconscious. She immediately phoned for an ambulance.

The paramedics worked on him for some time before transferring him to hospital, where he was pronounced dead.

I stayed with Anne for a few days to help organize the funeral and contact his workplace. In the end, I had to return home. We were all heartbroken, and Anne was now on her own. In her own words, her "magic carpet ride" was over.

In time, there was a fatal accident inquiry, where I represented Anne in court in Dumbarton. The recommendations that followed made it compulsory to triage suspected heart attack patients, and the role of NHS 24 was reviewed. But nothing could bring Gordon back.

He was buried in the Green family grave at Hawkhead Cemetery in Paisley. His family called him "The Golden Shilling"—a phrase now inscribed on his headstone.

Gordon Grieg "The Golden Shilling"

Back to Northern Ireland

Working as a freelance consultant with Motts gave me the opportunity to become a truly polished professional, as the standards they expected were of the highest level. After two years, I was working on both onshore and offshore renewable projects, including wind farms. By 2010, I was appointed Senior Consultant with Motts and became a shareholder.

I had the opportunity to conduct due diligence on a contractor called Novera, who were building a wind farm in Lissett, near Driffield in England. Novera had hired a consultancy firm called PMSS, based in Romsey, Kent, to handle their health and safety consultancy on-site.

When I arrived, it was clear that PMSS were not performing. I criticized the safety conditions on-site and submitted my report.

The consultant advising the site was Nick Chivers, son of Alan Chivers the Managing Director. It wasn't long before Alan called me for a chat. Expecting to defend my report, I was surprised when Alan instead made me a proposal. He asked if I would like to join PMSS, specifically their Glasgow office in Queen Street. He offered me £72,000 per annum plus bonuses, with the prospect of becoming a Principal Consultant.

Although I was settled at Motts and my career was progressing well, I liked Alan, and PMSS was a well-known consultancy firm specializing in renewables. Taking a chance, I resigned from Motts and handed back my shareholding.

After a few days in the PMSS Romsey office, sorting out my laptop and phone, I faced one issue—I would be reporting to Nick Chivers. To Nick's credit, he was always a good boss and allowed me to get on with things.

One of my PMSS projects was supporting Aquamarine's Oyster Wave Energy Converter. I was informed that the HSE Manager I would be reporting to was Eddie Scott, the former Pelamis HSE Manager. Eddie and I had some tough conversations on this project, but we maintained our friendship. When he moved to Aquamarine, which was building the Oyster Wave Energy

Convertor, he found that I had been appointed by Motts as CDM-C for the project.

The Oyster was built and shipped to the European Offshore Energy Test Centre in Stromness, Orkney. The design aimed to extract energy from waves by pumping high-pressure water onshore to drive a turbine and export electricity to the grid. When Scotland's First Minister, Alex Salmond, inaugurated the Oyster 800 at a high-profile PR event at the Bi-Fab site in Leith, the project was at its peak. However, in the end, the design failed, and Aquamarine was wound up—much like Alex Salmond himself, who later ended up on Russian TV station RT and dropped dead in 2024.

The project was not without incidents. On one occasion, a diver suffered decompression sickness ('the bends') and had to be transferred to the hyperbaric chamber in Stromness. He was an older man with an undeclared medical condition. Though he made a full recovery, he was not allowed to dive again on the project.

A few months into my role at PMSS, Nick called to see if I could source a consultant for construction operations at Edinbane Wind Farm on the Isle of Skye. Around the same time, my son Jamie had been working with his building company. I suggested he complete his offshore and NEBOSH training, and being a graduate in business and management, he was well- suited for the project.

Jamie Graduates with BA

Jamie wasted no time and was soon at Edinbane, where he did a great job and became well-regarded at PMSS. He later worked on Thanet Offshore Wind Farm, Baltic 2, and Ormonde Wind Farm construction projects.

I was then appointed to an ESB project in Northern Ireland at Curryfree, near Derry—or Londonderry, depending on your political perspective. I had no desire to return to Northern Ireland due to past experiences, but I had no choice. My work required me to travel between the ESB offices in Dublin and Curryfree. On the plus side, I was able to stay at the Beech Hill Hotel on the outskirts of Derry, where Bill Clinton had stayed during the peace talks.

There were few problems on-site, but one evening I received a call informing me that a security advisor had been attacked and was in hospital. The investigation revealed that he had been working alone, armed only with a radio and a mobile phone. While on his rounds, he had disturbed three men attempting to steal copper cable cuttings. They smashed his radio and phone

before beating him up. Rumors suggested paramilitary involvement, but I believed it was more likely local scrap dealers.

At the end of the project, I had a great night out in Dublin's Temple Bar with Gerry O'Keenaghan and the project team. I have no recollection of the evening whatsoever!

Despite my initial hesitation about Northern Ireland, I grew to appreciate the scenery and the warmth of the people. I even returned to the Beech Hill a year later while on holiday with John and Marjorie Waters. After some lunch, we made our way to the Gweedore Hotel near Bunbeg in Donegal.

On the second day, I noticed several vehicles on the beach. Taking Elaine onto the hard sand, I decided to try out the Mitsubishi Warrior. To get the perfect shot, I edged the 4x4 closer to the sea—a big mistake. When I tried to reverse, the rear wheels sank into the softer sand.

With the tide coming in, I began to panic. I tried using driftwood planks and digging the wheels out, but nothing worked. A nearby group of German teenagers attempted to help push the car, to no avail. I phoned the hotel, but they could only call a local fisherman—who turned out to be drunk.

With no other option, I contacted emergency services. The sea was only a few feet away and advancing quickly. Marjorie and John joined me as I prepared to watch my new 4x4 disappear into the Atlantic.

Just in time, the drunken Irishman arrived in his tractor. Within minutes, he had pulled the car free. What a relief! I offered him payment, but he refused and drove off, leaving me a very grateful man. God bless the Irish!

Back at PMSS, I was appointed to a new project in Colchester, where a company called Empower was building a modular power station for sub- Saharan Africa. The existing consultant had failed in his duties, so I had to resolve several issues. This required producing all the necessary HSE documents for a CDM 2007 construction project.

Captain of the ship on PMSS weekend adventure

CHAPTER 50:
ELLEN DIES

The construction site was at the MAN Diesel & Turbo factory on Hythe Hill, about half a mile from the Army barracks in Colchester. I stayed at the Rose and Crown Hotel and travelled back and forth from the beginning of 2009.

On 5th March, I received a call informing me that my sister, Ellen, had been taken into hospital and was seriously ill. I left immediately, travelling back to Glasgow via Stansted Airport. From there, I drove straight to the RAH Hospital, where I met Ellen's husband, Bob Gibb, and their two sons, Barry and Chris.

Ellen was in a room being worked on by doctors and nurses. I tried to see her, but by then, she was already dying—or had passed. Eventually, the consultant came in and told us she was gone. We buried her next to Mum and Dad in Hawkhead Cemetery. Ellen was a beautiful person and liked and loved by all and our loss was hard to take. Her work colleagues at the SSEC in Glasgow placed a memorial plaque in the garden at the main entrance to the Exhibition Centre. One of the great sadnesses about Ellen's death was that she did not live to see her sons get married and produce wonderful grandchildren. She was also denied the benefit of the £1 million pounds inheritance that her next-door friend and neighbour bequeathed to her for looking after her during the final years of her life.

My beautiful sister Ellen

CHAPTER 51:
TEESSIDE

In 2011, I was appointed as CDM-C for the Teesside Windfarm project, owned by EDF Energy. The project team was based at the ex-ICI building at the Wilton Centre near Redcar. I joined at the design stage and travelled regularly between London Victoria and Teesside.

The project was led by Tim Black, who I didn't get on with particularly well. We had many awkward conversations, as he wasn't always focused on safety. The project HSE manager, Andy Trotter, was useless—he spent most of his day outside having a cigarette.

During construction, the jack-up barge got stuck in the mudstone, and the entire crew had to be evacuated. With so many things going wrong, the EDF project director eventually got involved. I was finally allowed to speak openly about the project, which put Tim Black and me on a collision course. PMSS directors stepped in, realizing they could be removed from the contract.

By 2012, things had settled down, and my routine involved taking a taxi to Glasgow Airport, hiring a car from Avis, and driving to Teesside. In September, I had become well known to the Avis team, and the local rep upgraded me to a brand-new Alfa Romeo Giulietta, advising me to take care of it. However, on my way into Middlesbrough, a young mother—who was in the wrong lane—crashed into the Alfa. It was a low-impact collision, and no one was hurt, but the car was severely damaged. It was a bit embarrassing handing the keys back, and to this day, I think I must be blacklisted by Avis!

In the project office, we had started a competition for the "fat folk" to lose weight. At over 15 stone, I took on the challenge and was leading the competition. In November, I took Elaine with me to Teesside, and we booked into the Thistle Hotel. She planned to do some Christmas shopping and use the hotel's swimming pool. That week, I had been in back-to-back meetings since Monday, and on Thursday evening, Elaine and I went to Fellini's restaurant for dinner, followed by a film.

When we returned to the hotel, I felt a sharp pain in my stomach—I knew instantly it was a burst ulcer. I should have gone straight to hospital, however based on my previous ulcer episode, I thought I could wait until morning. I barely slept, my stomach was making loud gurgling noises, and by morning, I knew I needed to leave.

I decided to go into the project office in Redcar to let them know I was heading home as I wasn't feeling well. By the time I arrived at the Wilton Centre, I could hardly walk—my legs felt as if I had lead boots on. I managed to find Mal Plunkett, the interface manager, who immediately said I looked very unwell. Mal was sympathetic, and I slowly walked back to my car and drove to the hotel reception.

I barely made it inside before asking the receptionist to call an ambulance and find Elaine. When she arrived, I was slipping into unconsciousness, sitting in a chair in the reception area. The last thing I remember was handing her my wallet and PIN numbers, convinced this was the end.

The paramedics wired me up and rushed me to the James Cook Military Hospital, straight to triage. Elaine later told me that I suddenly "exploded," with blood spurting from my mouth and backside, and I was gone. Around ten doctors and nurses whisked me into theatre, where surgeons managed to stop the bleeding and save my life.

I spent five days in hospital before going home to rest for a couple of weeks. What struck me most was how little my employers cared. Nobody from PMSS made any effort to see me. From that moment, I knew that if another opportunity arose, I would leave PMSS.

That said, in fairness to Alan Chivers and PMSS, they gave Jamie and me the chance to earn good money and develop as consultants. We also enjoyed some fantastic paid trips to Austria, Longleat, and Nice.

In Austria, the entire team had the option to climb the Via Ferrata into the mountains between Austria and Italy. Instead, I chose to paint the Marmolada mountain range with the help of an artist in a one-to-one session. I was dropped off at the base of the mountain, took a cable car to the top, and had a lovely lunch before starting my lesson. It was, without doubt, one of the best days of my life.

Longleat was a team-building exercise. Jamie, Steve Loft, and I were joined by Dr David, our new environmental consultant. David had only been with us for a few days and had been tasked with improving the business in Scotland. We enjoyed the day but were eager to get back home in the evening.

Every Friday, we had a business planning meeting at our Queen Street offices in Glasgow. David agreed to visit potential customers in Aberdeen, Edinburgh, and Dundee, as he lived near the Aberdeen/Dundee area.

Early in 2012, David was on his way home after visiting lawyers in Dundee, driving along some B-class roads. We never learned the full details, but his 4x4 overturned on a bad bend, and he was killed instantly.

On Monday morning, Alan briefed the company. Steve and I tried to contact David's family, but they held a private funeral, and no one from PMSS attended. For days, Steve and I sat staring at his empty desk and his untouched tea mug. When we asked if we could pack up his belongings and send them to his family, we were told not to. (RIP David.)

After this, I was appointed to the Kelburn Windfarm project, run by the RES Group. Their offices were in Glasgow's STV building and in Kings Langley, just off the M25 north of London. Kelburn was about a 30-minute drive from my home in Caldwell, near the seaside town of Largs in Ayrshire.

In the early stages, I travelled frequently between Glasgow and Kings Langley. Eventually, we established a site high in the hills above Largs on the west coast of Ayrshire. The windfarm consisted of 14 turbines spread over the hills, with a substation and education centre overlooking the windfarm and the sea. The views were spectacular.

The site project manager was Fergal Duffy, an Irishman, while the overall project manager was Alan McMahon. The project went very smoothly, with only one major incident—a heavy-lifting crane got stuck in a ditch. It took about 18 months to complete, and it was one of the most enjoyable projects I ever worked on.

Like most construction sites, the men had set things up so there was always a warm place to take a break and decent food available. On particularly bad weather days, Gary Scowther, the site manager, would often take me into Largs for a big Scottish breakfast. The windfarm became fully operational in September 2012.

One of the more unusual aspects of the Kelburn Windfarm was the presence of an old aircraft wreck high in the hills. Within the boundaries of the windfarm lay the remains of a Dakota C-47B, which crashed on 28th March 1956, killing one of its pilots on Greenside Hill.

The aircraft had been flying from Speke Airport near Liverpool to Renfrew Airport near Glasgow, carrying only three crew members. The pilot, Geoffrey Moss, miraculously survived despite severe injuries, including a broken back. He managed to pull the air hostess, Hilda Pearson, free from the wreckage, saving her life. He then crawled nearly a mile to find help before returning to the crash site.

Standing there, looking at the miserable pile of broken aircraft parts, I couldn't help but think of his heroism. I was fit and had walked that site before, and even in good health, it was tough going. How he managed to carry out the rescue and then crawl a mile for help is almost beyond belief. The pilot who died that day was Noel C. A. Stanley.

CHAPTER 52:
GENEVA, HAMBURG, ESBJERG, AND HOME

Towards the end of 2012, one of my colleagues from the past invited me for a coffee in Glasgow. He had recently moved for a new job in London. We popped into Costa Coffee near Glasgow Central. He asked if I was thinking of leaving PMSS, but I said no—I had just secured a £1 million-plus order for the Glasgow office and felt I might be in line for a promotion. As a principal consultant, a regional director's role seemed within reach.

However, my colleague, who was also a good friend, advised me that PMSS was about to be taken over and that the Glasgow office could close. This was unwelcome news, as I enjoyed working there despite the demanding pace and project pressures.

Unexpectedly, I received a call from Dan Hill, Vice President of SGS in Hamburg, responsible for the SGS Renewables Global Team. He offered me the role of HSE Manager for the HSE Global Team, responsible for business development. The offer was £80K plus a 20% bonus and a new Mercedes. It was a no-brainer for me, but I was also aware that Jamie was about to lose his job.

Renewables Consultant speaker at Offshore Conference for SGS

Stewart Herbert, Dan's HR Manager, finalized the details in the SGS offices in Camberwell, London. He also mentioned that SGS was looking for an HSE Manager to oversee wind turbine inspectors in the UK. I sent him a redacted version of Jamie's CV so that if Jamie secured an interview, it would be on his own merit. Within a few days, they offered him the job. In October 2012, both Jamie and I left PMSS and joined SGS.

By early 2013, PMSS had been taken over by TÜV, forming PMSS TÜV SÜD. Later that year, they closed the Glasgow office.

Jamie settled in well with the wind turbine teams, and his new car and salary were well above standard. We considered ourselves incredibly fortunate and got on with our work at SGS. I frequently travelled to Hamburg to meet Dan and other team members, the most memorable being Dr Tom Louis. A Swiss national fluent in several languages, Tom and I collaborated on various initiatives to develop the business, including exhibitions in Germany and the UK. I was also tasked with identifying consultancy firms suitable for acquisition. Dan asked me to lead a tender for Wikinger Windfarm and another for windfarms in Morocco. Tom and I worked on these bids, which were overly complex, requiring international conference calls across multiple time zones—not easy when our American colleagues were still in bed.

I had secured this role based on my success in building the PMSS business— I was seen as a "rainmaker." However, SGS lacked a strong UK consultancy team, and I had to rely on German project engineers, whose performance at that time was inconsistent. Their cost structure was uncompetitive, and they had little awareness of Iberdrola's and ScottishPower's requirements. Despite our efforts, we failed to win the bid.

I then focused on ACWA, which was set to be Africa's largest wind farm, based in Akhfenir, Morocco. SGS made it to the final two bidders for this multi-million-dollar contract.

Meanwhile, Tom was experiencing difficulties with Dan, and I was privy to several tense conversations between them. By the summer of 2013, the situation had worsened, and in July, Tom was given notice. He subsequently took legal action against SGS.

During my frequent trips to Geneva, I had met Dan's superiors. I had proposed acquiring a marine consultancy firm, Marex, based in Aberdeen, and presented the business case to SGS leadership. I was also aware that since taking on his role as VP, Dan had a l l e g e d l y incurred £2 million in losses.

I was asked me to justify the Marex acquisition. I explained that it would strengthen SGS's offshore consultancy capability, enabling us to lead competitive bids. As Marex was already profitable, its earnings could offset existing losses while positioning SGS for lucrative renewable energy contracts. The response was telling: "If I wanted to make more profits, I'd should open a chain of coffee shops." At that moment, I knew my time at SGS was coming to an end. The board had already decided to close Dan's global renewables team.

In September, Dan asked me to attend a business strategy meeting at an SGS office in Clydebank, near Glasgow. During that meeting, I was handed my notice. Ultimately, I received a cheque for about £20K and was allowed to keep my Mercedes for three months.

Initially, I felt bitter about how things had ended, especially as Jamie was also about to lose his job. I believe Dan had recognized that his time was running out and had hoped that having Tom and me as "rainmakers" would turn things around. However, he had not accounted for the weaknesses in the German consultancy team.

Yet, as I would soon discover, life had other plans for me.

I started applying for jobs every day, and it was soul-destroying as the pile of rejection letters grew on my home office desk. I now had a new problem— Elaine was beginning to be crippled by osteoarthritis and needed two new hip joints. I used some of the redundancy money to start a consultancy company, Excuria QHSE Ltd, and kept the rest as a working reserve to pay bills. I relied on some of my professional contacts at SGS, including Tom Louis and Dr Gregory Dudziak, to secure contracts for the ABC Group— Tom handled technical translations, while Gregory produced wind farm documents for French developers.

By March 2014, Elaine had undergone both operations and was once again able to dance. Although I was struggling with the stress of not finding another job, nursing Elaine was good for both of us as a couple. At 63 years old, with no money left, I was preparing to go back to being a jobbing builder. Desperation was setting in as the house was falling into disrepair.

I was then contacted by a recruitment company in Manchester called G2. The agent, Drew Roberts, was keen for me to attend Skype interviews, and I had an interview with two managers from a Swedish company Vattenfall.

Trying to get a job often means building some bias into your CV— it's effectively a hook, much like choosing the right fly for salmon fishing. After a year of trying every hook without success, I was out of options when I got my last interview. On Friday, 28th March, I was interviewed by Kim Rasmussen and Enrico Jacobi, the senior HSE managers for Vattenfall. They were looking for an offshore HSE specialist for a project in Denmark— DanTysk Offshore Wind Farm, located in the German sector of the North Sea. Since I had already gone through three interviews, I knew it was down to me and one other candidate. I had to secure this contract, or it would be gone.

Enrico asked if I had my offshore certificates in place—sea survival, helicopter escape, fire awareness, first aid, and manual handling. I had a BOSIET certificate, but it was out of date. So, I was economic with the truth.

Kim, the senior manager, then asked if I could start on Monday, 31st March, and come to the Vattenfall offices in Esbjerg, Denmark. I agreed. He told me that the G2 agent would be in touch to sort out the contract.

Getting ready to take the helicopter offshore to Dan Tysk
offshore windfarm Substation

I was elated but also anxious—I had no money, no accommodation, and had to organize travel.

In the early hours of Monday, 31st March, Jennifer watched her old Dad step out of her car with two hold-all bags and wave goodbye outside Queen Street Station in Glasgow. She couldn't stop crying as she drove away.

I took the first train of the day from Queen Street to Dyce. The train was full of men and women heading north to Aberdeen for offshore work on the oil rigs. Some of them fell asleep on the 2-hour, 30-minute journey. I looked at their faces—mostly young to middle-aged men, all looking tired. I took a sharp breath as I realised—I was now an old man.

At Dyce, I struggled with my baggage while crossing the station to catch the bus to the airport. A young oil worker helped me. Every instinct told me to get back on the train and go home. But I didn't.

At 12:30, I boarded a Flybe flight to Esbjerg. With the one-hour time difference, I arrived at 13:00 CET. I got through border control without issue and took a taxi to the Vattenfall offices. Dressed in a grey suit with a shirt and tie, I climbed four flights of stairs of the office with my two holdalls. At the top, I stood for five minutes, catching my breath and composing myself before entering the project office.

Inside, I was met by Find Poulsen, the Project Director. I was relieved—he was closer to my age than the others. I liked Find immediately; he was well- seasoned and spoke excellent English.

I was introduced to the rest of the DanTysk Offshore Wind Farm project team and placed in the capable hands of Jette Mortensen , the office manageress.

On my second day, Stefan Kahlen from Vattenfall's Hamburg office came to onboard me. He had set aside three days for the process, but instead, he handed me a USB stick and said, "Everything you need to know is on this." He then informed me that we wouldn't have time to go through it, as we had a diving drill in the Port of Esbjerg that afternoon.

Stefan left me to browse the USB stick before taking me to the quayside, where we inspected a vessel and observed a diving drill—rescuing a diver from the seabed using another diver. The operation went smoothly; within minutes, the rescue diver brought up the other man, who was then transferred onboard and into the hyperbaric chamber on deck.

Afterwards, the vessel master invited us to lunch, which was both welcome and friendly. Once we disembarked, Stefan told me he had to return to Hamburg the next day. He said to call him if needed and to write a report on the diving drill. He then dropped me off at the Vattenfall offices and disappeared. That was my induction into Vattenfall's HSE operations.

Back in the office, I had to use my own laptop and mobile phone, as my company devices would take time to arrive.

At the end of the first day, I had to figure out where I would live and how to get there. Over the weekend, I had tried unsuccessfully to book a hotel or B&B, but I had managed to secure a room on a farm seven miles north of Esbjerg. The only way to get there was by taxi.

Jette called a taxi company, and after work, I was taken to the Guldager Urups B&B farm, next to the Tulip Bacon factory on the town's outskirts.

The taxi cost me 30 euros. I quickly realised I didn't have enough money to do this every day—I needed a plan.

I was met by the landlady, Birgitte, a pleasant middle-aged woman who took a credit card payment for the room in advance. She showed me to my room— small and sparse, like a prison cell, but clean. She gave me a tour of the house and mentioned they didn't serve evening meals, but I could order a pizza delivery. Which I did.

I checked out the local shops and found a supermarket about two miles away that stayed open late.

After having my pizza, I went to the communal kitchen to make some tea and met a few other people using the farm. One man, a painter working on boats in the harbour at Esbjerg, advised me to store food in the fridge and cook in the kitchen—it was far cheaper than eating pizza.

I phoned Elaine to let her know I was safe and sent her some pictures of my new home. Then, I set off for the supermarket, where I bought enough food for the week and stored it in the kitchen fridge.

That night, I had a good sleep. In the morning, I washed and shaved while staring at the farm's rusty equipment. I made up my mind that this was going to be very temporary. However, I calculated that by the following Friday, I would be out of money and have no flexibility left on my credit card. The next day, I called my agent, Drew Roberts at G2, and told him I needed to be paid by Friday. Drew assured me I would receive payment as long as I had submitted my timesheets and invoices.

I completed my diving report and began attending the construction meetings for the DanTysk offshore wind farm project. The construction manager, Rasmus Wandrop, chaired these meetings daily, giving me a chance to better understand the project. It was clear the project was behind schedule. All 80 monopiles had been piled into the seabed, and the transition pieces (TPs) were fitted, but due to the delay, mould had started forming inside the TPs, affecting the equipment. Some of the TPs had also been colonized by gulls, and the guano posed a health risk to the technicians. I immersed myself in making operations to clean the mould and remove the guano as safe as possible for the operatives.

On Friday at lunchtime, I walked into Esbjerg town and checked my balance at the nearest cash machine. To my relief, my account had gone from a £2,000 overdraft to a £3,000 balance. I couldn't stop smiling—"Yes, yes, fucking yes!" I could finally make some moves.

The next morning, I went to the Europcar depot near Esbjerg station and hired a Ford Fiesta on a micro lease. Life is so much easier with a car. I then started looking at rental accommodation and found a few suitable options. I was about to settle on one and told Birgitte when she mentioned that a friend of hers had a rental in Store Darum a small village about 15 km south of Esbjerg. It was incredibly kind of her, as she would lose my rental, but like many Danish people, she was honest and willing to help.

I contacted Jytte Friss, the wife of the local doctor, Hans Christian Friss, and arranged a visit over the weekend. The property was perfect—a self- contained unit that had once been a barn. It had a bedroom, kitchen, shower room, and a section of the garden with a table, chairs, and a lounger for al fresco dining. I shook hands on the deal and paid the first month's rent in advance. That second weekend, I left the farm and moved into my new home.

Now, I had a car, a nice place to live, and money in the bank—though I was still 2,000 miles from home.

Writing my story in Store Darum near Esbjerg in Denmark

In my third week, Find informed me that there had been too many blade- lifting incidents offshore and that he needed me to investigate. The problem was that my certificates were out of date. It was awkward, as I hadn't been entirely truthful during my interview. Find was incredibly supportive and told me to contact Tomas Henning, who oversaw offshore training. A training programme was put into action immediately.

I was booked into two training facilities: Falck and Maersk. I completed Working at Height, First Aid, Manual Handling, and Firefighting training with Falck, while I did Sea Survival and Helicopter Escape training with Maersk. I had already done the latter with Petrofac in Aberdeen, but Working at Height was new. On the two-day course, I had to jump out of a nacelle with only a descender between me and instant death. After two weeks, all my training was in place.

Working at Height Training Esbjerg Denmark

Find paired me up with Christof Huss, the turbine package manager. So, on a cold April morning, I presented myself at 05:00 for offshore duties on the Crew Transfer Vessel Celtic Wind, fully kitted out. I had been offshore before and was prepared for the trip, but the journey to the wind farm in the North Sea took 3.5 hours.

At first, I felt a bit queasy, but after an hour, I settled down. Fifteen minutes before our arrival at DT06 offshore wind turbine, we received the warning to prepare for the boat transfer. I had never done a real boat transfer before. The sea state was about one meter, meaning the CTV was rising and falling by about the same— roughly five ladder rungs on the landing. The deckhand waited until the boat was at the top of the rungs before instructing us to jump, ensuring the next wave wouldn't send the boat crashing into us.

I had on all my kit: immersion suit, climbing harnesses, life jacket, double hooks, gloves, glasses, and hard hat.

Christof went first, followed by the Siemens investigator, Andrej Risteski. Our mission was to board the installation vessel Pacific Osprey and carry out a series of investigations to determine the root cause of the incidents. The only way to board was to climb up the monopile boat landing and transfer via a gangway attached to the turbine installation platform.

Christof went first and, in true Teutonic fashion, ignored his colleagues behind him. By the time I reached the gangway, I was exhausted.

Eventually, I made it to the Osprey's changing rooms, where I ditched my climbing kit and survival suit. I was then invited onto the bridge , where I handed over my passport to the first officer. He assigned me a cabin, and we completed the vessel induction.

That Friday evening, the vessel carried out a muster drill. I was on the wrong side of the ship when the alarm sounded. Although I was fairly certain it was just a drill, seeing the lifeboats deploying and fire hoses being readied was a stark reminder that this was real. Suddenly, all that training seemed invaluable—I knew exactly what to do.

The officers guided us to the life jackets and then into the lifeboats. I braced myself, ready to be lowered into the sea—my very own Titanic moment. Just as I prepared for the plunge, we were informed that the drill had been successful and were instructed to return to the ship.

Working on these large construction vessels operates on a 24-hour basis with two shifts. The evening shift was about to begin, but we had suspended all lifting operations until the root cause of recent lifting incidents had been established.

We conducted interviews with the night shift lifting supervisors, riggers, and crane drivers, as well as the vessel's officers and master. Vattenfall had placed a €1 million penalty on the table for any company found culpable.

As we spoke with various individuals, it became clear that the vessel owners, Swire Blue Ocean, were blaming Siemens, the turbine suppliers, for the errors. Given that there had already been nine incidents, I had little difficulty identifying the sub-root cause: a failure in the Safety Management System. The final root cause was even more apparent—a failure in the overall Management System.

With these findings presented, we agreed that they would update their procedures with a focus on human error and communication during lifts. Additionally, the next blade lift would be designated as a test lift, conducted under full supervision. The test lifts were successful, and production was allowed to resume.

After three days, I transferred via CTV to a flotel nearby in the North Sea near the sea battle site of the battle of Jutland and then took another CTV home.

The following day, I presented my report to Find Poulsen, advising him that he would need to be prepared to defend it at higher levels. From experience, I knew that when you criticize management—especially from large corporations—and when €1 million is at stake, the claws come out quickly. Find read the report and instructed me to issue it.

I also got full support from the Vattenfall European HSE Manager Chris Bartliff who would in the fulness of time become my boss for the next decade. Chris was the same age as my son Jamie and smart with intelligence and capability of an older man.

The fallout was swift. The shit hit the fan. Both SBO and Siemens launched heavy criticisms of my report. In response, we invited them to our head office in Esbjerg, where each party gave presentations on communication and lifting controls, while I presented on human error. The meeting started out tense, but Find's skillful chairmanship and Chris's management skills eventually steered it towards a productive outcome. By the end, all parties understood the required remedial actions.

There were no further blade incidents, offshore production proceeded smoothly, and the project finished a month ahead of schedule—saving approximately €2 million. I had earned my laurels with Vattenfall.

In April of 2015 Jennifer and Gus got Married in the University of Glasgow Chapel and a family reception at the Oran Mor at thew top of Byres Rd.

Jennifer's Wedding Day

I was commissioned to report to Ormonde Offshore Windfarm based in Barrow in Furness in the lake District in England.

In September, I was reassigned to the Operations team in Aberdeen, also supporting the team at Ormonde—my old stamping ground. Kevin Jones had been promoted to Head of Operations for both Aberdeen and Horns Rev 3 (both North Sea projects). He was set to step down as Operations Manager at Ormonde, to be replaced—his second-in- command for the past year—taking his place.

My role required frequent travel between Aberdeen and Barrow-in-Furness, Cumbria, providing HSE support until August 2019, when Louise Smith, the HSSE Specialist for Aberdeen and Ormonde, was due to return from maternity leave. I was permitted to keep my rental home in Dyce, but every other week, I stayed at the Swan Hotel at Newby Bridge on Lake Windermere. On many of these trips, I took Elaine with me, and we enjoyed the excellent facilities at the Swan, and on one occasion, the Whitewater Hotel at Backbarrow.

It quickly became clear that my working relationship with the new Manager would be difficult. His management style was chaotic and rigid—his way or no way. He was not particularly health and safety conscious and often tried to dodge responsibility, leading to frequent clashes between us.

Matters came to a head when he asked to speak to me privately in the main stores, away from the workforce. He seemed unusually strained. Having recently run a programme on mental health first aid, I asked if he needed support. He insisted he was fine, but I had my doubts. His personal life was complicated, and he had a history of struggling to work with colleagues. Worse still, he constantly shifted blame for problems of his own making.

Meanwhile, my workload was becoming increasingly demanding. The Aberdeen site still required construction work, while the Operations team had to meet day one readiness. A new temporary Operations Manager, ex- Ormonde's Mike Herdman, had been brought in to help. I had a strong team of HSE Advisers reporting to me including Jamie who had responsibilities for both onshore and offshore construction.

Aberdeen Offshore Windfarm also known as the Offshore Wind Deployment Centre was constructed without any loss of life and opened by the First Minister of Scotland Nicola Sturgeon on the 7th September 2018 despite strong opposition from Donald Trump as in his opinion spoiled the view from his Golf course.

*Donald Trump was not happy about Aberdeen Offshore
Windfarm spoiling the view from his golf course*

In November, we planned a gearbox exchange offshore at
Ormonde, with Vattenfall's project support team overseeing the
MCR (Major Component Exchange).A Danish project manager,
Casper Sønderby, had been appointed to lead the GBX (Gearbox
Exchange) project. Tensions arose immediately over
responsibilities, and the O/M Manager withdrew, leaving Casper
to take full charge. To Casper's credit, he did a solid job despite
Paul's reluctance to engage.

We prepared for offshore operations. I reviewed all documents
and plans, then travelled to Belfast to meet the offshore GBX team
before boarding the installation vessel Bold Tern, a construction
jack-up. There, I met with the vessel's project team and our
technicians, led by my Scottish colleague, John Sharp, based at
Ormonde.

I was assigned as the HSE representative, while Casper was due
to join the vessel later, on Friday 30th November, as the Client
Representative. However, at the last minute, he informed us of a
personal situation preventing his attendance. The vessel sailed,
leaving me to cover both roles—HSE and Client Representative.

When we arrived at the Ormonde offshore site in the early hours of 1st December, I was allocated the client cabin onboard the Bold Tern and was well looked after.

During an MCR, the most crucial factor is ensuring the weather conditions are suitable for the lift. As we prepared to remove the old gearbox from the O3 offshore wind turbine location, the weather window closed. The Bold Tern project team was not pleased—each day at sea cost them £50,000, and since they were on a fixed-price contract, they attempted to blame the delays on Vattenfall. I firmly rejected this.

Over the next few days, we successfully removed the old gearbox and installed the new one. On 4th December at 06:30, I was transferred by CTV back to Barrow-in-Furness, where I immediately set off home to attend a family funeral for my cousin, Robert Armstrong, who had passed away a few days earlier.

When I returned to Ormonde, the GBX campaign was deemed a success, thanks to Jim Green and the Ormonde technicians. Paul was delighted and posted a plaudit on Vattenfall's internal platform, Connect-Us. However, this led to complications. My new boss at the time was aware that all major offshore lifts had to be reported to the HSE Inspectorate UK. Had I known, I would have done so, but this requirement was never communicated to me—something he later admitted. As a result, Vattenfall had to notify the HSE retrospectively, causing some embarrassment, particularly for others, who had been aware of the requirement.

Jim and Jamie on the opening day of Aberdeen Offshore Windfarm

The HSE response was to request all documentation to verify that a safe system of work had been in place. The HSE Inspector, whom I had spent time with earlier that year during construction —was not convinced. He instructed Vattenfall to update all documentation to his specifications, which we did. He also requested a meeting to discuss future MCRs. Not long after this meeting, in early 2019, we learned that Casper had been let go.

In the end, the issue was smoothed over, and the HSE UK allowed Vattenfall to continue with future MCRs.

Over the following months, I travelled between Aberdeen and Barrow as the workload increased. I raised this with Kevin Jomes, now the Manager for Aberdeen and Horns Rev 3 wind farms. He arranged for me to report full-time to Aberdeen, while Jamie took over at Ormonde. As freelancers, Jamie and I were a costly resource for operational wind farms, and it was only a matter of time before local hires were appointed.

My last day at Ormonde was 6th March 2019, and I was glad to leave.

I continued working in Aberdeen, planning for a blade exchange. On 25th March, I transferred offshore to the jack-up vessel Seajacks Scylla, where we swapped out a damaged blade. In the early hours of 26th March, I returned to shore.

However, behind the scenes, dark clouds were gathering for both Jamie and me. Freelancers are well paid—Jamie and I earned around £3,000 per week, which bred resentment among permanent HSE specialists. Vattenfall was comfortable with project freelancers but not in operations. At least one internal HSE specialist had an active campaign to push us out. He had more than one reason to target me: he had applied for the HSE lead role for onshore, and I was the only other person in the company with experience across all UK onshore wind farms. Freelancers can sometimes be persuaded to take permanent roles, and he clearly saw me as a threat.

Several factors worked against me. Ormonde had the trust of HSE Inspector and relied on Ormond for HSE advice. The reality was that I knew the HSE inspector better than anyone, but others wanted to keep me out of any discussions—likely because it would expose management failure to inform me about reporting MCRs. Ormonde wasted no time in advising Vattenfall HSE to retrospectively report the Ormonde MCR, effectively making me the scapegoat for the lack of reporting.

Steve Lewis then requested all documents for the contract lift and found that the Lifting Plan did not constitute a safe system of work, prompting a review. This gave Ormonde and Vattenfall Management the perfect opportunity to shift the blame onto me. Casper, who had organised the contract lift, was let go, and I was tasked with producing new plans that met the required safety standards.

At this point, Vattenfall appointed a new HSE Manager for Offshore who had previously worked for a German utility company and had a consultancy background within Germany. It didn't take me a too long to realise that he was a change agent—and that my time at Vattenfall was likely coming to an end.

At an HSE team meeting in Amsterdam in May, the new manager remained silent, simply observing. On the last day, after three days of meetings, I asked if he planned to visit Aberdeen, and he dismissively replied that it was unlikely. That was the moment I knew my time with Vattenfall was over.

Within a month, I had to align with a new HSE Manager, meaning he needed to be fully briefed on Aberdeen operations.

I had taken Aberdeen Offshore Windfarm from design through to construction and into Operations successfully and so I wanted to mark the event in some way. I decided that I would commission John Byrne to do a painting for me depicting life during his time and mine in Ferguslie.(See the front cover of this book) John was very gracious and accepted the commission. On the 28th of April 2018 I met up with John to collect the painting in his Edinburgh Gallery. I took him a bottle of malt whisky and 200 cigarettes which he was delighted to accept. Elaine was with me, and he engaged in a long conversation about life and Ferguslie which lasted for about two hours. We were so sad when John passed away in 2024.

Jim Green with John Byrne two Fegs together

CHAPTER 53:
LIFE AND DEATH

Elaine and I booked the first week of June for a holiday in Sorrento, Italy. However, three weeks before our departure, I visited my dentist in Aberdeen, Jonathan Aspey from the Hilton Dental Practice, for some routine repairs. During the appointment, he noticed an abnormality and referred me to a colleague at Aberdeen Royal Infirmary for further examination.

Two weeks later, I received an appointment with the Maxillofacial Oral Cancer Unit in Aberdeen. The moment I saw the letter, fear set in, but I wasted no time in attending—though first, I had to go on holiday. I didn't want to upset Elaine or spoil the trip, so I kept it to myself. I spent three days sleeping by the pool in Sorrento, my mind weighed down by thoughts of my own mortality. We visited Capri for a day and had a lovely time, but I couldn't shake the anxiety.

When we returned home, I attended my appointment with the professor, who reassured me that I didn't have cancer. Instead, I was diagnosed with an incurable condition called Lichen Planus. He handed me a leaflet explaining that I needed to be diligent with oral hygiene, avoid smoking and drinking, and steer clear of spicy foods. While Lichen Planus can, in rare cases, lead to cancer, the likelihood is exceptionally low. That was good enough for me. At last, I could explain to Elaine why I hadn't been myself on holiday. I felt immense relief, knowing I had avoided the horrors of facial cancer.

However, my relief was short-lived. Back home in Caldwell, I attended a routine medical check at my local medical centre with a new nurse. During the examination, she detected an irregularity in my heartbeat and referred me to a cardiologist at the Royal Alexandra Hospital in Paisley. The appointment was set for the 3rd of July, and I took Elaine with me, just in case it was bad news.

The cardiologist explained that the test would go one of two ways: either my heart trace would be normal, and I'd be discharged, or if it was abnormal, I'd be admitted to the Cardio Ward or referred for immediate anticoagulant treatment. He wired me up to the machine, attached multiple sensors to my body, and then delivered the news—I had a sound heart with no problems. I asked him to repeat this to Elaine, which he did. As we left, standing by the lift, I broke down in sheer relief.

On the 27th of May 2022, I suffered a near-fatal heart attack and underwent triple bypass surgery, which they say, successful.

I added this note on the 31st of July 2023. ☺

At that time, I recalibrated my outlook on life and came to terms with my mortality. I chose to live by two mottos:

"Sans Peur" (Without Fear) – my father's regimental motto.

"I Remain Unvanquished" – the motto of my mother's clan, the Armstrongs.

At this point in the book, I wanted to make a clear break for Book 2 as not only had my life changed but the whole world had changed because of COVID 19.

Another Feg Book 2 (Lock-Down) (Fishing for Spanners)

CHAPTER 1:
LOCKDOWN STARTS

I left Aberdeen on 27th February 2020, and the following week, Nicola Sturgeon, the First Minister of Scotland, announced a total lockdown due to COVID-19.

A few years earlier, during the H1N1 bird flu pandemic, my employer, Mott MacDonald Group, had appointed me as the health coordinator for contingency plans to mitigate infection in the offices. I was well aware of the need for social distancing, hygiene, masks, and other sensible precautions. I posted my concerns for family and friends on Facebook, along with a picture of myself in full PPE—including a mask, protective suit, goggles, and gloves.

Most of my friends and family welcomed the post, but some reacted badly, accusing me of scaremongering. They were among the first wave of deniers who refused to be persuaded—until the death toll began to rise worldwide. Within a few weeks, three members of our family had contracted the virus.

At the time of writing, worldwide deaths exceeded three million. The world hopes the vaccines will prevail, although thousands of sceptics and deniers continue to do immeasurable harm.

I hadn't been feeling well, so on 11th March, I had an appointment with the doctor. I was met by Nurse Heather Mitchell, who took the usual blood and urine tests, as well as measuring my height, weight, and blood pressure.

A week later, I returned for my results. The nurse told me I was Type 2 diabetic and obese at 20 stone 4 lbs.—no wonder I hadn't been feeling well. All my key health indicators were alarming: high cholesterol, high blood pressure, and high blood sugar. In the old-fashioned way, she gave me a good earbashing and frightened the life out of me. She put me on statins, blood pressure tablets, and Metformin for diabetes. Furthermore, I was officially registered as diabetic and advised to follow an 800-calorie-per-day diet and exercise for at least 30 minutes a day.

If I wanted to live, I had to completely change my lifestyle. I discussed the situation with Elaine, and she immediately committed to helping me.

One of the effects of diabetes and being overweight was a severe lack of energy—I would often fall asleep, making driving extremely dangerous. I also experienced intense pain when moving.

The first time Elaine and I set out to walk up the hill outside our house, I had to stop five times in 200 yards, nearly collapsing. Over the next few days, I still felt pain but needed fewer stops. After a month, I had lost a stone and could reach the top without stopping.

During these walks, I also wore a mask. Using country roads, we gradually increased our distance to 10K and started walking faster. Jenni helped me with resistance band exercises, and I tracked my progress on an app. I could see my weight coming off and was feeling much better and fitter.

I also started several garden projects, including renewing the courtyard fence and clearing the back garden for a kitchen garden. I hired my grandsons Gabriel and Robin to help at the weekends— Gabriel on Saturdays and Robin on Sundays— paying them a bit more than normal pocket money.

By July, I was able to fit into some of my old clothes and donated 10 bags of clothing to the Salvation Army. We were able to go out for meals at the Uplawmoor Hotel with friends. However, as the death toll rose, we avoided restaurants and relied on home-cooked meals or takeaways.

In April, I refocused the business so I could work from home. We registered our existing company with a name change, Excuria Ltd, as CDM Plus Ltd. Fortunately, we had a reasonable income from pensions, so I didn't need to work.

I focused on improving the house and garden. I cleared a lot of debris, built a new log store, and hired a JCB with a driver to level the back garden after Gabriel, Robin, and I removed the trees and shrubs. The trees provided plenty of logs for the new store, and when we lost another old pine tree, Jamie and Robin harvested even more.

I also hired George the joiner, to fit a new attic access and flooring for storage. Gabriel helped catalogue the contents of the storage containers.

By early September, with my newfound health and a five-stone weight loss, I decided to update all my GWO certifications and medicals. I was surprised by how much I enjoyed the training at Clyde Training Centre in Clydebank— it was great to be out of the house again. The doctor also gave me the turbine climb exertion test, which I passed. He strongly advised me to avoid catching COVID-19.

In September, our new neighbours arrived. They were a young family. It was great to have the house occupied again, as the previous owner, Tony, our old neighbour, had not spent much time there in recent years. I met up with him in the courtyard a few days before handover to say our goodbyes. Tony had been a great neighbour, once loaning me £5,000 to pay off the bank. I repaid him shortly afterwards, but in gratitude, I did some work on his part of the house for free.

No sooner had I recertified when, in early October, I received a call from Andy Gillan, the site manager for South Kyle Windfarm, about 40 miles south of Caldwell. He asked if I could help them prepare for a Vattenfall HSE Audit in November. I agreed to a rate of £450 per day for one month.

I had to be onsite at 07:00, so I left home at 05:30. I was based in the site office and reported to the existing HSE Manager, Mrs Lee Steward, who was very busy with work. The office was chaotic and a COVID-19 hotspot, so I immediately started making changes. I handled worker inductions, created new presentations on winterization, modern slavery, and site risks, and constantly reminded workers to wear masks.

One presentation to around 20 workers highlighted a major concern—when I asked how many had downloaded the NHS Track and Trace app, not a single hand went up.

There were two serious incidents during my time on site. The first involved a logging wagon colliding with a MOXI dumper, damaging the log support pillar. The driver attempted to leave the site, but Lee stopped him. I investigated the incident and explained that if he had left, we would have had to report him to the police for driving a dangerous vehicle—potentially costing him his license. He quickly calmed down.

The second incident occurred in my final week when a Stobart lorry carrying timber chippings went off the road into a ditch on the Strathwiggan Forest tracks. We arranged overnight accommodation for the driver and a recovery unit. I supervised the recovery operation, ensuring safety. It took five hours, and I was relieved to finally get home and warm up.

In my last week, I prepared the Principal Contractor for the Vattenfall Audit. During a test audit, I scored them 4.3 out of 5. I later heard they achieved 4.3.

One of the site's Client Owner's Engineers, Alan McDonald, had been the Site Manager at Aberdeen Substation—it was great to catch up. I also got on well with the Vattenfall HSE Rep, Neil Buswell. He later recommended me to Ionic Consultants, who needed a temporary Resident Engineer for the Windy Rig wind farm, owned by Statkraft. I got the appointment and started in early November.

The site, high in the Scottish Borders, offered spectacular views of Cumbria.

At Windy Rig, I witnessed concrete pours for turbine foundations and submitted daily reports. The site conditions were rough, worsened by heavy rain and snow, but we completed the work.

After this, I settled in for the winter, preparing for Christmas with Elaine. COVID-19 made it especially hard, as we couldn't have family over, but we made the best of it—decorating the house, putting up outdoor lights, and even projecting a laser show onto the stable walls.

Then, during the Christmas-New Year recess, I received a call from an old colleague, Mark Pollard who had been one of the engineers on the MAN diesel modular power station project in Colchester.

Mark had been appointed as senior engineering manager with a company called AGR who needed a Principal Designer for an energy centre they were building near Cambridge.

After agreeing a good rate, I got started on the project.

CHAPTER 2:
COVID AND OMICRON

Around early 2021, it became clear that COVID-19 was not going away, even though vaccines were on the horizon. I had most arrangements in place so that, if I were infected and did not survive, I could leave a final message for my family. I wrote down some rough notes and began recording my death video on my laptop. I never expected it to be so difficult—because as I started speaking, I realised these would be my final words. It took me an hour to say what I wanted, and in the process, I was fundamentally changed.

Here are the decisions I made:

Family will always come first—Elaine, the children, and the grandchildren.

Eliminate negativity and practice love, kindness, respect, understanding, and tolerance.

I decided to continue working for as long as I could "die with my boots on." Working in the renewables sector and specializing in health and safety was more than just a job; it was a noble calling. I loved my work.

I had considered my mortality before—when dealing with cancer scares, coronary issues, and now diabetes. I knew that if I caught COVID-19, I would be extremely ill and, in all likelihood, would not survive. I recalled the doctor who conducted my GWO Offshore medical was blunt: "Mr Green, you do not want to get this virus." At 70, I had no illusions about living a long and healthy life.

Coming to terms with my mortality, I felt at peace. I took comfort in knowing I had lived a good life and done my best for my family. Billy Connolly once quoted an old Indian saying: "Death is the way of all things." I accepted that and put my house in order.

In mid-February, both Elaine and I received the Pfizer vaccine, which gave us some hope of surviving an infection. AGR required me to work from home, but in mid-March, I was asked to carry out my first site tour to complete an audit and ensure due diligence was in place regarding the project and contractors.

Work was steady and well within my capabilities. I arranged for BT to install fiber broadband, and with Gabriel's help, we remodeled the home office.

At weekends, we worked in the garden, constructing raised beds for our kitchen garden. Indoors, we sorted out archive materials, storing them in the attic, and over the weeks since Christmas, we burned old papers and other combustible materials. January and February were bitterly cold, and in March, the boiler broke down, taking a week to fix. We relied on our standby electric heaters in the meantime.

We also had a few tentative outdoor meetings with our new neighbours, Peter and Jayne. I helped them with some water supply and burst pipe issues. Jayne, a doctor, was incredibly busy with COVID-19 patients at her Hospital.

Normally, Gabriel would visit on Saturdays and Robin on Sundays, and I paid them £40 per shift. However, Robin had to focus on his studies, hoping to secure a place at university or college. This meant Gabriel benefited from double wages, but both boys worked incredibly hard—sometimes until they had to sit down from exhaustion. I saw them developing into young men, and it was wonderful to hear them becoming more articulate over time. I also provided them with workwear and basic tools.

I sourced all the materials for the raised beds and concrete work, and the first raised bed was given to Leo for his ninth birthday.

By April, I had completed all the concrete foundations for the garden, including the summerhouse, composting area, and a base for Elaine's pergola—purchased by the children and built by Jamie and Robin. At the end of April, Elaine saw an opportunity to use the large composting area as a "sitootery" for the back garden, so I devised a new composting system using two spare raised beds.

In May, we received news that our gardener, Ian, was too ill to return to work, so the boys and I took over. All the raised beds were set in the ground and pegged, and we began working on the pathways, using a plastic grid system on Terramesh and finishing with small chippings. We also needed large amounts of quality soil, and by July, we had moved around 12 tonnes of soil, sand, chippings, and cement, plus two pallets of bricks for the summerhouse construction.

We planted vegetables and flowers experimentally to plan better for the following year. By June, the kitchen garden was well established, and Gabriel was confident using the ride-on mower.

Recognizing how quickly the boys were growing up, I decided to equip them with better tools and provide them with training. This proved invaluable— Robin helped build the framework and decking for the new sitootery, which Elaine furnished with new garden furniture. We also moved her arbor onto the decking.

In July, Gabriel and I started the brickwork for the summerhouse. Once completed, we constructed the frame and roof trusses, framing out the roof together. By August, we strengthened the structure in preparation for installing the glass and polycarbonate sheeting.

Meanwhile, we had some regular visitors—an incredibly tame pheasant and his mate, who came in for crumbs every morning. They became so comfortable that they even wandered upstairs inside the house!

The summer was particularly successful for our actress daughter Jennifer, who landed a role in a TV production called Murder Island and a film called Tetris. Later in the year, she was cast in a film about refugees. In Murder Island, she played the lead role, and in the final episode, it was revealed she was the murderer— exceptional acting.

My project with AGR Group required monthly trips to Cambridge, where I consolidated my position Principal Designer. I usually drove down, stayed two days on-site, and returned on the fourth day. Sometimes, Elaine joined me, and we stayed in an apartment or at the Varsity Hotel, celebrating our wedding anniversary at their rooftop restaurant. On other occasions, we stayed at the Hilton on Downing Street in Cambridge, booking a junior suite. Eventually the contract was completed successfully, and I looked to new Horizons.

In June, I continued my contract with AGR. Soon after I got a call from my old boss Chris Bartliff who was now a senior manager with Light Source BP and major developer of solar and battery energy storage systems on a global scale.

Chris advised that there had been a serious incident on one of their construction sites where an electrical engineer suffered significant injuries to his head, knee, and hand when 7,000 volts passed through him.

Chris asked me to investigate and provide a root cause analysis of the incident.

I travelled to King's Lynn, arriving at the Thornham Solar Farm near the Sandringham Estate in Norfolk. The site team was clearly traumatized by the accident. The substation where it occurred had been sealed, and a Health and Safety Executive inspector had already been on-site. I was granted full access to reports and interviewed key managers and workers.

Chris tasked me with conducting a root cause analysis and compiling a full report. While working on it from home, I was instructed to lead a *collaborative report* with all the duty holders involved, working with the Principal Contractor, Groupotec, and Greenfrog Connect. After a month, the report was published in mid-August, having been reviewed by BP's legal department.

Now working for two clients I required to be meticulous with my organization.

Both the Principal Contractor and Contractor initially concluded the root cause of the incident was human error. However, I debunked this, clarifying that while human error was a causal factor, the true root cause was a failure of managerial control. This was reflected in the final collaborative report.

By August, I had completed several key documents for LSBP, and Chris advised that their activity would ramp up significantly in 2022.

At home, we celebrated several birthdays, including Emma Robin's 18th and Lily's 7th. Robin and Gabriel spent their weekends working hard to build the summer house (Pavilion) in the garden.

In early August, I had my routine medical review for diabetes. I was advised to stop taking Metformin, and if my next blood sugar reading remained stable, my records would be updated to "Diabetes Resolved." This was great news. However, the nurse noted that my cholesterol had risen slightly and recommended going back on statins. This was problematic for me, as statins made me feel "fuzzy." I resolved to manage it through diet instead. Additionally, I was referred—once again—to the cardiologist due to an unusual heart rhythm. It was my third referral, and although I protested, I accepted that it was better to be safe than sorry. The cardiologist carried out all the necessary tests on 24th August and gave me the all-clear.

I was delighted to receive confirmation from my client at Black & Veatch that my proposal had been accepted for QHSE support on a research project involving a wave hub device. It would be deployed at the BiMep test centre in the Bay of Biscay near Bilbao, Basque Country. The contract, set to start in 2022, would run for two years and provide £36,000 on a part-time basis.

In the garden, Gabriel and Robin continued helping me with the Pavilion's construction. September also saw Robin's 18th birthday, and Jamie, Robin, and I had our first beer together in a small pub in Stewarton.

The grandchildren were growing up fast. Angelina and Bear both started secondary school. Angelina excelled in gymnastics, winning two golds, a bronze, and the highest overall points in her club competition. She aspires to become a stuntwoman. Gabriel secured a place at PACE acting group in Paisley and began studying at HoC with two tutors for Maths and English.

Lucy was also thriving—fully engaged as a pupil ambassador in her second year at Eastwood High. She joined several clubs, including Art, Drama, Boxing, Swimming, and Saxophone. Leo joined the local Neilston Football Club (WASPs) and was named Footballer of the Month. Lily was appointed to the Pupil Council at Uplawmoor Primary, and Melissa took up swimming.

James our youngest grandson started school and was developing impressive language skills. He even told me to stop calling him "darling," so we now address him formally as James Richard Mowbray!

In early September, Elaine and I took a short holiday with John and Cath on Arran, staying in a cottage near Corrie. We wanted to spend quality time with them, as John's Alzheimer's had worsened. He managed the journey well, including the ferry trip, though he needed a little support as his balance and speech were affected. Despite these challenges, he still enjoyed the holiday. It was a special time for Elaine and I and Cath, his primary carer. We ate out, explored the island, visited the Arran Distillery, and had a lovely picnic in Lamlash, opposite Holy Island.

On the ferry, as I held John's hand, I could sense his anxiety— particularly as we navigated the lift from the car deck to the restaurant. It was a stark reminder of how much the disease had progressed. Yet, despite the difficulties, it was a good trip for us all. Before leaving Arran, we collected some large stones from the beach near Lochranza.

In October, I continued working with LightSource BP, visiting Cambridge in the second week for an AGR site audit and to chair the Joint Contractors HSE Committee meeting. I also oversaw the delivery of safety training for 250 immigrant workers from Ukraine and Bulgaria, certifying a trainer and working with two interpreters. By the end of November, the programme had been successfully completed.

I had agreed with AGR Group to complete my contract by the end of the year, so I prepared a handover plan. My final committee meeting was on 15th November. Elaine accompanied me on this trip, and in the evenings, we enjoyed diners at The Ivy in Cambridge.

Towards the end of November, we received worrying news about Elaine's brother, John. She visited him, and it was clear that his condition had deteriorated significantly.

On 1st December, I took Gabriel to Glasgow University, where I had agreed to donate £3,000 to UG Racing—a university-led renewables project focused on driverless, clean combustion and electric cars. We handed over the cheque to the team lead and toured the project facilities. After the visit, we decided to offer Gabriel an internship, allowing him to represent CDM Plus Ltd while also taking on a role as an IT and Development intern.

December also brought fantastic news for Angelina—after an assessment, she was granted "Elite Status" in gymnastics. Seeing the video of her performance made it clear she was exceptionally talented.

Early in the month, we attended a G4 festive concert in Ayr Town Hall, where masks were mandatory. We also went to the Dunlop Players' Christmas pantomime, where Bear had a lead role and Harris made his debut. At the final performance, Bear was awarded the "Best Actor" trophy.

Elaine and I were so please and proud with all our grandchildren and full credit to the mums and dads. Jamie& Maggie, Jennifer& Gus and Emma and Neil.

I made my final trip to Cambridge on 15th December, but Elaine stayed home as John's condition had worsened. With the Omicron variant spreading rapidly, it was safer for her to remain nearby. John had been admitted to the RAH hospital, slipping into a coma.

We visited John several times in Ward 3 as tests were carried out to determine the cause of his sudden decline. Elaine and I were grateful to be there for him and to support Cath. Sadly, on 3rd December, John passed away.

His funeral was held on 18th December at St Charles Chapel in Paisley. Despite COVID and the Omicron variant, the chapel was nearly full. He was laid to rest in Hawkhead Cemetery, near his grandfather John Keenan's grave. We marked his resting place with the Arran stones we had collected on our September holiday.

Christmas was difficult, as expected, but we still managed to gather the family for dinner and presents. On Hogmanay, Elaine and I had dinner with Jennifer and Gus her family and their neighbours, Mark, and Lorna Street, at the Dalmeny Park Hotel. We saw in the New Year at Mark and Lorna's house, relieved to leave 2021 behind and welcome 2022 with hope.

CHAPTER 3:
MINI-COOPER

The passing of my brother-in-law John on 3rd December 2021 shook the whole family to the core, especially Elaine. Watching him decline slowly and then catastrophically was deeply painful. Though we were relieved to see an end to his suffering, his passing left a huge hole in the family.

My awesome brother-in-law John

I first met John when I was only 15 and working for Elaine's mother, May, as a grocer's boy in Hay & Co shop on Causeyside Street, Paisley, where May was the manageress. One of my duties was delivering boxes of groceries to various addresses. Near Christmas 1960, May asked me to deliver a box to her home at 84 Glenburn Road, Paisley. I lifted the box onto my shoulders, carried it to the nearest bus stop, and took the bus to Glenburn.

May's house was on the first floor of a tenement building, one I knew well— my great-grandfather lived at No. 80, and my aunt May and uncle Robert Armstrong lived at No. 88. I knocked on the door, and May's father-in-law answered. A bright and polite retired gentleman in his seventies, he welcomed me kindly as I delivered the groceries. Over the following weeks, I made a few more deliveries, and at the beginning of 1967, May took on her only daughter, Elaine, as a part-time assistant, just like me.

Over the weeks, I grew fond of Elaine and looked forward to her coming into the shop after school and working all day on Saturdays. There was always a good atmosphere and although Saturdays were hard work, they were also great fun with all the staff.

In April 1967, I plucked up the courage to ask Elaine on a date, and she agreed to go to the pictures with me. We went to the Regal Cinema to see My Fair Lady. I didn't realise at the time that I had found my soulmate—I just knew I loved spending time with her.

On Saturday evenings, after returning from the pictures, we would stand kissing on the half-landing in the close until the last bus made its way down Glenburn Road. On its way up to the terminus, John would usually be on it,

having travelled home after a date with Elaine's school friend, Cath Gordon. We often met on the stair or at the bus stop.

John was great fun. As the eldest in my family, I had never had an older brother, and he filled that role for me. He worked as an apprentice cooper (barrel maker) at Clark Hunter's yard on Greenhill Road, Paisley. He was two years older than me and full of enthusiasm for life, earning him the nickname Mini Cooper— partly because he was only 5ft 4 inches. John always dressed well, rode a scooter, and played drums in a band, sometimes with my cousin, Robert Armstrong. It was the sixties—life was good.

Losing a loved one is never easy, and Elaine was devastated by her brother's passing. As 2021 came to an end, we all hoped for a better 2022. Unfortunately, over the New Year period, the whole family was struck down with either COVID or winter flu. Elaine and I took multiple lateral flow and PCR tests, all negative, but we were still laid low with a horrible flu that drained us for three weeks.

Then, on Monday, 17th January, we got a call from a very distraught Emma our youngest daughter—her house had caught fire in the early hours of the morning. At 5:00 am, a neighbour spotted flames rising from the side shed up to the roof. They raised the alarm, called the fire brigade, and got Emma, Neil, and the four kids to safety. While the women cared for the children, the men helped Neil fight the fire with garden hoses. When the fire brigade arrived, they managed to extinguish the flames, but the shed was completely destroyed, and a section of the roof was badly damaged. Thankfully, the inside of the house was mostly spared, aside from some minor smoke damage.

When Elaine and I visited, the house and the sight of the damage was horrifying. The whole family looked pale with stress and shock. We did what we could to help, bringing spare heaters as the boiler had been damaged, and treated them to a pizza dinner.

We couldn't stop thinking about how much worse it could have been. If the neighbour hadn't been awake at 5:00 am to raise the alarm, they might have lost the entire house—and worse, their lives.

It brought back memories of the fire that happened to my own family in Ferguslie in the 1960s.

In the middle of January, everyone in the family had COVID or some other winter flu. On the 23rd, I took Gabriel to Braehead to get a new laptop. Jenni came over to discuss his school report, which was actually very encouraging. I thought a new laptop and a Microsoft 365 package would help with his studies and also prepare him for working life.

February started off as an incredibly busy month for me, with my workload at LSbp increasing, along with heightened requirements from my other client, Black & Veatch (BV). It was Elaine's birthday on the 23rd, and we were delighted to be able to celebrate normally. However, the next day, on the 24th, the world changed as Russia invaded Ukraine. We watched in horror as news reports and video footage showed the devastation caused by the Russian war machine.

The only good news at this time was that Angelina had done extremely well in the Scottish National Gymnastics competition in Perth, ranking 4th in her age group.

We watched in admiration as the President of Ukraine, Volodymyr Zelenskyy, stood his ground against Putin and the Russian army, even as Kyiv was besieged. At the time of writing (1/4/25), he was still alive and leading his country in its defense. Putin must lose—this battle is one of democracy versus totalitarianism.

In my lifetime, I have never had to go to war. I watched as we fought in the Falklands, Serbia, Afghanistan, and the ongoing conflicts with the IRA and ISIS. As a peace-loving old man, I would still be willing to die to preserve the basic principles of love, humanity, kindness, and democracy.

On 9th March, I packed up my kit and travelled to Rugby to be available the next day for a site inspection at LSbp's newest solar farm at Streetfield and Northfield House near Lutterworth. I met up with Jeff Perkins, the site HSE adviser for LSbp. We toured both sites in an electric rover vehicle, and on our return, we debriefed the site principal contractor (PC) on key issues. The LSbp site manager, Liam Henry, was very responsive. We got on well, and he was glad to see me, as he needed support with the PC due to strained relations.

I identified three key risk areas:

Arrangements at a crossover point with a gas main Traffic management Security threats, including theft and damage to equipment and materials.

I produced my report the next day and issued it. The shit hit the fan. The Principal Contractor did not like some of my content. However, my boss, Chris Bartliff, had approved the report and agreed to issue it. The following week, Chris and Jeff returned to the site and upheld my findings. It's easy in these situations to try and appease the more difficult site characters, but that's not in my nature—I held my ground and so did Chris and Jeff.

Later that week, Chris Bartliff's mum passed away after a knee operation, so I remained on standby to support the team.

At home, Cath asked if we could help her find the keys to the gun safes in John's study, as she believed he had locked her passport inside before he died. She suspected he had hidden the keys somewhere in the room.

Jamie, who is skilled at picking locks, came with me. As a backup, we brought grinders in case we had to cut the doors open. We searched the room for over an hour without success.

I remember calling out, "Hey John, help us find the keys!"

Within a minute, Jamie and I were drawn to the bookcase behind the door. Jamie checked high, then low. I got on my knees and noticed a small opening in a radiator cover at floor level. I reached in—nothing. Then I thought, if these keys were really important, John might have pushed them in further. I stretched my arm as far as I could and finally touched the lost keys.

Unfortunately, the passport wasn't inside the safes. However, we found 12 guns, one musket, and some gold coins. Cath was relieved to have the keys at last. As a reward, Jamie got a gun, and I got two, plus holsters all made legal by rendering unable to fire bullets.

Going through a loved one's belongings is emotional, and Jamie was already struggling, as he had been close to his uncle John. Cath offered us some of John's tools from his workshop. After ten minutes, Jamie found it overwhelming, so I told him I'd finish the task. In the end, we each took home a box of tools—I'm sure John would have approved.

John had so much stuff that we barely made a dent. He had been a true enthusiast, collecting miniature soldiers, Dinky cars, re-enactment uniforms, leatherworks, and books. Seeing his collection was incredibly moving, revealing the complexity of the man and his incredible intelligence. We will always miss him.

On Saturday, 26th March, I took Gabriel to Slater Menswear in Howard Street, Glasgow, to get his first three-piece suit. We had both been invited to a university function at the Grosvenor Hotel in Glasgow, where we were guests of the Adam Smith Economic Society (ASES) Competition Case Study event and dinner on 1st April this was an event that CDM Plus Ltd sponsored.

Gabriel's eyes widened as he took in the sights and sounds of Slater's. He told me he loved the experience. We left with a full outfit—two pairs of shoes, three shirts, ten ties, a belt, socks, and underwear. When I saw him in the suit, I was so proud of my grandson—he had grown into an exceptional young man.

I was especially proud because I had earlier rewarded him for getting an A+ in his business exam. In our family, we give a gold star badge and £100 for exceptional performance in school or life. However, Gabriel surprised me by asking me to take the star back—he admitted he had cheated.

When he explained how he had done it, I agreed to take the star back. I had also cheated to get through a math's exam in the '70s while studying for my HNC—I knew it was wrong, but in my case, it had been necessary.

Overnight, I reflected on Gabriel's honesty. It was important that we had a relationship where he not only respected me but also himself enough to tell the truth. "Let me earn it properly," he said.

Because of that, I decided to reward him—not for the exam result, but for his honesty. He became my +1 at the ASES event, where he was also the CDM Plus Ltd intern.

The event was a great success, and it was inspiring to see Gabriel engage with the other students. We had a superb dinner, courtesy of Barclays and Santander, who sponsored the event.

I dropped Gabriel off at his house and then headed home to HoC. When I reached the back door, I noticed that a stray cat had somehow made its way inside. This cat had visited us several times before—an unneutered young male, spraying everywhere to mark its territory, stealing our cat Lizzie's food, and terrorizing her.

As soon as it saw me, it bolted upstairs. I tried to chase it out, but it seemed to have decided this was its house now. It darted from room to room while I pursued it with a small brush. Every room it entered, it managed to knock things over. Half an hour later, it was still inside. I eventually cornered it in the pantry, but it leapt onto a shelf, knocking over five of Elaine's best vases, smashing them to pieces. I opened the back doors, hoping it would flee, but instead, it ran back upstairs to the half-landing, where the window is at least ten feet high. In desperation, it climbed the curtains, destroying them and bringing down the pelmet in the process. It then tore back downstairs into the kitchen, sending more ornaments and vases crashing from the window ledge.

Finally, it bolted out of the back door. It took me an hour to clean up, then I had to take the pelmet to the workshop to rebuild it before refitting both it and the curtains. I thought I'd scared it off for good—but on Monday, Elaine spotted it in the garden. (Where's my gun?)

On Friday, 8th April, I got a call from Mark Pollard about a new issue at the AGR site in East Cambridge. Two workers from the owners had fallen through the glasshouse roof, and the owners had allegedly tried to cover it up. The HSE advisor was brought in to investigate but faced heavy pressure from the glasshouses managing director and withdrew from the case.

Mark had done some digging and suspected that the incident might also involve a modern slavery issue. I advised him to seek legal counsel and report the accident to the HSE UK, and to inform the police about the modern slavery concerns.

On Saturday, I picked up Robin from his home in Dunlop. Almost immediately, he told me he'd split up with his girlfriend. He was trying to keep his emotions in check. Back at HoC, his gran made him a good breakfast, but he barely ate a thing.

We started work, but after a few hours, he was struggling. I told him to take a break in the pavilion. It's easy for us older folk to forget how tender a young heart can be. His girlfriend had her own demons, and to be honest, I was relieved for Robin that the relationship had ended.

Elaine was beginning to feel more like herself again. She spent time with her cousins, enjoying a long weekend in the Highlands with Linda, Pauline, and Eleanor. On the 11th, she met up with Von and Ian for a day out at Luss on Loch Lomond.

On Easter Sunday, 17th April, the whole family got together. It was great to be together again without COVID-19 restrictions hanging over us.

Jamie was told by Vattenfall that his contract would be terminated at the end of the month. We immediately started looking for new opportunities, and within a few days, he had several promising leads.

On 19th April, Elaine and I travelled south to the Rugby area to visit the LSbp solar farm construction sites at Streetfield and Northfield House. We stayed overnight at the Ullesthorpe Court Hotel—Elaine made the most of the spa and pool while I prepared for the site visit the next day.

On-site, I met as usual with Jeff Perkins, the LSbp HSE auditor, and we started early with the site tour. At Laydown Area 1, it quickly became clear that both the site and construction work were well below LSbp's required safety standards. I immediately advised the LSbp executive and the principal contractor to implement a full safety standdown.

I called an emergency meeting with LSbp and METKA. After identifying several critical issues, we agreed on remedial actions. I issued an interim report to the LSbp Head of Construction and the HSE Lead.

That evening, I picked up Elaine from the hotel, and we arrived home around 22:30.

The next morning, I finalized the full report and sent it to all relevant parties. Within a few days, the contractor had resolved the issues. The HSE Director later issued a plaudit for my actions and professionalism.

CHAPTER 4:
SPANNER IN THE WORKS

Life was beginning to return to normal in May, but the war in Ukraine remained ever-present in the background—deeply upsetting as each day revealed new horrors. Elaine and I decided to donate to aid the humanitarian effort both in Ukraine and in the UK. My comrade, Ian Fulton, had family contacts in Italy who were transporting medical equipment to Poland for transfer to Ukraine. We covered their fuel costs with a £1,000 donation.

Ian was also a director of the Scottish Refugee Council. While the world's attention was on Ukrainian refugees, we knew that people from other crisis- stricken countries, such as Syria, were still suffering. Wanting to help, we donated another £1,000 to the SRC.

At work, my boss, Chris, renewed my contract for another year, and my other client, Black & Veatch, wanted to integrate me further into the project in the Bay of Biscay, Spain. I was managing my portfolio well—it was enjoyable and well paid.

On Sunday, 22nd May, Robin worked his last day at HoC before leaving for his summer job in Aviemore. Over the two years we had worked together— along with Gabriel—we had completely transformed the back garden, creating a vegetable patch, a pavilion, and new concrete work. Robin had learned a great deal, gaining new skills while also managing his type 1 diabetes. Over time, I had helped him build up his tool kit, and it was good to hear that, after his first week in Aviemore, his new employer was putting those skills to use.

Jamie received news from Vattenfall that his current contract was ending, but he would be moving from Operations to Projects, based in Esbjerg, Denmark—just as I was.

I was feeling good and working well. On 26th May, as usual, I went out for a meal and a movie with my two old friends, Ian Johnson and Fred Thorley. We dined at an Italian restaurant in Linwood before heading to the Showcase Cinema in Paisley to watch Top Gun: Maverick. We had the best reclining seats, so I settled in comfortably to enjoy the film.

About 30 minutes before the end, I became aware of a chest pain. At first, I assumed it was indigestion, then food poisoning. But when the pain grew more intense and began radiating down my left arm and under my jaw, I knew—I was having a heart attack.

I excused myself from Ian and Fred, went to reception, and requested a bottle of water. I crushed and dissolved 3 x 300mg of soluble aspirin in it and drank it down. I also asked the manager to call an ambulance.

By the time the paramedics arrived—30 minutes later—the film had ended, and Ian and Fred were by my side. I asked Ian to phone Elaine and Fred to accompany me to the hospital, though he wasn't allowed in. The paramedics wired me up to a heart monitor and a defibrillator and gave me another tablet to chew. My heart trace looked stable, but my blood pressure was dangerously high—over 200. They administered a nitro-lingual spray under my tongue to dilate my arteries, which helped but gave me a splitting headache.

I arrived at the RAH around midnight, still conscious, and was admitted and triaged. However, I was then left in a corridor for about five hours before seeing a doctor. Some of the other patients there were gravely ill. Since I was starting to feel better, I suggested to a nurse that I should go home. She was emphatic—absolutely not—I needed to stay for blood tests.

The consultant later told me that taking the aspirin so quickly had saved me from severe heart damage. (Note to self: always keep aspirin to hand.)

Eventually, a doctor took blood and sent me for an X-ray. After a few hours, he confirmed the results—I had suffered a heart attack. I was admitted to the Coronary Care Unit, given oral and injected medication, and wired up to a monitor for round-the-clock care. Despite the circumstances, I even made friends with some of the other patients.

Over the weekend, my entire family visited me. Seeing the worry etched on their faces as they came to terms with my illness was heartbreaking. I also received numerous well-wishes from friends and colleagues.

The cardiology consultant, Mr Stuart Hood, informed me that I needed an echocardiogram before they could determine the next steps. Since echocardiograms weren't performed on weekends; I remained in hospital until Monday morning. The results confirmed heart damage, meaning I now required an angiogram at the Golden Jubilee Hospital in Glasgow. I was discharged with a bag of medication—blood thinners, statins, blood pressure pills, aspirin, and beta blockers.

This event was truly life-changing for several reasons. I had always been aware of heart attacks, particularly after the loss of my brother-in-law, Gordon Greig. His death was subject to a fatal accident inquiry, during which I acted as the legal representative for my sister, Anne.

Having trained for offshore work, I had been recertified as a first aider multiple times—I knew what to do for others in a cardiac emergency, including CPR and defibrillator use. But what if it was me?

Since the 1980s, I had suspected heart problems. One night, after a heavy meal with friends, back when Elaine and I lived in Tantallon Drive, I felt unwell—so much so that I genuinely thought my heart might stop. Unable to sleep, I got up at 4:00 a.m. and walked for two hours, trying to shake the discomfort.

That moment sparked a change—I committed to getting fit. I started walking, then built up to running marathons over the next two years. I completed the Glasgow and Inverclyde marathons, the Stirling half marathon, and numerous fun runs across Scotland. It became a family affair—I fondly remember us all running around Arthur's Seat in Edinburgh and Glasgow Green, where the race compère announced, "Here come maw, paw, and the weans over the finish line!"

Fitness remained a core part of my life. In 1985, I started my own construction business, spending years doing physical, manual labour.

However, by 2010, I began noticing problems—particularly after big breakfasts or fast-food meals. I had a large appetite and wasn't one to skimp on fries or meal deals. During a holiday in Spain, Elaine and I went out for a meal, and on the walk home, I was so uncomfortable I had to stop and sit down.

There were other minor episodes, but I always managed them with soluble aspirin.

One of the more concerning incidents happened in Aalborg, Denmark. I was with a team from Vattenfall, visiting Vestas wind turbine suppliers for the Aberdeen Offshore Windfarm. After a grueling travel schedule—Aberdeen to London, London to Schiphol, Schiphol to Billund—I arrived at my hotel at 2:00 a.m., exhausted and hungry. The night porter offered me a bottle of water and a baton salad sandwich.

By morning, I could barely walk. Every step was slow and labored. I eventually made my way, inch by inch, across the road to Steve Burns's hotel. Steve was the new Security Manager for Vattenfall. As soon as I got inside, I told him I wasn't well and asked him to get me some aspirin, which, foolishly, I had forgotten to bring. Steve reassured me that there was no need to worry—our hotel was hosting an international cardiology conference!

Thankfully, I recovered and managed to complete my visit and return home without further incident. At the time, home was a corporate townhouse in Dyce, Aberdeen, provided while I worked on the wind farm project.

Looking back, the signs had been there all along. I knew something was wrong. I had tried dieting, but I definitely had a food problem. Comfort eating was all too easy, especially with my Aberdeen house situated right next to an M&S Food Hall.

Now, everything had changed. There was no avoiding the truth—if I wanted to keep living, I had to take my health seriously.

During this time, I was also having regular medical check-ups at our local health centre. One particular blood test raised alarm as my cholesterol levels were off the scale. The culprit? Kefir. I had been taking it to improve my gut health after a course of antibiotics for a chest infection. However, Kefir is loaded with cholesterol.

It was clear that I wasn't well. As mentioned in Chapter One, I was also type 2 diabetic. Following that diagnosis, I spent the next year getting fit and losing about five stone. By 2019–2020, I was back at work and on Metformin for my diabetes. In May 2021, the practice nurse noted that my blood sugars and other readings were good, so I was taken off Metformin. However, she detected an unusual heartbeat. For the third time, I was sent to the cardiologist at the RAH. Once again, I was told my heart was strong and functioning well.

So, there I was—heart fine, diabetes in remission. But in the summer of 2021, I made the mistake of returning to a normal diet and limiting my exercise to weekends.

That uncomfortable feeling returned, stronger than before. As my 71st birthday approached, I couldn't shake the thought that I might not have much time left. I started preparing mentally wanting to do right by my family, make the most of each day, and try not to overeat.

On 22nd June, I underwent an angiogram to determine whether I was "fixable." Gus and Elaine accompanied me, though I was already breathless by the time we reached the cardio unit on the first floor. The reception area was crowded around twenty other men were also waiting for angiograms. Elaine got a lift home with Gus while I was taken to a cubicle to be prepped for surgery.

I changed into a surgical gown, signed forms, and answered various health questionnaires. A cannula was fitted, bloods were taken, and my blood pressure was checked. After a few hours, I was led to the operating room. A nurse quickly covered my exposed backside with a blanket, which led to some laughter in the ward.

On the operating table, I exchanged some banter with the staff about how my heart attack had occurred while watching Top Gun: Maverick—a film advertised as "heart-stopping action." I was given an injection in my hand, and Dr Stuart Hood began the procedure, positioning the X-ray equipment over my chest. It was over quickly, and I barely felt a thing before I was wheeled back to my cubicle.

Dr Hood came to see me with the results. No stents. Instead, I needed a triple bypass. He warned that the waiting list was long—this would take months rather than weeks. I was discharged later that day, and Gus took me home. A pressure dressing covered my right arm, where they had inserted the angiogram dye.

In the following days, a series of appointments were lined up—Pharmacist, Dietitian, Cardio Rehab. On 2nd July, I received a letter from Dr Hood confirming that my case had been reviewed by the surgical team. They agreed I needed the bypass, but no date was set. In the meantime, I was placed under the support team to manage my diet and exercise while waiting for the operation.

On 3rd July, I was invited next door to chat with Dr Jayne McLaren and her father, Ian, who had undergone a triple bypass a decade earlier. Jayne, a cardiothoracic surgeon, provided invaluable insight into the procedure, while Ian shared his personal experience of recovery—his story was reassuring.

Despite the looming uncertainty, Elaine and I did our best to keep life as normal as possible. We continued celebrating birthdays and anniversaries and enjoying meals out with family and friends. However, bad news kept coming—many friends were falling seriously ill, and more deaths reached us.

It's easy to become fatalistic in such circumstances, but that's not a solution. We stuck to the old adage: hope for the best, plan for the worst.

A source of comfort was the excellent NHS support from the multidisciplinary team—Pharmacists, Cardio Rehab specialists, Dietitians, and Cardio Consultants. It also helped to stay focused on work, as the business was doing well and provided a positive distraction.

Beyond my personal challenges, the country faced escalating energy costs on an unprecedented scale. Many people struggled to afford their utility bills, particularly electricity and gas. For us, the cost of LPG gas was set to soar from £5,000 per year to £20,000.

It became clear that we needed to act. In June 2022, I placed an order for a solar and battery system to meet our needs.

On 22nd July, Elaine and I celebrated our Golden Wedding Anniversary with a quiet dinner at Scott's Restaurant in Troon. I arranged 50 red roses, champagne, and chocolates for Elaine. The day before, I had travelled to Glasgow, where the staff at Mappin & Webb's Jewelers in Argyll Arcade helped me choose a solid gold bracelet—one diamond for each child and grandchild, plus a hidden ruby for Cailin our deceased grandson.

July was also packed with medical tests in preparation for surgery. After an angiogram, echocardiogram, and pre-op assessment, I finally met my surgeon, Ms. Rashmi Birla. It was Dr Stuart Hood who confirmed I wasn't eligible for stents and required a triple bypass.

There was a lot to take in, and I had my fair share of sleepless nights. But I had to accept the reality—I had serious cardiovascular disease and needed surgery to prevent another heart attack.

On 5th August, Elaine and I hosted a Golden Wedding Anniversary celebration at the Lynnhurst Hotel in Johnstone, inviting 65 guests for dinner and a party.

Golden Wedding and family celebrations August 2022

Leading up to this, we celebrated Gabriel's 16th birthday by taking him to Ralph Slaters' in Glasgow for another three-piece suit and accessories. Elaine and I then took him to The Ivy for his birthday dinner.

Just two weeks earlier, we had attended John and Marjorie Waters' Golden Wedding Anniversary at the Inverkip Hotel. Guests had heard about my heart attack and were incredibly kind. I had a long conversation with Rosemary, who had been battling terminal illness for years, and Mary Elliot, Marjorie's sister-in-law. Both were in good spirits. The next day, we were shocked to learn that Mary had suffered a stroke and passed away in early August.

I took a short break from work between 5th and 12th August. Elaine and I enjoyed a few trips—to the Ayrshire coast, Loch Lomond, and Glasgow's Kelvin Art Galleries for the John Byrne Exhibition. We also treated Lucy to a "Pretty Woman" shopping day for her 14th birthday.

August brought some good news too. Gabriel received his NAT 5 results— five As and four Bs. Another highlight was the Glasgow University Racing Team, which we had been sponsoring, winning the overall Formula event at Silverstone. Both Gabriel and Lucy had attended the car launch before the races, making it all the more special.

Congratulations to University of Glasgow, winners of Formula Student 2022.

University of Glasgow win FS2022

CDM Plus Ltd Sponsors UG Racing

CHAPTER 5:
A COLD WIND IN AUGUST

During August, I attended several medical appointments in preparation for my surgery. These included blood tests, dental preparedness, swab tests, an echocardiogram, lung function tests, and an angiogram. Eventually, I had an interview and examination with my surgeon, Ms. Birla. This gave me the opportunity to discuss the procedure, and Elaine came with me.

My surgery was initially scheduled for 5th September but was deferred until the 9th. Processing this surgery—and the fact that I would die without it— was not easy. I could see the stress on the rest of the family, especially Elaine, who was incredibly supportive and stoic.

I had briefed my client at LightSource bp, where Chris Bartliff was very understanding and told me to take whatever time I needed to recover before returning to work.

In preparation for winter, Jamie, Robin, Jenni, and Gabriel came over the weekend before my surgery to help stack logs, as we anticipated the winter fuel and energy crisis. To stay ahead of this crisis—brought on by Putin's war in Ukraine—we had an electric boiler installed to reduce our gas consumption. I had also contracted a company, Eco-Energy Ltd to install a 14kW solar plant in the back garden, scheduled for early October.

I am writing this part of my story three days before surgery, aware that these words could be my last. Hopefully, I will be back soon to continue this book. My surgery date has already been postponed twice, and at the time of writing, it is now planned for Friday 16th. Last week was a historic one for the nation, as the Queen passed away, and we now have King Charles III.

My overall philosophy regarding the heart surgery was to hope for the best but plan for the worst. I had already ensured that Elaine had access to all bank accounts and was a director of the business. I also arranged for Jamie to start getting involved. After discussions with Ms. Birla, I was under no illusions about the risks—death, stroke, or other debilitating consequences. My chances of a successful outcome were better than 95%, which I was pleased to accept. My only alternative was to wait for another heart attack, which I might not survive.

If I do not survive, I want everyone to know that I did my best and loved my family with all my heart. My only regret would be not continuing life with them.

Jim Green, 5/9/22

Not yet for the Grim Reaper

On Thursday, 15th September, I was admitted to the Golden Jubilee Hospital in Glasgow, and on the 16th, I underwent triple bypass surgery. After the operation, I was moved to intensive care, where my left lung collapsed, and I developed an infection. The care staff were outstanding in fighting for my life. After two days in high dependency, I was transferred to the cardiac ward.

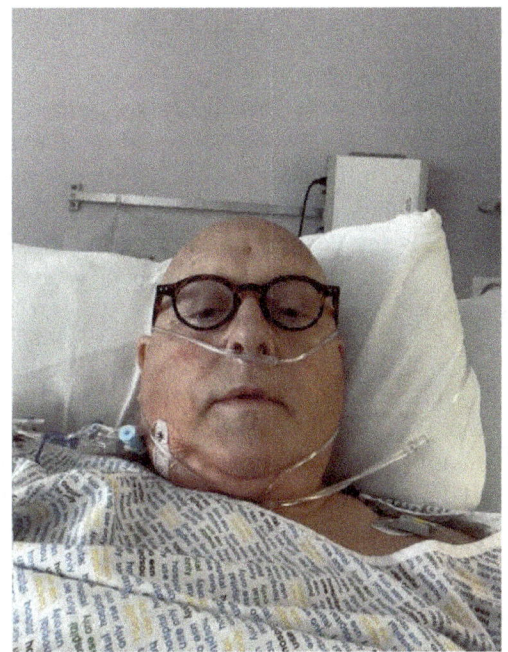

Bypass heart surgery complete

On 26th September, I was discharged and allowed to return home.

During this time, Elaine was incredibly supportive, visiting me under what must have been highly stressful circumstances. Over the following days, I continued to recover, with discomfort mainly from the pain in my legs. The wounds where the grafts had been taken from my left leg leaked, requiring the district nurse to change dressings every three days. I was also restricted from driving for six weeks.

By the end of October, my wounds were healing well, except for a section on my left leg that became infected, requiring ongoing treatment at the Barrhead health centre. By then, I could drive again, which meant I no longer needed nursing visits. However, on 29th October, I had a minor accident while parking in Linwood Retail Park, bumping into another car. It was only a small knock, and after exchanging details, we both moved on.

By November, I had returned to work part-time and was enjoying the routine. Under normal circumstances, I would have started the Cardio Rehab programme at the RAH in Paisley, but the infection in my leg delayed this until my wounds had fully healed.

Plans to install the solar plant at HoC faced a setback when Eco-Energy unexpectedly cancelled the order without explanation. I then had to fight to get my £6,000 deposit refunded. Fortunately, the sales engineer who placed my order contacted me, admitting he was embarrassed by his company's poor service. He then helped arrange for another contractor, CircoTech Group, to provide a quote for the work.

Some good news during this time was Gabriel's outstanding academic results—he achieved seven A's in his SAT5 exams. Jamie also left Vattenfall after nine years and started a new job as an HSE Advisor for Scottish and Southern Energy on the Sea Green offshore wind farm. Robin secured a job on a construction site in Burnside, applying the skills he had learned while working for me at HoC.

Through November and into December, I had multiple check-ups at Barrhead Medical Centre and the doctor in Neilston to monitor the healing of my left leg. The graft site at my ankle was slow to recover.

On 28th October, Elaine and I travelled south to Retford, where I had a site visit at Tiln Solar Farm on the 29th. This trip was important to me—it was my first post-surgery work visit, and I needed to ensure I could handle it without health issues. The site spanned hundreds of acres, and access roads posed a challenge, as local anglers could only reach their fishing zones via our construction tracks. I had to meet with the contractor and landlord to resolve the issue. Additionally, the site had been robbed over the weekend by an organised crime gang, who subdued the guard and stole all construction cables and equipment. Despite these setbacks, my meetings and audit were successful, and Elaine and I returned to Glasgow on the 30th, stopping at Mainsgill Farm Shop on the A66. It was an enjoyable visit, where we stocked up on Christmas treats and had high tea.

During the first weekend of December, Gabriel came over to the Hall. After a McDonald's breakfast in Darnley, we set about putting up the Christmas lights in the garden. On the first Saturday, Elaine and I decorated the Christmas tree—a ritual that made me reflect on how lucky I was to be here for another year.

On 13th December, my mother's birthday, I had a follow-up appointment at the Golden Jubilee Hospital with Ms. Birla. After completing a questionnaire with one of her team's female surgeons, I was officially discharged. Elaine was with me, and I attempted to present Ms. Birla with a cash donation as a token of gratitude for her and her team's excellent care, but she declined due to protocol.

Jenni had organised and directed a Christmas show, The Nutcracker, for her dance students from the villages of Dunlop, Neilston, and Uplawmoor. Leo did a reading at Uplawmoor Church, while Bear narrated The Nutcracker.

Angelina supported her mum on stage, helping to organize the children and performing in several sketches. I was incredibly proud of them all.

Bear   *Jennifer*   *Angelina*

On 17th December, I took Gabriel to Glasgow, where we had lunch at Princes Square. Afterwards, we visited Argyll Arcade to look at watches for his Christmas present. After browsing several shops, we settled at Chisholm Hunter at the arcade entrance on Buchanan Street. Over a few coffees, I purchased Gabriel's first Swiss watch—a Longines Hydro-Conquest diver's watch—as a reward for his exceptional performance in his SAT5 exams.

Christmas was wonderful as the whole family gathered on Christmas Day to exchange presents and enjoy the buffet Elaine had prepared. As I put up the tree, I felt incredibly grateful to be alive and wondered if it would be my last one. Gabriel helped me put up the lights outside.

I had taken two weeks off work and attended the Cardio Rehab unit at the RA Hospital in Paisley. It was tough, but I managed. During January, I attended two more sessions and could feel the benefits. I also travelled to Greenock Esplanade, where I walked 3K to test out my new heart.

On 25th January, we were invited to Emma and Neil's for a Burns supper. I did the Address to the Haggis, Emma sang and played the dulcimer to Wild Mountain Thyme, and Neil played Auld Lang Syne. It was a lovely evening with the children. On 31st January, we attended a Cherish the Ladies concert at Glasgow Concert Hall with John, Marjory, Susan, and Bob.

At work, my boss, Chris, asked me to support a project in Kotun, Poland, and prepared me to assist with projects in South East Asia (Singapore, Australia, and New Zealand) and Azerbaijan.

I had a few accidents and breakdowns with my Land Rover Discovery. I collided with a woman parking her car in a car park in Linwood, then later hit a barrier in the ASDA car park in Barrhead. On Saturday, 28th January, the steering failed while visiting Jamie in Dunlop, leaving me stranded. Eventually, I had to get a recovery vehicle to take the car to Taggarts in Darnley and reschedule the collision repair for later in February. I was beginning to wonder if the beta blockers were affecting my driving.

The solar project restarted, with the new contractor, CircoTech, beginning excavation and cable-laying. The plan was to have everything commissioned by mid-February. It had become more urgent, as I had been monitoring the cost of running the electric boiler during winter. Despite increasing my monthly payments to Scottish Power from £200 to £800, by January, I was £3,001 in the red. I shut the electric boiler down and switched back to the gas boiler.

In February, we celebrated Elaine's 72nd birthday with a family dinner at The Vine restaurant in Prestwick. I also continued attending my cardio rehab classes at the RAH in Paisley.

At work, I continued supporting LSbp with solar projects in Kotun (Poland) and Retford (UK).

At the end of March, Elaine and I travelled to Great Yarmouth for her cousin Brenda's Golden Anniversary. We broke up the journey by staying at the Majestic Hotel in Harrogate and, on the way home, stopped at Mainsgill Farm Shop for afternoon tea and to buy some Barnsley chops.

This month, my contract with LightSource BP was renewed for £156,000, covering me until the end of the year.

The solar installation progressed well, and early results showed strong performance, meaning Scottish Power could no longer charge me thousands each month.

In March, we took Gabriel and Lucy to the business competition with the Adam Smith Economic Society at Glasgow University, where CDM Plus Ltd sponsored the prizes. It was a fantastic day for them both—they participated with the judges and gave a great account of themselves. The day ended with a dinner sponsored by Amazon at the Grosvenor Hotel.

Jim Green with Gabriel and Lucy as Sponsors

In April, Angelina won gold at the Perth Scottish Championship, securing her place in the British Competition in May.

Despite both Elaine and me having the flu, we pushed on with the complete makeover of the main bedroom. Leo started working with me as Gabriel was fully immersed in studying for his Highers exams.

The solar farm was fully commissioned, and we not only enjoyed using our own electricity but also began exporting power back to the Scottish Power grid.

We renewed our sponsorship with the GU Racing Team, handing over a £3,000 cheque.

April also brought devastating news—our dear friend Johnny Morrow passed away from prostate cancer. Johnny had taken the family photographs at our Golden Anniversary last year. He is buried just a few yards from Elaine's brother, John, in Hawkhead Cemetery.

After completing the cardio rehab programme, I renewed my membership at Bowfield Country Club to access the gym and pool.

On 12th–13th April, Elaine and I travelled to Retford, where I conducted an audit on the Tiln SV and BESS construction site.

Also, this month, the forest of 90 trees at the bottom of the McClaren's garden was cut down due to Ash Dieback disease. It was sad to see them go, but it significantly brightened our garden and improved the performance of the solar farm

CHAPTER 6:
LET THE SUNSHINE IN

As an older man who had gone through an existential experience, I was acutely aware of how quickly life—mine and others'—could be snuffed out. Many of our friends and family were becoming seriously ill. So, what would be my strategy to get the best out of life now that so little time was left?

Many of my friends and family were trying to persuade me to retire or telling me, "You need to take it easy."

The problem was that I didn't know how to take it easy. I loved my family, my work, and my life. My biggest danger was my love of food. I was still seeing the doctor, my weight was still in the obese range, and my blood pressure remained high despite strong medication.

My consultancy provided a regular structure, working in renewables on a global scale—work that was both enjoyable and self-affirming. It also gave me the flexibility of working from home, meaning I could still take Elaine a cup of tea in the morning and sometimes help throughout the day—whether visiting garden centers, spending time with family, or attending medical appointments. The money was extremely helpful, allowing us to do good things for ourselves, our family, and others.

I was determined to remain as positive as possible, to move forward with love and kindness, to put my family first, and to focus on being as fit and healthy as I could.

Challenges never go away prostate cancer was in my family DNA and I had been considering a PSA test myself, so I ordered a kit from Amazon. However, when I was about to use it, I noticed a note inside advising against it if taking blood thinners. I resolved to get a test the next time my bloods were taken at the medical centre.

I hesitated over the PSA test because my grandfather, Joe Armstrong, had died of prostate cancer at 72—the same age I was now. All reports suggested that many men my age had prostate cancer. Having just survived one existential health scare with my heart attack and bypass surgery, I was in no hurry to face another potential diagnosis.

April's troubles weren't over, as on the 26th, I fell on the stairs at Caldwell, injuring my fingers, bruising my thigh, knee, and chin, and sustaining open wounds on my knee and fingers. This wasn't a result of senility but rather the cocktail of medication I had to take each morning—including strong beta blockers that left me drowsy and disoriented. My entire body ached, and I could feel movement in the breastbone join from my previous surgery.

At this time, my salvation was my work and daily routine. I was managing solar projects in Poland (Kotun) and the UK (Retford), where we were also installing a Battery Energy Storage System (BESS).

Elaine was busy refurbishing our main bedroom, while Gabriel had moved in to focus on studying for his Highers.

My next mission was to get an electric car. I test-drove the Polestar EV and was thoroughly impressed with the drive up to Whitehill Wind Farm Visitor Centre.

At the end of May, Elaine and I took a trip to London by train, combining business and pleasure. We stayed at the Landmark Hotel in Marylebone from Saturday, 20th May, to Wednesday, 24th May. The hotel was fabulous, and Elaine loved it—spending two days to herself visiting Chelsea and enjoying the hotel pool and spa.

I attended management meetings and training at LightSource BP's head offices in Holborn. I remember having to take a bus from Glasgow to Carlisle due to train strikes, then being dropped off some distance from the station, leaving us exhausted by the time we boarded the train. We upgraded to first class for £60.

At the hotel, we were warmly received by uniformed porters and pleasantly surprised by our suite. That evening, we took a short walk to the Globe pub, where we had a casual dinner with beer and wine.

On Sunday, we walked to Regent's Park, enjoying a lovely summer's day with cappuccinos and Danish pastries at the coffee house. In the evening, we visited the Mirror Bar in the Landmark hotel for cocktails before dinner in the main restaurant, where we listened to a pianist playing in the foyer. Monday followed a similar pattern, though after work, I had dinner by the Thames at Blackfriars with the LSbp team. On Tuesday, Elaine and I went to the sports bar opposite Marylebone Station for a shared platter, beer, and wine.

On Wednesday, we travelled home by train from Euston Station to Glasgow Central, then on to Neilston, where Neil our son-in-law, picked us up for the final stretch home.

At this time of year, the grandchildren were looking forward to the school holidays. It's worth mentioning how well all the children were doing.

Robin was working as a barman in Dunlop while pursuing his driving license.

Bear and Harris were both acting in a series of plays by the Dunlop Players Drama Group and helping Maggie with the annual Dunlop Gala Fête.

Gabriel had completed his Highers and was one of ten boys nominated for Head Boy at Eastwood High School.

Angelina won four medals at the Gymnastics Club Championships in Cumbernauld. She also supported her mum, Jennifer, at the Dunlop Fête's dancing school demonstration event.

Leo continued to score goals with his football club, Neilston Wasps. Lucy completed her Silver Level Duke of Edinburgh Award.

Lily, Melissa, and James were all doing well at Uplawmoor Primary School.

James had been unwell for about a week but rallied quickly, especially after I bought him a gel pellet machine gun—he spent hours firing off rounds in our garden.

Elaine and I were nearing completion of the main bedroom at Caldwell and looking forward to moving into our new super-king-size bed.

By chance, I bumped into Robbie Paton at the Land Rover garage in Paisley. Robbie had been one of my lecturers during my MBA days in the 1980s and 1990s, when I was also a visiting lecturer. He was now Dean of the University of Glasgow's Adam Smith Business School. We hadn't seen each other in 30 years, so we agreed to catch up later in June.

Robbie had done his checks and was keen to discuss extending CDM Plus Ltd.'s sponsorship to the Business School. I was happy to oblige and set an annual budget of £5k to support various initiatives, including mentoring, events, prizes, and trophies—all linked to renewables and sustainability.

The children all had a fantastic month at school. Gabriel was appointed Deputy Head Boy at Eastwood High School, Lucy landed the lead role in the school's summer show, and Angelina continued her gymnastics success, winning multiple medals—including gold—and ranking number one in her category in Scotland.

Angelina No 1

In Stewarton, Bear received a medal for his role as the Herald in the Stewarton Trades Guild fete.

Bear Medalist

Robin, now in his twenties, secured a job as a barman in his local village in Dunlop and found himself a new girlfriend.

I took Gabriel to the Arnold Clark Innovation Centre in Glasgow for the launch of GU Racing's new electric racing car. It was raced at Silverstone this month, finishing in third place—compared to last year's first-place finish for the clean combustion car.

Elaine and I took a well-earned week's holiday, taking the ferry to Arran and spending a few days at the Auchrannie Hotel while

456

touring the island. We also visited Maureen and Ian Brough and family to celebrate their 80th birthdays. Meanwhile, Emma, Neil, and the children travelled to Tuscany via London, and Jamie, Maggie, and the boys headed north to Carradale for a camping trip.

On the 22nd, we took Emma to Mappin & Webb and a few other shops to pick out birthday presents and celebrate her publishing success in Woman Magazine's September issue.

I also managed to get the fencing contractor to complete work on the solar farm boundary, while Elaine finished remodeling the main bedroom— meaning we could finally move in.

One unexpected success in this rollercoaster month was receiving a cheque for £4,000 from Scottish Power, thanks to the success of our new solar farm and the resulting reduced monthly payments.

Life, as they say, is a rollercoaster, and we were deeply saddened to hear of the passing of Jackie Collins, daughter of Linda and Danny Collins from the Labour Party, after her battle with cancer. Tragically, when Danny visited her shortly before she passed, he suffered a near-fatal heart attack. Thankfully, he underwent surgery for a new heart valve and recovered. Jackie was only 52, but she had lived long enough to raise four children and meet her first grandchild. Her funeral at St John's Church in Barrhead was packed, with hundreds standing outside. We followed the cortège to St Conval's Cemetery, where she was laid to rest. Elaine and I helped Linda into her car, as she was overwhelmed with grief.

On a brighter note, the grandchildren continued to excel. At the school awards ceremony, Gabriel won top prizes for English and Business Studies—an incredible achievement given his dyslexia.

Gabriel Prizewinner

Lucy earned her Duke of Edinburgh Award, Angelina received the overall champion trophy at her gymnastics club in East Kilbride, and Leo was made team captain for his football team. We all—parents included—celebrated at the Uplawmoor Hotel.

Lucy with Ken MacIntosh the Presiding Officer and Paul O'Kane MSP at the Scottish Parliament in Edinburgh

During weekends we settled into a routine. Saturdays were designated as couple's days for Elaine and me, while Sundays became workdays, with Lucy, Gabriel, and Leo helping with garden and house projects in exchange for wages. Sundays typically started with a 10:30 am pickup, followed by a McDonald's breakfast in Barrhead before heading back to Caldwell for work. Tasks included grass cutting, weeding, pruning, logging for winter, window cleaning, flat-pack furniture assembly, composting, strimming, driveway resurfacing (20 tonnes of chips!), roof repairs, and general maintenance.

The 17th of September marked one year since my heart surgery. I was profoundly grateful to be alive. The body's ability to heal is remarkable, but the psychological journey was far more challenging. Facing an existential crisis like that forces you to recalibrate, to strike a new balance between maximizing life's joys and minimising risks.

I made several key decisions:

To prioritise my health, though resisting unhealthy food remains a challenge.

To keep taking my medication, despite the overwhelming negative information about beta blockers, statins, and antacids.

To spend as much time as possible with family and close friends. To let love, kindness, and happiness guide my actions.

To hope for the best but plan for the worst.

On 22nd September, I packed my bags and headed to Snowdonia for a painting class with three friends. I drove down with Fred Thorley and John Waters, meeting Malcolm Trehorn (Fred's ex-police friend from Norfolk) at the Royal Ship Hotel in Dolgellau, Gwynedd.

Our plan was to spend the weekend painting with Sammi and Jan Wilson, who run a painting school and gallery just outside Dolgellau. We met them for dinner at the hotel, where Sammi outlined the training schedule for the next two days. After a pleasant evening, I retired to my twin room with John. It was comfortable enough—until John started snoring. Feeling deeply sorry for Marjorie, his wife of 50 years, I eventually fell asleep.

On Saturday morning, we set off with Sammi and Jan, stopping at various scenic locations to take reference photos. We visited Barmouth Bay, a slate quarry and mine, and finally, at my suggestion, Portmeirion—the stunning village where The Prisoner, starring Patrick McGoohan, was filmed. I was in awe, taking photos at every turn. Sammi, who is wheelchair-bound, found it more challenging, but I managed the hills without issue and enjoyed a flat white at the Angel Café.

Malcolm drove us back to the hotel, where we freshened up before dinner at Y Sospan, a restaurant adjacent to the hotel. Located in a 17th-century courthouse, the building still had the hook outside where people were once hanged—a chilling detail.

I turned in early and managed a solid nine hours of sleep. The next morning, after a full Welsh breakfast, we headed to Sammi's home, Sleepy Hollow, in Twywn Rd Y Friog Gwynedd, for our painting session. Sammi had set up four workstations, each with a full set of art materials.

She guided us through selecting a subject from our printed photos. I chose a colorful scene from Portmeirion, while Malcolm painted a coastal slate mine, Fred depicted a boat, and John recreated Barmouth Bay. Jan prepared a lovely lunch with sandwiches, cakes, tea, and coffee, and we all focused intently on our work.

Portmeirion in Wales

At the end of the session, we were allowed to keep our paintings and art materials. To round off the trip, we had dinner at the Richard III Restaurant in Penmaenpool before returning to the Royal Ship Hotel for our final night.

The next morning, after another hearty Welsh breakfast, John and I said goodbye to Malcolm and Fred, who were heading back to Norfolk. We took a leisurely drive north, stopping in Carlisle for a break, and arrived in Caldwell by 4:30 pm, where John picked up his car and continued to Inverkip.

CHAPTER 7:
A WARM WIND IN OCTOBER.

On Tuesday, 3rd October, Elaine, and I joined Jenni, Gus, Gabriel, Angelina, and Leo for a holiday in Gran Canaria.

We set off at 04:30, taking both Land Rovers to Prestwick Airport for our 06:00 flight. However, due to a computer fault with the Ryanair aircraft, we faced a two-hour delay. Eventually, we arrived in Gran Canaria at 14:00 local time. We hired a nine-seater minibus, which I drove as I had the most left- hand drive experience.

We reached the villa at around 15:00, nestled in the rocky hills above Tauro. The temperature was over 30°C, with clear blue skies. Jenni had done an exceptional job choosing the villa—it was fabulous, spread over four floors with excellent facilities, a swimming pool, and an outdoor BBQ area. Elaine and I had a double room on the first floor, while Gus, Jenni, Leo, and Angelina stayed on the ground floor. Gabriel also had a room on the first floor.

Later, we drove down to the local shop at the foot of the mountains to stock up on supplies before heading to a nearby restaurant for drinks and dinner.

Over the next few days, we enjoyed the villa and pool, taking day trips to Costa Rica Beach, where the kids had fun at the water park while we relaxed with drinks in the shade.

One day I was in the pool and Jenni asked me not to move as she took a picture. I was not aware that a dragon fly had laded on my head apparently a symbol of transformation change and self-realization and a sign of good fortune (Google)

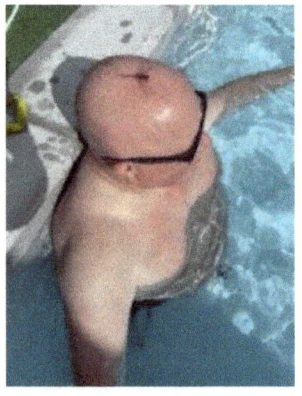

Lucky me

We tried to enjoy ourselves, but the horrific news of the Hamas atrocities in Israel was difficult to ignore. In the evenings, we turned off the news and watched Netflix to distract ourselves.

It was a good holiday, and on the 11th, we made our way back to the airport, flying home to a wet and cold evening in Prestwick. I returned to work the next day to catch up on my projects.

In early November, Elaine and I took a trip to Retford, where my solar and battery project at Tiln Farm was entering the winter period. The site was in poor condition, and my report reflected that. We stayed at the Best Western Hotel in Retford, taking a suite for our stay. On the way home, we visited Mainsgill Farm Shop not far from Scotch Corner in Cumbria and stocked up on Christmas supplies.

Christmas arrived, and Gabriel, Leo, and Lucy helped with the preparations—decorating the tree and putting up the outdoor lights. I sat down to prepare the Christmas newsletter, which I usually included with our cards.

As I began writing the letter, I reflected on how grateful I was to have made it through another year. The number of friends we had lost was painfully long, and many deaths had come as a shock:

Kenny Gibb, my childhood friend, employee at 1st Addition Ltd, and schoolmate. I was Kenny's best man when he married.

Johnny Morrow, our dear friend, and family photographer. He had taken the pictures for our Golden Wedding just months before he passed.

Roy Garscadden, who died of a heart attack, leaving behind his wife Anne and their two children. He had been in the Labour Party with Elaine and me and served as the Councillor for Barrhead.

Jackie Collins, daughter of Danny and Linda Collins, a young woman in her forties with children, died of spinal cancer. Her father, Danny, suffered a heart attack while visiting her in hospital. I visited him at the RAH—his loss was immense, compounded by the earlier deaths of his three sisters.

John Wilson, Director of Education in East Renfrewshire during Elaine's tenure as Convenor of Education, died suddenly of a heart attack.

Gordon Lennie, husband of Margaret, suffered a fatal brain hemorrhage, leaving Margaret a widow with no children.

Carolyn Burns, my cousin John's wife, was found dead in her bath at just 56 years old. Although she and John were estranged, he was utterly heartbroken, crying throughout the funeral. It was devastating to see how deeply he still loved her.

May they rest in peace.

Christmas Day followed its usual pattern, with Jamie, Jennifer, and Emma bringing the children over to open their presents. As always, I took on my role as 'the black bin bag man.'

Hogmanay was a traditional celebration with our neighbours— Valerie Dempster, Colin and Anne Sparrow, and Emma and Neil, along with Lucy, Lily, Melissa, and James. With Scottish music and songs, it felt just like old times.

On 22nd January, I travelled to Retford to inspect the solar and battery site at Tiln before the start of commissioning.

January ended as it often does—cold, dark, and wet, with the usual wave of winter illnesses. The month reached a low point when we found ourselves back at the crematorium at the Hurlet Crematorium on 29th January, saying goodbye to Richard Elliot, who had passed away after a long struggle with Alzheimer's.

On Tuesday, 6th February, Elaine, and I travelled first class from Glasgow to London, checking into the Rubens at the Palace Hotel. We dined at the hotel that evening.

On Wednesday, Elaine visited Buckingham Palace while I worked from the hotel. That evening, we had dinner at Zédel's in Piccadilly before seeing Moulin Rouge at the theatre an excellent immersive show.

On Thursday, Elaine had arranged to meet Susan Green (Marjorie's sister) and her daughters, Vicky, and Natalie, at the RAF Club. In the evening, they went to the theatre to see Hamilton. Meanwhile, I attended a team meeting at LightSource

BP's head office at 22 Holborn (Sainsbury's building). After the meeting, my boss, Chris Bartliff, took us out for dinner at a local restaurant. I left early to meet Elaine at the Victoria Palace Theatre, which was just a short walk from our hotel.

When I returned to the Rubens at around 21:00, I felt unwell. I had eaten a light meal and unusually had two pints of Guinness, but I suddenly felt as though I were having a heart attack. I took extra aspirin and used my Nitrolingual spray. After a while, I managed to walk to the theatre, taking my time. I met up with Elaine, and we made it back to the hotel without further incident. By morning, I felt fine, and we set off for Euston. Definitely no more alcohol for me now.

As our taxi approached Buckingham Palace and passed Clarence House on the Mall, we noticed a crowd gathered, cameras poised. Suddenly, a limousine escorted by outriders passed us on the right—it was the King, on route to meet Prince Harry amid his cancer diagnosis.

We arrived back in Glasgow that evening, as always, glad to be home safe.

On the world stage, on 19th February, we received news that Alexei Navalny had died in a Russian prison—Putin once again eliminating competition, whether by imprisonment or assassination. In the West, we have failed to support Ukraine adequately, leading to unnecessary loss of life each day while Putin continues his harassment of the West. It all feels deeply depressing.

At home, the Tories continue to infight as the country spirals further downward.

In East Renfrewshire, we committed to supporting Blair McDougall, the Labour Party candidate for the 2024 General Election. Before his selection, we worked behind the scenes to ensure his constituency victory.

On 14th February, we celebrated Valentine's Day. On the 22nd, we marked James's birthday, and on the 23rd, Elaine's 73rd. It was lovely having Jennifer and Emma visit and spend time with their mum.

On 3rd March, we installed a CCTV camera at the tennis court to cover the substation and the solar farm.

Thursday evenings were my night out with the boys from the Purple Socks Club*, usually for a meal and sometimes a film. Most often, it was me, Fred Thorley, and Ian Johnston, and occasionally John Waters, meeting at the Royal Taj Mahal in Gourock. On 7th March, the group met up with Duncan, Fred's son, at the Royal Polo Club Indian restaurant in Maryhill.

On 8th March, I took time to remember my Granny, Isa Green, as it would have been her 124th birthday. On the 9th, we attended a fundraiser for Blair McDougall in Giffnock.

Angelina continued to amaze us—on 10th March, she won three gold medals in the Scottish Championship Gymnastics event. On 15th March, we celebrated Leo's birthday, gifting him a new computer desk for his room. Also, that day, Gabriel's team won the Team Journey business award at his school.

On 22nd March, Gabriel passed his driving test. With a new car from his Mum and Dad and some help with insurance, he was officially on the road.

On 28th March, I attended the Adam Smith Business School competition for the Adam Smith Economic Society's best business proposal event, which we co-sponsored with Barclays Bank. Elaine, Gabriel, and Lucy also attended as CDM Plus interns. Unlike last year, when we were on the judging panel, this time we were merely observers—and we strongly disagreed with the judges' choice of winner!

After the event, we had dinner at Café Andaluz in Ashton Lane.

In April, I travelled to Retford for a final site walkover and to complete my report. It was a good chance to catch up with Grant Ward, the Site Manager, and Jeff Perkins, my team colleague. We had brunch at the local Morrisons, and in the evening, Jeff and I had dinner at his hotel, The Bell Inn. On the way home, I stopped again at Mainsgill Farm Shop near Scotch Corner to stock up on groceries for HoC.

At the end of the month, Chris Bartliff informed our team that he would be leaving LSbp in July—a disappointing surprise, as he had been my boss for 13 out of the last 16 years.

In mid-May, Elaine and I took some time off to travel to Majorca for a holiday in the sun, staying in the north of the island in Alcudia. The last time we were there was with the children, during what turned into a disastrous trip—Emma ran through a plate glass patio door, suffering severe lacerations, and ended up in Palma Hospital. This time, we found some comfort in the new hospital located next door to our resort, and we noticed that every glass door now had three white dots to mark it.

We returned home thoroughly refreshed. It was good for me to switch off, enjoy some swimming, and listen to audiobooks.

Weekends were spent working in the garden with Gabriel and Leo after their exams and school shows. Lucy had a principal role in her school's production of Sister Act. Jenni directed and produced her annual show in Dunlop, with support from nearly everyone in the family. On stage, Angelina was brilliant, while Gabriel, Leo, Bear, and Lucy worked hard behind the scenes.

On 31st May, Neil and Emma got married on the banks of Loch Lomond at Firkin Point. It was a charming, intimate event, conducted by registered celebrant Stuart Roger. The ceremony was very Scottish—Neil wore his kilt, and Emma looked stunning in her dress. The wedding party on the loch's beach included Elaine and me, Neil's mum Marilyn and the children—Lucy, Lily, Melissa, and James.

As part of the ceremony, they observed the Scottish tradition of handfasting, tying together two pieces of tartan—hence the phrase "tying the knot." Later, Emma and Neil toasted each other with a quaich filled with Scottish whisky, the last drops used by the celebrant to declare them husband and wife—the beginning of the Mowbray-Green dynasty.

The Mowbray-Greens Wedding on the banks of Loch Lomond

After signing the marriage papers in Helensburgh, we moved to the picnic area, where Elaine had prepared finger food and champagne.

We then travelled to Glasgow, following the wedding car, which Jenny and Leo had decorated with the usual "Just Married" signs and tin cans on strings. It was a genuinely joyous occasion.

We parked in Glasgow and met the rest of the family at Little Italy on Byres Road, where we enjoyed a wonderful wedding reception and a feast. As the evening was beautiful, we later headed to the Botanic Gardens for some fun with the children and took great photos for the wedding album.

Emma and Neil's wedding celebration at the Kibble Palace

On Wednesday 12th June, my brother Charlie and his wife Christine visited us for lunch while they were in the area on car business. As an extra birthday present, I gave Charlie a Hoshen Jewish ring to celebrate our shared Ashkenazi ancestry. I based this on the fact that I had been part of a DNA research project at Edinburgh University which was in collaboration with the BBC and presented by Dr Michael Mosley called Scotland's DNA. I found out that on my Father DNA I am Ancient Irish and on my mother's I am an Ashkenazi Jew.

It is worth noting that Dad who had served in Palestine and saw his comrades killed in acts of terrorism by the Irgun and Stern Jewish underground was anti-semetic who had without knowing married a Jewish woman.

On 15th June, we visited my sister Anne in Helensburgh for her birthday. It was lovely catching up in her beautiful home, sharing family news. In the evening, we had a birthday dinner at the Sugar Boat restaurant in town. Since losing her husband Gordon, Anne has overcome her heartbreak and continues a successful career in child psychology.

On Sunday 16th June, I was delighted to have the whole family over for Father's Day—I was showered with cards, presents, and love. I am an incredibly lucky man.

On 17th June, we watched the Scotland football team underperform at the Euros and make an early exit.

At work, I was appointed to consult on solar projects in Antikythera, Greece, and battery energy storage systems in Ireland and Northern Ireland. I continued supporting LightSource BP with other solar projects in Kotun, Poland, and battery storage in Tiln, near Retford, both of which were nearing completion.

On the weekend of 21st June, I travelled north to Montrose with the Purple Sox Club—John Waters, Fred Thorley, and Malcolm Trehorn—where we stayed at the Links Hotel. On Saturday, we attended the Drumtochty Highland Games near Laurencekirk. It was a very enjoyable day, though I suffered slight heatstroke and had to go to bed early to recover.

The next day, we drove to Aberdeen and took a stroll along the esplanade, admiring the view of the Aberdeen Offshore Windfarm, which I helped build. We then continued north to Blackdog, booked dinner at the Cock and Bull Restaurant, and travelled further to Cruden Bay, where we enjoyed a pleasant walk at Port Errol Harbour, chatting with anglers on the pier wall. That evening, we returned in time to watch the Scottish football team exit the Euros, comforted only by some good cider.

We drove home on Monday, bidding farewell to everyone except John, who had left on Sunday.

On 26th June, we attended a service at Uplawmoor Church, where Leo and his class said their goodbyes to Uplawmoor Primary School before moving up to Eastwood High. We were so proud of Leo as he delivered his farewell speech—we could see our grandson turning into a handsome and clever young man. Afterwards, Elaine and I treated Emma, Jennifer, and the children to lunch at the Uplawmoor Hotel.

On 28th June, I met with Prof. Robbie Paton and Frederica Farolfi at the Adam Smith Business School, along with three other professors, to discuss the strategy for the Green Prize, which our company CDM Plus Ltd was sponsoring. The prize was designed to provide financial support for students working on sustainability-related economic behaviour projects. It was agreed that I would contribute cash prizes, mentoring, and speak at seminars planned for 2025.

The following week, Jenni, Gus, and the kids went on holiday to Gran Canaria. With the boys away, Lucy helped me in the garden—cleaning the solar panels, cutting the grass, and sorting the recycling.

On Friday, 5th July, we celebrated the Labour Party's landslide victory over the Tories, as well as Blair McDougall's winning in East Renfrewshire and was now our new MP at Westminster Parliament.

On Saturday, we took Leo to the Rangers Shop at Ibrox to replace his football strip with a larger size. We then went to the Arnold Clark showroom in Maryhill, where we test-drove the Vauxhall

Mokka and Astra EVs, only to be disappointed—they were too small.

On Monday, 8th July, Elaine, Gabriel, Lucy, and Bear attended the UG Racing launch of the Student Formula EV car at the University Quadrangle. We also attended the prize presentations upstairs, where Elaine and I sponsored the three winners. The car was set to race at Silverstone the following week. After the launch, we had lunch at Café Andaluz in Ashton Lane.

On Tuesday, we visited Harris in Dunlop to give him a music keyboard for his 11th birthday.

July was a busy month, with our anniversary and Emma's birthday both falling on 22nd July, followed by Gabriel's 18th on 26th July. Elaine and I spent the whole week dining out.

We had a pizza party for Gabriel in Glasgow, followed by a men-only cinema trip with Gus, Gabriel, and Aaron—Gus's son from his first marriage. We also had a Greek dinner party with the Mowbray-Greens on 22nd July.

On 24th July, Neil, Emma, and the children travelled south to Cambridge before heading to France for their summer holiday, basing themselves in a small, remote village in the Dordogne called Condom—to our amusement. They had a great time and returned safely, stopping overnight in Bath on 6th August.

That same day, Scottish students received their exam results. We were delighted that Lucy achieved six As in her NAT5s, and Gabriel completed his set of six As at Higher level—he was now ready for university.

The weekend before, we hosted afternoon tea for the Elliot family— Marjorie, John, Susan, Bob, Billy, and Catherine. It was a lovely afternoon filled with good food and shared stories. We all felt lucky to be alive—both Billy and I were heart attack survivors.

On 18th August, Ian Fulton organised a dinner for the old Labour campaign team to celebrate Blair McDougall's election victory in East Renfrewshire. Ken (former Presiding Officer of the Scottish Parliament), Nasim, Ian, and I met Blair at the Malletsheugh restaurant in the outskirts of Newton Mearns for a lovely Indian dinner. Blair shared insights from his first week at Westminster.

Gabriel enrolled at the Adam Smith Business School to study Business and Management, to our delight. Meanwhile, Lucy and Angelina were now joined by Leo at high school, and the other grandchildren returned to school.

On Saturday, 25th August, I took Emma and Lucy to PC World and bought them both laptops—one for Lucy's studies and one for Emma's writing. The previous week, I had also bought a new laptop for Leo.

On 31st August, I took Gabriel and Angelina to PC World again, this time purchasing an iPad with a keyboard and pen for Angelina. We spent £5,000 in total, but it was worth every penny to support the grandchildren's education.

The following weekend, Elaine and I travelled to Edinburgh and checked into the DoubleTree Hilton at the airport before heading to Dundas Castle for Mike and Nicky's wedding. We had attended my nephew Kenny Green's wedding there 20 years ago. It was great catching up with Mike, Nicky, and Kevin Jones, my former boss from Vattenfall. The evening was filled with music, fireworks, and good food.

The next morning, after breakfast at the hotel, we drove to Bathgate to meet Charlie and Christine for a family catch-up.

On Monday, I had the stressful task of informing my client, LightSource BP, that I would be leaving my contract. The week before, I had signed with Aukera Energy to provide Principal Designer services through my company, CDM Plus Ltd. My direct boss at LSBP Sandra Perera became quite emotional as she was sorry to see me go. I had offered to stay on for two projects until they found a replacement. I then had to inform Sandra's boss, James Wilson, and his boss, Nick Much. James was understanding—he suspected I might follow Chris Bartliff to Aukera, as Chris had been my boss for more than a decade.

I started the onboarding process with Aukera, balancing it with LSbp meetings. My new laptop arrived on Tuesday, and Aukera's IT team helped set it up. Then, unexpectedly, Chris informed me that HR and Legal had voided my contract, mistakenly treating it as an employee agreement rather than a service contract. After discussing IR35 implications, Chris reassured me that the issue would be resolved, but I was told to hold off work until a new contract was in place.

I was now in limbo—having resigned from LSbp but without a valid contract at Aukera.

On 10th September, my contract with Aukera was confirmed, and by the end of the month, I had already attended several meetings and produced my first documents for five UK projects, including a BESS project at Benthead near Kilwinning, just 20 minutes from our house at Caldwell.

We celebrated Jennifer's 49th birthday on 13th September, gifting her a nice watch—she was thrilled.

By 18th September, Gabriel had started at Glasgow University, and after his first week, he was loving it.

By month's end, everyone in the family had the flu—thanks to school reopening and Gabriel's Freshers' flu.

In early December, I successfully juggled work for Aukera and LightSource, and I also secured a small contract with AGR Group again.

On 4th December, Elaine and I received our winter flu and COVID vaccines. That night, my heart started racing—eerily similar to the night after my last COVID booster when I suffered my near-fatal heart attack.

On 7th December, I travelled to Edinburgh with Elaine, where we stayed in the Castle Suite on the 7th floor of the Sheraton Hotel. We enjoyed the VIP facilities and a lovely dinner, with spectacular views of the castle at night.

The next day, after breakfast, Elaine went shopping in the city while I met with my replacement, from LSbp. We had a productive handover meeting in the VIP meeting room before saying our goodbyes at 14:00. I picked up Elaine outside the Edinburgh Playhouse, and we returned home via a short visit to Dean Village.

Death was now staring me in the face.

I contemplated I was in "sniper alley" and should tie up all loose ends. I completed the draft manuscripts for both books and submitted them to Amazon. I also spoke with Books for Anyone (AI), which, after an hour of interrogation, produced a book for me called Renewables for Dummies Like Me. A few weeks later, I received hard copies and gave them to friends as stocking fillers for Christmas. Despite my reservations about AI, the book was insightful and very entertaining.

My AI Book

Who among us knows what the future will bring?

My life has been eventful, challenging, frightening, sad, happy, adventurous, and wonderful.

I remain without fear and unvanquished.

I am hoping this book is part of my legacy as a life lived as "Another Feg" where I have been able to survive despite the slings and arrows of outrageous fortune.

I wanted to write it before some AI App grabs all my information and data store up there in the cloud and produces it's version of Jim Green's life.

I hope you enjoy the life and times of "Another Feg"

POSTSCRIPT

*The Purple Socks Club (PSC) was formed about 10 years ago when me and Fred and Ian my longtime friends since my teenage years were out on our regular Thursday evening dinner sand cinema date. I noticed that by chance Ian was wearing the same color of purple socks. Fred then pulled up his trouser legs to also reveal a pair of purple sox.

As the weeks passed bye we formalized some rules and created the PSC and in order to differentiate with other organizations we changed the name to the Purple Sox Club.

Our ethos was simple we wanted to be there for each other and on Thursdays we would always wear purple sox. We wanted to really try and enjoy at least one day a week and celebrate our friendship a positive and happy way. As the days and months moved on we invited others who were of a similar mind to also become members. We invited John Waters and Malcolm Trayhorn to join us and, on occasion, people who were nice to us and of a similar mind. At the time of writing there are 300 members.

It's just about having fun at least one day a week with friends.

With the second book I wanted to demonstrate that after the heart attack I could go on to lead a full and active life despite the "Sword of Damocles" hanging over me. I was so inspired by Sir Chris Hoy the British Olympian going public with his terminal prostate cancer diagnosis and being so positive and helpful to his fellow men who are afraid to get that PSA test and subsequent treatment.

I now work full time as a Principal Designer specializing in solar and battery renewable energy projects. As PD I like the idea that I am focused on designing, building, and commissioning projects safely so that workers and others go home without injury and at the same time these projects help to make the world a cleaner and more sustainable place.

There will be friends family and colleagues who read this book and will wonder why they are not mentioned. I have deliberately kept a lot of material for my next book called "Blue-Note"

Blue-Note for those who are Jazz fans will recognize this special term and the significance of that special sound. In life there are times when events hit the Blue-Note of life, and those moments are completely special and unforgettable.

I have included many Blue-Note moments in my narrative above however my next book will include all other Blue-Note events and those people who are for ever in my memory. Those individuals will be referred to by name and will be known as the Blue-Note people.

Blessings and Shalome to you all Jim Green 2025

BACK COVER

The picture on the back cover was painted by my friend Fergus Hall the famous Scottish artist who painted the Tarot cards for the opening scenes of the Bond movie "Live and Let Die" I had carried out work for Fergus in the past with my building company and I recognized his magnificent and kindred spirit. I commissioned the picture towards the end of 2024 and on the 26th April 2025 Elaine and I visited Fergus and Julie his partner at their home studio on the Scottish Borders where I was able to discuss final adjustments to complete the picture. The essence of this picture is in the words:

"I am cut down in the corn, Yet I shall not perish"

Having survived the heart attack and several other life-threatening situations this sentiment ties together the whole book. The front and back cover pictures were completed by two of my artistic friends who had in their lifetimes the challenges of life-threatening health issues.

John Byrne died in 2024 and no doubt both me and Fergus will perish in time however through the art legacy of both John and Fergus and hopefully my book our spirits will never perish.

The End

www.ingramcontent.com/pod-product-compliance
Lightning Source LLC
Chambersburg PA
CBHW070857120626
46546CB00001B/36